CHILDREN'S ISSUES, LAWS AND PROGRAMS

SCHOOL HEALTH SCREENING SYSTEMS

CHILDREN'S ISSUES, LAWS AND PROGRAMS

Additional books in this series can be found on Nova's website under the Series tab.

Additional e-books in this series can be found on Nova's website under the e-book tab.

CHILDREN'S ISSUES, LAWS AND PROGRAMS

SCHOOL HEALTH SCREENING SYSTEMS

BRADLEY MCPHERSON
AND
CARLIE J. DRISCOLL
EDITORS

nova publishers
New York

For permission to use material from this book please contact us:
Telephone 631-231-7269; Fax 631-231-8175
Web Site: http://www.novapublishers.com

Library of Congress Cataloging-in-Publication Data

ISBN: 978-1-63117-942-6

Published by Nova Science Publishers, Inc. † New York

CONTENTS

PREFACE

School health screening is important. It is important for children, their families, their teachers, and their communities. For over a hundred years, health care services have been linked to the education systems of young children. Medical and education professionals have long recognized the linkage between physical and mental health and educational performance. School health screening programs are, in many countries, a large component of school health services. For many children, elementary school screening programs offer early detection of health problems that could otherwise harm their educational, social, and economic future. Effective school screening programs provide access to health care for all children within an educational jurisdiction and are a base for preventive interventions among whole communities.

School health programs have always been influenced by wider health and economic trends within societies. For example, school screening programs in the industrialized world that previously were concerned with signs of under-nutrition in children are now increasingly focused on obesity, and are also beginning to pay greater attention to mental health issues. These same concerns increasingly drive school screening programs in low and middle income economies that are in epidemiological transition to disorders more prevalent in developed regions. *School Health Screening Systems* is primarily based on work undertaken in the developed world but we feel it contains lessons for all school screening professionals.

This book gives an overview of contemporary school health screening procedures, protocols, problems and progress. The history and principles underlying school health screening are outlined and detailed information on ways to objectively analyse the effectiveness of screening programs is provided in Chapter 1 (School health screening: History, principles, and analysis). Young school children are prone to a range of health conditions and these are discussed in Chapter 2 (The young school child: Common diseases and disorders). As mentioned above, children are routinely monitored in many school health systems for weight and height. Current considerations related to this activity are detailed in Chapter 3 (Screening for growth and development). Screening programs for sensory system disorders were some of the earliest school health activities and hearing screening for school children is highlighted in Chapter 4. Increasing emphasis is being placed on the communicative competencies of school children and this has created a greater recent interest in screening in this area, as noted in Chapter 5 (Speech and language screening for school children). Likewise, mental health is an emerging area in elementary school screening and recent developments in this field are reviewed in Chapter 6 (Mental health screening for school children). Elementary school children commonly have dental problems that may go untreated without expert screening (Chapter 7—Dental screening for school children) or spinal disorders that require early detection (Chapter 8—Scoliosis screening for school children). They may also have complaints such as head lice, which can lead to educational and social disadvantage, and are often best treated within a school health screening framework (Chapter 9—Pediculosis screening for school children). Throughout this book screening is viewed as part of the wider school health care system. To support this emphasis we have included essential chapters on the relationship of screeners to children and their caregivers (Chapter 10—Communicating screening results to parents and children) and the organization of information-rich school health screening systems (Chapter 11—Data management in school health screening systems).

This book does not claim to be a definitive guide to all school health screening issues but aims to offer the professional reader a detailed background understanding of many of the main areas associated with elementary school health screening. The editors are indebted to our respected international network of authors for their willingness to share their expertise. We hope that this book assists those engaged in the policy and practice of school health screening, who every day guide so many young children on the path to better health.

ACKNOWLEDGMENTS

The editors would like to thank Dr. Asad Khan, Statistician, School of Health & Rehabilitation Sciences, University of Queensland, for his help in reviewing the statistical concepts and data presented in this book.

CONTRIBUTING AUTHORS

Wendy Arnott School of Health and Rehabilitation Sciences, University of Queensland, Australia. Chapter 5.

Donald C. Brown Child Life and Health, University of Edinburgh, UK. Chapter 2.

Kelly J. Brown School of Speech-Language Pathology and Audiology, University of Akron, USA. Chapter 11.

Deon V. Canyon Office of Public Health Studies JABSOM, University of Hawaii at Manoa, USA. Chapter 9.

Kenneth M C. Cheung Department of Orthopaedics and Traumatology, University of Hong Kong, China. Chapter 8.

Megan Counahan Epidemiologist, AusAID, Samoa. Chapter 9.

Dianne DeBell Professor of Policy in Health and Social Care, Anglia Ruskin University, UK. Chapter 3.

Chris Del Mar Faculty of Health Sciences and Medicine, Bond University, Australia. Chapter 10.

Carlie J Driscoll School of Health and Rehabilitation Sciences, University of Queensland, Australia. Preface, Chapters 1 and 4, Glossary.

Anne M. Fleming School of Speech-Language Pathology and Audiology, University of Akron, USA. Chapter 11.

Daniel Y.T. Fong School of Nursing, University of Hong Kong, China. Chapter 8.

Tammy Hoffmann Faculty of Health Sciences and Medicine, Bond University, Australia. Chapter 10.

K. Todd Houston School of Speech-Language Pathology and Audiology, University of Akron, USA. Chapter 11.

Keith D.K. Luk Department of Orthopaedics and Traumatology, University of Hong Kong, China. Chapter 8.

Colman McGrath Faculty of Dentistry, University of Hong Kong, China. Chapter 7.

Bradley McPherson Centre for Communication Disorders, University of Hong Kong. China. Preface, Chapters 1 and 4, Glossary.

Maura Mulloy Independent Scholar, Ethiopia. Chapter 6.

Ashley Jones Philp Richland Two School District, Columbia, South Carolina, USA. Chapter 6.

Rick Speare Anton Breinl Centre for Public Health and Tropical Medicine, James Cook University, Australia; Tropical Health Solutions Pty Ltd, Townsville, Australia. Chapter 9.

Joni Williams Splett School Mental Health Team, University of South Carolina, USA. Chapter 6.

Rae Thomas Faculty of Health Sciences and Medicine, Bond University, Australia. Chapter 10.

Carol To Centre for Communication Disorders, Faculty of Education, University of Hong Kong, China. Chapter 5.

Tali R. Weinberg School of Speech-Language Pathology and Audiology, University of Akron, USA. Chapter 11.

Mark D. Weist School Mental Health Team, University of South Carolina, USA. Chapter 6.

Helen Weld Public health nurse consultant, Yungaburra, Queensland, Australia. Chapter 9.

Wayne J. Wilson School of Health and Rehabilitation Sciences, University of Queensland, Australia. Chapter 4.

Yat-Wa Wong Department of Orthopaedics and Traumatology, University of Hong Kong, China. Chapter 8.

PART I: GENERAL CONSIDERATIONS IN SCHOOL HEALTH SCREENING

In: School Health Screening Systems
Editors: Bradley McPherson and Carlie J. Driscoll
ISBN: 978-1-63117-942-6

Chapter 1

SCHOOL HEALTH SCREENING: HISTORY, PRINCIPLES AND ANALYSIS

Bradley McPherson[1,*] and Carlie J. Driscoll[2]
[1]University of Hong Kong, Pokfulam, Hong Kong
[2]University of Queensland, Brisbane, St Lucia QLD, Australia

ABSTRACT

For over a century school health services have provided children with an important safety net—identifying those with disorders that may not be readily apparent to parents or teachers, or to the children themselves. These services became more sophisticated over time, with formal screening of targeted age groups of school children for specific disorders replacing the general medical checks of earlier years. Screening tests now are standard procedures in all school health services and tests cover a wide range of disorders. Growth and development, hearing and vision, speech and language, and dental problems are some of the many health issues handled by school health screening systems. Health screening has developed ethical principles that apply to school-based testing and that aid the qualitative evaluation of screening programs. The history of school health screening and the principles that guide school health screening systems are outlined in this chapter. In addition, procedures can be rigorously evaluated using quantitative methodologies that are often specific to the practice of screening. This chapter details these methods and includes examples of screening programs that have been appraised using quantitative techniques. School screening systems have a valued place within both the health care and education sectors. Systems that are constantly reflected upon and critically evaluated will continue to serve our children well, far into the future.

INTRODUCTION

For any society, the well-being of its children is a fundamental concern. Families universally want their children to grow in a healthy manner and realize their full potential.

* Corresponding author: Bradley McPherson. University of Hong Kong, E-mail: dbmcpher@hku.hk.

Governments generally see pediatric health care as an area of legitimate interest and intervention. Educators understand there is a strong connection between child health status and the learning process in schools—healthy children are better learners (Clark, Clasen, Stolfi, and Jaballas, 2002). For these reasons and many others, school health screening has developed into a globally accepted component of the health care and education systems. Screening in this context refers to "the examination of a whole population of apparently healthy children, using simple tests to distinguish those who probably have a condition from those who probably do not, so that the outcome can be improved by treating the condition before it produces obvious symptoms or signs" (Hall, Williams, and Elliman, 2009, p. 177). Screening is usually more rapid and much less costly than definitive diagnosis, with positive screening outcomes needing further, diagnostic, tests for confirming them (Braveman, and Tarimo, 1994). It is important to keep in mind that school health screening is a *component* of the systems it is embedded in. Screening is part of a wider strategy that includes diagnostic assessment for children with a positive screening result, a health care management plan for each affected child, feedback to schools on the educational and social implications of the health disorders identified, and placement of the screening procedure within the wider school health program.

Screening differs in many ways from other health care procedures. By definition it is devoted to the identification of health issues in "apparently healthy children", that is, to detect conditions that may otherwise be overlooked by parents, teachers, and health care professionals (Hall, Williams, and Elliman, 2009). Health screening has a specialized knowledge base of principles and methods of analysis. This chapter outlines the history of school health screening, its ethical foundations, and the basic analytic tools used to gauge the effectiveness of screening procedures.

History of School Health Screening

School health screening has a long history, dating back to the 19th century. Interest in improving the health of children at school led to the appointment of school doctors to teacher training colleges in Sweden, commencing in 1840. In the 1880s, medical officers were appointed to schools in France, Germany, and Switzerland (Henderson, 1975). In the same decade, a large scale vision screening program for school children was undertaken in England (Ferdinands, 1891) and the first textbooks in English on school health were published (Hirst, 1991). In Britain, school doctors were appointed to some schools in the 1890s and these professionals regularly reported high levels of ill-health, malnutrition, and disability among school children (Henderson, 1975). Subsequently, a formal school medical service was created in 1908 to better serve the health needs of students in elementary schools. This service was mandated to include routine health screening activities for growth and development, hearing, and vision (Henderson, 1975). Influenced by British trends, groups within the Australian medical profession began to call for the regular health examination of school children. In response, school health services were introduced in Australia in the early years of the 20th century. By 1907, two part-time medical officers were employed by the Sydney City Council to examine the health status of school children (Gandevia, 1978). In the United States, a similar timeline can be seen, with Boston establishing school health services in 1890, followed soon after by Chicago in 1895, New York City in 1897, and Philadelphia in 1898. State-mandated school screening followed, with eye, ear, and throat examinations compulsory for school children in Vermont from 1904 (Veselak, 1959). World War I medical examinations for military personnel exposed the poor health of many young men and, between 1918 and 1921, almost all states enacted laws related to school health issues, including screening (Means, 1975). Influenced by European concepts of school hygiene, in 1898 school doctors were placed in public schools in Japan. Their duties included biannual examination of students for "height, weight, chest circumference, spinal column, physique, visual acuity, eye disease, hearing acuity, ear disease, teeth, and other diseases" (Uchida, 2008, p. 7).

By the 1930s, ad hoc examinations conducted by medical doctors or nurses were superseded in many countries by formal, standardized screening tests and protocols. Universal (or "mass") screening of an entire population (such as all school children in a school district) gave way to targeted screening (or selective screening), which confines tests to groups (such as all incoming grade 1 students) who are considered to be at particular risk for a health condition. For example, hearing and vision screening is often conducted on children first entering the school system, to ensure prompt identification and early treatment to limit the adverse educational consequences of sensory disorders. A highly targeted procedure is screening for Tay Sachs disease carrier status in Montreal, where screening is restricted to high schools in which the Ashkenazi Jewish community resides, as the community has a tenfold increased carrier risk for this genetic disorder (Mitchell, Capua, Clow, and Scriver, 1996).

An influential World Bank report (World Bank, 1993) highlighted the strong link between poor health and school failure, and this association has been noted by others (Devaney, Schochet, Thornton, Fasciang, and Gavin, 1993). School achievement levels and school completion rates tend to be higher where quality school health programs are in place (Murray, Low, Hollis, Cross, and Davis, 2007; Vinciullo and Bradley, 2009). School health screening, as an important part of an overall school health program, is now advocated in both developed countries and developing countries (Bundy, 2011; McPherson and Olusanya, 2008) for this reason.

PRINCIPLES OF SCHOOL HEALTH SCREENING

There are a number of well-accepted criteria for deciding whether a health screening procedure is acceptable. Governmental and nongovernmental agencies and professional organizations often publish screening policy documents that consider such criteria. Most of these policy statements are based on the classic work of Wilson and Jungner (Andermann, Blanquaert, Beauchamp, and Déry, 2008; Wilson and Jungner, 1968), who framed 10 basic health and socioeconomic principles with which health screening should be consistent. These basic principles are listed in the form of questions below, with examples of school health screening procedures that relate to each issue.

1. Is the condition to be screened of public health importance? *Example:* Many school authorities arrange for screening of pediculosis (head lice). This may initially be seen as a low priority issue from a public health perspective but pediculosis infections have been found to result in high rates of absence from school—an adverse educational outcome (Counahan,

Andrews, Weld, Helen, and Speare, 2007). Given this information school health managers may appraise pediculosis as indeed having important effects on public health.

2. Is there an accepted and effective treatment for identified cases? *Example:* Modern genetic technology allows screening in childhood for a wide range of adult-onset genetic diseases (such as Huntington's disease, early-onset Alzheimer's disease, and Charcot-Marie-Tooth disease). However, many policy makers advise that such testing should not be carried out because the harms involved in testing (including possible damage to self-esteem and injury to family relationships) are not offset by benefits, since there is no accepted and effective treatment for these genetic conditions (Duncan, Savulescu, Gillam, Williamson, and Delatycki, 2005).

3. Are facilities for diagnosis and treatment available? *Example:* Screening programs are not worthwhile unless they include provision of follow-up services for diagnosis and treatment. These services need to be accessible to children and parents. Kimel (2006), in a study of compliance with elementary school vision screening, noted many economic and social barriers to children receiving follow-up exams, with less than 40% of students with positive screening outcomes attending follow-up services. In this situation, effort needs to be made to improve access to diagnostic and treatment services or the viability of the screening program should be reconsidered.

4. Is there a recognizable latent (early, asymptomatic) stage in the condition? *Example:* Typically, scoliosis—abnormal lateral curvature of the spine—is clinically apparent by age 10 years. Screening at this early stage allows for non-invasive treatments for children with scoliosis, such as back braces which stop the progression of spinal curvature (Bunnell, 2005).

5. Is there a suitable test to employ in screening? *Example:* There is a longstanding consensus that mental health screening and treatment programs are important for young school children (Hendren, Birrell Weisen, and Orley, 1994; WHO, 2003). A number of 'broadband' screening tests are available, which test for overall psycho-social functioning, and also 'narrowband' screening instruments, which test for specific disorders such as depression. Guzman et al. (2011), using data from two broadband tests, found that positive screen results in first grade students were strong predictors of low achievement scores in fourth grade. This study showed that suitable tests were available for use in mental health screening and that positive test results were of educational significance.

6. Is the test acceptable to the population to be screened? *Example:* Increasing attention is being paid to childhood obesity in many developed and developing countries (Ben-Sefer, Ben-Natan, and Ehrenfeld, 2009). Many school screening programs that assess height and weight now include body mass index (BMI) information when reporting results to children and parents, as part of an obesity prevention plan. It is important that any screening test is acceptable to the population being screened—and their parents, in the case of children. The level of parental support for BMI screening was found to be high in one North American study (Kubik, Fulkerson, Story, and Rieland, 2006), indicating that this test is acceptable to the test population.

7. Is the natural history of the condition understood? *Example:* Natural history refers to the uninterrupted timeline of a disorder from exposure to a causative agent to resolution or death. Peripheral hearing loss has many known causes, with a clearly understood natural history in most cases (Davis, Davis, and Mencher, 2009).

Both newborn hearing screening programs (Leigh, Schmulian-Taljaard, and Poulakis, 2010) and school-based hearing screening programs (see Chapter 4) make use of this information in developing test protocols. Based on knowledge of the natural history of many progressive genetic hearing disorders, school-based hearing screening is typically focused on younger children upon entry to elementary school.

8. Is there an agreed policy on whom to treat as patients? *Example:* School dental health screening often involves visual examination for caries with a recommendation for dental follow-up in positive cases (Donaldson and Kinirons, 2001). In this screening procedure, there is a consensus that all children who fail the screen should be treated and a consensus on the standard treatment options.

9. Is the cost of case finding (including diagnosis and treatment of those diagnosed) non-wastefully balanced in relation to expenditure on medical care as a whole? *Example:* Targeted cardiac screening has been suggested for school children who are commencing stimulant medication for attention deficit-hyperactivity disorder (Denchev, Kaltman, Schoenbaum, and Vitiello, 2010). However, analysis suggests that due to the very low prevalence of the cardiac disorders to be screened the cost-effectiveness of such screening is poor (Leslie et al., 2012).

10. Is case finding an ongoing process and not a "one-off" project? *Example:* School health screening systems have both initial and recurrent costs. These costs can be high (Bamford et al., 2007; Fayter et al., 2008; Yawn and Yawn, 2000) and unless a screening program is established as a long-term proposition the costs of case finding may be unacceptably high. In addition, many disorders targeted in school health screening have a low prevalence and cases will not be identified unless there is sustained program activity.

Other principles that should be considered in health screening have also been formulated. Haggard (1990) included four further principles that should be considered. These were suggested in relation to hearing screening but also have a much wider relevance.

1. The incidental harm should be very minor compared to the overall benefits. *Example:* There are four broad types of harm that can be caused by screening programs: physical, psychological, social, and ethical (Marshall, 1996a). Physical harm includes the discomfort caused by the screening process itself, or from the diagnostic assessment, or treatment procedures associated with positive findings. Psychological harm includes any stress or anxiety linked with the screening procedure, and any anxiety due to the results of a screening test (including stress related to false re-assurance in the case of incorrect negative results). Social harm includes the costs of participating in a screening program. These can include time, travel, and loss of productivity concerns that impact on children and their caregivers, as well as wider societal issues, such as generating an exaggerated fear of a disorder through screening. Ethical harm may arise when school health screening programs fail to obtain proper informed consent from parents (Marshall, 1996b). All types of harm should be carefully considered and compared to the overall benefits for any school health screening procedure.

2. There should be guidelines on how to explain results to parents with appropriate support. *Example:* School health screening programs may provide screening services to many thousands of children within a school district and it is important that positive findings that require follow-up are clearly communicated to parents and acted upon. At times, programs work hard to provide quality screening procedures but find it difficult to ensure that parents are fully informed and that appropriate follow-up action is taken. Parents may be unaware that their children have received screening or need extensive support from the school health system to access referral services (Clark, Clasen, Stolfi, and Jaballas, 2002). In this situation, guidelines that seek to improve current system limitations need to be developed.

3. All screening arrangements should be reviewed in the light of changes in demography, epidemiology, and other factors. *Example:* Certain groups of school children may be at greater than normal risk of health disorders that can be identified by school screening programs. When epidemiological findings flag this at-risk status then consideration needs to be given to changes in school screening arrangements. Studies that note the greater prevalence of vision and hearing disorders in children who are in foster care (Festinger and Duckman, 2000) or hearing loss in indigenous children (Leach, 1999) should lead to review of the school screening systems that support such groups of children.

4. Costs and effectiveness of screening should be examined on a case-type basis to maximize the effectiveness and benefit for each type before considering overall costs, effectiveness, and benefits. *Example:* Children with hearing loss are typically categorized as having mild, moderate, severe, or profound impairment, based on their average hearing threshold level. When considering costs and benefits of screening for hearing loss, it is important to distinguish the relatively modest benefits that detection of mild cases of hearing loss may bring from the potentially greater benefits that can be gained from the detection of severe or profound hearing loss (Haggard and Hughes, 1991).

Appraising the Performance of Screening

In general, screening program evaluation is an essential responsibility of managerial staff, one that should be conducted on an ongoing basis in order to identify and modify factors that may impede achievement of optimum performance and patient care (AAA, 2011). Rigorous and critical data analysis can serve many purposes, not least of all, its documentation can assist in demonstrating the worth and effectiveness of the screening program. On a finer level, appraising program data may identify shortfalls such as under-and over-referrals, training and equipment needs, high loss to follow-up rates, among other issues (AAA, 2011).

Program evaluation often begins with comprehensive analysis of the performance of screening tests included in the screening program. Such analysis allows management to competently judge test functionality, that is, can the test distinguish children at risk of the target disease/disorder from those who are not at risk? It is not adequate to merely keep a running count of the number of diseased/disordered cases who have failed screening or the number of normal cases who have passed screening. More valuable information can be provided by applying an array of test performance measures. Bristow, Fortnum, Fonseca, and Bamford (2008), in their investigation of the UK's school-entry hearing screening practices, found it impossible to recommend policy decisions regarding continuation or cessation of screening due to a distinct lack of robust test performance studies. As major decisions may hinge upon analysis of test performance measures, it is vital for program management to be familiar with at least the typical computations, as described below.

Reliability and Validity

In any program analysis, management would likely want to be reassured that the tests they have employed are reliable, repeatable, and precise in nature. The measurement of reliability involves determining whether test outcomes are consistent through time (test-retest reliability), across different examiners (inter-test reliability), within the same examiner (intra-test reliability), within the same child (subject reliability), and using different equipment (instrument reliability). If variation is found to be due to child, equipment, or examiner factors, it is important that this variation is minimal when compared with the natural variation found between diseased and non-diseased cases (Riegelman, 2000).

Program management must also feel confident that the screening tests are, indeed, appropriate for their given application. Can these tests actually determine the true risk of a particular disease or disorder? Hence, it is necessary to investigate the validity of the tests. This is defined as the degree in which the screening test results are consistent with the presence or absence of the target disease/disorder (Roeser and Clark, 2004). Test performance measures obtained through comparison with a reference standard diagnostic test, as described throughout this chapter, are often a chosen means of establishing validity. The reference standard must be reputable, reliable, and precisely capable of delineating those with the target condition, for example, an objective or subjective set of clinical findings that have received the approval of the professional community (Miller, Dunn, and Wei, 2007). Without such a 'gold standard', test performance measures can be hard to elucidate (Miller et al., 2007).

Sensitivity and Specificity

It is an imperative responsibility of a program manager to ensure optimal performance of the screening system. Central to such is examining their programs' ability to differentiate those children who would be classified as diseased/disordered by a reference standard from those that would be classified as without the target condition. One way that this may be achieved is through the use of a simple 2x2 frequency table, based upon signal detection theory (which operates from the assumption that decision-making will always involve a degree of uncertainty and attempts to quantify and display the separation of "signal" from the "noise", revealing in the process whether the test is suitable for its given aim).

As shown in Table 1.1 below, screening and reference standard tests can align positively in two ways: as true positive cases and true negative cases. True positives are the cases with the target condition that are correctly identified by a positive screening test result. True negatives are those without the target condition that are correctly identified by a negative screening test result. Similarly, screening and reference standard results can align negatively in two ways: as false positive cases and false negative cases. False positives are the cases without the target condition that are incorrectly identified by a positive screening test result. False negatives are those with the target condition that are incorrectly identified by a negative screening test result. Notably, these cases are expressed as number counts, not percentages or proportions, and will alter with the frequency of the target condition in the study group. On the other hand, sensitivity is the *proportion* of cases with the target condition that are correctly identified by screening, and specificity is the *proportion* of cases without the target condition that are correctly rejected by screening.

Table 1.1. Calculation of common test performance measures

	Reference Standard Positive (Failed)	Reference Standard Negative (Passed)	*TOTAL*
Screening Positive (Failed)	A = True Positive cases [aka Hits] True-positive rate = A/(A + C) [aka Hit rate or Sensitivity]	B = False Positive cases [aka False Alarms] False-positive rate = B/(B + D) [aka False-alarm rate]	*A + B*
Screening Negative (Passed)	C = False Negative cases [aka Misses] False-negative rate = C/(A + C)	D = True Negative cases [aka Correct Rejections] True-negative rate = D/(B + D) [aka Specificity]	*C + D*
TOTAL	*A + C* *(proportions added = 1)*	*B + D* *(proportions added = 1)*	*(N) =* *A + B + C + D*

These performance measures are valued, as they generally remain the same regardless of whether a disease/disorder is rare or highly prevalent. Table 1.1 shows the calculations for these proportions or rates. Note: Sensitivity is also referred to as the hit rate or true-positive rate, and specificity as the true-negative rate. The complements of each are the false-negative rate and false-positive (or false-alarm) rate, respectively. Further note that all such proportions may be altered by shifting the cut-off points for the pass/fail criteria of the screening test and/or the reference standard. A trade-off is usually produced, whereby the hit rate and false-positive rate increase or decrease in tandem (Turner, 1991).

So, once armed with these proportions, how does the program manager determine their worth? A full, formal cost-benefit analysis would likely answer the question, but it is not easy to put a price on, say, the cost of disruption to family dynamics or the benefits of early medical intervention. The determination of worth is a complex issue, one best made in consultation with all key stakeholders in a local, if not national, capacity. To illustrate the complexity, one may consider some of the disadvantages of a false positive outcome, which include but are not limited to: financial costs of unnecessary diagnostic assessments, psychological distress of both child and family, disruption to family dynamics, financial costs and potential harms should the diagnostic assessment also fail to correctly categorize the child (Roeser and Clark, 2004), contribution to excessive referral rates in turn over-extending resources and delaying the identification of true positive cases, and overall diminishment of stakeholder confidence in the screening system (Driscoll and McPherson, 2010). Similarly, consider the disadvantages of a false negative outcome: false reassurance delaying diagnosis, reduced benefits from early detection (Roeser and Clark, 2004), and, again, a decline in stakeholder confidence in the system (Driscoll and McPherson, 2010). Balancing the effects of screening systems is a difficult task for any manager. In some cases, it is of great assistance to be supported by professional position statements. For instance, the European consensus statement for preschool and school-age hearing screening (Skarzynski and Piotrowska, 2012) clearly states that such an endeavor will always produce over-referrals and, henceforth, for the benefit of the children, false positives are preferred over false negatives (p. 121).

Finally, it is of interest to note that in the medical field, many common diagnostic (not screening tests) only achieve sensitivity and specificity values of 80% and 90%, respectively (Driscoll and McPherson, 2010; Riegelman, 2000). Tests, be they diagnostic or screening, are rarely perfect in nature. Turner (1991) explains these imperfections in test performance as being due to the overlapping distribution phenomenon—tests can produce a wide range of scores and overlap is likely to exist between those obtained from diseased/disordered cases and those obtained from non-diseased/disordered cases. Sources of bias that may also contribute to fallible test systems are further discussed in a later section of this chapter.

An example: In Queensland, Australia, it is recommended by the state public health authority that all children are screened for visual acuity defects around the age of school-entry. The district manager of south-east Queensland conducted an analysis of test performance for all assessments in the school-entry health screen for the year 2011. During this year, a total of 49,851 children were screened under the program. Concerning the performance of the visual acuity screen (the Linear STYCAR 7 letter chart); it was found that 2,495 cases were referred to an optometrist for full diagnostic evaluation. Referred cases were asked to provide records of the diagnostic tests to the school health nurses. Records were obtained from 1,788 cases only. Of these, it was revealed that 1,602 cases had failed the diagnostic tests and had been correctly identified by the screening program (they were true positive cases). However, 186 cases had actually passed the diagnostic stage (they were false_positives). [Extrapolating these figures, had reports been collected for all 2,495 cases, 2,235 true positive and 258 false positive cases would have been expected.]

If a disease prevalence of 4.5% is assumed in this population, it can be inferred that 2,243 cases would have failed diagnostic testing, had such testing been completed for all cases rather than just those who were referred due to screening failure. The screening program is likely to have detected 2,235 of these cases. Thus, detection of eight cases were most likely missed (they are the system's false negatives). Furthermore, if a non-disease prevalence of 95.5% is assumed, and with the knowledge that 258 false positive cases were likely, it is possible to estimate that 47,350 cases were correctly rejected by the screening system (they were true negatives). The above mentioned values now allow the district manager to perform some test performance calculations:

A = True Positives = 2,235 C = False Negatives = 8
B = False Positives = 258 D = True Negatives = 47,350

Sensitivity = A/(A+C) = 2,235/(2,235+8) = 0.99
Specificity = D/(B+D) = 47,350/(258+47,350) = 0.99
False-Negative Rate = 1 – Sensitivity = 0.01
False-Positive Rate = 1 – Specificity = 0.01

Understandably, the district manager was highly pleased with these results and declared the visual acuity screener to be a valid inclusion in the school health screening battery!

Posterior Probabilities

Calculations of test sensitivity and specificity make the assumption that the results of the diagnostic test are foreknown, that is, a particular screening test may provide a passing result for a case definitively known to have the target condition. Posterior probabilities differ in that they provide an estimate of the chance that a case will have the target condition, knowing only the results of the screening test. Thus, some argue that posterior probabilities are a more clinically-appropriate measure of screening performance than hit rates and false-alarm rates, given that the screener usually does not know the diagnostic status of the case until after the screening has been performed, if at all. This is the most realistic of clinical scenarios—a child appears for screening and the tester must determine the risk of the child having a particular disease/disorder, having only the screening test results to work with.

Therefore, not only should program managers investigate the common measures of sensitivity and specificity, they should also see value in the calculation of posterior probabilities. The positive posterior probability (Pr[D/+]), otherwise known as the positive predictive value, is the probability that the presenting case does have the target condition given that a positive screening test result has been obtained.

Conversely, the negative posterior probability (Pr[N/-]), or the negative predictive value, is the probability that the presenting case does not have the target condition given that a negative test result has been obtained.

$$Pr[D/+] = HR/(HR + FA)$$

$$Pr[N/-] = TN/(TN + FN)$$

where HR = Hit rate, FA = False-alarm rate, TN = True-negative rate, and FN = False-negative rate.

In view of posterior probabilities being susceptible to the prevalence (PD) of the target condition, Miller et al. (2007) provides the additional equations below for consideration.

$$Pr[D/+] = HR \times PD/ (HR \times PD) + (FA \times [1 - PD])$$

$$Pr[N/-] = HR \times PD/ (FN \times PD) + (TN \times [1 - PD])$$

An important point to note in the interpretation of posterior probabilities is that these metrics are heavily affected by the false-negative and false-positive rates. Hence, when screening for a condition that has a typically low prevalence, a very high Pr[N/-] may be observed, in addition to a very low and unappealing Pr[D/+] (Turner, 1991). Such does not immediately render the test unsuitable for its purposes, rather the manager should choose to acknowledge the effect of prevalence on the measure and employ Miller et al.'s (2007) version of the posterior probability equations.

Accuracy and Efficiency

Some screening tests provide simple dichotomous results, for example, pass or fail. Others commonly include the capacity to manipulate the pass/fail criterion by altering a cut-off point. For instance, in hearing screening, passing of otoacoustic emission (OAE) testing may occur when a signal-to-noise ratio of 6 dB has been reached. Movement of the decision threshold will affect a test's performance measures. Thus, if the OAE pass criterion was set at 4 dB instead of 6 dB, one would likely see an increase in sensitivity but decrease in specificity as is generally the case. Conversely, raising the cut-off to 9 dB could increase specificity but decrease sensitivity (Miller et al., 2007).

When the program manager is dealing with continuous as opposed to dichotomous outcomes, the receiver operating characteristic (ROC) curve is an opportune way of visually displaying the effects of different pass/fail cut-off points upon the hit rate and false alarm rate. ROC curves are usually plotted on linear coordinates, and Swets (1988) suggests that at least five data points (cut-off values) are needed to adequately define the curve. The ROC display can also be used to judge the overall performance of a screening test, in that tests with poor performance will have curves that lie close to the rising diagonal, whereas perfect tests would have curves that approach the upper left hand corner, where the hit rate is 1 and the false alarm rate is 0 (Deeks, 2001; Driscoll and McPherson, 2010). Another way of expressing the same information is to use the curve to establish a test's accuracy (A'). This commonly used, quantitative index is depicted by the area under the curve (AUC) of the ROC display (see Figure 1.1). Effectively, it establishes the probability that a randomly chosen case with the target condition will be rated with greater suspicion than a case without the target condition.

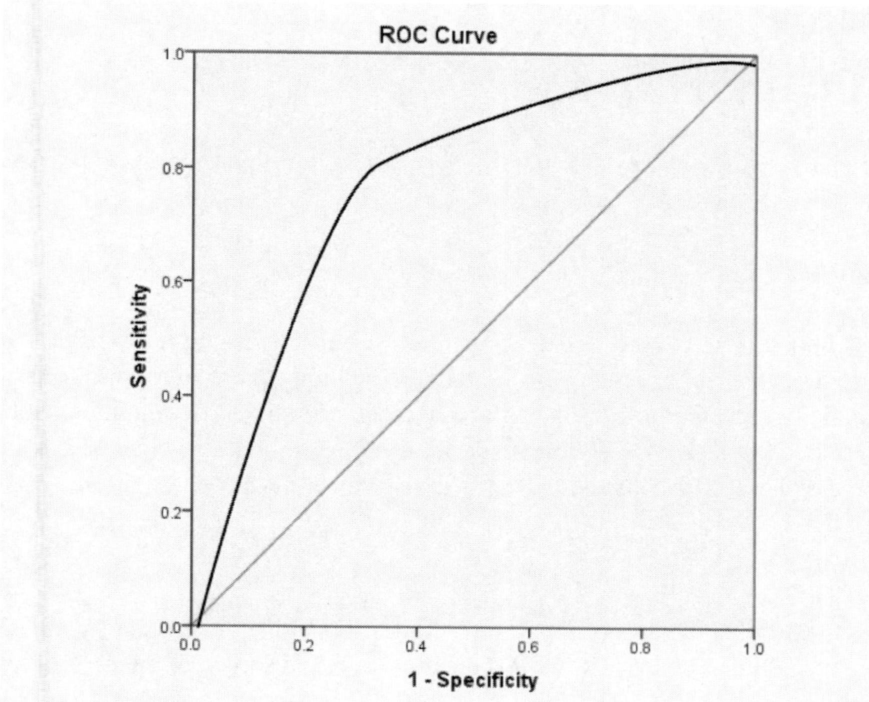

Figure 1.1. Example of a ROC curve.

A statistical computer program is usually used to calculate accuracy (Turner's, 1991, equation is given below) and, advantageously, a normal distribution of cases is not required.

Each single data point on the curve, in other words, each plotted cut-off criterion corresponding to one pair of hit and false alarm rates, is used to determine the accuracy of the test. Resulting values vary from 0.5 to 1 and can be interpreted as follows: Accuracy values approximating 0.5 indicate that the test is unable to discriminate between diseased and non-diseased cases and is no better than pure chance at the task, whereas a value of 1 indicates perfect performance with maximum sensitivity and specificity. The precision of the accuracy values should also be reported through inclusion of confidence intervals, the 95% range being conventional (Bossuyt et al., 2003).

Further, management may be interested in comparing the accuracy of different tests or of different cut-off criteria within the same test. In this case, the differences in accuracy values can be assessed for statistical significance using a critical-ratio test or *t*-test (Swets, 1988) or a modified Wilcoxon rank-sum test (Dawson-Sanders, 1994).

$$A' = 0.5 + (HR - FA) \times (1 + HR - FA) / 4HR \times (1 - FA)$$

Finally, another measure that may be employed to determine the overall performance of a screening test or system is the efficiency index (EF). By comparison of screening and reference standard results, it establishes the proportion of screening results that are truly correct (cases that have correctly passed or correctly failed). However, this measure is also influenced by the prevalence of the target condition, a relationship which is summarized by Turner (1991) in the second equation below.

$$EF = A + D / (A + B + C + D)$$

$$EF = (HR \times PD) + (TN \times [1 - PD])$$

where A = hits, B = false alarms, C = misses, D = correct rejections, and PD = prevalence.

Likelihood Ratios

The likelihood ratio is used to determine how well the screening test performs in ruling in, or ruling out, the likely presence of the target condition. These ratios specify how many times more likely particular test results will be in cases with the target condition than in those without (Deeks, 2001). A positive likelihood ratio refers to the occurrence of a positive test result, whereas the negative likelihood ratio deals with a negative test result, as described below.

Likelihood Ratio (+) =

Probability of positive test result if disease/disorder present (or HR) /
Probability of positive test result if disease/disorder absent (or FA)

Likelihood Ratio (-) =

Probability of negative test result if disease/disorder present (or FN) /
Probability of negative test result if disease/disorder absent (or TN)

Regarding interpretation of likelihood ratios, which can be of infinite value, the positive ratio (+) if above 10 provides the program manager with credible evidence of the likely presence of the target condition; above 5 is considered as strong evidence (Deeks, 2001). A low positive ratio (e.g., 1) would suggest to the program manager that the screening test does not offer any additional information that could assist with ruling in the target condition (Riegelman, 2000). The negative ratio (-) if below 0.1 provides convincing evidence of the likely absence of the target condition; below 0.2 is considered as strong evidence (Deeks, 2001), and a perfect test would display a value of zero. A high ratio (e.g., 1) would indicate that the test does not offer any additional information that could assist with ruling out the target condition (Riegelman, 2000).

Clinical Odds Ratios and Relative Risk

In technical terms, the odds ratio (OR) describes the strength of association between two binary data values. In clinical practice, however, it is often used to specify the risk of occurrence of a particular disease/disease/condition in one group of cases compared to another group. The groups may be categorized by experimental versus control, or any other dichotomous separation. An OR of 1 indicates that the condition is equally likely to be found in both groups. An OR >1 implies that the condition is more likely to occur in those of the first group than those of the second group and an OR <1 suggests that the condition is less likely to occur in those of the first group than in those of the second group. ORs are typically reported along with their 95% confidence intervals, which provide the OR range within which one can be 95% confident that the true value lies.

$$OR = AD / BC$$

where A = number of cases in Group 1 with the condition of interest, B = number of cases in Group 1 without the condition of interest, C = number of cases in Group 2 with the condition of interest, and D = number of cases in Group 2 without the condition of interest.

An example: A manager of a school hearing screening program is interested in whether children with a recurrent history of middle ear disease (as reported on the pre-screening parental questionnaire) are more likely to fail screening than those with no history of middle ear disease. This question has arisen as she has been informed that finances will not allow for annual screening of children in all grades in the district, thus, she must decide which high-risk children to screen beyond school-entry level.

Her calculations, using the above equation, provided an OR of 5.0 (CI: 4.6 – 5.7). This indicates that hearing screening failure was 5 times more likely to occur in those with a recurrent history of middle ear disease than in those without such a history. The program manager uses this result to add weight to her argument that children with a history of recurrent middle ear disease should be screened each year.

ORs are a suitable measure to perform in the event that a condition is rare (i.e., ≤10%) rather than highly prevalent. A more appropriate choice in that latter event is the use of relative risk (RR) measures. The RR is the risk of an event, or developing a condition, relative to exposure and is often seen in the medical literature in relation to randomized control trials. It is the ratio of the probability of the condition occurring in the exposed versus non-exposed group. Interpretation of the obtained values is as per described above for the OR. If the rare disease assumption holds, then, mathematically, the OR will approximate the RR regardless. Conversely, if the assumption is not true, the OR may overestimate the RR. Thus, the OR and the RR are not always interchangeable.

RR of a negative event or no condition = D(C + D) / B(A + B)
RR of a positive event or condition = C(C + D) / A(A + B)

where A = number of cases in Group 1 with the condition of interest, B = number of cases in Group 1 without the condition of interest, C = number of cases in Group 2 with the condition of interest, and D = number of cases in Group 2 without the condition of interest.

A Complete Example of Test Performance Analysis

The following is a hypothetical case, based upon a school-entry hearing screening program in Queensland, Australia. The state public health authority is considering the use of new technology (otoacoustic emission testing, OAEs) to replace the traditional pure tone test, in view of its vastly superior test-time efficiency. Thus, a senior project officer is charged with running a pilot study in a single district, to compare the performance of programs: Program 1 uses OAEs and Program 2 uses the pure tone test. Full diagnostic assessment is performed on the same day as the screening, using pure tone audiometry, and is conducted for all cases (screening passes and failures), in order to thoroughly appraise the performance of each program.

Finances have been allocated to the research endeavor for this purpose. Programs 1 and 2, as well as diagnostic testing, are performed by different testers who are blinded to the results of the other tests. Raw data obtained during the study appears in Table 1.2. This data was then used to construct a tetrachordic frequency table (see Table 1.3), from which multiple measures of test performance were calculated (see Table 1.4). [Note: Accuracy was not measured as the programs produced only one data set each (one set of hit and false-alarm rates). This was due to the pass/fail criteria for each test being set to a fixed point; alternative pass/fail criteria to alter test performance were not investigated in this instance.]

Based upon this appraisal, the project officer reports back to management that Program 2 is preferred as the screening tool of choice. Program 2 is marginally superior to Program 1 in most test performance values and clearly superior in the others. Notably, sensitivity, specificity, posterior probabilities, and efficiency are actually high for both programs, while the false-negative and false-positive rates are both low. The positive likelihood ratios are high for both programs and indicate that both tests are capable of predicting the likely occurrence of hearing loss.

Table 1.2. Raw data obtained from school hearing screening project, comparing the performance of two different screening tests (OAEs and pure tone screening) to a reference standard of diagnostic pure tone audiometry

	Program 1 OAEs	Program 2 Pure tones
Total screened	1,211	1,211
Positive screening cases (failed)	140	107
Negative screening cases (passed)	1,071	1,104
Positive reference standard (failed)	120	120
Negative reference standard (passed)	1,091	1,091
Hearing loss diagnoses in positive screening cases	112	100
Hearing loss diagnoses in negative screening cases	8	2

Table 1.3. Frequencies of pass/fail results, where 1 denotes the OAE screening program and 2 denotes the pure tone screening program

	Reference Standard Positive (Failed)	Reference Standard Negative (Passed)
Screening Positive (Failed)	A1 = 112 A2 = 100	B1 = 28 B2 = 7
Screening Negative (Passed)	C1 = 8 C2 = 2	D1 = 1,063 D2 = 1,102

Table 1.4. Standard test performance measures for each program

Test Performance Measure	Program 1 OAEs	Program 2 Pure tones
Hit rate = A/(A + C)	0.93	0.98
False-alarm rate = B/(B + D)	0.03	0.01
False-negative rate = C/(A + C)	0.07	0.02
True-negative rate = D/(B + D)	0.97	0.99
Positive posterior probability = HR/(HR + FA)	0.97	0.99
Negative posterior probability = TN/(TN + FN)	0.93	0.98
Efficiency index = A + D/(A + B + C + D)	0.97	0.99
Likelihood ratio (+) = HR/FA	31	98
Likelihood ratio (-) = FN/TN	0.07	0.02

Where A = true positive cases, B = false positive cases, C = false negative cases, D = true negative cases, HR = hit rate, FA = false-alarm rate, TN = true-negative rate, and FN = false-negative rate.

Similarly, the negative likelihood ratios are low for each program and indicate that both tests can provide convincing evidence of the likely absence of hearing loss. However, the project officer also cleverly notes that such a global decision regarding which test to employ cannot be truly reached until thought is given to the other critical factors described in the "Other Considerations" section of this chapter!

Other Considerations

First, the true performance of a screening system can be obscured by many sources of potential bias, as summarized below. An awareness of such issues and their latent effects on test performance measures is highly worthwhile, regardless of whether the screening tests in question produce quantitative or qualitative results, or whether they are performed by trained professionals or automated devices. A well-constructed screening program should make an effort to control for all sources of bias, as far as is feasible.

- Selection bias: Results of the screening may be influenced by differences between cohorts, for example, those who voluntarily participate in the screen and those who do not. Disparities may be based on baseline health status, socio-demographic characteristics, screening history, risk-factor spread, and severity of the target condition (Miller et al., 2007). It is also referred to as 'spectrum' bias (Bossuyt et al., 2008).
- Length-time bias: Screening systems may have a propensity to detect progressive conditions rather than aggressive states, as in the latter case symptoms may be obvious prompting detection through routine diagnostic pathways (Miller et al., 1997).
- Context bias: Screeners may be more likely to interpret a subjective test's result as being abnormal if it occurs in an environment where prevalence of the target condition is high (Bossuyt et al., 2008).
- Test review bias: If screeners are aware of the results of reference standard testing, this may influence their interpretation of screening results, potentially inflating the measured accuracy of the screening test (Bossuyt et al., 2008).
- Diagnostic review bias: Conversely, knowing the results of the screening test may influence interpretation of the reference standard test (Bossuyt et al., 2008).
- Clinical review bias: The screeners' interpretation of a test may be buoyed by the seeking of addition clinical information concerning the child, again boosting measured accuracy of the screening test (Bossuyt et al., 2008).

Second, it should be noted that in the event that the screening system involves multiple stages with repeat use of the same test or use of different tests, it is necessary to recalculate or model the test performance for each stage and the system as a whole, rather than just examining the component tests. Amalgamation of screening tests is referred to as a test protocol and may be chosen as a means of improving overall test performance or to manipulate hit and false-alarm rates (Driscoll and McPherson, 2010; Turner, 1991). Application of a test protocol, as opposed to a single test, however, does not guarantee enhanced performance—it may, conversely, worsen it (Turner, 1991). For further information concerning the use of tests in series or parallel, with strict or loose criterion, and with significant correlation between tests, the reader is referred to Turner (1991) and Turner and Hurley (2009).

Third, it is worth considering that program evaluation encompasses more than simple test performance analyses. To ensure the effectiveness of the program in its entirety, data pertaining to follow-up management pathways should also be explored. In particular, it would be useful to record and further evaluate the number of cases referred for follow-up against the number that do receive such follow-up, the number of diagnosed cases along with details of the diseases/disorders (the "yield" being the number of new cases diagnosed per 100 children screened), and the number of cases that receive medical or other intervention post diagnosis. Such would require a sophisticated data management system, of the kind described in Chapter 11. Considering data beyond the standard test performance measures is especially important when needing to compare the accomplishments of two or more screening tests. The final choice of screening test should also be based on knowledge of test feasibility, associated harms/benefits, cost-effectiveness, and the availability of effective pass/fail criteria (Driscoll and McPherson, 2010). All information must be enmeshed to provide an accurate answer to the question of how satisfactorily does each test meet the primary objective of screening—does it alter the natural history of the condition and/or improve the child's prognosis (Driscoll and McPherson, 2010)?

Conclusion

School health screening should always be considered within the wider context of children's health and educational needs. From the earliest days of school health services, the fundamental aim has been to improve children's lives and improve children's learning. Screening supports this objective by identifying disorders that may otherwise go undetected and disadvantage affected children. School health screening systems have firm historical and ethical foundations and a large research literature supporting their practice.

Professionals involved in school screening need to be aware of this research to confirm that their own programs have a secure evidence base. Program managers need to ensure that regular program review is conducted and make use of appropriate program evaluation methods. Examples given in the present chapter highlight the way reflection and evaluation can give school health managers confidence in their screening systems.

References

American Academy of Audiology. (2011). *Childhood hearing screening guidelines*. Retrieved from http://www.audiology.org/resources/documentlibrary/Documents/20110926_ChildhoodHearingScreeningGuidelines.pdf.

Andermann, A., Blanquaert, I., Beauchamp, S., and Déry, V. (2008). Revisiting Wilson and Jungner in the genomic age: A review of screening criteria over the past 40 years. *Bulletin of the World Health Organization*, 86(4), 317-319.

Bamford, J. Fortnum, H., Bristow, K., Smith, J., Vamvakas, G., Davies, L., Hind, S. (2007). Current practice, accuracy, effectiveness and cost-effectiveness of the school entry hearing screen. *Health Technology Assessment*, 11(32), 1-168.

Ben-Sefer, E., Ben-Natan, M. and Ehrenfeld, M. (2009). Childhood obesity: Current literature, policy and implications for practice. *International Nursing Review*, 56(2), 166-173.

Bossuyt, P. M., Reitsma, J. B., Bruns, D. E., Gatsonis, C. A., Glasziou, P. P., Irwig, L. M., … Lijmer, J. G. (2003). The STARD statement for reporting of diagnostic accuracy: Explanation and elaboration. *Clinical Chemistry*, 49(1), 7-18.

Braveman, P. A. and Tarimo, E. (1994). *Screening in primary health care*. Geneva: WHO.

Bristow, K., Fortnum, H., Fonseca, S., and Bamford, J. (2008). United Kingdom school-entry hearing screening: Current practice. *Archives of Disease in Childhood*, 93, 232-235.

Bundy, D. (2011). *Rethinking school health. A key component of education for all.* Washington, DC: World Bank.

Bunnell, W. P. (2005). Selective screening for scoliosis. *Clinical Orthopaedics and Related Research*, 434, 40-45.

Clark, D., Clasen, C., Stolfi, A., and Jaballas, E. R. (2002). Parent knowledge and opinions of school health services in an urban public school system. *Journal of School Health*, 72(1), 18-22.

Counahan, M. L, Andrews, R. M., Weld, H., Helen, W., and Speare, R. (2007). What parents in Australia know and do about head lice. *Rural and Remote Health*, 7(3), 687.

Davis, A., Davis, K. and Mencher, G. (2009). Epidemiology of permanent childhood hearing impairment. In: V. E. Newton (Ed.), *Paediatric audiological medicine* (2nd ed.) (pp. 1-28). Chichester: John Wiley and Sons.

Dawson-Saunders, B. (1994). *Basic and clinical biostatistics* (2nd ed.). Norwalk, CT: Appleton and Lange.

Deeks, J. J. (2001). Systematic reviews of evaluations of diagnostic and screening tests. *British Medical Journal*, 323, 157-162.

Denchev, P., Kaltman, J. R., Schoenbaum, M., and Vitiello, B. (2010). Modeled economic evaluation of alternative strategies to reduce sudden cardiac death among children treated for attention deficit/hyperactivity disorder. *Circulation,* 121(11), 1329-1337.

Devaney, B., Schochet, P., Thornton, C., Fasciang, N., and Gavin, A. (1993). *Evaluating the effects of school health interventions on school performance: Design report.* Princeton, NJ: Mathematics Policy Research Inc.

Donaldson, M. and Kinirons, M. (2001). Effectiveness of the school dental screening programme in stimulating dental attendance for children in need of treatment in Northern Ireland. *Community Dentistry and Oral Epidemiology*, 29(2), 143-149.

Driscoll, C. J. and McPherson, B. (2010). Newborn screening: History, principles, and analysis. In: C. J. Driscoll and B. McPherson (Eds.), *Newborn screening systems: The complete perspective* (pp. 3-24). San Diego, CA: Plural.

Duncan, R. E., Savulescu, J., Gillam, L., Williamson, R., and Delatycki, M. B. (2005). An international survey of predictive genetic testing in children for adult onset conditions. *Genetics in Medicine*, 7(6), 390-396.

Fayter, D., Nixon, J., Hartley, S., Rithalia, A., Butler, G., Rudolf, M., … Westwood, M. (2008). Effectiveness and cost-effectiveness of height-screening programmes during the primary school years: A systematic review. *Archives of Disease in Childhood*, 93(4), 278-284.

Ferdinands, G. (1891). Investigations into the eyesight of children attending some of the Aberdeenshire Board Schools. *British Medical Journal*, 2(1602), 585-588.

Festinger, T. and Duckman, R. (2000). Seeing and hearing: Vision and audiology status of foster children in New York City. *Journal of Behavioral Optometry*, 4, 77-81.

Gandevia, B. (1978). *Child health and welfare*. Sydney: Pergamon Press.

Guzman, M. P., Jellinek, M., George, M., Hartley, M., Squicciarini, A. M., Canenguez, K. M., ... Murphy, J. M. (2011). Mental health matters in elementary school: First-grade screening predicts fourth grade achievement test scores. *European Child and Adolescent Psychiatry*, 20(8), 401-411.

Haggard, M. and Hughes, E. (1991). *Screening children's hearing*. London: HMSO.

Haggard, M. P. (1990). Hearing screening in children--state of the art(s). *Archives of Disease in Childhood*, 65(11), 1193-1195.

Hall, D. and Elliman, D. (Eds.). (2006). *Health for all children* (4th ed., revised). Oxford: OUP.

Hall, D., Williams, J. and Elliman, D. (2009). *The child surveillance handbook* (3rd ed.). Abingdon, UK: Radcliffe Publishing.

Henderson, P. (1975). *The School Health Service 1908-1974*. London: HMSO.

Hendren, R., Birrell Weisen, R. and Orley, J. (1994). *Mental health programmes in schools*. Geneva: WHO.

Hirst, J. D (1991). Public health and the public elementary schools, 1870-1907. *History of Education*, 20(2), 107-118.

Kimel, L. S. (2006). Lack of follow-up exams after failed school vision screenings: An investigation of contributing factors. *Journal of School Nursing*, 22(3), 156-162.

Kubik, M. Y., Fulkerson, J. A., Story, M., and Rieland, G. (2006). Parents of elementary school students weigh in on height, weight, and body mass index screening at school. *Journal of School Health*, 76(10), 496-501.

Leach, A. (1999). Otitis media in Australian Aboriginal children: An overview. *International Journal of Pediatric Otorhinolaryngology*, 49, S173-S178.

Leigh, G., Schmulian-Taljaard, D. and Poulakis, Z. (2010). Newborn hearing screening. In: C. J. Driscoll and B. McPherson, *Newborn screening systems: The complete perspective* (pp. 95-115). San Diego: Plural.

Leslie, L. K., Cohen, J. T., Newburger, J. W., Alexander, M. E., Wong, J. B., Sherwin, E. D., ...Triedman, J. K. (2012). Costs and benefits of targeted screening for causes of sudden cardiac death in children and adolescents. *Circulation*, 125(21), 2621-2629.

Marshall, K. G. (1996a). Prevention, How much harm? How much benefit? 3. Physical, psychological and social harm. *Canadian Medical Association Journal*, 155(2), 169-176.

Marshall, K. G. (1996b). Prevention, How much harm? How much benefit? 4. The ethics of informed consent for preventive screening programs. *Canadian Medical Association Journal*, 155(4), 377-383.

McPherson, B. and Olusanya, B. O. (2008). Screening for hearing loss in developing countries. In: B. McPherson and R. Brouillette (Eds.), *Audiology in developing countries* (pp. 73-105). NY: Nova Science.

Means, R. K. (1975). *Historical perspectives on school health*. Thorofare, NJ: Charles B. Stack.

Miller, D. C., Dunn, R. L. and Wei, J. T. (2007). Assessing the performance and validity of diagnostic tests and screening programs. In: D. F. Penson and J. T. Wei (Eds.), *Clinical research methods for surgeons* (pp. 157-173). Towata, NJ: Humana Press.

Mitchell, J. J., Capua, A., Clow, C., and Scriver, C. R. (1996). Twenty-year outcome analysis of genetic screening programs for Tay-Sachs and beta-thalassemia disease cariers in high schools. *American Journal of Human Genetics*, 59, 793-798.

Murray, N. G., Low, B. J., Hollis, C., Cross, A. W., and Davis, S. M. (2007). Coordinated school health programs and academic achievement: A systematic review of the literature. *Journal of School Health*, 77, 589-600.

Riegelman, R. R. (2000). *Studying a study and testing a test* (4th ed.). Philadelphia, PA: Lippincott Williams and Wilkins.

Roeser, R. J. and Clark, J. L. (2004). Screening for auditory disorders. In: R. J. Roeser and M. P. Downs (Eds.), *Auditory disorders in school children: The law, identification, remediation* (4th ed.) (pp. 96-123). NY: Thieme.

Skarzynski, H. and Piotrowska, A. (2012). Screening for pre-school and school-aged hearing problems: European consensus statement. *International Journal of Pediatric Otorhinolaryngology*, 76, 120-121.

Swets, J. A. (1988). Measuring the accuracy of diagnostic systems. *Science*, 240, 1285-1293.

Turner, R. G. (1991). Making clinical decisions. In: W. F. Rintelmann (Ed.), *Hearing assessment* (2nd ed.) (pp. 679-738). Austin TX: Pro-Ed.

Turner, R. G. and Hurley, A. (2009). Evaluating a model to predict protocol performance. *Journal of the American Academy of Audiology*, 20, 644-651.

Uchida, T. (2008). School health activities in Japan. *Japan Medical Association Journal*, 51 (1), 5-11.

Veselak, K. E. (1959). Historical steps in the development of the modern school health program. *Journal of School Health*, 29(7), 262-269.

Vinciullo, F. M. and Bradley, B. J. (2009). A correlational study of the relationship between a coordinated school health program and school achievement: A case for school health. *Journal of School Nursing*, 25, 453-465.

Wilson, J. M. G. and Jungner, G. (1968). *Principles and practice of screening for disease*. Geneva: WHO.

World Bank. (1993). *World development report 1993*. NY: Oxford University Press.

World Health Organization (WHO). (2003). *Caring for children and adolescents with mental disorders: Setting WHO directions*. Geneva: WHO.

Yawn, B. P. and Yawn, R. A. (2000). The estimated cost of school scoliosis screening. *Spine*, 25(18), 2387-2391.

In: School Health Screening Systems
Editors: Bradley McPherson and Carlie J. Driscoll
ISBN: 978-1-63117-942-6

Chapter 2

THE YOUNG SCHOOL CHILD: COMMON DISEASES AND DISORDERS

Donald C. Brown*
University of Edinburgh, Edinburgh, Scotland, UK

ABSTRACT

The disorders affecting children during the early years of their education range from simple short-lived illness to life-long chronic conditions. The majority of children will have their schooling interrupted by disease only occasionally and for a few days at a time. Viral infection and minor injury will account for most of these. Schoolchildren with ongoing disorders, for example, asthma, diabetes, and epilepsy, may be affected by the condition while at school, or need to take time off to attend hospital or have treatment delivered elsewhere. Most children will experience conditions affecting their teeth, hair, or skin at some stage during primary education, whereas only a few will be affected by hematological or malignant disease. Disorders of the senses and learning disability may require significant adaptation of curricula, or result in education being delivered outside mainstream systems. Significant mobility disorders, for example, cerebral palsy and arthritis will cause difficulty moving around school premises and taking part fully in physical education. Regarding behavioral, emotional, and social difficulties, the factors causing and maintaining such problems are seen to change from family-based to peer-related as the early years of formal education proceed.

INTRODUCTION

During the first few years of life, children become increasingly mobile and mix more with other children. Their opportunities to contract infectious illness via contact with others are numerous. Viral and bacterial diseases are common. Curiosity and mobility combine with lack of judgment and inexperience to result in many accidents. The growing child's sense of identity, peer jealousy and personality conflicts mean that behavior disorders, trivial and

* Email: donald.brown@nhs.net.

significant, are common. The school environment presents foci for socialization and transfer of infections. The introduction of formal teaching and assessment exposes problems related to intelligence and deficiencies of the sense organs. At this stage, learning and psychological problems may become more evident. Hearing loss, visual impairment, physical abnormality and neurodevelopmental handicap all modify children's education and lifestyle during this period.

INFECTIONS AND INJURIES

Infections

Viral illnesses and minor injuries are extremely common in early childhood. They may be viewed as challenges for the child to overcome and opportunities to learn to cope and adapt. Viral and bacterial illnesses aid the development of immunity and allow the child to develop appropriate responses, recognizing short-lived illness as a natural part of growing up and life in general. Minor injuries play a similar role. Children can learn, through the experience of falls, bruises, cuts and minor burns, how to avoid more serious injury.

Short periods or single days of absence from primary education due to illness usually involve viral upper respiratory tract infections or gastroenteritis. Symptoms include *coryza*, cough, sore throat, diarrhea and vomiting with or without fever. Whether, and for how long, a child stays off school will depend not only on the severity of symptoms. Parental attitude to illness, work patterns, family dynamics, and the availability of child care may all influence the last-minute decision whether to dispatch children to school or keep them at home.

The prevalence of infective illness varies by geography, age, and season. It can be reduced or interrupted by immunization and public health campaigns. However, the winter months in general remain times of epidemics and outbreaks of influenza and other viral respiratory tract pathogens along with similar organisms affecting the gastrointestinal tract. Some infectious illnesses are quickly recognized because the disease is known to be affecting the local community or when a typical rash is present, for example, varicella (chickenpox) or parvovirus (fifth disease). Streptococcal pharyngitis, conjunctivitis, otitis media, ringworm and scabies all have typical symptoms and clinical courses. Transmission of tuberculosis is by droplet spread from an individual with open disease. This may be an elderly relative, or in the case of school children, an adult with undetected tuberculosis who is working in the school. Many infections are subclinical.

Viral illness may affect the liver (hepatitis, Epstein Barr virus). Lyme borreliosis (Lyme disease) is a spirochetal infection with ticks as the vectors of spread. During the early stage of infection there may be a typical rash (erythema migrans), fever, aches and pains and lymph node enlargement. The infection can progress to cause malaise, fatigue, headache, meningism and arthralgia, culminating in severe cases with arthritis, meningitis, encephalitis, neuritis and carditis. Urinary tract infection is frequently asymptomatic, at least in the early stage. Older children may present with enuresis, frequency, dysuria and/or pyrexia.

Injuries

Accidents and traumatic injuries are the leading cause of death of children and a major reason for hospital admission and outpatient attendances. They occur due to high impact trauma (such as falls from a height or motor vehicle collisions) or during free play and organized sports. Fortunately, the commonest injuries affecting children are minor ones, such as small lacerations, abrasions, minor burns, and insect bites and stings. Similarly, although children have frequent episodes of head trauma, most are minor. During primary education, bicycle accidents become a more common cause of head injury than falls or motor vehicle collisions. Fractures in childhood can involve any part of a bone. Growth plate fractures are specific to children. The growth plate is a cartilaginous disc near the end of the long bones, responsible for the longitudinal growth of the bone. Injury to it can result in subsequent abnormal growth.

PHYSICAL PROBLEMS

Asthma

Asthma affects many children – between one in five and one in ten at some stage in their lives. It can be understood by most children by explaining that it is a condition that affects the airways – the small tubes that guide air in and out of the lungs. These airways are more likely to be sensitive and inflamed than average. When the child with asthma comes into contact with something that irritates their airways (a trigger) the airways become narrower, making it more difficult to breathe. Many children are introduced to human biology during primary education, and can comprehend explanation of the pathophysiology of asthma. For example, they can be told how the muscles around the walls of the airways can tighten as the lining of the airway becomes inflamed, and how mucus gets in the way of air that is heading towards, or away from, the lungs. This is turn helps children to understand why and when their preventer and reliever medications are required.

It is important that children, parents and staff are trained to recognize the typical symptoms of asthma – cough (particularly at night and during exercise), wheeze (a whistling sound in the chest) and becoming short of breath, or experiencing difficulty talking or moving. School children with asthma, and their peers, should know that asthma is not an infectious disease, but may run in families and be associated with other allergic conditions such as eczema and rhinitis. The negative effects of smoking should be emphasized so that children with and without asthma can make healthy lifestyle choices.

The treatment of asthma involves two types of medication – preventer (prophylactic) and reliever (emergency). As with all preventative treatments, children may find it difficult to understand why they would need to take any medicine while they are feeling quite well. It is important for them to understand how preventer medication is designed to reduce airway inflammation and sensitivity. Hence, they are more likely to adhere to a once or twice daily dose of oral or inhaled medication. The most important aspect of reliever therapy is that it is freely available for the child to take when they perceive their symptoms are increasing, or an asthma attack occurs.

On average, asthma will affect two children in every classroom. Campaigns by public health and voluntary organizations can aim to make school staff more aware of how to deal with asthma at school. School health staff and teachers should be made aware of individual children's medications and any likely triggers of exacerbations. School activities involving animals, exercise or fumes, and those in the playground and outside may require special consideration. The benefits of exercise can be promoted, both in terms of overall fitness and a tendency to improve asthma control. Adherence to preventer therapy, having relievers freely available, and the judicious use of warm up/down activities are all ways to ensure that the child with asthma can participate enthusiastically in exercise and sport. Anxiety regarding asthma being triggered by exercise can be reduced by making clear plans that allow the child to stop, take their reliever inhaler and wait five minutes or until they feel better before resuming.

Children with asthma may be at a disadvantage because people may believe that their asthma should prevent them from joining in with sporting activity and exercise. Full participation should be the goal for all but the most severely affected. It should be ensured that everyone involved in physical education is aware of the needs of children with asthma. There should be an opportunity for children who have exercise-induced asthma to take a dose of their inhaler before they start exercise. Teachers should be aware that some children are shy of doing this in public. Children should make sure that they bring their inhalers to the gym, the sports field, or the swimming pool.

It can be very reassuring for school children with asthma to know that their school has an asthma policy with appropriate guiding principles. The school should welcome all children with asthma, encouraging them to participate fully in all aspects of school life. The school can recognize that asthma is an important condition affecting many children and that immediate access to the appropriate therapy is vital. The school can aim to make its environment favorable to children with asthma. For example, it can be ensured that pupils are never exposed to passive smoking, that school pets are accommodated away from classrooms, and that pupils are allowed to leave science lessons involving irritant fumes. Staff should have a clear understanding of what to do in the event of a child having an asthma attack. Training sessions for teaching and non-teaching staff will increase their confidence in implementing treatment. Guidance on what to do in the event of an asthma attack can be displayed prominently, particularly in staff rooms, gyms, and other physical education areas.

Blood Disorders and Tumors

The onset and progression of iron deficiency are usually gradual. Most children will not have major symptoms, but instead ill-defined weakness, irritability, fatigability, headaches, anorexia and poor weight gain. There is an association between iron deficiency anemia, impaired learning, and decreased school achievement. Children with hemophilia have inadequate amounts of blood coagulation factors and hence unreliable blood clotting ability. They experience bleeding into the joints, mouth, and renal tracts. Idiopathic thrombocytopenic purpura is caused by the production of antibodies that bind to platelets, resulting in their destruction. Typically, a previously well child develops easy bruising and petichiae, but there is the possibility of serious gastrointestinal or intracranial bleeding with very low platelet counts. Sickle cell disease is a genetic disorder of hemoglobin which results in abnormal red blood cells and subsequent anemia, and pain from infarction. Thalassemia involves a different abnormality of hemoglobin that results in anemia and enlargement of the spleen. Henoch Schonlein purpura (HSP, anaphylactoid purpura, allergic purpura) is a diffuse necrotizing vasculitis, presumed to have an immune origin. The main manifestations are non-blanching skin rash, arthritis, abdominal pain and hematuria. As the cause is essentially unknown and the prognosis varies – most children have no lasting complications while a few may develop renal failure – HSP is a worrying condition for children and their families, who can be given little definite reassurance during the early days of the illness.

Leukemia is the most common form of malignancy seen in childhood and the second commonest cause of death in children between five and fourteen years of age in the western world. What were once invariably fatal conditions, the childhood leukemias are now more frequently considered treatable and curable. Leukemia is caused by over-proliferation of immature blood cells resulting in suppression of normal blood-forming processes and infiltration of various organs. Fever, pallor, fatigue, purpura, and anorexia are common presenting symptoms. Therapies such as chemotherapy, bone marrow transplantation, treatment for relapse, and supportive care are becoming more sophisticated and successful.

The solid tumors seen in the pediatric population include Wilm's tumor or nephroblastoma (affecting the kidney), neuroblastoma (nervous system), rhabdomyosarcoma (embryonic muscle), germ cell tumor and teratoma (primordial germ cells), retinoblastoma (eye), Ewing sarcoma, and osteogenic sarcoma (bone).

Cerebral Palsy

Cerebral palsy is a persistent but not unchanging disorder of posture and movement appearing early in life following any pathological interference with brain function. It is the commonest cause of physical handicap in childhood. Cerebral palsy is classified according to the status of neuromuscular tone and the limbs affected. Schools can provide for the education and some of the medical needs of children with cerebral palsy. There may be requirement for physical therapy, speech therapy, special nursing, hydrotherapy, and other aids and resources. Where and how the child's education is delivered will depend on a number of factors, not least whether problems with mobility can be overcome.

Congenital Heart Disease

Most children born with congenital cardiac abnormalities will have these repaired fully before school age. Some will require repeat assessment, investigation, or further operative procedures during their school years. They may require long term medication, or need to adapt their lifestyle or physical activity to varying degrees.

Cystic Fibrosis

School children with cystic fibrosis suffer a combination of recurrent purulent chest infection and difficulties with poor weight gain and diarrhea due to fat malabsorption.

Treatment of cystic fibrosis is arduous and time consuming, involving physiotherapy, antibiotics, pancreatic enzyme supplementation, physical exercise, vitamins and nutritional support. Time off school may be necessary for treatment, clinic attendance, hospitalization, and intercurrent illness. The condition is likely to interfere with school trips, musical, sporting and other extracurricular activities.

Dental Caries

Tooth brushing is one of the earliest activities of daily living introduced as a routine to preschool children. Although careful parental supervision is recommended in order to ensure children's dental care is adequate, the actual degree of supervision, and the attention paid to regular tooth brushing vary widely. Young children differ in their knowledge of how diet and dental care can help prevent dental caries. Attractive facial appearance may not be as important an outcome to them as it will be during adolescence. Adherence with a routine chore, the outcome of which offers no immediate reward, may therefore be low. Enlightened schools offer education and training in dental hygiene methods and healthy diet in the early years. However, the damage may already be done and dental caries remains the commonest condition affecting British school entrants.

Together with head lice, dental caries prevention is based in public health education during the early years, as discussed further in Chapter 6. Education of parents and, subsequently, of children and their peers, aims to instill knowledge of, and adherence with, preventative strategies to improve the dental and oral health of all children. Aside from inadequate dental hygiene, poor dietary habits, particularly consumption of confectionery with high sugar content, increase the tendency to develop caries. As with tooth brushing, parents have the greatest influence, both as supervisors and role models. Children's understanding and attitudes can be improved by education of parents at their own dental checks, or targeted campaigns at schools, libraries, dentists, or via social media.

Diabetes

Juvenile diabetes is so called because it usually begins during childhood or early adulthood. Insulin therapy, via injection or infusion through the skin, is nearly always required from when the condition is first diagnosed. In the absence of insulin, glucose remains in the bloodstream and the blood glucose level rises, particularly after meals. Glucose may then be excreted in the urine, accompanied by water leading to increased amounts of urine being passed, and subsequently increased thirst, in the period leading up to diagnosis.

If diabetes is diagnosed during school years, children may spend between two days and two weeks in hospital while blood glucose levels are brought under control and the nature and management of the condition are introduced and explained. During the days or weeks just prior to diagnosis, diabetic children's schooling may have been affected by changes in their appetite, weight, or energy. They may have suffered urinary problems, such as frequency or day or night incontinence, abdominal pain, or mood changes. Diagnosis may provide an opportunity to explain these difficulties to the child, their family, their friends, and their teachers. Diabetes liaison staff are best placed to deliver such information and provide knowledge of the condition required by the child's friends and carers.

Most diabetes treatment regimens require several injections per day of insulin, meaning that at least one injection will require to be administered during the school day. The support offered, in terms of a room in which to inject, and staff to supervise, will vary from school to school depending on available resources. Similarly, how families react to intercurrent illness will depend on how carefully sick day plans are explained and implemented. A child with diabetes will be more likely to miss a day's schooling with a straightforward viral illness if they or their family are unnecessarily anxious that there will be a deleterious effect on diabetic control. These concerns can be alleviated by prior explanation, to family and relevant school staff, about how blood testing and insulin administration should be altered during episodes of infectious illness.

Epilepsy

Epilepsy, the tendency for a temporary disturbance in brain activity to cause seizures, is relatively common in school age children. Most schools will have at least one pupil with epilepsy that currently affects them. For the most part children respond well to treatment and their seizures eventually stop. Thus, many will grow out of the condition and no longer require regular treatment. Fits and faints are common in children, and less than half of such episodes turn out to be epileptic seizures. There may be a significant period of time before children, and those around them, know for certain that they have epilepsy. School friends or staff may be the first witnesses who see the affected child having a seizure. The child and their peers may experience fear and misunderstanding until the condition is identified, explained, and managed appropriately.

After diagnosis, the affected child, their family, friends and teachers will require accurate and appropriate information about the condition. This may include explanation regarding the type of epilepsy, its treatment and how the child's day-to-day activities may be affected. Epilepsy nurse specialists and voluntary organizations may be well placed to discuss relevant issues in an understandable way.

In addition to attendance at hospital, or inpatient admission, for seizures or intercurrent illness, children with epilepsy may need to miss school to attend medical review or investigation. They may miss out on trips unless the school is resourced to provide the supervision necessary to reassure the child and their family that they will be as safe as possible away from the home or school environment. As far as possible, children with epilepsy should be encouraged and supported to take part in a wide range of school activities. Some children with epilepsy have difficulties with learning and behavior. Educational and clinical psychologists can provide support in these areas.

Eye and Vision Abnormalities

Severe visual abnormalities requiring special education are rare. In tropical areas, blindness is more common, where keratomalacia due to vitamin A deficiency may be exacerbated by viral infection. In Britain, nearly half of blindness has a genetic cause, and is frequently associated with learning disability, hearing loss, cerebral palsy, and epilepsy.

The commonest eye problems affecting school entrants are refractive errors. These may have been diagnosed prior to school entry and already managed with corrective lenses. Otherwise, they may be revealed by entrance screening examinations (see Logan & Gilmartin, 2004) or after classes begin following difficulties with visualizing educational material. Abnormalities of refraction are treated with convex (for hypermetropia) or concave (for myopia) lenses. Adherence with corrective lenses (usually spectacles) varies depending on children's confidence, self-esteem, and peer reaction. The acceptance of spectacles by school children may be in proportion to the popularity of media figures who wear them. Explanation of the reasons corrective lenses are required can prevent peers from ridiculing or bullying those who require spectacles. Children with a marked error of refraction in one eye who do not wear their glasses may develop amblyopia (lazy eye) on that side.

Squints originate early in life, when stereoscopic vision develops in the first six months as a function of the brain that depends on the visual axis of each eye being directed at the same point of fixation. In young children the presentation of two different images causes suppression of the less distinct one, and subsequently amblyopia of that eye. The majority of squints in childhood are, thus, due to errors of refraction.

Gastrointestinal Problems

Repeated abdominal pain affects up to one in ten school children. It is often associated with a family history of similar pain, migraine, peptic ulcer, and anxiety. Gastroesophageal reflux, celiac disease, and inflammatory or irritable bowel disease are the sorts of conditions to be excluded before an emotional or psychological origin is ascribed.

Appendicitis is the most common cause of an acute surgical problem in the abdomen during childhood. It is rare in early childhood but becomes more common after the age of ten years. An increased incidence in the spring and fall months has been observed.

Food allergy is a common but frequently unconfirmed diagnosis in children. Although food intolerance is caused by allergy in some children, adverse reactions to foods are a feature of many other gastrointestinal conditions. Causes such as malabsorption, temporary lactase deficiency, effects of contaminants and additives, and psychological upset should be considered. Cow milk and soy protein allergies are the best defined allergic disorders affecting the gastrointestinal tract. Gluten sensitive enteropathy (celiac disease) is characterized by malabsorption, frequently resulting in diarrhea and poor weight gain, which improve when gluten is removed from the diet and recur when it is reintroduced.

Headache

Headache is common in childhood. Frequent headaches may impede a child's educational progress. Migraine, dental, hearing or visual problems and sinusitis are treatable causes.

Hearing Loss

Hearing loss is usefully divided into sensorineural hearing loss, due to nerve or cochlear abnormalities, and conductive hearing loss, due to disorders of the middle ear, including the bones and air spaces responsible for transmitting sound vibration from the outside world to the neuronal pathways responsible for auditory perception. The early detection of mild, moderate and severe hearing loss is important to prevent or minimize the delayed language development, poor educational performance, and behavioral problems which can follow. Refer to Chapter 4 for full discussion of hearing screening in school children.

Although sensorineural hearing loss is less common than conductive hearing loss, it tends to be more severe and therefore more likely to require special education. Children with persistent conductive hearing loss may respond to medical decongestant therapy, long term antibiotics, or surgical management involving adenoidectomy, myringotomy, or ventilator insertion into the tympanic membranes.

Musculoskeletal Problems

Although arthritis is frequently thought of as a condition affecting the elderly, around one in a thousand children is affected by it. Some episodes of arthritis are brief, due to infection in the joint or a reaction in the joint to infection or inflammation elsewhere. Chronic (or long term) arthritis will usually only be diagnosed after a minimum of three months' symptoms. Polyarticular arthritis is defined as arthritis affecting more than four joints. Girls are more frequently affected than boys. This type of arthritis often involves the joints of the hands and feet and produces pain, swelling, and stiffness. Involvement of the legs may cause difficulty walking. Involvement of the wrists and hands may lead to difficulty with manipulative tasks, for example writing, drawing, and using keyboards and musical instruments. Often, children feel generally unwell and may have high temperature when the disease is active. As well as non-steroidal anti-inflammatory drugs, disease-modifying or immunosuppressive therapy may be required to prevent future joint damage.

Systemic arthritis may begin without joint problems, but instead high temperatures that are more frequent in the evening after school. Boys and girls are affected with equal frequency. Blotchy red rashes may appear on the legs, arms and elsewhere. These may cause itch, and may initially be ascribed incorrectly to infection. The lymph nodes may become enlarged, most obviously on the neck, groin, and axillae. A third, less common variety of chronic arthritis affecting school children is that associated with the skin condition psoriasis.

Regarding diagnosis and treatment, time away from school can usually be reduced by delivering medical assessment and review on an outpatient basis. There may be occasional requirement for day patient admission for joint injections or commencement of more intensive therapy. At the clinic, measurement of the child's growth and evaluation of the current severity of their arthritis will take place. Examination and investigation results will be compared with previous visits in order to monitor disease activity and plan future treatment.

Drug therapy is only one part of the management of children with arthritis. General measures include healthy diet, making sure that the amount and type of food consumed will give enough calories and protein for growth, and calcium to keep the bones as strong as possible. Physiotherapy aims to counteract various effects of chronic arthritis. Pain can be reduced by the use of ice packs or heat packs and TENS (transcutaneous electrical nerve stimulation) devices. Stretches aim to loosen stiff joints in the morning and increase their range of movement. Muscle building exercises can help the muscles to support the joint more effectively and, therefore, reduce pain and stiffness. Building up muscle groups reduces the stress placed on joints during weight bearing, enables maximum function during activities such as dressing and walking, and maintains the range of movement achieved by stretching. Hydrotherapy (exercise or treatment in warm water) is useful in supporting the body or limb during mobilizing, assisting joint movement and strengthening muscles by resisting movement. Furthermore, the warmth of the water helps reduce muscle spasm and pain. Occupational therapy involves assessment and intervention in activities of daily living (washing, dressing, toilet, bathing), education, leisure, environment, and hand function. Therapists ensure that the child with arthritis can function as independently as possible at a level that is appropriate to their age and development. Aids (such as tools or reachers) and in some cases home adaptations, may be required to enable children with arthritis to bath, use stairs, the toilet or kitchen independently. Many children will experience temporary difficulties during a flare but will return to independence following therapy.

Arthritis can interrupt a child's ability to gain fully from their education. This may be due to absence for hospital admissions or therapy appointments. It may be that their hand function is affected, and writing may be painful and tiring. Getting around a busy school can be tiring and frightening for a child who has difficulty walking. A child may need their seating, desk height, and position in the classroom checked, and the possibility of eye involvement carefully monitored. At home and in school, assessments can be made to facilitate the child's independence.

The severity of orthopedic problems in schoolchildren varies from mild talipes to severe defects of the spine and limbs. Children with such conditions have decreased mobility and restriction of activity caused by the disorder and its treatment. Periods of immobilization and hospital admission may inhibit their educational and social development. Instability of the hip joints at birth may resolve spontaneously, or result in true dislocation with subsequent adverse effects on the development of the joint and the head of the femur. Scoliosis is important to detect early as progression can lead to cardiovascular and respiratory problems which can in turn shorten life (see Chapter 9).

Growing pains is a term frequently used to explain any discomfort in the lower limbs of children. Pain may be more obviously due to previous trauma. Cramps may suggest calcium or vitamin deficiency. Osgood Schlatter disease (*tibial apophysitis*) is seen particularly in association with sporting activities. Ligamentous injuries, *osteochondrosis*, and Perthes' disease of the hip can all invoke pain away from the site of the problem. Osteomyelitis, arthritis, and leukemia are serious causes of leg pain and tenderness which should be borne in mind when assessing the affected child.

Short Stature

Three groups of short children require further investigation, and potentially treatment. Firstly, children whose height velocity is low, evidenced by their crossing downwards through height centiles when plotted serially on a growth chart, secondly, children who lie well below (say three standard deviations) the mean height for their age, and lastly, short children of tall biological parents should give extra cause for concern. Full details of screening for growth in school children are provided in Chapter 3.

Skin and Hair Disorders

Eczema is the commonest skin condition and affects one in five children of school age. Symptoms include redness, dryness, cracking, itching, pain, and infection of the skin. Atopic eczema usually starts in infancy, tending to improve somewhat at a later age. Children with atopic eczema may also suffer from time to time from rhinitis and asthma, with all three conditions being more likely to affect children whose close relatives have been diagnosed with the same condition.

In atopic eczema the barrier function of the skin becomes less efficient. Dehydration causes the skin to crack and itch, leading to scratching and increased risk of infection. Commonly, the bend of the elbow and the area behind the knees are affected. Children may suffer from tiredness due to sleep disturbance following overnight itching and scratching. The most important aspect of eczema care is maintaining skin hydration by keeping up a good fluid intake and applying emollients to smooth, soften, hydrate, and protect affected areas.

Impetigo is a superficial bacterial infection of the skin, caused by Staphylococcus Aureus or Streptococcus Pyogenes. Lesions begin as small vesicles which develop into pustules and then crusting plaques with surrounding erythema. Scratching results in spread of lesions. Treatment involves topical or oral antibiotics, with intravenous therapy required in severe cases.

Warts and verrucae in young children on the hands, face, and feet often disappear spontaneously. They may, however, cause exclusion from swimming classes and difficulties with socialization.

Infestation with head lice (Pediculus Humanus) is one of the most common conditions affecting young schoolchildren, as described in Chapter 8. The commonest symptom is itching of the scalp, neck, ears, shoulders and back. The best therapeutic cream rinses remain on the scalp long enough to kill unhatched eggs (nits) and a second application a week later increases their effectiveness. Fine toothed combs are used to remove nits from the hair shafts. All affected individuals in the same school class and family should be treated simultaneously, whether symptomatic or not.

Learning Problems

Normal Development

By the age of five, children should be able to skip and run, climb and swing. They show increasing skill in kicking, throwing and catching balls. Thereafter there are improvements in strength, precision, speed and stamina. The five-year-old can copy a square and a triangle. He can draw a house with a door, windows, a roof and a chimney. He is able to play games with complex rules. Themes, within play or school, can be developed and maintained. Five-year-olds learn to be protective of, and responsible to, sibling and friends, at least some of the time. Five-year-olds can learn to tell the time, recognize letters and numbers, and begin to read.

In general, during their primary education, children are acquiring a sense of industry and competence while at the same time trying to discard feelings of inferiority. They acquire the ability to think logically, and realize that objects and actions are distinct from words, thoughts, and rules. They learn to compare, to understand the relation of part to whole, to group items in time and space, and to appreciate conservation of mass and volume.

Learning Disability

Learning disability is a significantly reduced ability to understand new or complex information and learn new skills (impaired intelligence) associated with a reduced ability to cope independently (impaired social functioning). Mild learning disability (Intelligence Quotient, IQ 50-70) is usually due to a combination of genetic and environmental factors and in some cases represents the lower end of normal intelligence. Severe learning disability (IQ 20-34) is more commonly due to genetic or physical abnormalities such as cerebral palsy, trisomy 21 (Down syndrome), or Fragile X syndrome.

Learning disorders are abnormalities in one or more of the psychological processes involved in understanding or using language (spoken or written) that manifest as difficulties in listening, speaking, reading, writing, spelling, or mathematics.

Most learning disorders lie within four areas of information processing – input, integration, storage, and output. Input is the information received via the senses such as sound and vision. The child may have problems with recognizing shape, position, size, and sequence. Auditory perception problems may lead to difficulty screening out competing sounds and focusing on a teacher's voice. Integration involves the interpretation of perceived input, categorizing it, and relating it to previous learning. Affected children may be unable to tell ordered stories, memorize sequences (such as days of the week), or learn facts or vocabulary. Storage disorders lead to memory and spelling problems, and difficulty learning new material without much repetition. Output includes speech, gestures, writing, and drawing.

Children with spoken language disorders have difficulty answering questions on demand. Those with gross motor disorders may be clumsy and prone to stumble, fall, or bump into people or objects. They may have difficulty running, jumping, climbing and bicycle riding. Children with fine motor disorders have trouble buttoning clothes, tying shoelaces, and handwriting. Eighty percent of children with learning disorders have reading problems. Children with learning disorders may suffer from low self-esteem.

Speech, Language and Communication Problems

Over a million children and young people in Britain have a speech, language, or communication impairment, equivalent to an average of two children in every classroom. Many skills are needed for speech and language to develop, so there are many ways that children's speech and language can go wrong. Children may have difficulty in moving the muscles which control speech, or may not understand how a conversation works or the meaning of a sentence. Some children cannot understand or use language at all. Some children can overcome these difficulties with appropriate therapy, but one in five hundred has severe or permanent problems.

Young school children with speech, language or communication difficulties may jump inappropriately from one topic of conversation to another, or talk about only one subject and find it hard to switch to others. They may find reading difficult, and struggle to understand time, emotions, or language which is not literal. They may have trouble remembering instructions, or forget conversation very quickly. They may find it difficult to pay attention, give inappropriate answers, or make irrelevant comments. They may not understand how to take turns in a conversation.

Thus, children with speech, language, and communication difficulties may struggle with school lessons and making friends. They may become isolated and unhappy. With the right help, such as speech and language therapy and specialist support at school, they can be helped to minimize these consequences. The reader is referred to Chapter 5 for full discussion of speech and language screening in schools.

Behavioral and Social Problems

Cognitive Development

The second half of the preoperational phase of cognitive development takes place during the first few years of school. During this period, language development facilitates cognition by allowing the child to start representing objects by symbols and words. Meanwhile, the child tends to regard the world solely from his own position with the inability to see a situation from another viewpoint. Everything, including inanimate objects, is endowed with feelings, thoughts, and wishes. At this stage, the child has problems with conservation of number, volume, and weight. For example, there appears to be more objects if they are spaced out compared to the same number more densely packed together. Similarly, there appears to be more water in a tall, narrow beaker than the same volume in a short, wide one. Young children deny chance or coincidence, believing that every event has a preceding cause. Moral sense is rigid and inflexible, so that punishment is invariably appropriate, irrespective of the circumstances. The child's concept of illness is that it is a consequence for misdeeds, a punishment for a misdemeanor.

During the concrete operational phase that follows between seven and twelve years of age, thinking becomes more logical and less dominated by immediate perceptual experience or events, such as changes of shape or arrangement. Conservation of number, weight, and volume is successfully achieved during this period. The child becomes less egocentric, capable of seeing events from another's standpoint. The child is able to appreciate and utilize reversibility (for example, if one and one make two, then two minus one leaves one).

Origins of Abnormal Behavior

In general, behavior is the result of learning. We do something because we have been reinforced or rewarded for doing it, or something very similar, in the past. We refrain from doing something because we have found either that it brings no reward or that the consequences of such an act are unpleasant. Before the first day of formal education, the factors affecting how children think of themselves and how they behave are genetic, prenatal, environmental, and largely family centered. Thereafter, the school and the child's peers gradually take over as substantial determinants of behavior.

As well as difficulties in defining what family means, there are further complexities in how families influence the behavior of their children. Children differ at birth as a result of genetic and prenatal factors and are, therefore, differentially susceptible to environmental influences. Children are born into different environments; therefore the effect of some traumatic episodes may be dissipated in high socioeconomic families and magnified in poor environments. Any single aspect of behavior is likely to be dependent on multiple influences which may interact. Behavior may, therefore, be governed more by a pattern of events rather than one. For example, the absence of a parent in early childhood may have a greater effect if combined with poverty. Family relationships change with time and children are more susceptible to influence at certain times in their lives than others. A change in behavior may not appear until some time after the event. For example, the effect of the departure of a parent may not show its effect until months or years later.

Children will bring abnormalities of behavior with them to their early years at school, but the school can effect change of these abnormalities given the opportunity. Attending a nursery school or preschool playgroup can provide a good preparation for later encounters with peers. Children who have satisfactory relations in the preschool period may find it easier to make friends once they are at school. By three or four years of age, children will have begun to talk to each other while playing, will have the habit of selecting playmates, and will have begun to watch each other while playing.

The first day at school is a major event in childhood and the child's first teacher is a key figure in subsequent development. Of particular influence is the prevailing atmosphere in the classroom, which depends in turn on the personality of the teacher. A mainly authoritarian style of leadership may produce children who are hostile to each other, a permissive style may induce boredom, and a democratic style tends to produce more productivity and less hostility.

From around six years of age onwards, gangs, more or less formal groups created by children themselves, become increasingly important. They offer relief from adult supervision and meet needs not usually catered for in adult-orientated societies. A typical gang is centered on play, their primary purpose being enjoyment. Gangs develop at about the same age that the genders voluntarily segregate themselves. They vary in size and activity, and in behavior from benign to antisocial. They all offer children an opportunity to measure themselves against others and to learn cooperation between peers.

Social discrimination refers to the tendency to make a distinction among people according to certain cues. Gang membership fosters social discrimination, not always to the good since it encourages notions of being in or out, of us and them. Awareness of social difference is rare before the age of three but may grow rapidly thereafter. Prejudice may be fostered by parents or peers, and encouraged by prevailing trends in society. Schools can prevent prejudice from becoming bullying if the indifference or hostility shown by one individual or group to another can be interrupted.

Attention Deficit

This involves an inconsistent, but not persistent, absence of attention and, therefore, wide, unpredictable ranges of academic achievement are typical. Children with attention deficit can concentrate some of the time on some subjects. They may have written language learning disability, particularly of content, usage, punctuation, and spelling.

Autism

Children with autism are normal at birth but later develop characteristic features, usually before the age of thirty months. They fail to develop normal interpersonal relationships, for example, they dislike cuddling and fail to make eye contact or become attached, even to parents. They make few, if any, friends and do not join group activities. There is delay in speech and language development. Ritualistic, repetitive, and compulsive phenomena are characteristic. Only around one in three children with autism go on to obtain employment and lead an independent existence. Good prognostic factors are the early development of useful language and IQ greater than 70.

Bullying

Schools that are best at tackling bullying accept, and make a clear statement, that bullying is wrong and unacceptable, and that no one has the right to hurt others by striking them, calling them names, spreading rumors about them, or sending threatening or hurtful messages via social media. Bullies may try to justify their actions by claiming that it is the victim's fault, because of their "difference". They may pick on others who are tall, short, fat, thin, shy, clever, attractive or have a different accent, hair color, or religion.

The victim should be reminded that it is not their fault, and that the bully, not they themselves, needs to change. Every school should have a policy to deal with bullying and children should know they have the right to ask a teacher or other adult for help. It is most important that concerns are addressed, and something is done before someone is seriously upset or hurt.

Busy Children

A typical busy childhood begins in infancy with parents rushing to feed solids to, and complete the toilet training of, their children so that day care is more of an option. Then, from the age of five, children are rushed from school to afterschool to extracurricular activities with little or no unstructured time. They are molded physically, socially, and psychologically into little adults before they are ready. Under such pressure children may suffer burnout and other stress related problems, which may manifest as headache, abdominal pain, sleeplessness, difficulty with toileting, tiredness, or bad behavior. Such children have no time for the most enriching and maturing activity of childhood; play, and in particular play that is designed and directed by the child himself.

Conduct Disorder

All children misbehave at some stage in their lives. Many behavioral problems resolve with time during the process of development, while some indicate lifelong patterns. For example, infantile temper tantrums affect fewer than ten percent of five-year-olds and two percent of fifteen-year-olds. Conduct disorder involves the persistent violation of the rights of others or the rules of society. Early in their cognitive development, a child's moral reasoning centers around avoiding punishment and seeking reward. Thus, young school children may tell lies to gain favor or avoid chores or punishment. Conduct disorder is usually diagnosed following at least six months of abnormal behavior such as aggression to people and animals, destruction of property, deceitfulness or theft, and serious violations of rules. Treatment requires the development of new attitudes and behavior patterns.

Emotional Difficulties

Young school children may be preoccupied due to anxiety, depression, and post-traumatic stress. Subsequently, they may have significant difficulties with concentration. They may ruminate about worries or escape into thoughts of fantasy. Subsequently, they have difficulty with reading comprehension and applied mathematics, tasks which require sustained, uninterrupted thought. The family history of such children may include divorce, bereavement, mental health or psychosocial problems, frequent changes of address, or domestic violence. Refer to Chapter 7 for consideration of mental health screening in school children.

Enuresis

Enuresis refers to the involuntary passage of urine and is generally acceptable until such time as there is parental expectation of continence and successful toilet training. Nocturnal enuresis is bedwetting, without daytime incontinence, frequency, or urgency. It will affect at least one or two children in a class of thirty. Schooling will be affected indirectly, as by any condition that lowers a child's self-esteem, and directly by the tiredness and reduced concentration associated with disturbed sleep. Overnight stays at friends' homes and school trips of longer than one day may seem inconceivable to affected children. Medications to reduce overnight urine production and alarm systems to train children to wake up in response to a full bladder are among the therapeutic interventions used. Diurnal enuresis is the tendency for a child's bladder to empty prematurely, frequently and at short notice. Bladder training exercises, ordered toileting habits, and bladder stabilizing medications are used.

Inactivity

Many children do not exercise properly or enough and may instead undertake several hours each day of computer screen time. Schools can assist in improving their pupils' fitness but are rarely officially charged with the task. The prevalence of childhood obesity is increasing in many countries. Schools can incorporate exercise and healthy eating programs into their curricula to counter the sedentary lifestyle and consumption of non-nutritious food promoted by television and other media. Today's children are less fit than their counterparts were two or three decades ago. It is not unusual to see children less than ten years of age becoming short of breath while walking for fifteen minutes. Demands of work mean many parents have less time to spend playing outdoors or walking their children to school. Children have downtime distractions that involve little or no activity. Children may be in a seated position for more than eight hours a day.

Lack of fitness at a young age may contribute, like obesity, to weight gain, poor cardiovascular health, weak bones and higher disease rates in general in later life. For under six-year-olds, children who are capable of walking should be physically active for at least three hours a day. Between the age of six and eight years, emphasis should be on developing the heart and lungs by exercising until children are out of breath, and on improving their balance and coordination. This is a good time for children to take up more organized sports, and learn to swim. Ball games involving throwing and catching can enhance hand-eye coordination. By nine to eleven years, children can begin to take part in competitive games and sports. Walking for pleasure in green spaces should be encouraged. If time is limited, solo exercise enhances strength and coordination, and short games of football, basketball, or tennis can be organized for groups.

Obesity

Obesity has become a global epidemic. In some parts of Britain, one out of every five school entrants is overweight or obese. Overweight or obese children are at increased risk of illnesses such as diabetes, and obese children tend to become obese adults. The increased prevalence of childhood obesity is the result of positive energy balance over time. This follows an imbalance between energy intake and expenditure. Physical activity and fitness are replaced by sedentary behavior, particularly prolonged periods of screen use. Although regular physical activity has a role to play in health outcomes, only one in four British school children meet recommended physical activity targets. This level of insufficient activity is a concern as these patterns of behavior may persist into adulthood. Therefore, the focus of several childhood obesity interventions is to increase physical activity and reduce sedentary behavior.

School Refusal

Illness accounts for the vast majority of absence from school. School refusal, where the prospect of attending school invokes a high level of anxiety or fear, usually accounts for only one percent of absence. It can be due to anxiety about separation from a parent, the journey to or from school, particular elements of school, lessons, teachers, other pupils, food, changing rooms, or toilets. Physical causes of somatic symptoms need to be excluded, and then an early return to school facilitated by addressing the source of the child's anxiety using family and external resources.

Sleep Disorders

One in four children will have sleep problems at some stage. Some have difficulty getting to sleep, some staying asleep, and some have their sleep interrupted by nightmares or night terrors. Most schoolchildren will sleep for eight to ten hours. School children may experience nightmares, night terrors, and sleepwalking. Some children have trouble getting to sleep, or wake too early in the morning. This may be related to various stresses, as children relive the day's events or worry about what will happen tomorrow.

Soiling

Soiling is the term given to involuntary or voluntary fecal leakage. Involuntary problems are usually associated with constipation. This may begin with, or become associated with, a painful perianal lesion such as a fissure, or dysfunctional toilet training. A poor diet, containing too much milk fat or too little fiber, may be contributory. In any case the child postpones or resists defecation and this may be exacerbated by an unwillingness to use school toilets. Children of school age who soil in the absence of constipation should be assessed to exclude physical, developmental, or emotional causes.

Conclusion

Health supervision systems for school age children recognize that such children are generally healthy and likely to be in need of little care. Their main function is to prevent or minimize morbidity. The real purpose of most health supervision assessments between the ages of three and five years is to determine school readiness and gauge the likelihood of subsequent intellectual and psychological success. At the same time, schools can plan staff, class size, and instructional equipment to suit the range of ability of their entrants. Despite careful screening for school readiness, some children are ill prepared for school entrance. Problems leading to school failure may not become apparent until a deficient ability or missing skill is required for success in a new part of the curriculum. For example, specific learning disorders reveal themselves during early primary education. Visual perception problems appear when reading and writing instruction begin.

Any child health service should respond to three basic requirements: first attending to acute illness; second providing surveillance, illness prevention, and health education; and third supplying care for children with chronic or handicapping conditions. The service is delivered from a variety of overlapping primary, secondary, and tertiary medical organizations. Similarly, the physical situation where acute care, illness prevention, health education, and care of chronic conditions is delivered may be home, school, clinic, or hospital depending on where abilities and resources are available. This, in turn, will depend on how health services are funded and organized, as dictated by governmental concepts of, and strategies for, pediatric care. The degree to which children with ongoing illness or disability can be integrated within ordinary schools will vary with how much advice and support can be provided there. For example, medical examinations may take place within schools or elsewhere in specialist clinics. Fully integrated school health services are involved in health education and work closely with teaching and community staff in the management of children with physical, learning, and behavioral problems.

Further Reading

Anderson, H. R., Bailey, P. A., Cooper, J. S., Palmer, J. C., & West, S. (1983). Morbidity and school absence caused by asthma and wheezing illness. *Archives of Disease in Childhood, 58,* 777-784.

Aronson, S. S., & Shope, T. R. (Eds.). (2009). *Managing infectious diseases in child care and schools: A quick reference guide* (2nd ed.). Elk Grove Village, IL: American Academy of Pediatrics.

Clay, D. (2004). *Helping schoolchildren with chronic health conditions: A practical guide.* New York, NY: Guilford Press.

Lightfoot, J., Wright, S., & Sloper, P. (1999) Supporting pupils in mainstream school with an illness or disability: Young people's views. *Child: Care, Health & Development, 25*, 267-283.

Logan, N.S., & Gilmartin, B. (2004). School vision screening, ages 5-16 years: the evidence-base for content, provision and efficacy. *Ophthalmic and Physiological Optics, 24*, 481-492.

Samuels, S. K., & Sikorsky, S. A. (1998). *Clinical evaluations of school-aged children: A structured approach to the diagnosis of child and adolescent mental disorders.* Sarasota, FL: Professional Resource Press.

Shaw, S. R., & McCabe, P. C. (2008). Hospital-to-school transition for children with chronic illness: Meeting the new challenges of an evolving health care system. *Psychology in the Schools, 45*(1), 74-87.

Thies, K. M. (1999). Identifying the educational implications of chronic illness in school children. *Journal of School Health, 69*, 392-397.

PART II: SCHOOL HEALTH SCREENING SYSTEMS—PRESENT AND FUTURE

In: School Health Screening Systems
Editors: Bradley McPherson and Carlie J. Driscoll

ISBN: 978-1-63117-942-6

Chapter 3

SCREENING FOR GROWTH AND DEVELOPMENT

Diane DeBell*
Anglia Ruskin University, Cambridge, UK

ABSTRACT

It is widely presumed that weighing and measuring school age children is both a straightforward task and one that is an important screening tool. Neither is necessarily the case. The need for precision and staff skill is one challenge. So too is the need to ensure that the findings can lead to appropriate clinical referral if necessary. This chapter clarifies the range of developmental problems that can be identified through growth monitoring. It also compares approaches to the task in different parts of the world and it indicates lessons for the future.

By school age (age 5 years), most birth to pre-school age screening will have uncovered growth development problems in children if there are any. Until recently, the justification for screening *school age* children for height and weight has been equivocal. However, two events have recently brought about a shift in this perspective. One is the increasing public health concern about childhood obesity and the second is the international implementation of growth standards for children under age 5 years. Together these have focused considerable attention on both the precision needed to measure and the public health findings that can inform child health improvement in areas such as nutrition and exercise (Butte, Garza, and de Onis, 2007).

This chapter investigates the rationale for growth development monitoring in school-age children and it also calls attention to the need for a distinction between public health monitoring and child health remedial care. In other words, current height, weight, and body mass index (BMI) measurements of school age children are used mainly for population monitoring purposes in order to identify patterns of overweight and obesity. The missing component in this process is a health promotion dimension that seeks to provide remedies for excess BMI. In 2004, Hall and Elliman wisely coupled growth monitoring with health promotion and renamed it *growth development and promotion.*

* Corresponding author: Diane DeBell. Anglia Ruskin University, Cambridge, UK. E-mail: ddebell@compuserve.com.

The key message of this chapter is that we make an error if we allow ourselves to believe that weighing and measuring school-age children is only about identifying obesity and/or excess weight gain.

INTRODUCTION

The International View

The measurement of growth in children is an essential component of monitoring health status, detecting deviations from normal development, and gauging the impact of interventions. "The significance of timely detection of poor growth in early life resides in its association with adverse functional consequences, including poor cognition and educational performance, low adult wages, lost productivity and, when accompanied by excessive weight gain later in childhood, increased risk of nutrition-related chronic diseases" (de Onis, Onyango, Borghi, Siyam, Blossner, and Lutter, 2012, p. 1603).

Hall and Elliman (2004) observed that routine measurement of babies and young children is presumed to be important by most health professionals. Nevertheless "there is still disagreement about the benefits, the ages when measurements should be made or recorded, and the threshold at which referral for specialist advice is desirable" (p. 169). The debate is mainly about whether or not to monitor the growth of children at school. Furthermore, weighing a school-age child is reasonably straightforward but accurately measuring height is more difficult. It is also the case that a single measurement is only minimally helpful as an indicator of health status. Measurements need to be repeated, recorded, and compared over time because of variations in professional skill and instrument reliability and also because of changes in child health.

It is also the case that growth measurement and weight measurement have been generally subsumed into a single screening category whereas they are different measures. In 2004, the Royal College of Paediatrics and Child Health for the United Kingdom (UK) accepted the principle of these measures but cautioned about the practice for children of school age, notably because of the danger of inappropriate referrals. The advice in the UK was to refer to growth monitoring (GM) rather than growth screening.

There is a commonplace presumption that weighing and measuring a growing child is a fairly simple and straightforward matter. Furthermore, there is a widespread presumption that the data we extract for a growing school-age child age 5 to 19 years (i.e., height-for-age, weight-for-age and BMI-for age) are reliable measures and are susceptible to relative comparisons for the purpose of population public health monitoring. Neither is entirely true.

Unlike the period from birth to age 5 years, there are consequences of sex, age, and cultural development that need to be factored. Furthermore, measurement precision requires instrument accuracy, staff training, and comparative growth charts. The World Health Organization (WHO) confronted this latter difficulty (comparative growth charts) in a 15-year study that culminated in a widely acceptable reference for measuring children from birth to the age of 19 years (De Onis, Garza, Victora, Onyango, Frongillo, and Martines, 2004; WHO, 2006). By 2011, 125 countries worldwide had adopted the WHO standards for growth measurement (De Onis et al., 2012). These standards include both weighing and measuring from birth and in the early school-age years. Previously, accepted UK growth measures were the 1977

National Center for Health Statistics (NCHS)/WHO charts. The United Kingdom adopted the 2006 WHO Child Growth Standards in 2007 (Department of Health, 2008) and they were endorsed by the European Childhood Obesity Group in May 2009 (ECOG, 2009). However, in advance of the WHO research, the United States released separate new growth charts in May 2000 in order to replace the 1977 NCHS reference. "The evaluation of child growth trajectories and the interventions designed to improve child health are highly dependent on the growth charts used" (de Onis, Garza, Onyango, and Borghi, 2007, p. 144). The Centers for Disease Control charts (for the United States) tend to reflect "a heavier, and somewhat shorter, sample than the WHO sample" (de Onis et al., 2007, p. 1). The consequence for the US is to imply lower rates of under-nutrition and higher rates of overweight and obesity when compared with WHO standards. The point here is that comparative growth charts are themselves a factor to be carefully considered when analyzing whole population height and weight trends for children of school age. The most recent, the easiest to use, and the most accurate measures are provided in the WHO (2013) AnthroPlus software. It presents international growth reference data for children and adolescents 6 months to 19 years. Nevertheless, the greatest difference in the various measurement charts arises in the pre-school period. For this reason, the Department of Health in England recommended that, from 2009, the new WHO charts should only be used for new births and that there is no need to re-plot for older children. "The UK 1990 charts should still be used for all children over age 4 years" (RCPCH, 2009, p. 1). Two events signaled a need to develop a single growth reference for the screening, surveillance and international monitoring of school-aged children and adolescents. One was the increasing public health concern about childhood obesity and the second was the international implementation of growth standards for children under age 5 (de Onis, Wijnhoven, and Onyango, 2004). The result of these latter evaluations has been a series of standardized growth measurements based on state of the art statistical methods and approaches appropriate for children under the age of 5 years.

The outcome has been the development of a single international growth reference for children in general, including school-aged children. It is a height-for-age and body mass index (BMI)-for-age measure. The weight-for-age charts extend only to age 10 years in order to accommodate those countries that routinely measure only weight but who would also like to monitor growth throughout childhood. But it is a significant achievement that there is now relative international consistency in childhood growth measurement with the infant to age 5 years and 5-19 years charts. The worldwide implementation of the WHO child growth standards had considerable positive consequences for many countries. Within five years of the release of the WHO standards, "countries have adopted and harmonized best practices in child growth assessment and established the breast-fed infant as the norm against which to assess compliance with children's right to achieve their full genetic growth potential" (de Onis et al., 2012, p. 1603). In addition, many countries have redesigned their child health records and have updated their recommendations to health workers since the launch of the WHO standards in April 2006.

Looking at the United Kingdom

Child growth and development screening in the United Kingdom (UK) was originally designed to identify a range of physical growth failures, including both Turner syndrome and growth hormone deficiency (GHD). The latter is an acute problem for about 1 in every 3800 of the child population. In fact, the figure for GHD is currently increasing, mainly due to the effects of radiotherapy amongst children who survive childhood cancers. However, it is no longer an explicit justification for growth screening in the UK.

By 2004, the Royal College of Paediatrics and Child Health in the UK took the position that growth *screening* for children of school age was no longer justifiable. The College noted that "with the possible exception of single height measurements, weighing and measuring children cannot be regarded as screening and therefore we have adopted the term growth monitoring (GM)" (Hall and Elliman, 2004, p. 169). The justification for this change in terminology and also change in practice was the consequence of considerable collective research that called into question all screening activities for children of school age. The highly influential work of David Hall and David Elliman proposed the need for a shift away from emphasis on screening activities toward a more dominant focus on preventive measures and health promotion work for children and young people after the age of 4/5 years. This position was based on evidence that pre-school children in the UK were sufficiently screened by the age of 4/5 years old and, thus, subsequent screening should be reduced to sight and hearing alone but with further reference to pre-school child records (e.g., for immunization history). Where early child health records or assessment were missing for a child, school-age assessment and screening would be necessary. Otherwise, all screening of children ages 5 to 19 years came under scrutiny in the UK at the beginning of the 21st century. On advice from the Child Health Sub-group of the National Screening Committee, the UK Screening Portal had already removed a number of screening programs for school age children by 2004 because they had become a matter of habit without research-based justification (Hall and Elliman, 2004). The National Screening Committee called attention to the requirement that screening is only justified if there is a remedy available for the problem being scrutinized. In addition, an international emphasis on the promotion of health had shifted attention toward national pressure to design public health activities that could confront the social and economic conditions that cause ill health in the first place (i.e., the health promotion agenda).

Yet in 2006, the emergence of a suspected and new pattern of childhood obesity triggered a national re-assessment of the child growth monitoring position across the UK. In 2006/07, the National Health Service (NHS) introduced the National Child Measurement Program (NCMP) and this has remained in place in England since that time. The NCMP measures the height, weight, and BMI at school for children in the reception class (ages 4 to 5 years) and again in Year 6 (ages 10 to 11 years).

Measurement of height and weight commonly takes place in the UK in schools. This is generally true across the United States as well. Children are measured without shoes and coats and in normal, light, indoor clothing. The English specification is that measurement should be undertaken by trained healthcare professionals. In other words, the measurements are not generally made by teachers, although in some countries teachers do weigh and measure school children. Children at each age 4 to 5 years and 10 to 11 years are measured over the course of a school year. (In most European countries, the second measurement occurs at child age 6 to 7 years.) This means that some children in a reported school year may well be many months older than children in the same school year at the point of measurement. For that reason alone, the child's age should be recorded in months rather than years. Comparisons between children for public health monitoring purposes do need to be made in terms of the child's age in months.

Participation in the English NCMP is for all children in reception classes and in Year 6 attending non-specialist maintained state schools. In the past, results were reported to the school's local Primary Care Trust and the Strategic Health Authority (until 1 April 2013). This has changed and reporting is now to local (county) Directors of Public Health under the new English regulations following restructure of the NHS. What remains the same is the fact that the school's address is the geographical marker for reporting—not the child's home address. This matters in so far as patterns of overweight or obesity may not necessarily be traced to neighborhoods. This makes it more difficult, for example, to assess possible relationships between socio-economic profile and overweight and/or obesity.

Scotland does not universally screen for growth in school age children but has a voluntary program in which families can opt in for measurement of a school-age child by a health professional at a GP surgery. Scotland uses a health promotion approach to growth and development that is focused on ages 5 to 11 years and on young people ages 12 to 15 years. Northern Ireland screens for height, weight, and BMI at only Year 1 of primary school. In all areas of Wales, school nurses weigh and measure children in primary schools but there is currently not a consistent set of standards for practice across the country. A research team carried out a study in 2009 and has recommended implementation of a program similar to England's NCMP but with measurements at year 4 rather than year 6 as well as measurements in the reception year of primary school (Public Health Wales, 2013). The recommendations have gone to Public Health Wales, a new local authority body created in April 2013

As a consequence of intense debate, systematic population screening programs for overweight/obesity were recommended by the UK Screening Portal from July 2006. This was the outcome of significant epidemiological pressure to measure for the purpose of population level assessments of what came to be called the "obesity epidemic". The next review of growth screening for children of school age is scheduled for 2013/14.

Monitoring Child Growth and Development – Contemporary Perspectives

When thinking about screening for child growth and development, the contemporary view presumes this work is about identifying obesity. This is a very recent presumption and it is a rationale that remains in debate. The guidelines in England reinforce this view of the reasons why we now measure height and weight at two age points for the school age child—in reception class (age 4 to 5 years) and in year 6 (age 10 to 11 years). The explicit NCMP rationale for its existence is "to assess overweight children and obese levels within primary schools" (Health and Social Care Information Centre, 2013). More fully, the "NCMP was set up in line with the Government's strategy to tackle obesity and to: inform local planning and delivery of services for children; gather population-level data to allow analysis of trends in growth patterns and obesity; increase public and professional understanding of weight issues in children; and be a vehicle for engaging with children and families about healthy lifestyles and weight issues (Health and Social Care Information Centre, 2013).

However, the history of screening for growth and development has not historically been about obesity. Instead, growth screening in the past focused on identifying cases in which the child may be suffering from a range of causes of under-development, including Turner syndrome and GHD. This latter condition affects the infant or the child at different ages and in different ways but it can be treated through growth hormone replacement and is the speciality of paediatric endocrinologists. This focus remains implicit in clinical practice but it is not specified in the NCMP. Growth failure is usually identified by ages 4 to 5 years via pre-school monitoring.

Growth screening of children (before and during school age) has always been at least an informal paediatric practice if not a public health practice. It was the emergence of childhood obesity as a relatively new health problem in the 21st century that produced the current practice of universal school-aged growth and development monitoring in England. From the outset in 2006/07, the recent British programme has been measuring and reporting BMI. In other words, the contemporary screening programme arises out of anxiety about what is understood to be the emergence of an obesogenic environment. At the same time, there are also anxieties that the present monitoring programme is designed for public health data gathering rather than for immediate assistance in providing care or cure for individual children—for example, where the child's failure to thrive has a physiological origin. In contrast for example, growth deficiency (or stunting), as a justification for a screening program does match the criteria we apply to decisions about what and whether to "look for health problems" in growing children. The classic protocol for putting screening in place should be derived from two factors, the incidence or prevalence of a potential health problem and the effectiveness of available interventions to deal with the problem. In other words, the criteria for screening include consequence. If we cannot offer assistance, help, effective intervention to manage the problems we find, then we need to ask ourselves if we are justified in measuring in the first place. If not amenable to intervention, then measurement becomes purely an epidemiological (i.e., population fact gathering) exercise and that raises questions about the ethical justification for measuring (see Chapter 1 for an overview of screening ethics). In other words, screening criteria specify that services must be available to "deal with the problem" in order to justify screening at all (Stevens and Raftery, 1997, p. xxxi). For example, when we look at screening with a view to identifying growth hormone deficiency, we can see that these classic criteria are met in the implementation of the screening programme. Thus we can justify the programme of surveillance—justify the financial investment and the human resource involved and the potential for intrusion into the child's life that is caused by measuring and weighing.

Early debates about the current (2006) growth screening programme in the UK were not only heated but they highlighted growth hormone deficiency (or other problems linked to failure of growth) as the key reason for implementing a screening programme. However, in the interim period since 2006 - 2007, the obesity argument has almost wholly replaced the original concerns about identifying growth failure. It is important to remember this when we analyze the existing growth and development screening programmes of school age children in any national context.

England's screening methods (and rationale) for measuring BMI do not necessarily meet the abovementioned screening criteria. In reality, the growth monitoring programme in England and in many other locations has been designed as a response to a sudden recognition that obesity is a new public health problem and is one of considerable seriousness. Both the UK and the US are now concerned that obesity may be the most serious non-infectious disease of childhood. In England, overweight and obesity (combined) affect 23.9% of the child population (unpublished Department of Health England data, 18 April 2013). What is missing, however, are effective methods of care as well as prevention for identifiable weight problems in children and young people. This is a complicated area of public health debate because countering or alleviating problems of overweight and obesity are social, cultural, economic, and attitudinal challenges. In fact, poor legal regulation of the food industry (advertising, labelling, packaging, and distribution) is considered a major factor in the causes of obesity and in overweight management but it is currently outside public health control in most countries, including the UK. It is further argued that it is social inequality and poverty that are at the heart of the emergence of contemporary obesogenic environments (Acheson, 1998; Marmot and Wilkin-son, 2006). Marmot terms this the "status syndrome".

Why, then, are we investing in the costly task of weighing and measuring all school-aged children in England if we can do little to alleviate the causes of overweight? The answer is that the existing growth measurement is a first step in establishing the extent of the obesity problem within the total population. At this point, investment is an epidemiological priority and not a priority for cure. By that we mean that the priority is to measure and establish the whole country profile of whether and to what degree there is a rising obesity problem in the UK. There are also questions to be answered about the financial and human resource costs of the contemporary measurement programs given that the remedies for obesity are under-developed and underfunded. By "financial cost" we mean the equipment and personnel costs of practical measurement tasks as well as the costs of paying for public health expertise. But, in terms of screening criteria, we need to continue to remind ourselves that any intrusive measurement is without justification if a remedy for a problem uncovered is not available, funded, or offered. For the time being, remedies for overweight or obese children are linked to matters of persuasion rather than medicine. In effect, they are public health responsibilities and require a range of population-based approaches to prevention and to health promotion.

For example, the UK government currently funds the National Obesity Observatory (NOO) out of Public Health England funding for the Public Health Observatories in England. In addition, the management and implementation of the National Child Measurement Programme (NCMP) in England has transferred from the Department of Health to local authority (local government) responsibility in England from April 2013. This raises questions about consistency of delivery, quality control, and professional skill when we talk about the NCMP in England.

Additional Rationales for Growth and Development Monitoring

The investment in the National Child Measurement Programme (NCMP) in England was actually triggered by public health (epidemiological) concerns about weight gain and obesity in children. Generally, we link this phenomenon to socio-economic factors that reflect income inequality or relative poverty. Poverty is a feature of the kinds of environments that tend to produce more children who are prone to becoming overweight and/or obese because of poor nutrition, excessive fats, sugars, and/or carbohydrates. We are finding that overweight and obesity are particularly linked to low income, overcrowding, and/or restricted exercise opportunities (Marmot and Wilkinson, 2006).

Yet a 2006 study of 13,000 school children in Leeds, England who were living in middle-affluent areas found this cohort to have the greatest probability of being obese within the metropolitan area of the city (Leeds Metropolitan University, 2013). In other words, poverty is frequently identified as a risk factor for obesity but it is not the only risk factor. In fact, overweight and obesity are likely to have become generalized within the population. In England, it is the function of NOO to track these socio-economic and neighborhood patterns.

In addition, there are also risk factors for overweight that are not linked to obesity. It is thereby important for health professionals to be prepared to diagnose a range of factors that could lead to overweight in school-age children. These can include: High birth weight; timing or rate of maturation; other behavioural or psychological factors; physical conditions such as endocrine causes (rare): hypothyroidism—especially Down syndrome; Cushing syndrome—associated with truncal obesity, hypertension, hirsutism; growth hormone deficiency—there may be weight gain with delayed puberty; muscular dystrophy and other causes of immobility; polycystic ovarian syndrome; hypothalamic damage; spina bifida; and genetic syndromes associated with hypogonadism (PatientPlus, 2013).

Overweight is not the only alert for screening. Growth failure historically has been the originating reason for growth screening of young children in most countries. It can be the consequence of a number of conditions that are treatable with human growth hormone (somatropin). It can also be the consequence of poor nutrition and food shortages. In May 2010, the National Institute for Health and Clinical Excellence (NICE) issued guidance for the treatment of growth failure in children. The guidance is scheduled for projected review in May 2013. The NICE guidance is only applicable in England and Wales but it is likely to be aligned with practices in other parts of the world.

Growth failure is associated with two main conditions; small birth weight for gestational age with subsequent growth failure at 4 years of age or later, and short stature homeobox-containing gene (SHOX) deficiency. Hormone treatment for growth failure is a specialist paediatric intervention and requires specialist expertise in endocrinology. The treatment is an option for children whose growth failure is associated with the two conditions mentioned above or any of the following disorders: growth hormone insufficiency; Turner syndrome; Prader-Willi syndrome; or chronic renal insufficiency.

There are a number of further conditions that can be detected by growth monitoring: juvenile hypothyroidism; growth impairment (presenting feature of many other disorders); cranial or total body irradiation and intracranial tumors; syndromes, such as Russell-Silver syndrome; some forms of bone dysplasia; idiopathic short stature; excessively tall stature; and psychosocial short stature.

On the whole, these conditions are generally discovered via other means and it is unusual for school-based measurement programs to be the first occasion for referral for these conditions. Nevertheless, a growth monitoring program, it is argued, can help to ensure against such conditions being missed altogether in developed countries that have good child health coverage.

An associated alert for children and young people occurs if there is concern about eating disorders associated with underweight, particularly if the child or young person also asks for advice on losing weight. This is the area of eating disorders and is not generally included in screening programmes for growth and development. Nevertheless, screening personnel need to be alert to the potential for need of clinical referral in such cases. In England and Wales, NICE clinical guideline no. 9 (NICE, 2010) recommends an appropriate clinical response if underweight is suspected to be the consequence of eating disorders. See Cole, Flegal, Nicholls and Jackson (2007) for definitions of thinness in children and adolescents.

The Obesity Problem

"Almost two thirds of global deaths result from non-communicable diseases and ... unhealthy diet has an important role in these. But what to do about it: cajole individuals to change their diets or get governments to use legislation, regulation, and taxation to project their populations towards the healthy option?" (Delamothe, 2013). The initial Foresight Report was explicit about the current absence of care and intervention services to remedy identifiable obesity problems (Government Office for Science, 2007).

In January 2013, the Royal College of Physicians published the first major report on obesity in the UK since 1983. The direct parallel in health damage potential identified in 2013 was the 1962 Doll report on the damage caused by tobacco smoking (Royal College of Physicians 1962). Obesity in the UK, which now has the second highest rate in the world, is currently estimated at a healthcare cost of "5 billion per year and predicted to double by 2050" (p. 12).

The epidemiological information that we have at this moment in time in England as elsewhere is partially a consequence of the investment in child growth monitoring that followed on from both the WHO and the UK debates in 2006. This is, therefore, an example of the use to which screening can be put (i.e., epidemiological population level measurement). It also makes apparent the critical need to find intervention methods that will include medical care and prevention strategies for poor nutrition, notably where it leads to overweight and obesity in children. Furthermore, it is now evident that the task of countering obesogenic environments will also "need multiple government department involvement" (National Audit Office, 2012) within individual countries.

The primary justification for the time being, therefore, for child growth monitoring internationally and in England is a public health analysis brief—either to identify malnutrition or to identify rates of overweight and obesity. In other words, investment in growth monitoring does not, as yet, include actions that are effective as health promotion interventions. Nevertheless, managing the seriousness of the danger to health caused by poor nutrition relies on ensuring that treatment, prevention, and intervention methods do actually follow in the immediate and longer term. Ideally, "the aim [of screening] would be to identify the tendency to excessive weight gain early and prevent or reverse it" (Hall and Elliman, 2004, p. 186).

Screening Tools Currently in Common Use for Child Measurement

The height measurement tools for school-age children in the UK (mainly England) are either a correctly installed stadometer or an approved portable measuring device. "For clinic or school use, good results are obtained with a Minimeter or the Leicester Height Measure. The latter has the advantage that no meter measuring stick is needed to check accuracy.

Although specialist clinics use more robust and expensive equipment, this does not necessarily increase accuracy" (Hall and Elliman, 2004, p. 169).

There are alternatives to weighing and measuring—e.g., directly measured by densitometry, scanning using dual-energy X-ray absorptiometry or indirectly measured via anthropomorphic measurements, bio-electrical impedance and air displacement plethysmography (Kiping, Jago, and Lawlor, 2008). But these methods are not practical for use in screening whole populations of children. Body mass index (BMI) *per se* is also not a precise way to assess obesity in children but it is practical and it is a measure that is supported by the 2006 WHO child growth standards (see DeOnis et al., 2007). "BMI (adjusted for age and gender) is recommended as a practical estimate of overweight in children and young people, but needs to be interpreted with caution because it is not a direct measure of adiposity" (NICE, 2006, p. 35). NICE is clear that there is insufficient evidence to support specific BMI cut-offs in children. Nevertheless, pragmatic indicators for action are the 91st and the 98th centiles (overweight and obese, respectively) (Box 1).

Interpreting Results

"Weighing and measuring have poor sensitivity and specificity in terms of identifying disease and normality. Measuring, plotting and interpreting the results are not simple ... Much harm can be done if staff do not understand the principles of how growth charts work, normal variation and regression to the mean. The problems with height monitoring are to do with quality, accuracy, unavoidable measurement error and low yield of genuinely new cases" (UK Screening Portal - UK National Screening Committee, 2004, p. 3).

Box 1. Body Mass Index reference data

Body mass index (BMI)
BMI = (weight in kg)/(height in meters) BMI is the most convenient and widely used proxy for obesity. It correlates with total body fat but does not distinguish between muscle and fat. It is possible that in less fit children muscle mass is replaced by fat mass. Body proportions affect BMI. Other measures of obesity, such as waistline and skinfold, are potentially helpful but are not yet in regular use. *British BMI reference cut-offs* BMI $\geq 91^{st}$ centile – overweight BMI $\geq 98^{th}$ centile – obese The International Task Force on Obesity derived cut-off points linked to the adult cut-offs of 25 kg/m^2 (overweight) and 30 kg/m^2 (obese) at age 18. These are under review.

From Hall and Elliman, 2004, p. 185.

Published online a decade ago, this assessment remains true for the simple reason that the personnel tasked with growth and weight measurement continue to be diversely trained. This is an underlying problem simply because national screening programmes continue to be unevenly allocated in terms of quality standards.

In some locations, trained health professionals conduct these measurements but in other locations staff who have marginal training are sub-contracted to do this work. This pattern of using untrained and/or minimally inducted staff to weigh and measure children is a reflection of the presumption that the task is relatively simple and straightforward. But the interpretation of measurement and the plotting of results on growth charts does require dedicated training. In the United States, for example, school teachers carry out BMI surveillance in some locations and the accuracy of the outcomes remain mixed (Berkson, Espinola, Corso, Cabral, McGowan, and Chomitz, 2013).

In England, prevalence rates for overweight/obesity are calculated by deriving every child's BMI plus the child's age and sex following NICE guidelines. The first report from the Department of Health Information Centre specified the categories of overweight and obesity.

"The following thresholds for defining healthy weight, overweight and obese children were then used:

- *Healthy weight* is defined as having BMI between the 2nd and 90th centiles;
- *Overweight* is defined as having BMI greater than or equal to the 91st and 97th BMI centiles; and
- *Very overweight (clinically obese)* is defined as having BMI at or above the 98th centile;
- *Underweight* [is] not examined but is specified as below the 2nd BMI centile classification." (Department of Health, 2013, p. 27)

And yet the National Obesity Observatory (NOO) in 2011 calls attention to the inappropriateness of fixed thresholds when applied to children because they can provide misleading findings. Assessing the BMI of children is more complex than for adults because a child's BMI undergoes developmental change. In addition, growth patterns vary between boys and girls, and hence both age and sex need to be taken into account when estimating whether BMI is within a normal range (Dinsdale, Ridler, and Ells, 2011). The body mass index (BMI) is calculated by dividing weight in kilograms by height in meters squared (see above). It does not, however, take muscle mass and body fat percentage into account. In addition, for children, the level of fatness changes over time. The serious question that arises is whether or not technical measurements of BMI are helpful mainly to the child or to public health monitoring.

Many countries have their own population-specific thresholds for assessing BMI. In January 2013, new growth charts were published for school age children and young people in England by the Royal College of Paediatrics and Child Health (RCPCH). The charts can be found at http://www.rcpch.ac.uk/child-health/research-projects/uk-who-growth-charts/uk-who-growth-chart-resources/uk-who-growth-ch-0. Note that they are consistent with the WHO (2006) charts and that these charts are recommended for the whole of England. Implementation of weighing and measuring school-age children in the UK remains within the jurisdiction of each of the four countries of the UK—England, Wales, Scotland, and Northern Ireland.

Advice for Parents/Carers

Only trained healthcare professionals have the expertise to interpret and to advise parents and carers. In some cases, this entails a referral to a medical practitioner. In other cases, it involves sensitive advice about diet, exercise, and family nutrition. Of course, making that initial distinction requires training. But, if the task involves alerting the parent(s) to a possibly emerging weight problem, knowledge and sensitivity are key requirements of a specific kind.

The task of raising the issue of excessive weight with the parent of a 4 to 5 year old or a 10 to 11 year old can be a difficult one. If the diagnosis is likely to be linked to diet, this can become a delicate matter to raise with a parent and can, in fact, strain the therapeutic relationship that is necessary in order to modify child weight gain. In fact, this may be the first time that weight has been discussed with the family as a problem. The following are recommended communication strategies for health professionals in England (PatientPlus, 2013):

- If the family expresses concern about the child's weight. Try: 'We can measure (child's) weight and see if he or she is overweight for his or her age'.
- If the child has weight-related comorbidities. Try: '(Condition) can sometimes be related to a child's weight. I think we should check (child's) weight'.
- If the child is visibly overweight. Try: 'I see more children these days who are a little overweight. Could we check (child's) weight?'

Single-strategy approaches to managing weight are not recommended for children or young people (NICE, 2006). Parents may also need to be encouraged to lose weight if they are also overweight or obese. In many cases, the child's weight may well be a reflection of the whole family's relationship to nutrition and exercise and/or, alternatively, a reflection of the family's historic growth patterns.

Areas for Caution

There are a range of difficulties in accurately screening for growth and development in children. They include: the skill and training of the person responsible for weighing and measuring; the precision of the reporting at the time; the accuracy of the instruments used; the time of year and the weight of the clothing and the range of child monthly age over the course of the year in which measurement takes place; the precision of the plotting on graph; inclusion of the child's age rounded up or down to years rather than in months; and the willingness of the parents/carers to approve measurement of their child. These are background factors to the knowledge and the skills that are needed in those who weigh and measure children at school. They range from interpersonal and communication skills to precision skills in measuring and precision skills in reporting outcomes.

The presumption that weighing and measuring a child is a simple task is fairly widespread and this has had the effect of transferring the task to untrained or under-trained staff. But the presumption is belied by a number of factors, including: the weight of the child's clothing at various times of the year will have an effect; height can vary depending on the child's hairstyle; observer variation and skill variation suggest that the same health professional should be weighing and measuring every child and every repeated screen – consistency; rounding up and rounding down is a pattern that varies between health professionals; instrument variation is as common as observer variation; the plotting of measurements is a further common source of error; there are arguments that community based charts are wise because of the variations that can exist between specific population growth patterns (see DHSSPS, 2010, p. 9); and variations in average body size exist between ethnic groups and for this reason a range of "acceptable" scales are needed in order to ensure subtlety of interpretation.

These are problems that attach to standardization and to staff skill and training. There are also more complex problems that suggest the need for sufficient levels of training for the manpower required. First, there are common national errors in growth monitoring such as: self-reported data; multiple measures; untrained staff conducting the measures; varied equipment or equipment that is not standardized; little attempt has been made to measure the cost effectiveness or the outcomes of screening for height and weight; little assurance of effective follow-up or measures of effective follow-up. Furthermore, and clinically serious, there can be: co-morbidities (e.g., sleep apnea or raised intracranial pressure) that require referral to a clinical setting; and psychological or physical problems that may require either pharmacological treatment or supplementation by micronutrient intake (NICE, 2006).

LOOKING TO THE FUTURE

It is fair to say that considerable resources have been invested in child growth measurement tools since at least 1977. In fact, the WHO, the United States CDC, and the UK have all committed considerable expertise and funding, particularly since the beginning of the 21st century—all committed to ensuring the sophistication of child height and weight measurement calculations. The recent driver has largely been pressure to counter a global increase in weight gain, particularly morbid weight gain amongst both adults and children in many developed countries but also in most of the increasingly industrialized countries such as China (Sun Jia, Peng, Dickerman, Compher, and Liu, 2013) and India (Raj, Sundaram, Paul, Deepa, and Kumar, 2007). Malnutrition continues to be a severe problem for some developing countries but it is also the case that over-weight and obesity are additional forms of malnutrition.

We now have the measurement sophistication we need in order to map accurately the changes in growth and development that are affecting children around the world. We have been able to identify some of the geographical, cultural and population locations that are most susceptible to excessive weight gain. Obesity is rapidly becoming one of the major non-infectious diseases worldwide that can significantly reduce life expectancy. This is a social as well as a medical challenge for healthcare professionals. Finding ways to reverse this trend is a matter for public health skills in addition to the clinical skills we already have in place.

Reversing a food and nutrition trend that may be damaging health requires new and different skills from those required to identify the trend in the first place. In other words, we have invested sufficient resources to track the fact of excessive weight gain amongst children and adults but we have not yet found ways to reverse this negative trend.

Weighing and measuring school-age children is likely to remain a monitoring task rather than a mainstream screening exercise. In other words, in populations where pre-school child growth is closely screened from birth there is little clinical need for weighing and measuring children during the school years. The responsibility for growth and development monitoring can arguably remain the responsibility of primary care practitioners. The challenge for the future will be how to use our epidemiological knowledge to underpin effective health promotion work, legislative control of the food industry, and the deleterious effects of poverty on child development.

Conclusion

The profile of growth (height and weight) that we measure in school age children can signal for us a variety of physical problems that we may have otherwise missed in the pre-school period. Thus growth development monitoring is a form of insurance. It can be a part of primary care practice as an annual health check or it can be carried out at school.

Measuring all children in their early school years can also tell us about the health of the population as a whole. For that to happen, however, we need to use standardized measures and appropriately trained staff. Furthermore, we need a public health approach that ensures epidemiological analyses of the whole of the population of children within a given geographic area. It is important to note that these are two separate measures. One is a tool for discovering any health difficulties that we may have missed in the growing child during the pre-school period. The second is a means of assessing the profile of health in the whole child population. In other words, weighing and measuring the child has a different purpose from weighing and measuring the child population.

By school age, we generally have a good understanding of most physical problems that are likely to have affected a child from birth and that might still be discovered via growth monitoring in the school years. Weighing and measuring school-age children may not really be essential, therefore, as a screening tool. For that reason, it is a matter of local judgment in each country whether or not to invest in the costs attached to weighing and measuring all school age children. There are a number of physical problems that can still be identified (for the first time) by measuring the school age child but they are few. (For example, highly mobile children, isolated children, families moving into the country from abroad.) Most are identifiable within a constellation of difficulties that emerge in other measures of child health. For a few it may be the first opportunity we have had to assess the health of children who were 'missed' before school entry. What is more important is that we need to ask ourselves what the purpose is of weighing and measuring all school age children. From around 2004 to 2006, an international alert to a growing problem of excessive weight gain and obesity emerged in the public consciousness. The health consequences of both overweight and obesity can be severe, can be life limiting, and can cause chronic and life threatening illnesses. Early 21st century reports identified obesity as a particularly serious problem, particularly in the United States, the UK, and in a range of developed and developing countries around the world. In England, the National Child Monitoring Programme (NCMP) was approved in 2006. It has been an important population measurement tool. This public health outcome has been its primary justification.

Other countries in Europe and most states in the US also monitor child growth and development at the population level. The long-term challenge will be in finding ways to modify, regulate, and quality assure the food industry and also ensure that children and families have access to healthy physical exercise.

REFERENCES

Acheson, D. (1998). *Inequalities in Health: Report of an independent inquiry*. London: HMSO.

Berkson, S. S., Espinola, J., Corso, K. A., Cabral, H., McGowan, R., and Chomitz, V. R. (2013) Reliability of height and weight measurements collected by physical education teachers for a school-based body mass index surveillance and screening system. *Journal of School Health*, 83, 1, 21-27.

Butte, N. F., Garza, C. and de Onis, M. (2007). Evaluation of the feasibility of international growth standards for school-aged children and adolescents. *Journal of Nutrition*, 137, 53-157.

Cole, T. J., Flegal, K. M., Nicholls, D., and Jackson, A. A. (2007). Body mass index cut-offs to define thinness in children and adolescents: international survey. *British Medical Journal*, 335, 194-202.

Delamothe, T. (2013). Food, inglorious food. *British Medical Journal*, 346, f2472.

De Onis, M., Onyango, A., Borghi, E., Siyam, A., Blossner, M., and Lutter, C. (2012). Worldwide implementation of the WHO Child Growth Standards. *Public Health Nutrition*, 15, 1603-1610.

De Onis, M., Garza, C., Onyango, A. W., and Borghi, E. (2007). Comparison of the WHO Child Growth Standards and the CDC 2000 Growth Charts. *Journal of Nutrition*, 137, 144-148.

De Onis, M., Garza, C., Victora, C. G., Onyango, A. W., Frongillo, E. A., and Martines, J. (2004). The WHO Multicentre Growth Reference Study: planning, study design, and methodology. *Food and Nutrition Bulletin*, 25(1), S15-S26.

De Onis, M., Wijnhoven, T. M. A. and Onyango, A. W. (2004). Worldwide practices in child growth monitoring. *Journal of Pediatrics*, 144, 461-465.

Department of Health. (2008). *National Child Measurement Programme: 2006/07 school year, headline results*. London: The Information Centre.

Department of Health, Social Services and Public Safety. (2010). *Healthy child, healthy future: A framework for the Universal Child Health Promotion Programme in Northern Ireland. Pregnancy to 19 years*. Belfast: DHSSPS.

Dinsdale, H., Ridler, C., Ells, L. (2011). *A simple guide to classifying body mass index in children*. Oxford: National Obesity Observatory. Retrieved from http://www.noo.org.uk/publications.

European Childhood Obesity Group. (2009). Endorsement of the new WHO Growth Standards for Infants and Young Children by the European Childhood Obesity Groups (ECOG).

Government Office for Science. (2007). *Foresight report: tackling obesities: future choices.* London: Government Office for Science. Retrieved from www.bis.gov.uk/assets/ foresight/docs/obesity/17.pdf.

Hall, D. and Elliman, D. (2004). *Health for all children.* 4th ed. Oxford: Oxford University Press.

Health and Social Care Information Centre. (2013). *National Child Measurement Programme.* London: Health and Social Care Information Centre. Retrieved from http:// www.hscic.gov.uk/ncmp.

Kipping, R. R., Jago, R. and Lawlor, D. A. (2008). Obesity in children. Part 1: Epidemiology, measurement, risk factors, and screening. *British Medical Journal*, 15, 335:a1824.

Leeds Metropolitan University. (2013, February 13). *Childhood obesity is not at its highest in the most deprived areas of the UK.* Retrieved from http://www.leedsmet.ac.uk/news/ childhood-obesity-is-not-at-its-highest-in-the-most-deprived-areas-of-the-uk12022013. htm.

Marmot, M. and Wilkinson, R. G. (Eds.). (2006). *Social determinants of health.* 2nd ed. Oxford: Oxford University Press.

National Audit Office. (2012). *An update on the government's approach to tackling obesity.* London: National Audit Office.

National Institute for Health and Clinical Excellence. (2010). *Clinical Guideline Practice No. CG9.* Eating disorders: Core interventions in the treatment and management of anorexia nervosa, bulima nervosa and related eating disorders. National Collaborating Centre for Mental Health. London: The British Psychological Society and the Royal College of Psychiatrists.

National Institute for Health and Clinical Excellence. (2006) Obesity: guidance on the prevention, identification, assessment and management of overweight and obesity in adults and children. *NICE clinical guideline 43: London: NICE.*

National Institute for Health and Clinical Excellence. (2010). *Human growth hormone (somatropin) for the treatment of growth failure in children.* London: NICE.

PatientPlus. (2013) *Obesity in children.* Retrieved from http://patient.co.uk/print/4037.

Public Health Wales. (2013). *Child Measurement Programme for Wales.* Retrieved from http://www.wales.nhs.uk/sitesplus/888/page/56237.

Public Health England. (27 August 2013). *National child measurement programme: operational guidance for the 2013 to 2014 school year.* London: Gov.uk. Retrieved from https:// www.gov.uk/government/publications/national-child-measurement-programme-operational-guidance-for-the-2013-to-2014-school-year.

Raj, M., Sundaram, K. R., Paul, M., Deepa, A. S., and Kumar, R. K. (2007). Obesity in Indian children: time trends and relationship with hypertension. *National Medical Journal of India,* 20, 288-293.

Royal College of Paediatrics and Child Health. (2004). *An approach to weight management in children and adolescents (2-18 years) in primary care.* London: Royal College of Paediatrics and Child Health.

Royal College of Paediatrics and Child Health. (2009). The UK-WHO growth charts: What is the difference? *UK-WHO Growth Charts – Fact Sheet 2.* Retrieved from www. growthcharts.rcpch.ac.uk.

Royal College of Physicians. (1962). *Smoking and health.* London: Pitman Medical Publishers.

Royal College of Physicians. (2013). *Action on obesity: comprehensive care for all*. Retrieved from www.rcplondon.ac.uk/sites/default/files/action-on-obesity/17.pdf.

Stevens, A. and Raftery, J. (1997). *Health care needs assessment: the epidemiologically based needs assessment reviews*. Oxford: Radcliffe Medical Press.

Sun, G., Jia, G., Peng, H., Dickerman, B., Compher, C., and Liu, J. (2013). Trends in childhood obesity in China and associated factors. *Clinical Nursing Research*, doi: 10.1177/1054773813493286.

UK Screening Portal – UK National Screening Committee. (2004). *Child Health Sub-Group Report on Growth Disorders: UK NSC policy on growth screening in children*. Institute of Child Health and Royal College of General Practitioners: London.

WHO Multicentre Growth Reference Study Group. (2006). *WHO Child Growth Standards: Length/height-for-age, weight-for-age, weight for length, weight-for-height and body mass index-for-age: Methods and development*. Geneva: World Health Organization.

World Health Organization. (2013). *WHO Reference 2007. Growth reference data for 5-19 years*. Retrieved from http://www.who.int/growthref/en/

In: School Health Screening Systems
Editors: Bradley McPherson and Carlie J. Driscoll

ISBN: 978-1-63117-942-6

Chapter 4

HEARING SCREENING FOR SCHOOL CHILDREN

Carlie J. Driscoll[1,*], Bradley McPherson[2] and Wayne J. Wilson[1]
[1]University of Queensland, Brisbane, QLD, Australia
[2]University of Hong Kong, Pokfulam, Hong Kong

ABSTRACT

Hearing screening is an integral component in virtually all school health screening programs. It has long been recognized that hearing loss will have negative consequences on children's communication abilities and educational performance unless early identification and management is arranged. School-based screening allows for the detection of children with hearing loss who have not been identified at an earlier stage (for example, in a newborn hearing screening program) and for children who have developed hearing loss after early childhood (for example, children with a progressive, inherited hearing disorder). This chapter provides an overview of pure-tone audiometry, the standard method for hearing screening in school children, and details the main established guidelines for screen protocols. Other hearing and ear health methods have also been considered for school-based programs, such as tympanometry, otoacoustic emission recording, and teacher/parent questionnaires. These procedures are discussed and their advantages and limitations outlined. Conventional hearing screening programs are not effective in detecting children with high tone, noise-induced hearing loss or children with auditory processing difficulties. Potential alternative screening protocols to identify children with such problems are presented. Advances in technology may alter the practice of hearing screening in the future. For example, telehealth-based screening may serve a useful role in future programs and genetic screening for hearing disorders may enhance the early detection of some cases of hearing loss.

DEVELOPMENT OF SCHOOL HEARING SCREENING

Children with sensory disorders have been of particular concern to school health screening services from their foundation.

* Corresponding author: Carlie J. Driscoll. University of Queensland. E-mail: carlie.driscoll@uq.edu.au.

Permanent childhood hearing loss may have a serious long-term impact on the communication abilities, educational achievement, socioeconomic status, and overall quality of life of an individual, as well as generating major financial costs for the community as a whole (Access Economics, 2006). School health services recognized that the early identification and management of hearing loss could mitigate the associated level of disability. Henderson (1975, p. 15) cites the Chief Medical Officer's 1908 report to the British Board of Education which stated that: "It is not usually practical during the routine examination of large numbers of children to test accurately the exact condition of the hearing capacity of a child ... [but] it is important that a careful examination should be made of all children in whom there is any reason to suspect defective hearing." By 1911, the Chief Medical Officer had revised this guidance and considered a hearing test should be given to "every child who is old enough to respond." A whispered voice test for school children was introduced in the United Kingdom in the 1920s, although its inadequacies were acknowledged (Henderson, 1975) and more scientific methods of hearing screening were introduced in the 1930s. By the 1940s pure-tone audiometry screening was a standard test throughout the country (Stevens and Parker, 2009). Australian school medical services incorporated a rudimentary hearing assessment component from the early 1900s (Skurr, 1978) and, in the United States, formal school hearing health examinations also developed as early as 1924 (McFarlan, 1927). Wall and Bührer (1987) noted that, by 1943, twenty American states had laws requiring school screening for hearing loss. With economic advancement, hearing screening was initiated in many other regions. For example, in Hong Kong audiometric screening for children in government primary (elementary) schools commenced in 1968 and became universal by 1981 (Lam et al., 2006). Screening audiometry has now come to be considered an established and essential aspect of school health practice throughout the developed world, and in many developing countries (McPherson and Olusanya, 2008).

School screening audiometry has concentrated on the detection of possible hearing disorders in elementary grade school children. This is appropriate because it is advantageous to arrange the earliest possible treatment or habilitation for hearing loss and because many cases of previously undetected hearing loss are noted at the time of school entry (Roeser and Northern, 1981). From the viewpoint of educators, intervention should be as early as possible so that is does not negatively affect academic performance.

In many countries, universal newborn hearing screening programs have now been established and the early detection of congenital hearing loss is common (Leigh, Schmulian-Taljaard, and Poulakis, 2010). However, the hearing screening of school children can be justified by the prevalence of hearing loss that is not detected by universal newborn hearing screening, due to factors such as delayed onset hearing loss or acquired hearing loss. British data suggests that the prevalence of bilateral, permanent hearing impairment increases by at least 50% (and perhaps up to 90%) between the newborn period and the ages of 9-16 years (Fortnum, Summerfield, Marshall, Davis, and Bamford, 2001).

In addition, there are limitations to newborn screening technology that mean it may not detect cases of mild hearing loss (Leigh, Schmulian-Taljaard, and Poulakis, 2010) and newborn screening programs may have a high non-compliance rate for follow-up (Danhauer, Pecile, Johnson, Mixon, and Sharp, 2008), leading to some children remaining unidentified until school entry. Approximately 3% of school age children in developed countries may have hearing loss in one or both ears (Marttila, 1986; Mehra, Eavey, and Keamy, 2009; Parving, 1999).

GOALS OF SCHOOL HEARING SCREENING

Screening programs need clear goals to be effective (Lescouflair, 1975). The two most influential sets of professional guidelines for hearing screening, both within and outside of North America, are those issued by the American Association for Speech, Language, and Hearing (ASHA) and the American Academy of Audiology (AAA). The broad ASHA (1997) goal for hearing screening is to identify children likely to have hearing impairment that may interfere with education, health, development, or communication and this aim is widely adopted in school programs. The AAA guidelines (2011) are similarly concerned with the identification of hearing loss that affects perception of speech and, hence, development of language-based skills. In both guidelines, it is implicitly or explicitly stated that this goal includes detection of children with unilateral as well as bilateral hearing loss.

PURE TONE SCREENING AUDIOMETRY

Nearly all school hearing health programs make use of pure tone screening audiometry as the fundamental component of their procedures (see Figure 8.1). This is for a number of reasons. Pure tone diagnostic audiometry is the gold standard for assessment of hearing loss. This involves measurement of perceived threshold intensities for a series of standard tones that cover the range of sounds required for optimal detection of speech.

It is convenient to base screening on the same procedure, using a pass/fail criterion intensity instead of determining threshold and to use a restricted range of test tones (test frequencies) that are critical for speech perception.

In addition, the sensitivity and specificity of pure tone screening audiometry has always been found to be better than that of any rival technique (Berg, Papri, Ferdous, Khan, and Durkin, 2006; Sideris and Glattke, 2006). FitzZaland and Zink (1984) noted sensitivity and specificity of 93% and 99%, respectively, in a well-conducted screening program.

Essentially, tones at fixed, single frequencies are presented at fixed intensity levels and the child is instructed to respond to a perceived signal by raising a hand, pressing a response button, or in some other standard manner. Earphones are the sound source and generally a practice tone is first presented to the child at a level clearly above the test tones (often at 40 or 60 dB HL) to introduce the child to the type of sound to be used. Test sounds are then presented first to one ear and later the other ear, and the presence or absence of a behavioral response from the child is recorded for each tone. No attempt is made to find the hearing threshold for a tone if the child does not respond at a particular frequency (Roeser and Northern, 1981).

Since the goal of screening is to detect hearing loss that may adversely affect speech perception, the test frequencies and intensities chosen should reflect this aim. ASHA guidelines (1997, p. 41) call for screening at 20 dB HL “in the frequency region most important for speech recognition”. Generally, this frequency region is considered to be from 500 Hz to 4000 Hz. However, ambient noise conditions in schools are rarely optimal for hearing screening (Choi and McPherson, 2005; Knight, Nelson, Whitelaw, and Feth, 2002; Shield, Greenland, and Dockrell, 2010) and low frequency ambient noise will often mask quiet test tones at 500 Hz, leading to high false-positive rates (McPherson, Law, and Wong, 2010).

The current ASHA guidelines recognize this constraint and recommend testing at 1000 Hz, 2000 Hz, and 4000 Hz only. The AAA (2011) guidelines make identical recommendations. A recent European consensus statement on hearing screening (Skarzynski and Piotrowska, 2012), while not making specific suggestions for test frequencies, states that hearing loss greater than 20 dB HL may have adverse effects on the development of communication skills, cognitive development, and academic achievement—in effect endorsing the ASHA and AAA recommendations for screening intensity level. It should be noted that many school screening agencies set their own criterion intensities and frequencies and these may not reflect standard guidelines (Meinke and Dice, 2007). However, any criterion set should be evidence-based (Wong and Hickson, 2012) and rigorously justified.

Pass/fail criteria may vary a great deal in pure-tone screening audiometry programs. Wall, Naples, Buhrer, and Capodanno (1985), in a large survey of American professionals involved in school screening, found that failure to detect a signal at two frequencies was deemed a test failure for about one-third of respondents, others used one frequency, more than two frequencies, two consecutive frequencies, or a pure-tone average greater than a pre-determined level as a criterion for 'failure'. Both ASHA and AAA guidelines define failure as a lack of response at any frequency in either ear.

The two guidelines differ somewhat in how 'failure' is determined. AAA (2011, p. 45) guidelines recommend "presenting a tone at least twice but no more than four times" if a child fails to respond. ASHA (1997) guidelines call for reinstruction, repositioning of earphones, and same day rescreening for any child who fails to respond at any frequency. Screening audiometers can be purchased specifically for this task.

These instruments provide a restricted test frequency range, usually from 500 Hz to 4000 Hz, and also limit earphone output intensity levels.

Figure 4.1. School screening using pure tone audiometry.

Periodicity of Screening

Ideally, it would be advantageous to screen all elementary school children for hearing and middle ear disorders on an annual basis. However, the associated practicalities rarely allow for this (Roeser and Clark, 2004). Guidelines tend to prioritize the screening of younger grades and/or high-risk populations, defined by Roeser and Clark (2004, p. 118) as those cases that are: new to a school, repeating a grade, commencing speech-language therapy, returning to school following serious illness, delayed in development, displaying emotional or behavioral problems, involved in noisy coursework, or are absent during previous routine screening. To assist in the decision-making regarding which particular grades to screen, AAA (2011) provided a summary of findings from an unpublished analysis of hearing screening results from three school districts in Colorado and Florida, US.

Notably, it was found that approximately 90% of new hearing losses were detected by screening in preschool, kindergarten, and grades 1, 2, and 3. This rate increased to up to 97% if including grade 5 or 6 also.

Alternatively, ASHA's (1997) guidelines specify annual screening of all children from kindergarten through to grade 3, as well as in grades 7 and 11. Furthermore, children should be screened as needed, requested, or mandated. ASHA is also a proponent of screening of high-risk cases as described above, with the addition of the factors of: concern from parent/ caregiver, health care provider, teacher, or other school personnel; family history of late or delayed onset hereditary hearing loss; recurrent or persistent otitis media with effusion (OME) for at least three months; craniofacial anomalies, including those with morphological abnormalities of the pinna and ear canal; stigmata or other findings associated with a syndrome known to include sensorineural and/or conductive hearing loss; head trauma with loss of consciousness; and, reported exposure to potentially damaging noise levels or ototoxic drugs.

Program managers should carefully consider the time of year when hearing screening is held. It is preferable to avoid times of the year that are known to be peak seasons for colds and influenza or for environment-related allergies (Richburg, Davie, and Smiley, 2012) since these are times of higher student absence rates and higher prevalence of transient conductive hearing loss.

Program Management

Hearing screening in the school environment may be performed by a variety of personnel, including, but not limited to: audiologists, audiometrists, speech-language pathologists, audiology assistants, school nurses, psychologists and specialist educators, and health workers. Personnel choices may be dictated by state licensure requirements or by district/ program managers. Richburg and Imhoff (2008) noted that when hearing screening programs were supervised by an educational audiologist, testing protocols were more uniform than when non-audiologists were in management positions. The World Health Organization (2001) reported significant variation in the screening results obtained by minimally trained, junior testers in comparison with experienced testers (with ≥ one year's experience in audiometry).

Further, Northern and Downs (2002) noted that inexperienced testers, by incorrectly placing headphones, can create a threshold shift of up to 35 dB HL.

They may also provide unsuitable instructions, provide verbal and physical cues, and use inappropriate stimulus presentation length. In recognition of such studies and of the fact that many school districts in the US use screening programs that are managed by personnel other than audiologists, AAA (2011) recommended that school hearing screening programs at least utilize a single or small group of local audiologists in an advisory capacity.

The audiologist(s) could provide valuable input regarding higher administrative functions of the program, such as choice of screening technology and protocols, training and monitoring of testers, equipment maintenance and calibration, and follow-up pathways and procedures (Roeser and Clark, 2004).

ASHA's (1997) guidelines clearly specified that performance of hearing and/or middle ear screening of children aged 0-18 years should be limited to clinically certified audiologists and speech-language pathologists, or support personnel under the direct supervision of a certified audiologist.

Test Environment

In order to minimize the false-positive rate, it is crucial that testing is performed in an environment with low ambient noise (Roeser and Clark, 2004). For instance, the school room selected for testing should be located away from high noise sources such as cafeterias, music rooms, air-conditioners and other mechanical equipment, high-volume road traffic, and high-volume pedestrian traffic as often occurs near offices and toilet facilities.

Alternatively, the use of mobile test vans and booths could be considered if finances allow. This is particularly important if wanting to ensure that under-identification does not occur for cases of unilateral and minimal/mild bilateral hearing loss (White and Munoz, 2008). Roeser and Clarke (2004) recommend against the routine use of noise-excluding headsets, in view of placement effects, unless utilized by experienced testers.

These authors also remind us of the importance of performing simple biological checks to assess whether background noise levels are appropriate (i.e., establishing hearing thresholds at least 10 dB below the screening level at all test frequencies for a person with known normal hearing, AAA, 2011) or, if possible, directly measuring noise levels using a sound level meter against ANSI standards (1999).

The maximum allowable noise levels for pure tone screening in accordance with ASHA (1997) protocols are: 49.5 dB SPL at 1000 Hz, 54.5 dB SPL at 2000 Hz, and 62 dB SPL at 4000 Hz. For AAA (2011) protocols, these are 50, 58, and 76 dB SPL at 1000, 2000, and 4000 Hz, respectively. Finally, testing should occur in environments with minimal visual distractions that could impact upon the child's concentration and contribute to elevated false-positive rates.

Accountability and Other Concerns

The program supervisor, preferably an audiologist, should assume responsibility for the screening system's accountability, risk management, and program evaluation (see AAA, 2011, and ASHA, 1997, for full details).

Accountability refers to adherence to confidentiality and consent requirements, maintenance of the system database, referral tracking, and counseling. Risk management requires the audiologist to evaluate risk factors associated with the screening program and to develop procedures to minimize or eliminate those factors (e.g., consideration of infection control, calibration of equipment, quality assurance procedures, and system errors at all levels).

Program evaluation to ascertain the effectiveness of a screening system is discussed in Chapter 1.

ALTERNATIVE SCREENING METHODS

As noted by Meinke (2011), school-based hearing screening has become synonymous with pure tone screening. Despite multiple, promising technological advances since the inception of school screening in the 1920's, very little has changed and the hearing screening landscape is still characterized by standard pure tone testing with a widespread lack of standardization between programs (Bamford et al., 2007; Meinke, 2011). It is certainly time for the everyday practice of school hearing screening to benefit from the type of rigorous research, systematic evaluation, and in-depth attention that has been typically afforded to universal newborn hearing screening programs worldwide. Presented below are some alternative screening methods that could be considered for inclusion in the modern school hearing screening test battery, followed by discussion of follow-up management pathways, and mention of some potential future directions in this field.

Tympanometry

Tympanometry is used in the assessment of middle ear function; it is not a test of hearing but, rather, a test of the mechanical properties of the tympanic membrane and other middle ear structures. The middle ear system is an essential component of the auditory pathway, conducting sound from the outer to the inner ear. Disruption of middle ear function can produce a conductive hearing loss that can be temporary, fluctuating, or permanent in nature.

Tympanometry is a minimally invasive, quick, painless, and objective test that involves placement of a small, disposable probe tip into the entrance of the external auditory canal in order to create an hermetic seal (refer to Figure 8.2).

As the air pressure within the canal is varied from +200 to -400 daPa, the volume of the canal alters accordingly due to movement of the middle ear. A tympanogram is produced; a graph of the admittance (compliance or mobility) of the middle ear system against pressure. When air is present in the middle ear cavity, the tympanogram will display a peak pressure that corresponds with the air pressure within the middle ear space (Roush, 2001).

Measurement parameters obtained typically include equivalent ear canal volume (Vea), peak compensated static acoustic admittance (Ytm), tympanometric peak pressure (TPP), and tympanometric width (TW).

The shape of the tympanogram, along with the associated values, is judged either against the classification system developed by Jerger (1970), against specific normative criteria, or against professional practice guidelines.

Under Jerger's system, a "type A" tympanogram is associated with normal middle ear compliance and pressure (usually indicative of normal middle ear function), a "type B" tympanogram is associated with no changes in compliance with changes in pressure (suggestive of middle ear pathology such as OME or tympanic membrane perforation if accompanied by an abnormally large ear canal volume), and a "type C" tympanogram is associated with normal compliance in the presence of excessively negative pressure (as is seen in Eustachian tube dysfunction). Refer to Figure 8.3 for display of these typical tympanogram shapes seen in school children.

In regard to the use of specific normative criteria, these may take into consideration the age, gender, ear, or even racial heritage of the child (e.g., Li, Bu, and Driscoll, 2006). Finally, tympanometric screening results for school children may be analyzed in accordance with professional practice guidelines, such as those produced by AAA (2011), whereby a "failed" screen would be indicated by a TW of ≥250 daPa (the preferred criteria), or Ytm of <0.2 mmhos, or TPP of -200 to -400 daPa (although this criterion alone should not trigger a medical referral).

As previously mentioned, although not a direct test of hearing status, tympanometry can be a useful addition to the audiological battery, as 49-66% of children with a type B tympanogram will have at least a mild degree of conductive hearing loss, compared with only 2-13% with other tympanometric profiles (National Health and Medical Research Council, NHMRC, 2002). For children aged 4-6 years, FitzZaland and Zink (1984) reported type B or C tympanograms to have a sensitivity ranging from 91.2 – 92.7% and a specificity ranging from 91.1 – 97.8% in the detection of hearing loss. These values increased to 100% and 97%, respectively, when tympanometry (type B tympanogram or Type C with ≤ -200 daPa) was used in conjunction with pure tone screening.

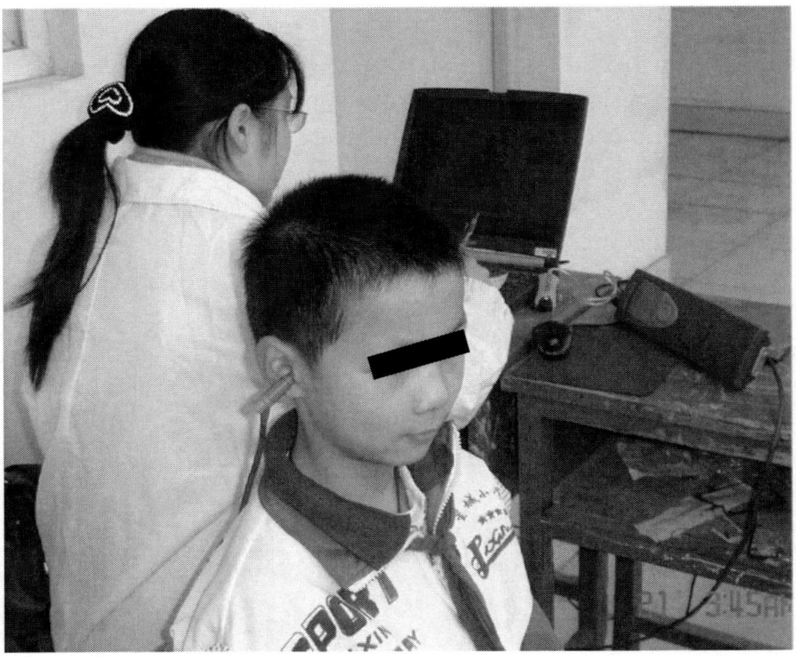

Figure 4.2. Tympanometry screening at a rural elementary school near Nanjing, Jiangsu province, People's Republic of China.

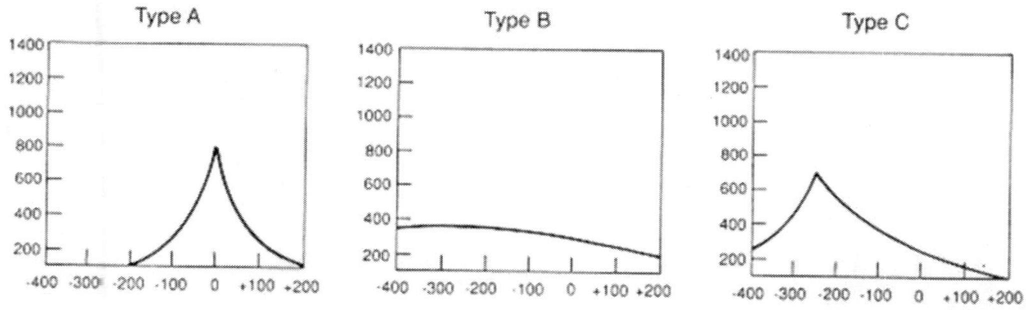

Figure 4.3. Typical tympanogram shapes observed during school screenings, using Jerger's (1970) classification system.

Furthermore, tympanometry demonstrates high sensitivity and specificity in the detection of OME when measured against a gold standard of myringotomy or pneumatic otoscopy (New Zealand Health Technology Assessment, 1998). In particular, type A tympanograms have a very high sensitivity in ruling out the presence of OME, and type B tympanograms have a sensitivity of 78-90% and a specificity of 63-94% in ruling in the presence of OME. These latter rates alter to 100% and 75%, respectively, if combined with type C tympanograms (New Zealand Health Technology Assessment, 1998).

Whilst there is little doubt concerning the appropriateness of tympanometry in detection of OME, support for its application in school-based screening programs is less conclusive. A suitable rationale for its inclusion might be if (a) OME was found to definitively cause long-lasting adverse effects upon a child's development and (b) that such effects could be averted by intervention (New Zealand Health Technology Assessment, 1998). However, the evidence to support these assumptions is conflicting and although a short-term correlation between OME and development has been recognized, a precise causal relationship has not. Adding to the uncertainty is the very nature of OME in childhood; it is a fluctuating disease subject also to seasonal variation, thus, single screening points throughout time are unlikely to detect all affected children. Furthermore, the rate of spontaneous resolution of OME is known to be high (Tos, 1984; Williamson, Dunleavy, Baine, and Robinson, 1994). Consequently, several professional bodies currently recommend against the routine, first-line use of tympanometry in school hearing screening programs (e.g., NHMRC, 2002; AAA, 2011).

It is suspected that the effects of OME on child development appear to be mediated by the associated hearing loss, although the exact degree and duration of loss needed to produce the negative sequelae remain unclear (AAA, 2011). In addition, of children with OME, 30-40% will experience recurrent episodes and 5-10% will experience episodes lasting in excess of one year (Tos, 1984; Williamson et al., 1994). Should the middle ear effusion be present for longer than three months, recovery is unlikely to occur in the absence of medical intervention (Tos, 1984; Williamson et al., 1994). Further, pure tone screening alone is not overly sensitive to middle ear disorders (Roeser and Clark, 2004). For these reasons, combined with the recognition of the noisy environments in which all school children must listen and learn and in which those with any degree or type of hearing loss can be considerably disadvantaged, some programs choose to include tympanometry in their basic test battery that is administered to all children. Others choose to apply tympanometry in the testing of those at high-risk of OME as per the AAA Position Statement on Identification of Hearing Loss and Middle Ear Dysfunction in Preschool and School-Age Children (1997).

Still others recommend its use as a follow-up or rescreening method. For instance, the AAA Childhood Hearing Screening Guidelines (2011, p. 46) state that tympanometry should be employed as an immediate next stage screening and/or a second stage screening for those who have failed pure tone or otoacoustic emission screening.

Tympanometry results should assist in clarifying the nature of the failure and in promoting the most efficient management pathway. Furthermore, AAA proposes that tympanometry could be considered as a first line screening tool for children in preschools, kindergartens, and grade 1 in situations where medical professionals and the school systems jointly decide to target OME in addition to cases with hearing loss.

The AAA guidelines also provide test protocol recommendations for tympanometry. Importantly, the tympanometer should be calibrated on a daily basis in accordance with manufacturer instruction. (A lightweight, easily portable device with a 226 Hz probe tone should be selected.) Prior to test commencement, visual inspection of the outer/middle ear using otoscopy should occur, in order to check for conditions that may necessitate medical referral or prohibit testing (e.g., tympanic membrane perforation, foreign bodies, blood in the ear canal, excessive cerumen, active discharge, etc.). Test results should be interpreted in accordance with the previously described criteria. Exceptions to these criteria include children with ventilation tubes who may be passed in the presence of a type B tympanogram with large Vea, and children of Asian heritage who may be passed with Ytm values of <0.2.

Otoacoustic Emissions

Otoacoustic emissions (OAEs) may be defined as low-intensity, acoustic energy produced by the cochlea and recorded in the ear canal (Probst, Lonsbury-Martin, and Martin, 1991). Originally described by Kemp (1978), such emissions are believed to reflect energy leakage that is radiated out by the cochlea as a result of its outer hair cells actively processing and amplifying incoming low-intensity sound. One particular class of OAEs occurs as a result of deliberate acoustic stimulation; evoked OAEs, which include both transient evoked OAEs (TEOAEs) and distortion product OAEs (DPOAEs). TEOAEs are so named as the emissions are commonly elicited by brief acoustic stimuli, such as Gaussian-shaped broadband clicks or tone bursts. Presentation of the stimulus results in a clear, frequency-dispersive response or "echo" detected in the ear canal within a short, time-locked window. The nomenclature of DPOAEs reflects the stimulus being a pair of pure tones that interact in the cochlea to produce a third tone (the distortion product).

To complete this electrophysiological test, the screener must place a small probe (comprised of a transducer and microphone/receiver) into the entrance of the ear canal, to create an acoustic seal. The adequacy of the probe fit is then assessed via visual analysis of the waveform display. Automatic stimulus presentation is followed by automatic amplification, filtering, and digitization of the response, after which the software can provide a programmed pass/fail judgment based on the OAEs signal-to-noise ratio (SNR) and other so desired measurement parameters, such as reproducibility (for TEOAEs, see Figure 8.4) or amplitude (for DPOAEs, see Figure 8.5). Refer to Roush (2001) for further details of the OAE test method.

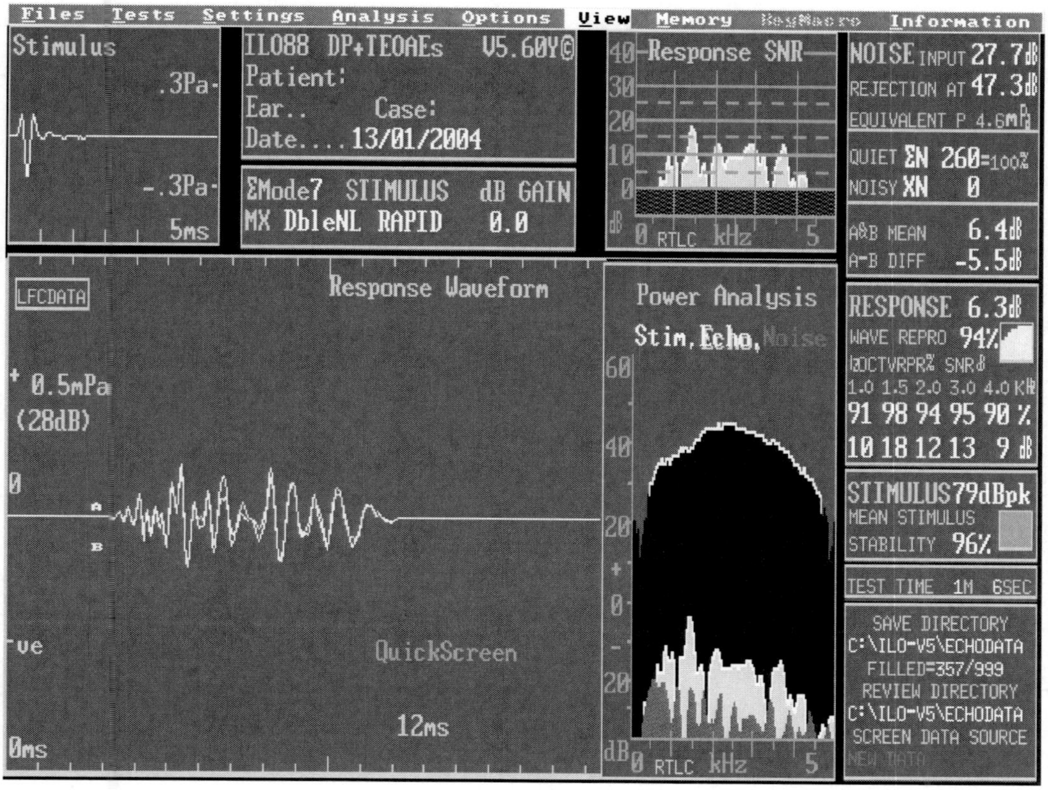

Figure 4.4. An example of the TEOAE test screen (taken using an Otodynamics ILO88 system).

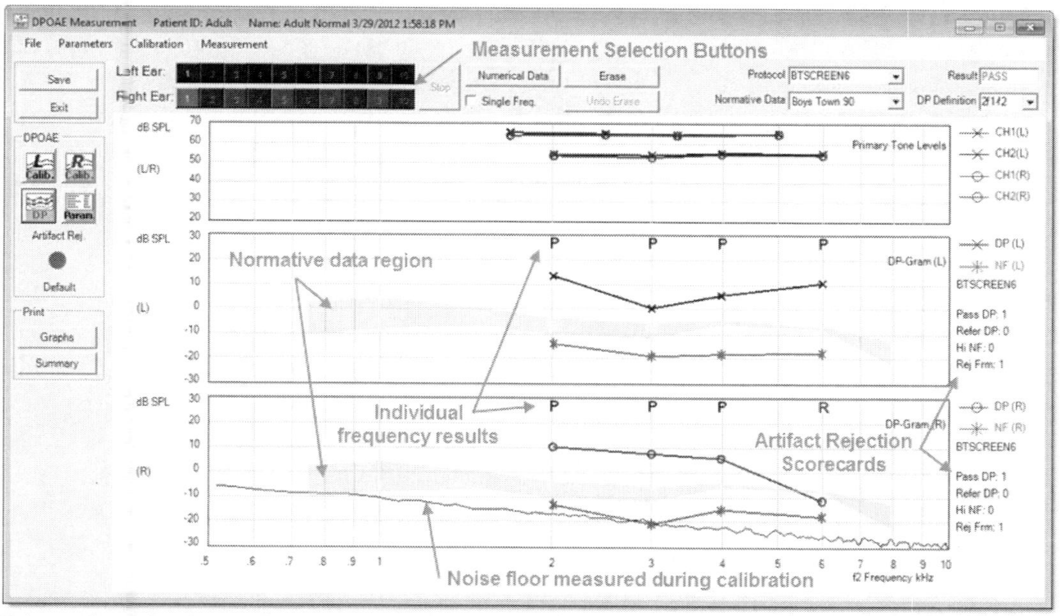

Taken using a Starkey DP2000 system, image courtesy of Starkey Laboratories.

Figure 4.5. An example of the DPOAE test screen. (Note: "DP" refers to the amplitude of the distortion product emission, and "NF" refers to the noise floor.)

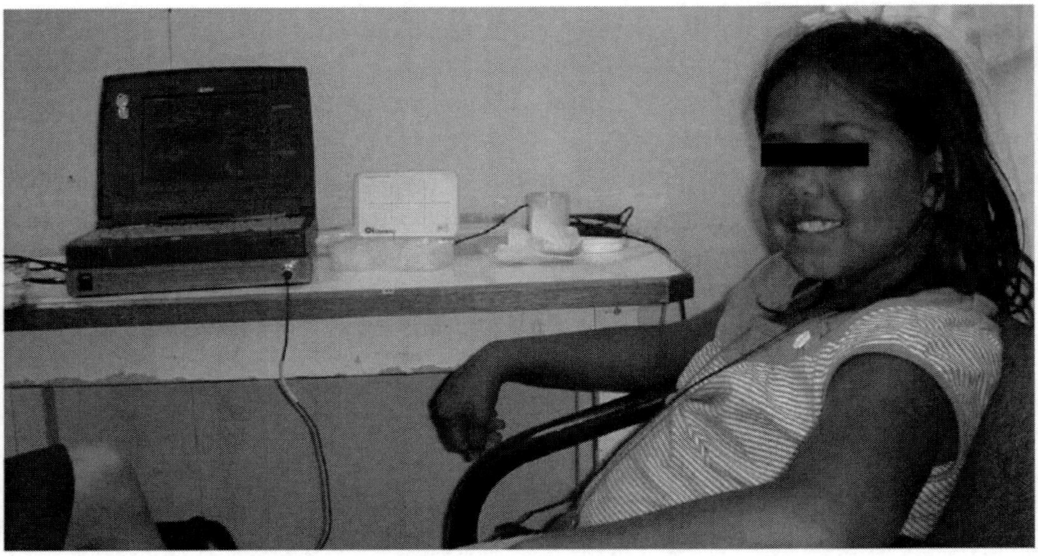

Figure 4.6. School-based screening using Otoacoustic Emissions testing.

Typically, TEOAEs can be detected in persons with normal hearing sensitivity and otological status. DPOAEs can be detected in those with less than a moderate degree of hearing loss (i.e., normal hearing or a mild loss). Although neither are tests of hearing per se, they are often used to suggest or confirm the presence of hearing loss. Their presence is usually interpreted as indicative of normal cochlear (inner ear) function, whilst their absence can suggest outer hair cell damage and, hence, hearing loss. However, it is worth keeping in mind that failure of OAE testing is also associated with a plethora of potential influences including middle ear dysfunction (e.g., OME), instrumental factors (e.g., inappropriate stimulus characteristics), and environmental factors (e.g., high levels of ambient noise).

In summary, passing of an OAE test is suggestive of normal audiological function up to the level of the cochlea; however, failure merely indicates increased risk of the presence of a conductive or sensory hearing loss and/or middle ear pathology.

Both tests carry the advantages of being simple in test administration, non-invasive, objective, and resilient in non-sound treated settings. The duration of testing is also remarkably short, at less than a minute, assuming low noise levels. For these reasons, OAEs have been employed extensively in universal newborn hearing screening programs across the world. Researchers are now interested in their application in the screening of older children, such as in elementary schools, as a potential replacement for the traditional pure tone test (see Figure 8.6). However, professional guidelines, including those of ASHA (1997), AAA (2011), and NHMRC (2002), have yet to endorse their routine use in this context, due to the inferior sensitivity and specificity of OAEs, as well as an extensive need for further research.

What is known to date concerning TEOAE screening in school-aged populations is that:

- The test is highly feasible for mass screening in elementary schools (AAA, 2011; Driscoll, Kei, and McPherson, 2001; Georgalas, Xenellis, Davilis, Tzangaroulakis, and Ferekidis, 2008; Nozza, Sabo, and Mandel, 1997; Taylor and Brooks, 2000);

- Sensitivity has been shown to range between 0.65-1.0, depending on the gold standard of choice (AAA, 2011; Driscoll et al., 2001; Georgalas et al., 2008; Nozza et al., 1997; Sabo, Winston, and Macias, 2000);
- Specificity has been shown to range between 0.8-0.969 (AAA, 2011; Driscoll et al., 2001; Nozza et al., 1997; Sabo et al., 2000; Sliwa, Hatzopoulos, Kochanek, Senderski, and Skarzynski, 2011; Taylor and Brooks, 2000);
- Negative predictive values tend to be high, for example, 0.98, whilst positive predictive values are typically low, for example, 0.25 (Driscoll et al., 2001; Georgalas et al., 2008);
- Accuracy and efficiency indices are also typically high, for example, up to 0.88 and 0.91, respectively (Driscoll et al., 2001);
- Combining tympanometry with TEOAE testing does not lead to improved sensitivity and specificity (AAA, 2011; Driscoll et al., 2001; Georgalas et al., 2008; Nozza et al., 1997);
- TEOAEs cannot predict middle ear status and, thus, cannot replace otoscopy or tympanometry (AAA, 2011; Driscoll et al., 2001; Georgalas et al., 2008; Nozza et al., 1997);
- Choice of pass/fail criteria is paramount to achieving adequate test performance, with criteria used for neonates not necessarily transferrable to older children (AAA, 2011; Driscoll et al., 2001);
- Failure rates can range up to 21%, dependent upon the pass/fail criteria selected among other factors (Driscoll et al., 2001; Sabo et al., 2000);
- Normal emissions may be recorded in children with mild hearing losses (20-30 dB HL) (AAA, 2011);
- Testing is unlikely to be able to be completed for low-frequency stimuli (e.g., <1000 Hz or <2000 Hz), even in sound-treated environments, due to physiological and ambient noise levels (AAA, 2011; McPherson and Olusanya, 2008);
- Low-frequency pass/fail criteria have not been established to date (AAA, 2011); and
- The test does not assess beyond the outer hair cells of the cochlea and, thus, cannot detect children with auditory neuropathy/dys-synchrony (AN/AD) whereby outer hair cell function is normal but neural transmission in the auditory pathway is impaired producing a neural hearing loss (AAA, 2011; Rance, 2005).

Regarding DPOAEs in school-based screening programs, it has been found that:

- The test is highly feasible for mass screening in elementary schools (Lyons, Kei, and Driscoll, 2004);
- Sensitivity and specificity have been shown to approximate 0.7 and 0.9, respectively, if excluding low frequencies such as 1.1 kHz (Lyons et al., 2004);
- Negative predictive values have been reported as high, for example, 0.94, whilst positive predictive values appear moderately high, for example, 0.76 (Lyons et al., 2004);
- A high efficiency index has also been reported, for example, 0.87-0.91 (Lyons et al., 2004);
- Combining tympanometry with DPOAE testing does not lead to improved sensitivity and specificity (Lyons et al., 2004);

- DPOAEs cannot predict middle ear status and, thus, cannot replace a screening battery comprised of both pure tone testing and tympanometry (AAA, 2011; Lyons et al., 2004);
- Choice of pass/fail criteria (SNR cut-offs) is frequency dependent (AAA, 2011; Lyons et al., 2004);
- Failure rates range up to 18% and may be reduced further by incorporating two-stage screening protocols, however, loss to follow-up then becomes a concern (AAA, 2011);
- Normal emissions may be recorded in children with mild hearing losses (up to 40 dB HL) (McPherson and Olusanya, 2008);
- Testing is unlikely to be able to be completed for low-frequency stimuli (e.g., <1000 Hz), even in sound-treated environments, due to physiological noise levels (AAA, 2011; McPherson and Olusanya, 2008);
- Low-frequency pass/fail criteria have not been established to date (AAA, 2011); and
- As per the TEOAE test, testing cannot detect children with AN/AD (AAA, 2011; Rance, 2005).

Based upon these findings, it is clear that further research is necessary before OAEs can be accepted as a replacement for the typical pure tone screening test. In particular, AAA (2011) noted that test and equipment parameters require additional investigation, along with blinded test performance studies, the establishment of developmental norms and associated pass/fail criteria, training protocols, cost analyses, noise reduction schemes, and, potentially, the development of technology that would mitigate the effects of abnormal middle ear function upon the recorded emissions.

Nonetheless, AAA (2011) concluded that the use of OAEs combined with reflectance measures of middle ear status may result in improved screening practices in the future.

Questionnaires

Although an obviously cost effective method, with the added benefit of raising awareness of childhood hearing loss and its consequences (McPherson and Olusanya, 2008), the use of questionnaires to detect children at risk of hearing loss and/or other otologic pathologies is limited by their dependency on third party observation and motivation (Newton, Macharia, Mugwe, Ototo, and Kan, 2001). Other limitations of the questionnaire method include its known weakness in detecting cases with milder degrees of hearing loss and unilateral impairments (Newton et al., 2001). In addition, although parental concern is an important risk factor for sensorineural hearing loss in children, the sensitivity and specificity of parental concern are low even in the presence of severe or profound hearing loss (NHMRC, 2002). Furthermore, at least 50% of children who develop a postnatal hearing loss do not display any notable risk factors (Kennedy, Kimm, Cafarelli Dees, Campbell, and Thornton, 1998; Mehl and Thomson, 2002), upon which questionnaires are usually based. In general, questionnaires, as a sole method, have not been viewed as suitable for hearing screening purposes.

Despite the common perception, several studies have shown questionnaires to possess some potential in school-based hearing screening applications (Hind, Aitkins, Haggard, Brady, and Grinham, 1999; Li, Driscoll, and Culbert, 2009; Newton et al., 2001). For instance, Li and colleagues (2009) examined the test performance of a questionnaire designed specifically for the screening of rural Chinese school children (the revised Chinese Hearing Questionnaire for School Children; CHQS-II).

This questionnaire, completed by parents/caregivers, consisted of an 11-item, Yes/No checklist constructed by the researchers to detect children at risk of otitis media with effusion (OME) and/or at least a moderate hearing loss in one or both ears. Analysis showed the CHQS-II to be moderately accurate (.62) as a screening system when compared with the gold standard diagnostic test battery of otoscopy, tympanometry, and pure tone audiometry. Its sensitivity or ability to detect those at risk of hearing loss or middle ear infection, was also moderate (.67). However, its overall efficiency was poor (.56). In essence, there was a high likelihood that a passing child would not have a hearing loss/middle ear disease but only a low likelihood that a failing child would actually have an otologic problem. As the CHQS-II test performances indices did not approximate those of conventional screening techniques, its immediate use was not recommended. A very similar pattern of findings was observed in a hearing questionnaire study of Brazilian preschoolers by Gomes and Lichtig (2005).

It appears that the potential of questionnaires in the hearing screening of school children may lie not so much in their use as an alternative to traditional methods but, perhaps, as an adjunct. In particular, questionnaires may provide valuable information concerning auditory status and history that is not otherwise easily obtained. For example, questionnaires could prompt parents/caregivers to ask their children about the occurrence of tinnitus and exposure to noise. Similarly, they may be used to collect risk factor data, such as: a family history of late-onset hearing loss; otitis media with effusion for at least three months; craniofacial anomalies; stigmata associated with syndromes including hearing loss; head trauma with loss of consciousness; ototoxic drug use; and parent/teacher/health care provider concern regarding hearing, speech, language, or learning abilities (ASHA, 1997).

Modifications to Traditional Pure Tone Screening

Liao, Lien, and Young (2010) commented on the limitations of traditional pure tone screening in school-aged children; notably that pure tone screening typically produces pass/fail results only, providing little information concerning exact hearing status. This does not allow for easy and accurate comparison of repeat or monitoring screenings, of the like that may be performed for cases of otitis media or noise-induced hearing loss. In addition, a simple "fail" result can lead to distrust from parents and teachers, who may be wary of false positives associated with school hearing screenings, leading to a lack of cooperation with management recommendations.

Thus, Liao and colleagues devised the Hearing Scale Test (HST), a modified pure tone screening method, based on the concept of the Landolt C vision-test chart. The HST utilizes 10 hearing scales from S_1 to S_{10}, with each scale containing four frequencies (0.5, 1, 2, and 4 kHz) and separated by 5 dB HL (range = 0 – 45 dB HL). Minimum audible hearing scales (the stimulus level at which the child responds correctly at all four test frequencies) are determined using a computerized, semi-automated audiometer. Scales S_1 to S_5 are equivalent to a typical pure tone screening "pass," whilst S_6 to S_{10} are comparable with a pure tone "fail." The procedure was trialed on 384 third-graders in a Taiwanese elementary school, taking approximately 2-3 minutes per child to complete. No significant difference (and a high level of agreement) was observed between the results of the HST and the results of traditional pure tone screening methods. Further analysis showed that the HST results could be interpreted as follows: S_1 to S_5 are indicative of normal hearing, S_6 and S_7 are suggestive of possible hearing loss, and S_8 to S_{10} or no response are symptomatic of confirmed hearing loss. With further widespread trials, the HST could be a successful alternative to the standard pure tone screen.

Other modifications to the traditional pure tone technique include the use of video testing (Bento, Albernaz, Di Francesco, Wiikmann, Frizzarini, and Castilho, 2003), whereby the four frequency sequence generated by an audiometer has been digitally recorded onto a video/CD. The disk can then be played in any test location that has access to a VCR or CD player. Bento et al. (2003) applied this method to 122 first-grade school children in Brazil and reported 100% sensitivity and 79.8% specificity when compared with pure tone audiometry. Although not capable of detecting unilateral hearing impairment, the researchers noted that such a modified technique may be useful for school screening in regions where standard test equipment and suitably qualified staff are not readily available.

With the increasing viability of computer-based audiometry, computerized screening audiometry methods deserve consideration. In the majority of school screening situations the screener is not an audiologist and a procedure that was based on an automatic test algorithm could enhance the quality of testing and reduce personnel training time and costs.

A recent pilot study of one commercially available audiometer software package found a good relationship between conventional hearing screening and computer-based screening in a group of 80 elementary school children (McPherson, Law, and Wong, 2010).

Finally, costs associated with false-positive cases could be reduced by development of noise-cancelling earphones for school screening purposes. Noise-cancelling technology is now commonly used in headphones (Schumacher, Kruger, Jeub, Vary, and Beaugeant, 2011). Lo (2012) reported, in a study of 232 elementary school students, that significantly fewer referrals were made in a screening program when noise-cancelling headphones were used compared to conventional audiometric earphones.

Other Methods

Alternatives for the hearing screening of school children such as acoustic reflex testing and the use of speech stimuli tests are currently not supported due to unacceptably high false-positive and high false-negative rates, respectively (AAA, 2011; NHMRC, 2002).

Furthermore, non-calibrated stimuli (e.g., the whisper test) should not be used in any capacity (ASHA, 1997).

Follow-Up Actions

A two-stage screening program is recommended by AAA (2011), in view of variables such as earphone placement, child behavior, and fluctuating/transient pathologies. By definition, AAA suggests that the two-stage protocol should include a same-day retest of failed cases, followed by a rescreening performed after a designated period of weeks (see Figure 8.7 for an example of a two-tiered program pathway).

For suspected cases of middle ear pathology, ASHA's (1997) guidelines recommend this period to be 6-8 weeks; AAA state a minimum of 8 and a maximum of 10 weeks.

As noted by AAA, there is a trend for lower failure and referral rates with increased periods between screenings. However, for suspected cases of permanent hearing loss, it would be wise to minimize delays in diagnostic assessment and, therefore, it would be wholly appropriate to refer immediately following same-day rescreen (refer to AAA, 2011, for full details of rescreening recommendations). In the event that referral to a medical practitioner is required for investigation of suspected middle ear pathology, AAA (2011, p. 50) suggests that the screener should include, if known, information concerning the duration and laterality of pathology, all test results from each test occasion, evidence/concern regarding speech and language abilities, and additional conditions that may exacerbate the effects of middle ear pathology in the referred case. Screening can be an almost useless endeavor if it does not lead on to diagnostic assessment and timely intervention. Unfortunately, receipt of follow-up care in school hearing screening programs has been not infrequently reported as sub-optimal. For example, Kemper, Fant, Bruckman, and Clark (2004), in their analysis of Michigan's program where 500,000 children are screened each year, found that only 73% of referred cases in grades 1-5 actually went on to receive follow-up services. This figure reduced to 57% for cases in grades 6-12. The most common reason cited by parents for failure to pursue follow-up was that the child had been previously evaluated for suspicion of hearing loss, followed by lack of concern, and doubt regarding screening accuracy.

To alleviate poor follow-up rates, AAA (2011) proposes: presenting results in the families' native language, including educational pamphlets on the effects of undiagnosed hearing loss, and propagating close relationships between screening personnel and the local medical community. Mundy (2001) further suggests engaging school personnel to facilitate receipt of follow-up, staff that may assist those with transportation problems, with lack of information concerning local medical resources, with lack of medical/health fluency in general, and those with second-language related issues.

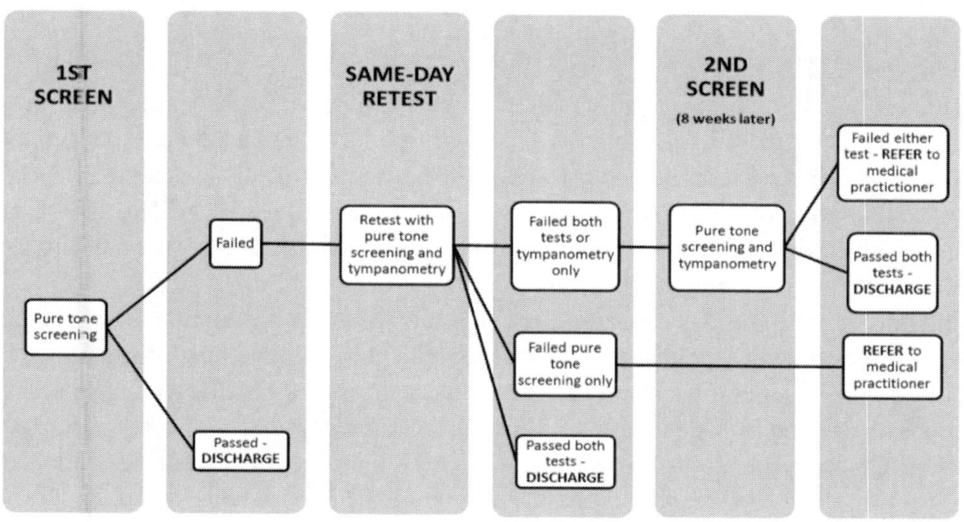

Figure 4.7. An example of a two-tiered hearing screening protocol based upon AAA (2011) recommendations.

FUTURE CONSIDERATIONS

Screening for Central Auditory Processing Disorder

Central auditory processing disorder (CAPD) has caught the attention of researchers, clinicians, educators, and parents alike, with a Google search for "central auditory processing disorder" in 2013 bringing up over a quarter of a million hits. Despite this attention, screening for central auditory processing disorder (CAPD) is as controversial as the disorder itself, and with this in mind, this section will briefly review the definition of CAPD before considering the current evidence for its screening.

Defining CAPD

Despite several decades of research, we still lack *gold standards* for defining and diagnosing CAPD (Wilson and Arnott, 2012). This led Dawes and Bishop (2009, p. 440) to postulate that "APD, as currently diagnosed, is not a coherent category". Through this controversy, the definition of CAPD offered by the American Speech-Language-Hearing Association's (ASHA) Working Group on Auditory Processing Disorders Technical Report (ASHA [2005]; an update on ASHA [1996]) has come to be the most cited.

They define CAPD as "a deficit in neural processing of auditory stimuli that is not due to higher order language, cognitive, or related factors" (ASHA, 2006, p. 2), and as difficulties in the perceptual processing of auditory information in the CNS as demonstrated by poor performance in sound localization and lateralization; auditory discrimination; auditory pattern recognition; temporal aspects of audition, including temporal integration, temporal discrimination (e.g., temporal gap detection), temporal ordering, and temporal masking; auditory performance in competing acoustic signals (including dichotic listening); and auditory performance with degraded acoustic signals (ASHA, 2006, p.2).

While this is the definition of CAPD that will be used in this section, the reader should consider other definitions such as those offered offered by AAA (2010) and BSA (2011a).

Screening for CAPD

Efforts to identify children with CAPD have been driven by at least three main factors. First is the incidence of CAPD, which is estimated to be as high as three to five percent in school-aged children (Chermak and Musiek, 1997). Second is the potential impact this disorder could have on listening, communication, and academic success (ASHA, 2005). Third is the need for early intervention "to exploit the plasticity of the CNS, maximize successful therapeutic outcomes, and minimize residual functional deficits" (ASHA, 2005, p. 11).

While the motivation to screen for CAPD appears to be strong, agreement is lacking on the "who, when, and how" of this screening. The guidelines for screening offered by Wilson and Jungner (1968) suggest we should screen children at risk for CAPD, who have access to appropriate diagnostic and treatment facilities at an affordable cost, who can be screened before CAPD becomes a problem or at least when they can benefit from intervention, and for whom we have suitable screening tools that can be applied by suitably qualified screening personnel.

Converting these principles into practice has remained a significant challenge, however.

Deciding who is at risk for CAPD has proven to be as controversial as the definition of CAPD itself. ASHA (2005, p. 5) state that individuals suspected of having CAPD frequently present with one or more behavioral characteristics, with their list being:

> Difficulty understanding spoken language in competing messages, noisy backgrounds, or in reverberant environments; misunderstanding messages; inconsistent or inappropriate responding; frequent requests for repetitions, saying "what" and "huh" frequently; taking longer to respond in oral communication situations; difficulty paying attention; being easily distracted; difficulty following complex auditory directions or commands; difficulty localizing sound; difficulty learning songs or nursery rhymes; poor musical and singing skills; and associated reading, spelling, and learning problems.

They also warn, however, that this list is illustrative and not exhaustive, and that these behavioral characteristics are not exclusive to CAPD.

How to Screen for CAPD

Deciding how to screen for CAPD is difficult. ASHA (2005) states that while there is no universally accepted method of screening for CAPD, current screening approaches typically involve systematic observation of listening behavior and/or performance on tests of auditory function that probe auditory behaviors related to academic achievement, listening skills, and communication. In the absence of an appropriate tool for primary screening for CAPD, Bellis (2003) has argued that such screening should be left to parents and teachers who are best positioned to regularly observe the child's behavior.

If a parent and/or teacher reported a child showed behaviors associated with CAPD, then Bellis (2003) recommends a secondary screening be conducted by a team of professionals that could include an audiologist, speech-language pathologist, educator, psychologist, social worker, the parents and a physician. The aim of this secondary screening is to gather information about the child's central auditory processing *and* educational, social, speech/ language, cognitive, and medical characteristics.

This aims to "provide a picture of the child's strengths and weaknesses across domains" so that the team can decide if there exists "sufficient evidence to support the likelihood that a CAPD is present" (Bellis, 2003, p. 170).

Suspected CAPD then triggers a referral to an audiologist for a diagnostic CAPD assessment, whereas suspicions of other disorders triggers referrals to more appropriate professionals (e.g., to a speech-language pathologist if a language disorder is suspected, to a psychologist if a cognitive disorder is suspected, etc.). Such a team approach does need to be balanced with practical issues including timing and cost (BSA, 2011b), which has left many researchers searching for the best single tool or small group of tools to screen for CAPD.

Tools Used to Screen for CAPD

It is beyond the scope of this section to describe all of the tools that have been used to screen for CAPD. Instead, this section will consider some of the tools that have been widely used by audiologists in the US (Chermak, Silva, Nye, Hasbrouck, and Musiek, 2007) where the diagnostic criteria for CAPD had been clearly stated and the data had been published in the peer reviewed, scientific literature.

Four questionnaires that have been used to screen for CAPD are the Children's Auditory Performance Scale (CHAPS), the Fisher's Auditory Problems Checklist (FAPC), the Listening Inventory For Education–Revised (LIFE-R), and the Screening Instrument for Targeting Educational Risk (SIFTER). The CHAPS (Smoski, Brunt, and Tannahill, 1998) requires teachers and/or parents to complete 36 questions rating a child's listening behavior in different listening conditions. Reports that the CHAPS cannot separate children with or without CAPD (Dawes, Bishop, Sirimanna, and Bamiou, 2008; Drake et al., 2006; Lam and Sanchez, 2007; Sharma, Purdy, and Kelly, 2009; W. J. Wilson et al., 2011) are evenly matched by those that report it can separate children with or without CAPD (Dawes and Bishop, 2010; Ferguson, Hall, Riley, and Moore, 2011; Iliadou and Bamiou, 2012; Moore, Ferguson, Edmondson-Jones, Ratib, and Riley, 2010).

The FAPC (Fisher, 1976) requires teachers and/or parents to use a simple checklist to identify any of 25 auditory behaviors of concern. A single study has reported it cannot separate children with or without CAPD (Dawes et al., 2008).

The LIFE-R series includes: the Before–LIFE-R (Anderson, Smaldino, and Spangler, 2011c), which requires students to mark items that describe their classroom setting; the LIFE-R Student Appraisal of Listening Difficulty (LIFE-R SALD) (Anderson, Smaldino, and Spangler, 2011a), which requires students to rate how difficult they find it to listen in 15 different classroom environments; and the After LIFE-R (Anderson, Smaldino, and Spangler, 2011b), which requires students to mark items that describe how they would respond in six difficult classroom environments. Teacher versions are also available (the LIFE-R Teacher Appraisal of Listening Difficulty [LIFE-R TALD] [Anderson, Smaldino, and Spangler, 2011d] and the LIFE-R Teacher Checklist: Self-Advocacy and Instructional Access [Anderson, Smaldino, and Spangler, 2011e]). A single study has reported one of the original LIFE questionnaires contained only two items that could separate children with or without CAPD (Johnston, John, Kreisman, Hall, and Crandell, 2009).

The SIFTER series includes the Preschool SIFTER (Anderson and Matkin, 1996), SIFTER (Anderson, 1989) and Secondary SIFTER (Anderson, 2004), each of which requires teachers and/or parents to rate a child's performance on 15 aspects of academics, attention, communication, class participation, and school behavior in the classroom setting. One study reported the SIFTER's academics subscore could (Johnston et al., 2009) and one study reported the whole questionnaire could not (W. J. Wilson et al., 2011) separate children with or without CAPD.

The most popular screening test for CAPD has been the Tests for Auditory Processing Disorders for Children, now in its third generation (SCAN-3:C; Keith, 2012), which requires professionals trained in standardized assessments to present children with pre-recorded stimuli to assess a range of central auditory processing tasks including gap detection, auditory-figure ground, and competing words. One study reported the original SCAN (Domitz and Schow, 2000) and one study reported the second generation SCAN-C (Madison, Hallberg, Anfinson, DeMaio, and Drake, 2005) could not separate children with or without CAPD.

Conclusion

Screening for CAPD remains controversial. Many screening tools have been offered and of the few that have been assessed the evidence for their use remains equivocal with no one tool standing out as a best candidate for screening for CAPD. Based on these results, it appears that two statements by AAA (2010, p. 13) on screening measures for CAPD should remain in place: 1. "While a number of questionnaires have been used to screen for CAPD ..., they generally have poor specificity, tend to over-refer, and have not been validated", and 2. "Further studies are needed to determine the efficiency of currently available screening instruments, including the efficiency of diagnostic tests used for screening purposes, and to develop new screening tools for CAPD."

Noise-Induced Hearing Loss

Recent research has drawn attention to the high prevalence of noise-induced hearing loss (NIHL) in adolescents, with preventative educational programs subsequently arising. For instance, the United States of America National Center for Health Statistics 2005-2006 NHAMES III data provided a prevalence rate of noise-induced hearing threshold changes of 16.8% (95% CI: 13.9%–19.7%) for adolescents aged 12 to 19 years (see Henderson, Testa, and Hartnick, 2011, for full details) and programs such as "Hear Today, Hear Tomorrow" a school curriculum based hearing health program by the National Acoustic Laboratories (www.nal.gov.au) and "Dangerous Decibels" by Oregon Health and Science University (www.dangerousdecibels.org) have been recommended to counteract this excessive occurrence of NIHL in older children. However, less is known about the prevalence of noise-induced hearing changes in younger, elementary school children. The Oregon Health and Science University's Hearing Research Centre has accumulated data from over 30,000 cases during 2002-2011 to show that approximately 17% of 5-12 year children have a hearing loss of at least 20 dB HL at 4 kHz – an indicator of NIHL (http://www.dangerousdecibels.org/research/omsi-research-data/). AAA (2011) also reported unpublished data from three US school districts that showed that there was a trend for decreased identification of new hearing losses in grades 1-3 but an increased identification rate at grade 5, suggesting a possible increased prevalence of high frequency hearing loss in the upper grades of elementary schools. Moreover, the role that routine screening in elementary schools could play in the immediate and long-term prevention of NIHL has been under-researched to date.

NIHL results from exposure to hazardous noise levels, be they very high levels for short periods of time (e.g., 120 dB A for 30 seconds) or lower levels for longer periods (e.g., 90 dB A for 3 hours per day). The increasing use of personal listening devices, such as iPods and MP3 players, has been frequently implicated in the causation of NIHL in children (Hendershot, Pakulski, Thompson, Dowling and Price, 2011; Niskar, Kieszak, Holmes, Esteban, Rubin, and Brody, 2001; Shargorodsky, Curhan, Curhan, and Eavey, 2010).

However, the World Health Organization (1997) have also noted that US children may receive more adverse noise exposure during a typical day at school than workers during an 8-hour factory shift. Such noise sources may include, but are not limited to: educational toys, musical equipment, sound field amplification systems, concerts, theatre productions, trade equipment, computers with headphones, and traffic noise.

NIHL is produced due to permanent damage to the delicate hair cells of the cochlea (see Figure 8.8). It is typically progressive, with a gradual onset, and appears on the audiogram as a high-frequency notched pattern. That is, "dips" in the audiogram will be seen in the high frequencies, most notably at the test frequencies of 3, 4, or 6 kHz with recovery at 8 kHz in the early stages. Niskar and colleagues in 2001 reported that 12.5% of 6- to 19-year-old children in the US were estimated to display such a notch in at least one ear, with 6 kHz being the most commonly affected frequency (Sekhar, Rhoades, Longenecker, Beiler, King, Widome, and Paul, 2011).

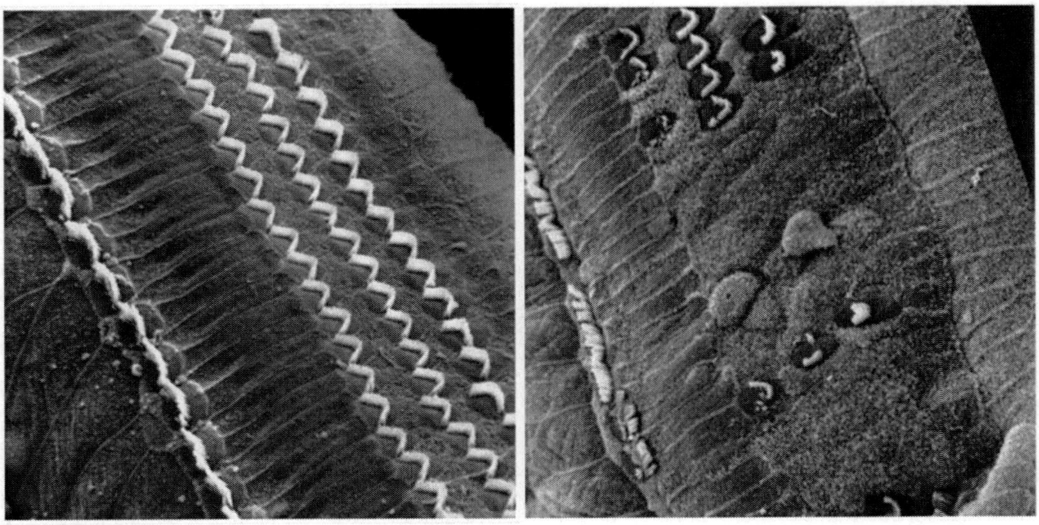

a b

Figure 8.8. (A) Normal cochlear hair cells showing three rows of healthy outer hair cells (OHCs) and one row of healthy inner hair cells (IHCs), (B) damaged cochlear hair cells producing a sensorineural hearing loss.

As the condition progresses, hearing loss will extend into the lower and higher ranges (Meinke and Dice, 2007). At this point, the typical negative consequences of permanent childhood hearing loss may be experienced, including delayed/disordered speech and language development, learning difficulties, social and behavioral problems, and, ultimately, reduced quality of life.

A hearing screening protocol capable of detecting NIHL (or, for that matter, any other form of hearing loss that produces a high-frequency notched audiometric configuration, such as is seen in ototoxicity or head trauma) must include assessment of the frequency range from 3 to 6 kHz. If utilizing pure tone screening as the method of choice, this will necessitate a longer test time with potential reliability implications when testing the younger grades in non-sound treated environments.

In addition, screening failure rates can be expected to dramatically increase. Sekhar et al. (2011) noted that when utilizing a pure tone screening criteria designed for detection of NIHL, 26.4% of 296 eleventh grade students received a failing result. Program management pathways would need to be carefully revised to deal with such a large proportion of follow-up cases – it would hardly be feasible to refer a quarter of all students for in-depth diagnostic testing. Schlauch and Carney (2010), in their examination of the NHANES III data, suggested that careful elimination of calibration errors, as well as utilizing headphones with low measurement variability, and repeating/averaging threshold measurements, may help to reduce the unacceptably high false-positive rate that could be associated with screening at 6 kHz.

An alternative to pure tone screening for NIHL may very well be the use of otoacoustic emissions to provide early detection of cochlear changes that occur prior to the advent of a measurable hearing loss (Meinke, 2011). Although further, extensive research is required regarding this application in elementary school settings, otoacoustic emission screening could serve as a useful adjunct to pure tone screening whereby, for instance, cases with normal pure tone results at the standard test frequencies of 0.5, 1, 2, and 4 kHz, but with abnormal otoacoustic emission SNRs at the frequency bands centered around 3 kHz, 4 kHz, and/or 6 kHz, would be marked for monitoring screens through time (perhaps on a yearly basis) and would receive preventative, educational counseling. A well-constructed computerized data management system (of the kind described in Chapter 11) would allow for easy analysis of changes in baseline measures.

Whilst true that NIHL is irreversible, its progression can be halted to a certain extent by avoidance of exposure to continual hazardous noise (Niskar, Kieszak, Holmes, Esteban, Rubin, and Brody, 1998). There is much scope for research to contribute toward hearing loss prevention at the earliest possible age and the investigation of otoacoustic emission protocols in elementary schools would be an obvious starting point.

Telehealth

Telehealth is the general term used to describe the application of medically-related services over a distance (Givens and Elangovan, 2003), typically associated with the use of telecommunication technology such as high-speed computer networks and the internet. Tele-audiology, providing audiological services using telehealth, has been studied by a few researchers using synchronous methods (where services are provided and results transmitted in real time) and asynchronous methods (where results are stored and forwarded for later analysis). Synchronous methods include the possibilities of (a) the audiologist utilizing interactive video to supervise a technician at a distant clinical site, then providing diagnosis and management recommendations or (b) the audiologist utilizing remote technology to directly test the case at a distant site, with the technician's role limited to headphone and probe placement, et cetera (Lancaster, Krumm, Ribera, and Klich, 2008).

Young and Ireson (2003) reported telehealth services in schools to be cost effective and highly acceptable to key stakeholders including parents, children, and school officials (Lancaster et al., 2008). Furthermore, Lancaster et al. (2008) conducted a thorough examination of the feasibility and test performance of a tele-audiology school hearing screening program. Forty-three third grade students in a Utah elementary school were screened by an audiologist on-site using otoscopy, tympanometry, and pure tone audiometry.

A second audiologist performed the tele-audiology screenings from a distance of approximately 30 miles, with the first examiner acting as a facilitator only. In the tele-audiology model, video otoscopy and pure tone testing results were synchronously interpreted by the distant examiner, with tympanometry results being asynchronously forwarded and analyzed. Full agreement between results obtained on-site and those obtained via tele-audiology was obtained for all otoscopy and tympanometry findings. For pure tone testing, disagreement occurred for 5/43 cases, although such was not considered statistically significant. These cases included four false-positive responses and one false-negative.

Therefore, in this study, although sensitivity for pure tone screening was found to be very high, specificity was less than optimal. The researchers concluded that tele-audiology demonstrated great potential for application in the hearing screening of school-aged children and suggested that further research should be conducted with larger cohorts and over greater distances, with attention given to proper training of technicians/facilitators and adherence to teleheath privacy requirements.

Tele-audiology may prove to be a very useful alternative to traditional on-site hearing screening in schools, helping to increase the productivity of pediatric audiologists who are, in many countries, in short supply. It may reduce the inefficiencies and inequities associated with hearing health care services in rural and remote locations.

Finally, it may be found to offer an improvement in the accuracy of screening, as it has been noted that school hearing screenings are often plagued by non-standardized protocols and procedures, non-calibrated equipment, inappropriate noise levels, and performed by poorly trained staff (Blair, 1991).

Genetic Screening

As it currently stands, many professional bodies concerned with the genetic testing of children advise against genetic analysis for adult-onset conditions. For instance, The Committee on Bioethics of the American Academy of Pediatrics state that such testing in general should be deferred until adulthood or until an adolescent is capable of mature decision-making (Committee on Bioethics, 2001).

Similarly, the United Kingdom's Clinical Genetics Society considers predictive genetic testing of children inappropriate until they can make such requests for themselves, as autonomous adults (Clarke and Working Party of the Clinical Genetics Society, 1994).

However, as noted by Caga-anan, Smith, Sharp, and Lantos (2012), not all adult-onset conditions are alike. For some conditions, the early diagnosis offered by genetic testing may promote improved management of the condition or psychological benefits regardless of the test outcome. In these cases, the ethical case for early genetic testing is clear (Caga-anan et al., 2012).

Further, the American Academy of Pediatrics' expert committee on the subject (AAP, 2013) advises against school-based genetic carrier testing or screening programs as "the school environment is unlikely to be conducive to voluntary participation, thoughtful consent, privacy, confidentiality, or appropriate counseling" (p. 621).

Currently, there are no known genetic screening programs available for operation in elementary schools. If programs of the like were to be devised, it would require extremely careful examination of the potential risks versus harms. Geneticists, genetic counselors, and bioethicists would be needed to determine the specific medical benefits, psychological risks (including the impact upon the child and upon family dynamics), and personal histories of the cohort (Caga-anan et al., 2012).

At present, no discussions of this kind have been published in regard to genetic screening of elementary school children for markers of late-onset hearing loss. Future applications, if considered at all, perhaps may be related to genetic testing for susceptibility markers associated with age-related or noise-induced hearing loss, which is still a relatively new and unexplored field. The potential benefits of predictive genetic screening of this nature might include access to preventative education and new treatment strategies, such as gene therapy, pharmacological interventions, stem cell implantation, et cetera, which are designed to halt or slow the development of hearing loss.

However, prior to implementation in elementary schools, it is likely that this new direction will first be explored in relation to adolescent screening.

CONCLUSION

To instigate the detection and re/habilitation of undiagnosed hearing loss in children, school hearing screening programs are a necessity. They present as a useful adjunct to newborn hearing screening, especially for postnatal cases, where the loss is acquired, progressive, or late-onset, as well as for milder cases that may have been missed by the newborn screen, and for cases where newborn screening was not available or desired. However, significant planning is required in order to operate an efficient and effective school hearing screening program. This chapter has provided an overview of the main methods and protocols for school screening. It has also offered suggestions for alternative screening techniques and has highlighted some potential future directions that may improve the current state of school hearing screening programs. It is posed that further, rigorous research and evaluation will soon lead to vast improvements in this screening endeavor.

REFERENCES

Access Economics. (2006). *Listen hear! The economic impact and cost of hearing loss in Australia*. Melbourne: Author.

American Academy of Audiology (AAA). (1997). *Position statement: Identification of hearing loss and middle ear dysfunction in preschool and school-age children*. Retrieved from http://www.audiology.org/resources/documentlibrary/Pages/HearingLossChildren.aspx.

American Academy of Audiology (AAA). (2010). *Clinical practice guidelines: Diagnosis, treatment and management of children and adults with central auditory processing disorder*. Retrieved from http://www.audiology.org/resources/documentlibrary/Documents/CAPD%20Guidelines%208-2010.pdf.

American Academy of Audiology (AAA). (2011). *Childhood hearing screening guidelines*. Retrieved from http://www.audiology.org/resources/documentlibrary/Documents/20110926_ChildhoodHearingScreeningGuidelines.pdf.

American Academy of Pediatrics Committee on Bioethics, Committee on Genetics, The American College of Medical Genetics, Genomics Social, Ethical and Legal Issues Committee (AAP). (2013). Ethical and policy issues in genetic testing and screening of children. *Pediatrics*, 130(1), 620-622.

American National Standards Institute (ANSI). (1999). *Maximum permissible ambient noise for audiometry testing (ANSI S3.1-1999)*. NY: Author.

American Speech-Language-Hearing Association (ASHA). (1996). Central auditory processing: Current status of research and implications for clinical practice. *American Journal of Audiology,* 5(2), 41-54.

American Speech-Language-Hearing Association (ASHA). (1997). *Guidelines for audiologic screening.* Retrieved from http://www.asha.org/docs/html/GL1997-00199.html#sec1.7.

American Speech-Language-Hearing Association (ASHA). (2005). *(Central) auditory processing disorders.* Retrieved from www.asha.org/policy/TR2005-00043.htm.

Anderson, K. L. (1989). *S.I.F.T.E.R.: Screening Identification For Targeting Educational Risk in children identified by hearing screening or who have known hearing loss.* Tampa, FL: The Educational Audiology Association.

Anderson, K. L. (2004). *Secondary S.I.F.T.E.R. Screening Instrument For Targeting Educational Risk in secondary students.* Westminster, CO: The Educational Audiology Association.

Anderson, K. L. and Matkin, N. D. (1996). *Preschool S.I.F.T.E.R. Screening Identification For Targeting Educational Risk in preschool children (age 3-kindergarten).* Westminster, CO: The Educational Audiology Association.

Anderson, K. L., Smaldino, J. J. and Spangler, C. (2011a). Listening Inventory For Education - Revised (L.I.F.E.-R.). *Student Appraisal of Listening Difficulty.* Retrieved from https://successforkidswithhearingloss.com/

Anderson, K. L., Smaldino, J. J. and Spangler, C. (2011b). Listening Inventory For Education - Revised (L.I.F.E.-R.). *Student Appraisal of Listening Difficulty: After-LIFE questions for students.* Retrieved from https://successforkidswithhearingloss.com/

Anderson, K. L., Smaldino, J. J. and Spangler, C. (2011c). Listening Inventory For Education - Revised (L.I.F.E.-R.). *Student Appraisal of Listening Difficulty: Before-LIFE questions for students.* Retrieved from https://successforkidswithhearingloss.com/

Anderson, K. L., Smaldino, J. J. and Spangler, C. (2011d). Listening Inventory For Education - Revised (L.I.F.E.-R.). *Teacher Appraisal of Listening Difficulty.* Retrieved from https://successforkidswithhearingloss.com/

Anderson, K. L., Smaldino, J. J. and Spangler, C. (2011e). Listening Inventory For Education - Revised (L.I.F.E.-R.). *Teacher checklist: Self-advocacy and instructional access.* Retrieved from https://successforkidswithhearingloss.com/

Bamford, J., Fortnum, H., Bristow, K., Smith, J., Vamvakas, G., Davies, L., … and Hind, S. (2007). Current practice, accuracy, effectiveness and cost-effectiveness of the school entry hearing screen. *Health Technology Assessment,* 11(32).

Bellis, T. J. (2003). *Assessment and management of central auditory processing disorders in the educational setting: From science to practice* (2nd ed.). San Diego, CA: Singular.

Bento, R. F., Albanez, P. L. M., Di Francesco, R. C., Wiikmann, C., Frizzarini, R., and Castilho, A. M. (2003). Video test for hearing screening in children. *International Congress Series,* 1240, 217-220.

Berg, A. L., Papri, H., Ferdous, S., Khan, N. Z., and Durkin, M. S. (2006). Screening methods for childhood hearing impairment in rural Bangladesh. *International Journal of Pediatric Otorhinolaryngology,* 70, 107-114.

Blair, J. (1991). Educational audiology and methods for bringing about change in schools. *Seminars in Hearing,* 12, 318-328.

British Society of Audiology (BSA). (2011a). *Position statement: Auditory processing disorder (APD).* Retrieved from http://www.thebsa.org.uk/images/stories/docs/BSA_APD_PositionPaper_31March11_FINAL.pdf.

British Society of Audiology (BSA). (2011b). Practice guidance: An overview of current management of auditory processing disorder (APD). *Draft document to Council for approval to press ahead with consultation.* Retrieved from http://www.thebsa.org.uk/images/stories/docs/BSA_APDMgmt_31March2011_Consultation.pdf.

Caga-anan, E. C. F., Smith, L., Sharp, R. R., and Lantos, J. D. (2012). Testing children for adult-onset genetic diseases. *Pediatrics*, 129(1), 163-167.

Chermak, G. D. and Musiek, F. E. (1997). *Central auditory processing disorders: New perspectives.* San Diego, CA: Singular.

Chermak, G. D., Silva, M. E., Nye, J., Hasbrouck, J., and Musiek, F. E. (2007). An update on professional education and clinical practices in central auditory processing. *Journal of the American Academy of Audiology,* 18(5), 428-452.

Choi, C. Y. and McPherson, B. (2005). Noise levels in Hong Kong primary schools: Implications for classroom listening. *International Journal of Disability, Development and Education*, 52, 345-360.

Clarke, A. and Working Party of the Clinical Genetics Society (UK). (1994). The genetic testing of children. *Journal of Medical Genetics*, 31(10), 785–797.

Committee on Bioethics. (2001). Ethical issues with genetic testing in pediatrics. *Pediatrics*, 107(6), 1451–1455.

Danhauer, J. L., Pecile, A. F., Johnson, C. E., Mixon, M., and Sharp, S. (2008). Parents' compliance with and impressions of a maturing community-based early hearing detection and intervention program: An update. *Journal of the American Academy of Audiology*, 19, 612-629.

Dawes, P. and Bishop, D. V. M. (2009). Auditory processing disorder in relation to developmental disorders of language, communication and attention: A review and critique. *International Journal of Language and Communication Disorders*, 44(4), 440-465.

Dawes, P. and Bishop, D. V. M. (2010). Psychometric profile of children with auditory processing disorder and children with dyslexia. *Archives of Disease in Childhood*, 95(6), 432-436.

Dawes, P., Bishop, D. V. M., Sirimanna, T., and Bamiou, D. E. (2008). Profile and aetiology of children diagnosed with auditory processing disorder (APD). *International Journal of Pediatric Otorhinolaryngology*, 72(4), 483-489.

Domitz, D. M. and Schow, R. L. (2000). A new CAPD battery - Multiple auditory processing assessment (MAPA): Factor analysis and comparisons with SCAN. *American Journal of Audiology,* 9, 101-111.

Drake, M., Brager, M., Leyendecker, J., Preston, M., Shorten, E., Stoos, R., and DeMaio, L. (2006). Comparison of the CHAPPS screening tool and APD diagnosis. Paper presented at the ASHA Convention, Miami Beach, FL. Retrieved from http://convention.asha.org/2006/handouts/855_0427Drake_Mary_072995_120106033139.pdf.

Driscoll, C., Kei., J. and McPherson, B. (2001). Outcomes of transient evoked otoacoustic emission testing in six-year-old school children: A comparison with pure tone screening and tympanometry. *International Journal of Pediatric Otorhinolaryngology*, 57, 67-76.

Ferguson, M. A., Hall, R. L., Riley, A., and Moore, D. R. (2011). Communication, listening, cognitive and speech perception skills in children with Auditory Processing Disorder

(APD) or Specific Language Impairment (SLI). *Journal of Speech, Language, and Hearing Research,* 54(1), 211-227.

Fisher, L. I. (1976). *Fisher's Auditory Problems Checklist.* Tampa, FL: The Educational Audiology Association.

FitzZaland, R. E. and Zink, G. D. (1984). A comparative study of hearing screening procedures. *Ear and Hearing*, 5, 205-210.

Fortnum, H. M., Summerfield, A. Q., Marshall, D. H., Davis, A. C., and Bamford, J. M. (2001). Prevalence of permanent childhood hearing impairment in the United Kingdom and implications for universal neonatal hearing screening: Questionnaire based ascertainment study. *British Medical Journal*, 323, 1-6.

Georgalas, C., Xenellis, J., Davilis, D., Tzangaroulakis, A., and Ferekidis, E. (2008). Screening for hearing loss and middle ear effusion in school-age children, using transient evoked otoacoustic emissions: A feasibility study. *Journal of Laryngology and Otology*, 122, 1299-1304.

Givens, G. and Elangovan, S. (2003). Internet application to tele-audiology: "Nothin' but net." *American Journal of Audiology*, 12, 59-65.

Gomes, M. and Lichtig, I. (2005). Evaluation of the use of a questionnaire by non-specialists to detect hearing loss in preschool Brazilian children. *International Journal of Rehabilitation Research*, 28, 171-174.

Hendershot, C., Pakulski, L. A., Thompson, A., Dowling, J., and Price, J. H. (2011). School nurses' role in identifying and referring children at risk of noise-induced hearing loss. *Journal of School Nursing*, 27, 380-389.

Henderson, E., Testa, M. A. and Hartnick, C. (2011). Prevalence of noise-induced hearing-threshold shifts and hearing loss among US youths. *Pediatrics*, 127, e39-e46.

Henderson, P. (1975). *The School Health Service 1908-1974.* London: HMSO.

Hind, S. E., Aitkins, R. L., Haggard, M. P., Brady, D., and Grinham, G. (1999). Alternatives in screening at school entry: Comparison of the childhood middle ear disease and hearing questionnaire (CMEDHQ) and the pure tone sweep test. *British Journal of Audiology*, 33, 403-414.

Iliadou, V. and Bamiou, D. E. (2012). Psychometric evaluation of children with auditory processing disorder (APD): Comparison with normal-hearing and clinical non-APD groups. *Journal of Speech, Language, and Hearing Research*, 55, 791-799.

Jerger, J. F. (1970). Clinical experience with impedance audiometry. *Archives of Otolaryngology*, 92, 311-324.

Johnston, K. N., John, A. B., Kreisman, N. V., Hall, J. W., and Crandell, C. C. (2009). Multiple benefits of personal FM system use by children with auditory processing disorder (APD). *International Journal of Audiology*, 48(6), 371-383.

Keith, R. W. (2012). *Technical report. SCAN-3 for Children.* Tests for auditory processing disorders. London: Pearson.

Kemp, D. T. (1978). Stimulated acoustic emissions from within the human auditory system. *Journal of the Acoustical Society of America*, 64(5), 1386-1391.

Kemper, A. R., Fant, K. E., Bruckman, D., and Clark, S. J. (2004). Hearing and vision screening program for school-aged children. *American Journal of Preventative Medicine*, 26(2), 141-146.

Kennedy, C., Kimm, L., Cafarelli Dees, D., Campbell, M., and Thornton, A. (1998). Controlled trial of universal neonatal screening for early identification of permanent childhood hearing impairment. Wessex Universal Neonatal Hearing Screening Trial Group. *Lancet*, 352(9145), 1957-1964.

Knecht, H. A., Nelson, P. B., Whitelaw, G. M., and Feth, L. L. (2002). Background noise levels and reverberation times in unoccupied classrooms: Predictions and measurements. *American Journal of Audiology*, 11, 65-71.

Lam, C. C. C., Poon, M. T., Doo, S., Lau, K. W. Y., Lo, Y. W. H., Chan, Y. B. V., and Wong, T. P. S. (2006). Hearing impairment. In: R. H. L. Mak, C. C. C. Lam, C. C. Y. Ho and M. M. Y. Wong (Eds.), *A primer in common developmental disabilities. Experience at Child Assessment Service, Hong Kong* (pp. 281-331). Hong Kong: Department of Health.

Lam, E. and Sanchez, L. (2007). Evaluation of screening instruments for auditory processing disorder (APD) in a sample of referred children. *Australian and New Zealand Journal of Audiology,* 29(1), 26-39.

Lancaster, P., Krumm, M., Ribera, J., and Klich, R. (2008). Remote hearing screenings via telehealth in a rural elementary school. *American Journal of Audiology*, 17(2), 114-122.

Leigh, G., Schmulian-Taljaard, D. and Poulakis, Z. (2010). Newborn hearing screening. In: C. J. Driscoll and B. McPherson (Eds.), *Newborn screening systems: The complete perspective* (pp. 95-115). San Diego: Plural.

Lescouflair, G. (1975). Critical view on audiometric screening in school. *Archives of Otolaryngology,* 101, 469-473.

Li, X., Bu, X. and Driscoll, C. (2006). Tympanometric norms in Chinese schoolchildren. *International Journal of Audiology*, 45, 55-59.

Li, X., Driscoll, C. and Culbert, N. (2009). Investigating the performance of a questionnaire for hearing screening of school children in China. *Australian and New Zealand Journal of Audiology,* 31(1), 45-52.

Liao, W.-H., Lien, C.-F. and Young, S.-T. (2010). The hearing scale test for hearing screening of school-age children. *International Journal of Pediatric Otorhinolaryngology*, 74, 760-764.

Lo, H. C. (2012). Hearing screening for school children: Utility of noise-cancelling headphones. *Master of Science (Audiology) dissertation*, University of Hong Kong.

Lyons, A., Kei, J. and Driscoll, C. (2004). Distortion product otoacoustic emissions in children at school entry: A comparison with pure tone screening and tympanometry results. *Journal of the American Academy of Audiology*, 15, 702-715.

Madison, W. I., Hallberg, A., Anfinson, J., DeMaio, L., and Drake, M. (2005). Comparison of composite SCAN scores to APD diagnosis. *Paper presented at the American Speech Language Hearing Association Annual Meeting*, San Diego, CA.

Marttila, T. I. (1986). Results of audiometrical screening in Finnish school children. *International Journal of Pediatric Otorhinolaryngology*, 11, 39-46.

McFarlan, D. (1927). The voice test of hearing. *Archives of Otolaryngology*, 5, 1-5.

McPherson, B., Law, M. M. S. and Wong, M. S. M. (2010). Hearing screening for school children: Comparison of low-cost, computer-based and conventional audiometry. *Child: Care, Health and Development,* 36(3), 323-331.

McPherson, B. and Olusanya, B. O. (2008). Screening for hearing loss in developing countries. In: B. McPherson and R. Brouillette (Eds.), *Audiology in Developing Countries* (pp. 73-105). NY: Nova Science.

Mehl, A. L. and Thomson, V. (2002). The Colorado newborn hearing screening project, 1992-1999: On the threshold of effective population-based universal newborn hearing screening. *Pediatrics*, 109(1), e7.

Mehra, S., Eavey, R. D. and Keamy, D. G. (2009). The epidemiology of hearing impairment in the United States: Newborns, children, and adolescents. *Otolaryngology-Head and Neck Surgery*, 140, 461-472.

Meinke, D. K. (2011). School-based hearing screening won't prevent noise-induced hearing loss. *Archives of Pediatrics and Adolescent Medicine*, 165(12), 1135-1136.

Meinke, D. K. and Dice, N. (2007). Comparison of audiometric screening criteria for the identification of noise-induced hearing loss in adolescents. *American Journal of Audiology,* 16, S190-S202.

Moore, D. R., Ferguson, M. A., Edmondson-Jones, A. M., Ratib, S., and Riley, A. (2010). Nature of auditory processing disorder in children. *Pediatrics*, 126(2), e382-390.

Mundy, M. R. (2001). The Chapel Hill-Carrboro (NC) schools: Hearing and middle ear screening for preschool and school-age children. In: J. Roush (Ed.), *Screening for Hearing Loss and Otitis Media in Children* (pp. 158-176). San Diego, CA: Singular Thomson Learning.

National Health and Medical Research Council (NHMRC). (2002). *Child health screening and surveillance: A critical review of the evidence*. Canberra: Author.

Newton, V. E., Macharia, I., Mugwe, P., Ototo, B., and Kan, S. W. (2001). Evaluation of the use of a questionnaire to detect hearing loss in Kenyan preschool children. *International Journal of Pediatric Otorhinolaryngology,* 57, 229–234.

New Zealand Health Technology Assessment. (1998). *Screening programs for the detection of otitis media with effusion and conductive hearing loss in preschool and new entrant school children: A critical appraisal of the literature.* Christchurch: Author.

Niskar, A. S., Kieszak, S. M., Holmes, A., Esteban, E., Rubin, C., and Brody, D. J. (1998). Prevalence of hearing loss among children 6 to 19 years of age: The third National Health and Nutrition Examination Survey. *Journal of the American Medical Association*, 279 (14), 1071-1075.

Niskar, A. S., Kieszak, S. M., Holmes, A. E., Esteban, E., Rubin, C., and Brody, D. J. (2001). Estimated prevalence of noise-induced hearing threshold shifts among children 6 to 19 years of age: The third National Health and Nutrition Examination Survey, 1988-1994, United States. *Pediatrics*, 108(1), 40-43.

Northern, J. and Downs, M. (2002). *Hearing in children* (5th ed.). Denver, CO: Lippincott Williams and Wilkins.

Nozza, R. J., Sabo, D. L. and Mandel, E. M. (1997). A role for otoacoustic emissions in screening for hearing impairment and middle ear disorders in school-age children. *Ear and Hearing,* 18(3), 227-239.

Parving, A. (1999). Hearing screening: Aspects of epidemiology and identification of hearing impaired children. *International Journal of Pediatric Otorhinolaryngology*, 49(Suppl. 1), S287-292.

Probst, R., Lonsbury-Martin, B. L. and Martin, G. K. (1991). A review of otoacoustic emissions. *Journal of the Acoustical Society of America*, 89(5), 2027-2067.

Rance, G. (2005). Auditory neuropathy/dys-synchrony and its perceptual consequences. *Trends in Amplification*, 9(1), 1-43.

Richburg, C. M., Davie, J. M. and Smiley, D. F. (2012). Hearing screenings in the schools. In: C. M. Richburg and D. F. Smiley (Eds.), *School-based audiology* (pp. 69-86). San Diego: Plural.

Richburg, C. and Imhoff, L. (2008). Survey of hearing screeners: Training and protocols used in two district school systems. *Journal of Educational Audiology*, 14, 31-41.

Roeser, R. J. and Clark, J. L. (2004). Screening for auditory disorders. In: R. J. Roeser and M. P. Downs (Eds.), *Auditory disorders in school children: The law, identification, remediation* (4th ed.) (pp. 96-123). NY: Thieme.

Roeser, R. J. and Northern, J. L. (1981). Screening for Hearing Loss and Middle Ear Disorders. In: R. J. Roeser and M. P. Downs (Eds.), *Auditory Disorders in School Children* (pp. 120-150). NY: Thieme-Stratton.

Roush, J. (2001). Methods of screening for hearing loss and otitis media. In: J. Roush (Ed.), *Screening for hearing loss and otitis media in children* (pp. 33-82). San Diego, CA: Singular Thomson Learning.

Sabo, M. P. Winston, R. and Macias, J. D. (2000). Comparison of pure tone and transient evoked otoacoustic emission screening in a grade school population. *American Journal of Otolaryngology,* 21, 88-91.

Schlauch, R. and Carney, E. (2010). Are false positive rates leading to an overestimation of noise-induced hearing loss? *Journal of Speech, Language, and Hearing Research*, 54(2), 679-692.

Schumacher, T., Kruger, H., Jeub, M., Vary, P., and Beaugeant, C. (2011, May 22-27). Active noise control in headsets: A new approach for broadband feedback ANC. *Paper presented at the IEEE International Conference on Acoustics, Speech and Signal Processing (ICASSP),* Prague, Czech Republic.

Sekhar, D. L., Rhoades, J. A., Longenecker, A. L., Beiler, J. S., King, T. S., Widome, M. D., and Paul, I. M. (2011). Improving detection of adolescent hearing loss. *Archives of Pediatrics and Adolescent Medicine,* 165(12), 1094-1100.

Shargorodsky, J., Curhan, S. G., Curhan, G. C., and Eavey, R. (2010). Change in prevalence of hearing loss in US adolescents. *Journal of the American Medical Association*, 304(7), 772-778.

Sharma, M., Purdy, S. C. and Kelly, A. S. (2009). Comorbidity of auditory processing, language, and reading disorders. *Journal of Speech, Language, and Hearing Research*, 52 (3), 706-722.

Shield, B., Greenland, E. and Dockrell, J. (2010). Noise in open plan classrooms in primary schools: A review. *Noise and Health*, 12(49), 225-234.

Sideris, I. and Glattke, T. J. (2006). A comparison of two methods of hearing screening in the preschool population. *Journal of Communication Disorders*, 39, 391-401.

Skarzynski, H. and Piotrowska, A. (2012). Screening for pre-school and school-age hearing problems: European consensus statement. *International Journal of Pediatric Otorhinolaryngology,* 76, 120-121.

Skurr, B. A. (1978). Hearing screening as a community health service in N.S.W. In: *Proceedings of the Third Conference of the Audiological Society of Australia* (pp. 115-129). Sydney: Audiological Society of Australia.

Sliwa, L., Hatzopoulos, S., Kochanek, K., Pilka, A., Senderski, A., and Skarzynski, P. H. (2011). A comparison of audiometric and objective methods in hearing screening of school children: A preliminary study. *International Journal of Pediatric Otorhinolaryngology,* 75, 483-488.

Smoski, W. J., Brunt, M. A. and Tannahill, J. C. (1998). *Children's auditory performance scale.* Tampa, FL: The Educational Audiology Association.

Stevens, J. and Parker, G. (2009). Screening and surveillance. In: V. E. Newton (Ed.), *Paediatric audiological medicine* (2nd ed.) (pp. 29-51). Chichester: Wiley-Blackwell.

Taylor, C. L. and Brooks, R. P. (2000). Screening for hearing loss and middle ear disorders in children using TEOAEs. *American Journal of Audiology*, 9, 50-55.

Tos, M. (1984). Epidemiology and natural history of secretory otitis. *American Journal of Otology,* 5, 459-462.

Wall, L. G. and Bührer, K. (1987). Hearing identification of the preschool child: A proposed training program. *Folia Phoniatrica*, 39, 145–152.

Wall, L. G., Naples, G. M., Buhrer, K., and Capodanno, C. (1985). A survey of audiological services within the school system. *ASHA*, 27, 31–34.

White, K. R. and Munoz, K. (2008). Screening. *Seminars in Hearing*, 29(2), 149-158.

Williamson, I., Dunleavy, J., Baine, J., and Robinson, D. (1994). The natural history of otitis media with effusion: A three-year study of the incidence and prevalence of abnormal tympanograms in four South West Hampshire infant and first schools. *Journal of Laryngology and Otology,* 108, 930-934.

Wilson, J. M. G. and Jungner, G. (1968). Principles and practice of screening for disease. *WHO Public Health Papers, No. 34.*

Wilson, W. J. and Arnott, W. (2012). Evidence about the effectiveness of interventions for auditory processing disorder. In: L. Wong and L. Hickson (Eds.), *Evidence-based practice in audiology* (pp. 283-308). San Diego: Plural.

Wilson, W. J., Jackson, A., Pender, A., Rose, C., Wilson, J., Heine, C., and Khan, A. (2011). The CHAPS, SIFTER, and TAPS–R as predictors of (C)AP skills and (C)APD. *Journal of Speech, Language, and Hearing Research*, 54, 278-291.

Wong, L. and Hickson, L. (2012). Evidence-based practice in audiology. In: L. Wong and L. Hickson (Eds.), *Evidence-based practice in audiology* (pp. 3-21). San Diego: Plural.

World Health Organization (WHO). (1997). *Report of a World Health Organization-Prevention of deafness/hearing impairment - Informal consultation III.* Geneva: Author.

World Health Organization (WHO). (2001). *Hearing aids for developing countries: Informal consultation.* Geneva: Author.

Young, T. and Ireson, C. (2003). Effectiveness of school-based telehealth care in urban and rural elementary schools. *Pediatrics*, 112, 1088-1094.

In: School Health Screening Systems
Editors: Bradley McPherson and Carlie J. Driscoll

ISBN: 978-1-63117-942-6

Chapter 5

SPEECH AND LANGUAGE SCREENING FOR SCHOOL CHILDREN

Carol K. S. To[1,*] ***and Wendy L. Arnott***[2]
[1]The University of Hong Kong, Pokfulam, Hong Kong
[2]The University of Queensland, Brisbane, St Lucia QLD, Australia

ABSTRACT

Speech and language difficulties are a common reason for referral to child health services during the preschool years. A speech and language problem in the early years may have significant implications for one's communication outcomes in adolescence and adulthood. However, there is considerable variation in what constitutes normal speech and language acquisition. Many preschool children who are late to talk improve spontaneously, while some apparently typical young children may decline in their speech and language performance in later years. The predictive power of an individual's speech-language ability for their later speech-language status improves with age. Speech and language problems at school-entry appear to be a stronger predicator for later communication issues than speech and language problems in the preschool years. With the potential long-term impact of speech and language problems, screening procedures for speech and language problems in school-age children have been developed. This chapter addresses some of the difficulties in implementing population-wide screening for speech and language problems in the early years and reviews some commonly used assessment tools for identifying school children with suspected speech and language problems.

Procedures for conducting language screening that are both beneficial to school-age children and cost-effective for society are also discussed.

INTRODUCTION

Speech and language are crucial prerequisites for children to access and obtain the most out of education and life. Children who have difficulties in attaining verbal competence at a

* Corresponding author: Carol K. S. To. The University of Hong Kong. E-mail: tokitsum@hku.hk.

young age are more likely to have persistent problems in the later stages of their lives if they are not identified and given appropriate intervention. The impacts of speech and language problems are diverse and can be considered at two levels – the individual and the population levels. At the individual level, children with early speech and language problems are more likely to develop reading and writing difficulties (Catts, Adolf, and Weismer, 2006; Catts, Fey, Tomblin, and Zhang, 2002). The risk of mental health and socio-emotional problems in adolescence is also higher (Baker and Cantwell, 1987, Cohen, Barwick, Horodezky, Vallance, and Im, 1998; Helland and Heimann, 2007). In adulthood, individuals with communication disorders may also have poorer vocational prospects (Ruben, 2000). To the very extreme, studies have also found that adults with a history of juvenile delinquency have a higher prevalence of communication disorders (Bryan, 2004). Such difficulties have the potential to impact not only on the individual concerned, but also on their family, their school, and, at the population level, on society. Health, education, and disability legislation and policies have, therefore, been developed to provide equal opportunities for these children to grow and learn as for their typical peers.

Types of Speech and Language Impairment

Speech and language refer to two different dimensions. Speech is the verbal means that conveys a language. Language encompasses the set of complex mental processes that allow speakers to encode linguistically their ideas ready for transmission. Speech then makes these ideas public. Conversely, language permits listeners to decode and understand the messages spoken by others. Speech and language problems are commonly labeled collectively as communication disorders.

Speech is sub-divided into the areas of articulation, fluency, and voice. Articulation concerns the way that speech sounds are produced. For example, if a person says the word "cat" as "tat", this is referred to as an articulation error. This problem, however, can have a number of different underlying causes. The cause can be linguistic in nature relating to the phonological or sound system of a child, or it can be the result of motor problems relating to motor execution or oromotor difficulties. A collective terminology for articulation and phonological problems is speech sound disorders (SSDs) (American Speech-Language-Hearing Association, n.d.).

Fluency refers to the rhythm of speech. If a person repeats letters or syllables, or prolongs certain sounds frequently, he/she may have a fluency problem. This condition is more commonly called stuttering. Voice is the power source for speech and refers to our ability to produce a smooth airstream via the vibration of our vocal folds. This airstream is then sent to the articulators (lips, tongue, etc.) to be changed into different sounds. Problems with voice can lead to changes in vocal quality perceived as harshness, roughness, or breathiness.

While speech is a physiological function, language refers to a knowledge system and, so, is relatively more abstract. Language can be considered as a means of communication, and can have various modalities including spoken, written, or gestural (e.g., sign language) forms. According to Bloom and Lahey (1978), the language system encompasses three main areas: language form or the rules governing the structure of words, sentences, and paragraphs (the linguistic areas of phonology, morphology, and syntax); language content or the rules governing the way meaning is conveyed (the linguistic area of semantics); and language use or the rules governing how language is used in different contexts (the linguistic area of pragmatics). Basically, language can serve receptive and expressive functions. Expressive language problems refer to difficulties producing language while receptive language problems refer to an impaired ability to comprehend language.

Speech and language impairments may be primary or secondary in origin. For primary speech and language impairment, the skills are delayed relative to other developmental skills while there is usually no clear cause for the delay. Specific Language Impairment (SLI) is a widely used diagnosis that describes a primary language disorder where there is a significant discrepancy between a child's receptive and/or expressive language skills and those of the age-matched population (Leonard, 2000). To allow for children who outgrow early language delays, the diagnosis of SLI is restricted to language difficulties that persist beyond early childhood (beyond 4 years). The hallmark feature of SLI is deficits in the structural aspects of language (morphosyntax and phonology) (Rice, 2004). In secondary problems, speech and/or language skills are impaired because of other developmental disabilities, for example, autism, cleft palate, hearing impairment, intellectual disability, or a combination of these (Law, Boyle, Harris, Harkness, and Nye, 1998).

The US Federal Individuals with Disabilities Education Improvement Act (IDEA, 2004; No Child Left Behind, NCLB, 2002) requires that special education services be provided to children who have learning difficulties, including those who have speech, language, and hearing problems. Services are available for children from birth to 21 years of age. In the UK, the "Every Child Matters" initiatives formed by the UK Government in 2002 have the mission of promoting all children and young people aged from 0 to 19 years (24 years for those with disabilities) to achieve five outcomes: to be healthy, to stay safe, to enjoy and achieve, to make a positive contribution, and to achieve economic well-being (Department for Children Schools and Families, 2003). Similarly, in Australia, the Disability Standards for Education (Australian Commonwealth Government, 2006) ensure that all children are able to access and participate in education and training.

Speech and language skills have been emphasized as a crucial component for achieving positive social, educational, and vocational outcomes (Bercow, 2008). The European Union member states have recently endorsed a consensus statement on hearing, vision, and speech screening in pre-school and school-age children to improve screening practice (Skarynski and Piotrowska, 2012). With these policies, administrators have devoted resources to establishing not only rehabilitation services, but also to developing effective procedures to identify the children who require such services.

PREVALENCE OF SPEECH AND LANGUAGE IMPAIRMENTS

Prevalence estimates of diseases can assist policy makers to evaluate the resources needed to support children with health and educational needs and their families. With respect to speech and language impairments, prevalence figures have revealed that these are common, not only during early childhood, but also in the school years and in adolescence.

Law et al. (2000) estimated that around 10% of school children and young people in the UK have speech, language, and communication needs. Broomfield and Dodd (2004) conducted a survey of the referrals to a child speech-language therapy service over a period of

15 months in the UK. The children referred were between the ages 2 and 6 years. Among the referrals, 14.9% did not attend the first assessment and 9.8% showed normal language ability. SSDs accounted for 29.1%; receptive language disorders, 20.4%; expressive language disorders, 16.9%; dysfluency, 5.3%; and voice problems, 2%. In 2007, McLeod and McKinnon (2007) studied a cohort of 14,514 Australian school children aged between 5 and 18 years old and involved both teachers and speech-language pathologists (SLPs) in the identification process. Teachers were trained to identify children who had communication problems based on a series of brief descriptors indicating the manifestation of different types of communication disorders, including difficulties in language, social communication, articulation, fluency, reading and writing, and voice. All decisions were confirmed by formal assessments conducted by SLPs. Using this method, a mean prevalence of 13.0% was reported. In a subsequent study based on a cohort of 286 preschool Australian children before their school entry, Jessup, Ward, Cahill, and Keating (2008) used SLPs as the main informants and reported prevalence rates for speech impairment and language disorders of 13.6-16.4% and 7.0-17.8%, respectively.

Looking more specifically at speech and stuttering, Keating, Turrell, and Ozanne (2001) surveyed the parents of 12,388 Australian children aged between 0 and 14 years. According to parental reports, speech and/or stuttering difficulties were present in only 1.7% of the sample. Later, McKinnon, McLeod, and Reilly (2007) examined the prevalence of speech disorders in Australian children from kindergarten to Grade 6. They stratified the prevalence rates into speech sound disorders, stuttering, and voice disorders and reported prevalence estimates for these three disorders of 1.06%, 0.33%, and 0.12%, respectively. For all disorders, there was a general decline of prevalence with age.

With respect to language, Law, Boyle, Harris, Harkness, and Nye (2000) conducted a systematic review of studies examining the prevalence of primary language delay in children from 10 months to 7 years of age. The estimates ranged from 2.02% to 24.6%. This large range may be due to the use of different diagnostic cut-offs as well as variability in the diagnostic assessments used. The estimates also varied as a function of age. For example, the estimate of language disorders for 5-year-olds was around 6.8%, while for 7-year-olds it was approximately 3.1%, indicating that while some children may catch up to their peers over time, many will continue to lag behind. Clearly, early identification of children with any communication disorders is important.

Speech and Language Screening: Considerations in the Preschool Years

Early identification through screening assumes: (a) detection of the problem before the client experiences significant clinical complaint and (b) that intervention is available for the detected disease/condition and that this intervention can be effectively implemented when the disease/condition is identified early (Gordis, 2009). Given the first assumption, a number of studies have been conducted to identify the risk factors for speech and language problems.

For speech problems, some studies have reported risk factors including being male, lower maternal education level (e.g., Campbell et al., 2003), recurrent hearing problems (e.g., Harrison and McLeod, 2010, Yoshinaga-Itano et al., 1998), late onset of talking or expressive language problems (e.g., Baker and Cantwell, 1987; Shriberg Kwiatkowski, and Gruber,

1994) and low stimulability of the error sounds (e.g., Haws, 1969 cited in Shriberg et al., 1994; Powell, Elbert, and Dinnsen, 1991).

For language impairment, a positive family history of speech and/or language disorders and being male are the most consistently reported risk factors across studies (e.g., Choudhury and Benasich, 2003; Tomblin, Smith, and Zhang, 1996). Other risk factors include premature birth, low birth weight (e.g., Weindrich, Jennen-Steinmetz, Laucht, Esser, and Schmidt, 2000; Yliherva, Olsén, Mäki-Torkko, and Järvelin, 2001), younger age of mothers (Tomblin et al., 1997), and higher birth order (Tomblin, Hardy, and Hein, 1991).

The second assumption for implementing population-wide screening concerns the availability of effective intervention. The evidence underpinning the effectiveness of speech and language therapy for improved communication outcomes has been emerging in the literature. Law, Garrett, and Nye (2003) conducted a systematic review on available speech and language therapy interventions and located 25 clinical trials. Evidence for speech interventions was relatively more elaborated than for language intervention. Overall, however, the level of evidence was low and came mainly from quasi-experimental and correlational studies (c.f., Law, Garret, and Nye, 2004; Williams, McLeod, and McCauley, 2010). Accordingly, further research involving randomized controlled trials of speech and language interventions is urgently needed.

Even though some significant risk factors have been identified for speech and language impairment and evidence for effective speech and language intervention is emerging, screening for speech and language problems in the early years as a population-based public health exercise is not currently recommended in Australia (National Health and Medical Research Council, 2002), UK (Law et al., 1998) or US (Nelson et al., 2006). This is because the risk factors identified are somewhat inconsistent across studies and evidence for speech and language treatment efficacy is limited with most evidence coming from small scale studies of weak design (Nelson et al., 2006).

In addition, screening tools that are sensitive, specific, repeatable, acceptable to the public, and simple to administer and interpret are lacking (Law et al., 1998; Nelson et al., 2006). Another concern relates to the potential harm of false-positive and false negative identifications in screening programs. False-positives refer to children with normal speech and language ability being erroneously identified as impaired. These children and their families may suffer personally, from stigmatization, and financially, by having to spend unnecessary time and money for further assessment and interventions. Conversely, false-negatives refer to children that have a true impairment but are missed in the screening process. For this group of children, progressive problems and delayed language intervention may have long-term impacts in their life.

Another factor that further complicates the feasibility of early speech and language screening is the wide variation in normal development. The growth trajectories of typical speech and language development, as well as their disorders, are very diverse. Reilly et al. (2007) summarized that about 30% of babies aged 8 to 10 months old have been reported to demonstrate early delay in communication skills. The delay continued to be observable in 50% to 80% of these children at 2 years of age (Law et al., 2000; Smith, 1998). Furthermore, late talking has been observed in about 15% of 2-year-olds (Rescorla, Dahlsgaard, and Roberts, 2000) and appears to resolve in 40% to 60% of children by 3 years and 70% by 4 years of age (Paul, Spangle-Looney, and Dahm, 1991).

A recent large scale study involving 13,016 UK children examined the predictive power of language performance at 3 years of age and other demographic factors for later language status at 5 years (Law, Rush, Anandan, Cox, and Wood, 2012). Law and colleagues followed not only those children with delayed language, but also those who exhibited normal language skills at 3 years. Based on the children's picture naming ability as measured by the British Ability Scales II (Elliott, Smith, and McCulloch, 1997), Law et al. identified four groups of children : (1) a typically developing group (n=12,066) who showed adequate performance at both time points, (2) a consistently weak group (n=201) who were delayed at both time points, (3) a resilient group (n=572) who showed delay at 3 years but not 5 years, and (4) a declining group (n=177) who showed typical performance at 3 years but delay at 5 years. Maternal education was a significant predictor for the last two groups. Cognitive functions such as pattern construction were useful predictors for the declining and resilient groups.

Even though significant predictors were identified, the model only explained 32% of the variance at age 5 suggesting a large amount of unexplained variance and emphasizing the multi-factorial nature of language disorders. These studies have highlighted the difficulty with speech and language screening in the preschool years. There is a wide range of normal individual variation with respect to the rate and pattern of speech and language acquisition in the early years. Further, even within the same child, his or her speed of speech or language acquisition may vary over time. As revealed in Law et al.'s resilient group (2012), a group of late talkers who showed a delay at age 3 may catch up to their peers by age 5, with or without language intervention, while some apparently typical children may show speech and language difficulties at an older age. These two groups of children, those whose language declines over time and those whose language problems resolve over time, present major challenges for the implementation of screening programs for speech and language problems. Accordingly, population-based screening programs specifically for young children's speech and language ability may not be significantly beneficial to the entire pediatric target population and, therefore, are not recommended in primary care settings for children up to 5 years of age.

Speech and Language Screening: Considerations for School-Age Children

While it is difficult accurately to predict one's language status and other language-related skills in adulthood based on language ability in the preschool years, particularly for borderline cases, the accuracy of prediction appears to improve with age. In a longitudinal study, Stothard, Snowling, Bishop, Chipchase, and Kaplan (1998) followed a group of 68 children with speech and language impairment at ages 4 years, 5 years 6 months, and 15-16 years. Of the 68 children diagnosed with SLI at age 4 years, 56 were successfully followed through to 15-16 years and, of these, 64.3% (36/56) continued to show speech and language difficulties. At age 5 years 6 months, 30 of the original 68 children appeared to resolve their language problems and showed satisfactory speech-language performance (the resolved group), whereas the remaining 38 children continued to show difficulties (persistent group). Based on language status at 5 years 6 months, the accuracy of predicting language outcomes at 15-16 years rose to 78.6% (44/56), with 17 of the 26 children in the resolved group maintaining their normal language status and 27 of the 30 children in the persistent group continuing to exhibit speech and language difficulties at 15-16 years. From these findings, it is clear that language outcomes are better predicted by performance at 5 years 6 months (90%, 27/30) than at 4 years (64.3%, 36/56). Stothard et al. concluded that if a child's speech and language difficulties are still observed at school entry, their prognosis is likely to be poor and may lead to poor language, literacy, and academic achievements in adolescence.

Besides Stothard et al. (1998), there are a number of other longitudinal studies examining the long term outcomes for children diagnosed with language impairment at around age 5. All of these studies conclude that children with early language difficulties at school entry are more likely to exhibit literacy, higher level education, psychosocial or mental health problems, and poorer employment outcomes in adolescence and adulthood.

Table 5.1 summarizes the longitudinal studies that followed children from 5 years to adolescence or adulthood and examined the predictive value of early language status. Most of these studies reported group data that would somewhat limit generalization of the findings to the individual level. However, it is worth noting that the consistency of predictions supports the notion that language testing at school entry may be a cost-effective and more accurate way of screening than during the preschool years.

AVAILABILITY OF TREATMENT FOR SCHOOL-AGE CHILDREN

As previously mentioned, the core assumption of any screening program is the availability of effective treatment. In the 2010 Cochrane review updates, the number of randomized controlled speech and language intervention studies increased to 54 (Law, Garrett, and Nye, 2010). However, the studies in the review remained focused mainly on children younger than 5 years of age. Outcome studies for school-age children are, however, emerging. In a systematic review of language intervention for school-age children, Cirrin and Gillam (2008) located 21 studies published between 1985 and 2006 that examined the efficacy or effectiveness of language intervention for school-age children. Subsequent to the review by Cirrin and Gillam (2008), James, Jeffries, and Worley (2008) identified an additional 50 outcome studies for children with speech and language problems by extending the time frame and including studies representing lower level evidence. The evidence from the review was generally encouraging in supporting the effectiveness of certain speech and language interventions for school-age children. However, the researchers called for more high-level outcome studies for school-age language intervention.

Evidence supporting speech and language screening at school entry as a population-based public health exercise is only emerging and further research is needed. However, given the potential long-term impacts of language difficulties, some school-wide screening and management approaches for speech and language impairment referrals have been proposed.

Schools may also develop their own screening procedures to identify children with speech and language impairment who may not otherwise be referred by teachers, parents, or other professionals. Speech problems tend to be more obvious than language problems and so are more easily identified by teachers (Antoniazzi, Snow, and Dickson-Swift, 2010).

Table 5.1. Longitudinal studies using the speech and language status of children 5 years or older to predict adult and adolescent outcomes

Study	Participant group	Duration	Data point and sample size	Outcome	Main findings
Beitchman et al. (1996)	Poor comprehender group at 5yrs Poor articulation group at 5 yrs Overall-low group at 5 yrs Overall-high group at 5 yrs	7 years	T1: 5 yrs (Poor comprehenders: n=28; poor articulation: n=49; low overall: n=45; high overall: n=14) T2: 12.5 yrs (same as T1)	Behavioral outcome Emotional outcome Social outcome	Early language is associated with behavioral and social competence at 12.5 years. Children without receptive problems showed better social adjustment.
Beitchman et al. (2001)	Speech impairment (SI) group at 5 yrs Language impairment group (LI) at 5 yrs Controls at 5 yrs	14 years	T1: 5 yrs SI: n=38; LI: n=77; controls: n=129) T2: 19 yrs (same as T1)	Psychiatric outcomes	Age 5 language impairment is associated with an increased risk of psychiatric disorder at age 19.
Young et al. (2002)	Speech impairment-only (SI-only) group at 5 yrs Language impairment-only (LI-only) group at 5 yrs Speech and language impairment (S+LI) group at 5 yrs Controls at 5 yrs	14 years	T1: 5 yrs (SI-only: n=35; LI-only: n=49; S+LI=25; controls: n=120) T2: 19 yrs (same as T1)	Academic outcomes	Early LI young adults lagged behind controls even after controlling for IQ. Early LI but not speech impairment is associated with continued academic difficulties into adulthood.
Johnson, Beitchman, and Brownlie (2010)	Speech and/or language impairment (S/LI) group at 5 yrs Controls at 5 yrs	20 years	T1: 5 yrs (S/LI: n =142; controls: n=142); T2: 12 yrs (S/LI: 101; control: n=114), T3: 19 yrs (S/LI: 114=; control: n =128), T4: 25 yrs (S/LI: 132; C: n =112),	Family life Education level SES of occupation Quality of life	LI group showed poorer outcomes in communication, cognitive/academic, educational level, and occupational status than control and speech-only impairment groups.
Stothard, Snowling, Bishop, Chipchase and Kaplan (1998)	Language impairment (LI) at 4;0 (subdivided into good (resolved language problem) and poor (persistent) outcome groups and general delay (GD) group at 5 yrs)	12 years	T1: 4 yrs (n=87) T2: 5;6 yrs (n=68 including 30 resolved, 38 persistent, 19 GD) T3: 15-16yrs (n=71 including resolved LI: n=26; Persistent n=30; GD: n=15)	Spoken language (vocabulary, sentence repetition, non-word repetition, spoonerism) Literacy and academic outcomes Nonverbal ability	Resolved group showed normal ability except sentence repetition, nonword repetition, and spoonerism. Persistent group showed continued language, literacy, and educational difficulties
Snowling, Adams, Bishop, and Stothard (2001)	In addition to the above groups, an age-matched control group was included	Same as above	Same as above	GCSE grades	The resolved at 5;6 group outperformed the persistent group but showed significant small number of passes in the top A-C band than the control.

Study	Participant group	Duration	Data point and sample size	Outcome	Main findings
Law, Rush, Schoon, and Parsons (2009)	Specific language impairment (SLI) group at age 5 Non-specific language impairment (N-SLI) group at age Typically-developing (TD) group at 5 years	Around 30 years	T1: 5 yrs (SLI: n=211; N-SLI: n=195; TD: n=8,726) T2: 34 yrs (same as before)	Literacy Mental health Employment	Logistic multiple regression model was used. Early language learning difficulties are associated with literacy, mental health, and employment outcomes in adulthood.
Clegg, Hollis, Mawhood, and Rutter (2005)	Severe developmental language disorders (DLD) group without known etiology and IQ>70 in middle childhood Sibling controls at T4 IQ match controls at T4 National cohort of 1384 adults at T4 for psychosocial outcomes	About 25 years	T1: middle childhood (mean age: 9.11 yrs) (DLD: n=17) T2: 13.04 yrs (DLD: n=9) T3: early 20s (DLD: n=17) T4: mid-30s DLD: n=17)	Intelligence, language and literacy Psychosocial functioning	DLD group was significantly impaired in their mid-thirties. Impairment was also observed in literacy and psychosocial domains.
Catts, Fey, Zhang, and Tomblin (2001)	Language impaired (LI) group Nonverbal cognitive impairment (CI) group Language and non-verbal cognitive impairment (LI+CI) group Controls	About 4 years	T1: KG (LI: n=123, CI: n=102; LI+CI: n=101; control n=276) T2: Second grade (N was the same)	Reading ability	Letter identification, sentence imitation, phonological awareness, rapid naming, and maternal education predict reading outcome.
Catts, Fey, Tomblin, and Zhang (2002)	Specific language impairment (SLI) group Nonspecific language impairment (NLI) group Low nonverbal IQ (LNIQ) group Non-impaired controls	About 4 years	T1: KG (SLI: n=117, NLI: n=91; LNIQ: n=94; NC: n=268) T2: Second grade (N was the same) T3: Fourth Grade	Reading ability	SLI at KG group who showed improvement in oral language skills by second and fourth grades had better reading outcomes than the persistent group. Literacy knowledge/experience at kindergarten, and reading achievement at second grade were good predictors of subsequent reading outcomes.

Note: CI=cognitive impairment; GD=general delay; DLD=developmental language disorders; LI=Language impaired; LI-only=Language impairment-only LI+CI=Language and non-verbal cognitive impairment; LNIQ=Low nonverbal IQ; N-SLI=Non-specific language impairment; NLI= Nonspecific language impairment; S+LI=Speech and language impairment; S/LI=Speech and/or language impairment; SI-only=Speech impairment-only; TD=Typically-developing; NC=Non-impaired control; T1 = Time point 1; T2 = Time point 2, etc.

In addition, in school years, speech problems are less prevalent than language problems (McKinnon et al., 2007; McLeod and McKinnon, 2007). The following section will describe some common school-based screening procedures, mainly for language impairment.

SPEECH AND LANGUAGE SCREENING PROCEDURES AND TOOLS USED IN SCHOOLS

While the objective of any speech and language screening program is to identify children whose skills in these areas require further, more extensive evaluation, the implicit aim of screening in school-aged children focuses on their educational potential by identifying children at risk of learning failure due to underlying speech and/or language problems. As with any screening program, the evaluation instruments used should be as sensitive and as specific as possible. Sensitivity refers to the accuracy with which the test instrument is able to identify a child with a disorder (true positives). Specificity, on the other hand, refers to the accuracy with which the test is able to identify the absence of a disorder (true negatives). The following section will first consider traditional pre-referral approaches to speech, language, and early literacy screening in this age group, followed by more contextualized curriculum-based preventative screening.

Pre-Referral Speech and Language Screening

Two of the most well-known standardized communication screening devices for school-age children are the Children's Communication Checklist Second Edition (CCC-2, Bishop, 2003) and the Clinical Evaluation of Language Fundamentals – Fourth Edition Screening Test (CELF-4 Screener, Semel, Wiig, and Secord, 2004). The CCC-2 provides an indirect assessment of a child's speech and language (semantic, syntactic, pragmatic) skills and was normed on over 500 UK children and check-normed on a smaller sample of Australian children (n=111). It is suitable for a wide age range (4 to 17 years), is quick to administer, and includes 70 items. The test items can be rated by either the child's parent or their teacher, however, parental ratings have been shown to be more accurate (Antoniazzi, et al., 2010; Bishop and Baird, 2001). The test manual outlines a validity study involving a group of 92 children with various communication disorders including SLI, pragmatic language impairment, and autism. The results of this study indicated that the CCC-2 General Communication Composite cut-off score (the 3rd percentile) correctly classified as language impaired, 93.8% of children with SLI and no control children, thereby indicating adequate sensitivity. A recent study of a Norwegian adaptation of the CCC-2 indicated, however, that while the CCC-2 can be used in other languages/cultures, optimal cut-off scores should be determined for those populations (Helland, Biringer, Helland, and Heimann, 2009).

The CELF-4 Screener is a criterion referenced test that involves direct assessment of a child's language skills. Like the CCC-2, it is quick to administer (approximately 15 mins), suitable for a wide age range (5 to 21 years), and examines a range of language domains.

Based on the larger, norm-referenced diagnostic battery, the Clinical Evaluation of Language Fundamentals-Fourth Edition (CELF-4, Semel, Wiig, and Secord, 2003), the CELF-4 Screener is purported to include the most discriminating tasks and items from its parent battery. For children under 9 years, there are 4 tasks involving 28 items, and for 9- to 21-year-olds, the screener includes 5 tasks and 34 items. Scoring is easy with each item being scored as correct or incorrect and criterion cut-off scores are provided. The test was normed on over 1200 American students and sensitivity and specificity were found to be high (both 88%).

Antoniazzi et al. (2010) examined the sensitivity and specificity of teacher ratings on the CCC-2 (Bishop, 2003) against the CELF-4 Screener in a group of 157 Australian first year preparatory students. The findings indicated that the CELF-4 screener was more sensitive to the presence of language impairment and that teacher ratings on the CCC-2 resulted in unacceptably high false positive and false negative identifications. The authors warned of the educational consequences of this high false negative rate suggesting that, based on their findings, as many as 13% of children in a preparatory cohort may have a language impairment that could go unrecognized by their teacher. It was suggested that the high number of false positive teacher ratings may be due to the ratings of language-related items being wrongly influenced by the presence of a speech deficit. It is important to note, however, that while the CELF-4 screener was administered by SLPs in this study, it is able to be administered by trained teachers. Accordingly, further research is needed to determine whether the poorer performance of the CCC-2 as compared to the CELF-4 Screener reported by Antoniazzi et al. was administrator-related or an artifact of the assessment method (i.e., indirect versus direct assessment of the student).

Other tasks that have potential utility as language screening instruments are nonword repetition and sentence repetition (also called sentence recall). Both are quick to administer and have been identified as reliable clinical markers of SLI. In particular, Conti-Ramsden, Botting, and Faragher (2001) reported very high sensitivity and specificity for the sentence recall task as a marker of SLI. More recently, Archibald and Joanisse (2009) devised a 5 minute screener comprising nonword repetition and sentence recall tasks and examined their effectiveness as screeners for language impairment in a group of 400 Canadian lower primary school children. While the two tasks together had high sensitivity (84%), specificity was poor (50%). Both measures rose to above 80%, however, for sentence recall alone, further supporting its utility as a sensitive clinical marker of, and screener for, SLI.

Also drawing on nonword and sentence repetition, the Grammar and Phonology Screening (GAPS) test (Gardner, Froud, McClelland, and van der Lely, 2006) was designed to identify children aged up to 6 years and 6 months who are at risk of academic failure due to underlying difficulties with language structure (van der Lely and Marshall, 2010). The GAPS employs novel elicitation procedures suitable for young children and was standardized in the UK on a large number of children (*n*=668). It can be administered by both speech pathologists and teachers and is quick to administer (approximately 10 mins). A smaller study, involving 30 typically developing children and 21 children diagnosed with SLI, reported very high sensitivity (91%) and specificity (100%) for the GAPS when using a cut-off of the 10th percentile (van der Lely and Marshall, 2010). While others have since confirmed the test's high specificity, low sensitivity of 20% was reported (Nash, Leavett, and Childs, 2011).

Another speech and language screening test recently developed for young Australian school children (4-5 years) is the Kindergarten Development Check (Jessup, Ward, Cahill, and Keating, 2008). A study involving 286 children revealed that teachers administering the Kindergarten Developmental Check had high specificity in recognizing children with typical speech and language skills (93% and 97%, respectively) but only low sensitivity (50%) in identifying children with speech impairments. This figure dropped to a very low 15% when identifying children with language impair-ment. The authors suggested that the low sensitivity may have been related to teachers erring on the side of caution. While preliminary results suggest that this test is currently ineffective as a teacher administered screener, further research is needed to examine the impact of teacher training on its sensitivity.

Finally, a test that is frequently utilized to screen the semantic and morphosyntactic skills of children aged 3-8 years is The Renfrew Language Scales Action Picture Test (Renfrew, 1997). Quick to administer, the test includes 10 picture cards and prompts to elicit sentence level responses. Sentences are then analyzed for informational content and grammar and raw scores totals for each are compared to normative bands. While this test appears to have considerable clinical support, its norms were collected in 1987-88 and yet, to date, limited research has been undertaken to establish its reliability and validity.

Pre-Referral Screening for Early Literacy Skills

Many countries have population-based screening for literacy skills. For example, in Australia, the National Assessment Program – Literacy and Numeracy (NAPLAN) (Australian Curriculum and Reporting Authority, ACARA, 2011) assesses the reading comprehension, writing, and numeracy skills of all children in Years 3, 5, 7, and 9. While national testing has not included early literacy skills such as word decoding, phonological awareness (PA) and phonics, screening programs for these foundational skills are beginning to emerge. In 2012, the UK government introduced a phonics screening program for Year 1 students (Department of Education, 2012). The screening test, which involves children reading aloud 20 regular real words (e.g., “best”) and 20 pseudo-words (e.g., “chom”), is based on psycholinguistic principles and assesses students’ ability to apply phonic knowledge during non-lexical reading. Further information including the actual test stimuli can be found at www.education.gov.uk/schools/teachingandlearning/pedagogy/phonics.

Given the important role of language and, in particular, phonological processing, in the development of literacy skills, SLPs are frequently involved in screening children for related pre-literacy skills. While a number of PA tests that are suitable for school screening are available, information regarding their sensitivity and specificity is extremely limited.

With this caveat in mind, two potential PA screeners, the Sutherland Phonological Awareness Test – Revised (SPAT-R, Neilson, 2003) and the Phonological Awareness Screening Test (Henty, 1994), will be briefly discussed below. Following this, a procedure for assessing word decoding will be outlined. The reader is also referred to Justice, Invernizzi, and Meier (2002) who provide comprehensive guidelines for designing and implementing clinician-based screening for early literacy skills.

The SPAT-R (Neilson, 2003) was normed on over 500 Australian children in Grades 1-4 and percentile ranks are provided. The test contains 13 PA-related tasks, each containing between four and eight test items and the entire test takes approximately 15 minutes to administer. While a special response form is provided for school screening purposes, the test manual advises that research regarding the test’s use as a screener is yet to be completed. In the meantime, the author suggests that children scoring below the 25th percentile for the cohort be considered at risk.

Like the SPAT-R, the Phonological Awareness Screening Test (Henty, 1994) was developed in Australia. This particular screener was designed to identify children with PA difficulties prior to them commencing Grade 1. The test was administered to 1302 preschool children and while some normative data is provided to guide the establishment of cut-offs, the test's sensitivity and specificity have not been examined.

To measure word reading proficiency, Coltheart and Leahy's (1996) word lists allow the examiner to take a psycholinguistic approach based on the dual route model of reading (Coltheart Curtis, Atkins, and Haller, 1993). The lists of 30 regular, irregular, and nonsense words are quick to administer and normative bands for 7- to 12-year-olds are provided. By comparing a student's performance across the lists, an indication can be gained regarding their ability to use lexical (using their sight word knowledge to read whole words) and non-lexical (using their knowledge of grapheme-phoneme correspondences to "sound out" words) reading.

Curriculum-Based Language Assessment

The aim of curriculum based language assessment is to determine whether a student has adequate language skills to learn their curriculum (Nelson, 2010). Accordingly, unlike the assessment measures outlined above, curriculum based assessment items represent more functional or contextualized means of evaluation, being drawn from or relevant to, the curriculum.

The Responsiveness to Intervention (RTI) Framework is an extension to curriculum relevant practice (Staskowski and Rivera, 2005). More specifically, the RTI model refers to an educational reform involving a school-wide approach that emphasizes prevention, universal screening, tiered instruction or intervention, and dynamic, curriculum-relevant assessment (Ehren and Nelson, 2005). RTI tends to focus mainly on reading and contrasts with traditional discrepancy approaches to diagnosis by identifying children with language or learning disabilities through their failure to respond to systematic and multi-layered intervention (Staskowski and Rivera, 2005). A typical RTI program incorporates three tiers of instruction with careful monitoring of each student as they progress through the tiers to ensure early identification and intervention for at-risk students (Troia, 2005). The first tier of RTI involves the provision of high quality evidence-based reading instruction for all children with frequent monitoring of their skills. For students who fail to achieve criterion levels of performance in response to first tier instruction, Tier 2 supplementary instruction, usually in the form of small groups, is provided.

Children who fail to respond adequately to this additional instruction are then carefully assessed and targeted individual intervention provided at the Tier 3 level. Because of the importance of speech and language for the development of literacy skills, SLPs have an important role to play at all levels of RTI in both the instructional and assessment aspects of the program (Ehren and Nelson, 2005; Justice, 2006; Robinson, 2012).

Fundamental to the success of the RTI framework is the use of sensitive test measures to audit class and individual student progress (Justice, 2006). Benchmark testing mainly informs teacher planning and employs either norm or criterion referenced tests to assess class performance in specific skill areas such as phonological awareness and sight word reading. Progress monitoring involves more frequent testing than benchmark testing and is designed to track students' rate of progress (Justice, 2006). Accordingly, tests need to be sensitive and quick to administer without strict test-retest restrictions.

The Dynamic Indicators of Basic Early Literacy Skills 6th Edition (DIBELS, Good and Kaminski, 2002) is an instrument that can be used for both benchmark testing and progress monitoring in the early grades. The DIBELS includes a series of tests designed to probe performance across a range of preliteracy and literacy skills including phonological, phonemic, and orthographic awareness. Each test takes only one minute to administer and students are scored on their fluency (number of correct items produced in one minute) for phonemic decoding, word reading, initial sound identification, and phoneme segmentation.

The test provides benchmark scores and cut-offs for classification of students as “at risk,” “some risk,” and “low risk” by task and grade level and recent updates have seen the sensitivity and specificity of these increased to 90% for benchmark scores and 80% for “at risk” cut-off points (University of Oregon Center on Teaching and Learning, 2012). The DIBELS and relevant technical reports are freely available from https://dibels.uoregon.edu.

Story telling or narrative has also received support as a sensitive curriculum-based screening tool for oral language and listening comprehension skills (Culatta, Page, and Ellis, 1983; Nelson, 2010; Robinson, 2012). Culatta et al. (1983) first described a quick procedure in which children’s receptive and expressive narrative skills were evaluated in response to a grade appropriate story. A total of 199 kindergarten and first grade children completed the story retelling screening procedure together with formal assessment of their language skills.

Based on his/her story-telling performance, each child was identified as suitable for (a) discharge, (b) further assessment, or (c) immediate language intervention. Comparisons of children identified as suitable for discharge or immediate intervention revealed that this more conservative three-pronged approach to screening resulted in very high specificity and sensitivity (92 % and 90%, respectively). While Culatta and colleagues’ (1983) procedure is now almost 30 years old, Nelson (2010) has proposed that it remains applicable for school-age children as a sensitive, curriculum relevant screening protocol and has offered suggestions for adapting Culatta et al.’s procedure for contemporary use. Also interested in the use of storytelling as a curriculum relevant method for examining both language comprehension and expression, Robinson (2012) recently examined the story retells of 52 children with language impairment and 52 matched controls. Based on the finding that measures of story grammar predicted group membership with 74% accuracy, Robinson proposed that narrative measures are an ecologically valid way to monitor response to treatment in school-age children.

The dynamic assessment approach of RTI and the tools outlined above appear to represent valid methods for universal school language and literacy screening. Such an approach is attractive as frequent monitoring means that the consequences of a false positive identification are not as dire for the child as with pre-referral screening.

The ultimate test of the RTI approach, however, will be a reduction in the number of children in the later primary years with literacy, language, and learning difficulties. Studies reporting positive outcomes are beginning to emerge (Koutsoftas, Harmon, and Gray, 2009; Lipka and Siegel, 2010); however, further research is needed.

CONCLUSION

Speech and language impairments are alarmingly common in school-age children and, if untreated, can have a profound impact on a child's educational, vocational, and social outcomes. Several pre-referral speech, language, and literacy screening options have been discussed but overall, there is a lack of quick, reliable, and valid speech and language screeners for school-age children. Some of the screeners examined offer potential when administered by SLPs but this is not always economically viable. More research is needed to examine the impact of teacher training on the validity of speech and language screening. The cost of high false negative identification rates is academic failure for the child. High false positive identification rates, on the other hand, have both resource and economic implications for educational teams. The RTI approach does appear to offer a solution to the problems associated with pre-referral screening instruments but RTI still relies on effective evaluation tools for benchmark and progress monitoring. The development of further suitable speech and language evaluation procedures is deserving of research attention. Also worthy of more research attention is the question of whether RTI does, in fact, accomplish early identification of all children with speech and language related learning difficulties and, therefore, whether it represents an effective universal screening approach.

REFERENCES

American Speech-Language-Hearing Association (n.d.). What are speech sound disorders? In: *Speech sound disorders: Articulation and phonological processes*. Retrieved Oct. 2012, from http://www.asha.org/public/speech/disorders/speechsounddisorders.htm.

Antoniazzi D., Snow, P. and Dickson-Swift, V. (2010). Teacher identification of children at risk for language impairment in the first year of school. *International Journal of Speech Language Pathology*, 12(3), 244-252.

Archibald, L. M. D. and Gathercole, S. E. (2006). Nonword repetition: A comparison of tests. *Journal of Speech, Language, and Hearing Research*, 49(5), 970-983.

Archibald, L. M. D. and Joanisse, M. F. (2009). On the sensitivity and specificity of nonword repetition and sentence recall to language and memory impairments in children. *Journal of Speech, Language, and Hearing Research,* 52(4), 899-914.

Australian Curriculum and Reporting Authority (ACARA, 2011). National Assessment Program Retrieved from http://www.nap.edu.au/index.html.

Baker, L. and Cantwell, D. P. (1987). A prospective psychiatric follow-up of children with speech/language disorders. *Journal of the American Academy of Child and Adolescent Psychiatry,* 26, 546-553.

Beitchman, J. H., Brownlie, E. B., Inglis, J. Wild, J., Ferguson, B., Schachter, D., … Mathews, R. (1996). Seven year follow up of speech/language impaired and control children: Psychiatric outcome. *Journal of Child Psychology and Psychiatry*, 37, 961–970.

Beitchman, J. H., Wilson, B., Johnson, C. J., Atkinson, L., Young, A., Adlaf, E.… Douglas, L. (2001). Fourteen-year follow-up of speech/language-impaired and control children: Psychiatric outcome. *Journal of American Academy of Child and Adolescent Psychiatry*, 40(1), 75-82.

Bercow, J. (2008) *The Bercow report: A review of service for children and young people (0-19) with speech, language and communication needs (SLCN).* London: DCSF.

Bishop, D. V. M. (2003). *The Children's Communication Checklist Second Edition* (CCC-2). London: The Psychological Corporation.

Bishop, D. V. M. and Baird, G. (2001). Parent and teacher report of pragmatic aspects of communication: Use of the Children's Communication Checklist in a clinical setting. *Developmental Medicine and Child Neurology*, 43, 809-818.

Bloom, L. and Lahey, M. (1978). *Language development and language disorders*. New York: John Wiley and Sons.

Broomfield, J. and Dodd, B. (2004). Children with speech and language disabilities: Caseload characteristics. *International Journal of Language and Communication Disorders*, 39, 303-324.

Bryan, K. (2004). Preliminary study of the prevalence of speech and language difficulties in young offenders. *International Journal of Language and Communication Disorders*, 39, 391–400.

Campbell, T. F., Dollaghan, C. A., Rockette, H. E., Paradise, J. L., Feldman, H. M., Shriberg, L., … Kurs-Lasky, M. (2003). Risk factors for speech delay of unknown origin in 3-year-old children. *Child Development*, 74, 346-357.

Catts, H. W., Adolf, S. M. and Weismer, S. E. (2006). Language deficits in poor comprehenders: A case for the simple view of reading. *Journal of Speech, Language, and Hearing Research*, 49(2), 278-293.

Catts, H. W., Fey, M. E., Tomblin, J. B., and Zhang, X. (2002). A longitudinal investigation of reading outcomes in children with language impairments. *Journal of Speech, Language, and Hearing Research*, 45(6), 1142–1157.

Catts, H. W., Fey, M., Zhang, X., and Tomblin, J. B. (2001). Estimating the risk of future reading difficulties in kindergarten children: A research-based model and its clinical implementation. *Language, Speech, and Hearing Services in Schools*, 32, 38-50.

Choudhury, N. and Benasich, A. A. (2003). A family aggregation study: The influence of family history and other risk factors on language development. *Journal of Speech, Language and Hearing Research,* 46(2), 261-272.

Cirrin, F. and Gillam, R. (2008). Language intervention practices for school- age children with spoken language disorders: A systematic review. *Language, Speech, and Hearing Services in Schools,* 39, S110–S137.

Clegg, J., Hollis, C., Mawhood, L., and Rutter, M. (2005). Developmental language disorders – a follow-up in later adult life. Cognitive, language and psychosocial outcomes. *Journal of Child Psychology and Psychiatry and Allied Disciplines*, 46, 128-149.

Cohen, N. J., Barwick, M., Horodezky, N., Vallance, D., and Im, N. (1998). Language, achievement and cognitive processing in psychometrically disturbed children with previously identified and unsuspected language impairment. *Journal of Child Psychology and Psychiatry,* 37, 865–877.

Coltheart, M., Curtis, B., Atkins, P., and Haller, M. (1993). Models of reading aloud: Dual route and parallel-distributed processing approaches. *Psychological Review*, 100, 589-608.

Coltheart, M. and Leahy, J. (1996). Assessment of lexical and nonlexical reading abilities in children: Some normative data. *Australian Journal of Psychology*, 48(3), 136-140.

Commonwealth of Australia (2006). *Disability Standards for Education (2005)*. Retrieved from http://www.deewr.gov.au/Schooling/Programs/Documents/Disability_Standards_for_Education_2005.pdf.

Conti-Ramsden, G., Botting, N. and Faragher, B., (2001). Psycholinguistic markers for specific language impairment (SLI). *Journal of Child Psychology and Psychiatry*, 42, 741-748.

Culatta, B , Page, J. L. and Ellis, J. (1983). Story retelling as a communicative performance screening tool. *Language, Speech and Hearing Services in Schools*, 14, 66-74.

Department of Education (2012). *Phonics screening check for year 1 pupils*. Retrieved from https://www.education.gov.uk/schools/teachingandlearning/pedagogy.

Department for Children Schools and Families (2003). *Every Child Matters*. Retrieved from https://www.education.gov.uk/publications/standard/publicationDetail/Page1/CM5860.

Ehren, B. J. and Nelson, N. W. (2005). The responsiveness to intervention approach and language impairment. *Topics in Language Disorders*, 25(2), 120-131.

Elliott, C., Smith, P. and McCulloch, K. (1997). *British Ability Scales* (2nd ed.). London, UK: NFER Nelson.

Gardner, H., Froud, K., McClelland, A., and van der Lely, H. K. J. (2006). The development of the Grammar and Phonology Screening (GAPS) test to assess key markers of specific language difficulties in young children. *International Journal of Language and Communication Disorders,* 41, 513-540.

Good, R. H. and Kaminski, R. Eds. (2002). *Dynamic Indicators of Early Literacy Skills* (6th ed.). Eugene, OR: Institute for the Development of Educational Achievement.

Gordis, L. (2009). *Epidemiology* (4th ed.). Philadelphia, PA: Saunders Elsevier.

Harrison, L. J. and McLeod, S. (2010). Risk and protective factors associated with speech and language impairment in a nationally representative sample of 4- to 5-year-old children. *Journal of Speech, Language and Hearing Research,* 53, 508-529.

Helland, W. A., Biringer, E., Helland, T., and Heimann, M. (2009). The usability of a Norwegian adaptation of the Children's Communication Checklist. Second Edition (CCC-2) in differentiating between language impaired and non-language impaired 6- to 12-year-olds. *Scandinavian Journal of Psychology*, 50, 287-292.

Helland, W. A. and Heimann, M. (2007). Assessment of pragmatic impairment in children referred to psychiatric services: A pilot study of the Children's Communication Checklist in a Norwegian sample. *Logopedics Phoniatrics Vocology*, 32, 23–30.

Henty, A. (1994). Phonological Awareness Screening Test. *Australian Communication Quarterly,* Suppl., 18-20.

Individuals with Disabilities Education Improvement Act of 2004, Pub. L. No. 108-144, (2004).

Johnson, C. J., Beitchman, J. and Brownlie, E. B. (2010). Twenty-year follow-up of children with and without speech-language impairments: Family, education, occupational and quality of life outcomes. *American Journal of Speech-Language Pathology*, 19, 51-65.

James, D. G. H., Jeffries, L. and Worley, A. (2008). *Speech and Language Therapy Service Model and Effectiveness Review: Stages II and III (5-18 year olds).* Centre for Allied Health Evidence, University of South Australia.

Jessup, B., Ward, E., Cahill, L., and Keating, D. (2008). Teacher identification of speech and language impairment in kindergarten students using the Kindergarten Development Check. *International Journal of Speech-Language Pathology*, 10(6), 449-459.

Justice, L. M. (2006). Evidence-based practice, response to intervention, and the prevention of reading difficulties. *Language, Speech and Hearing Services in Schools*, 37(4), 284-297.

Justice, L. M., Invernizzi, M. A. and Meier, J. D. (2002). Designing and implementing an early literacy screening protocol: Suggestions for the speech-language pathologist. *Language, Speech and Hearing Services in Schools*, 33(2), 84-101.

Keating, D., Turrell, G. and Ozanne, A. (2001). Childhood speech disorders: Reported prevalence, comorbidity and socioeconomic profile. *Journal of Paediatrics and Child Health*, 37(5), 431-436.

Koutsoftas, A. D., Harmon, M. T. and Gray, S. (2009). The effect of tier 2 intervention for phonemic awareness in a Response-to-Intervention Model in low-income preschool classrooms. *Language, Speech and Hearing Services in Schools*, 40(2), 116-130.

Law, J., Boyle, J., Harris, F., Harkness, A., and Nye, C. (1998). Screening for speech and language delay: A systematic review of the literature. *Health Technology Assessment, 2. Havant, UK: Health Technology Assessment NHS R and D HTA Programme*. Retrieved from http://www.hta.ac.uk/fullmono/mon209.pdf.

Law, J., Boyle, J., Harris, F., Harkness, A., and Nye, C. (2000). Prevalence and natural history of primary speech and language delay: Findings from a systematic review of the literature. *International Journal of Language and Communication Disorders*, 35(2), 165-188.

Law, J., Lindsay, G., Peacey, N. Gascoigne, M., Soloff, N., Radford, J. ... Fitzgerald, L. (2000). Provision for children's speech and language needs in England and Wales: Facilitating communication between education and health service. *DfES research report 239.* Retrieved from: https://www.education.gov.uk/publications/eOrderingDownload/RB239.pdf.

Law, J., Garrett, Z. and Nye, C. (2003). Speech and language therapy interventions for children with primary speech and language delay or disorder. *Cochrane Database of Systematic Reviews*, Issue 3 Art. No.: CD004110.

Law, J., Garrett, Z. and Nye, C. (2004). The efficacy of treatment for children with developmental speech and language delay/ disorder: A meta-analysis. *Journal of Speech, Language, and Hearing Research*, 47, 924-943.

Law, J., Garrett, Z. and Nye, C. (2010). Speech and language therapy interventions for children with primary speech and language delay or disorder. *Cochrane Database of Systematic Reviews,* Issue 5 Art. No.: CD004110.

Law, J., Lindsay, G., Peacey, N., Gascoigne, M., Soloff, N., Radford, J., and Band, S. (2000). Facilitating communication between education and health services: The provision for children with speech and language needs. *British Journal of Special Education*, 28(3), 133-137.

Law, J., Rush, R., Anandan, C., Cox, M., and Wood, R. (2012). Predicting language change between 3 and 5 years and its implications for education identification. *Pediatrics*, 130, e132-e138.

Law, J., Rush, R., Schoon, I., and Parsons, S. (2009). Modeling developmental language difficulties from school entry into adulthood: Literacy, mental health, and employment opportunities. *Journal of Speech, Language and Hearing Research*, 52, 1401-1416.

Leonard, L. B. (2000). *Children with specific language impairment*. Cambridge, MA: MIT Press.

Lipka, O. and Siegel, L. S. (2010). The improvement of reading skills of L1 and ESL children using a Response to Intervention (RtI) Model. *Psicothema*, 22(4), 963-969.

McKinnon, D. H., McLeod, S. and Reilly, S. (2007). The prevalence of stuttering, voice and speech–sound disorders in primary school students. *Language, Speech, and Hearing Services in Schools,* 38, 5–15.

McLeod, S. and McKinnon, D. H. (2007). Prevalence of communication disorders compared with other learning needs in 14 500 primary and secondary school students. *International Journal of Language and Communication Disorders*, 42, 37-59.

Nash, H., Leavett, R. and Childs, H. (2011). Evaluating the GAPS test as a screener for language impairment in young children. *International Journal of Language and Communication Disorders,* 46(6), 675-685.

National Health and Medical Research Council. (2002). Child health screening and surveillance: A critical review of the evidence. Reported prepared by Centre for Community Child Health, Royal Children's Hospital Melbourne for the National Health and Medical Research Council, Australia.

Neilson, R. (2003). *Sutherland Phonological Awareness Test – Revised*. Jamberoo, NSW, Australia: Neilson.

Nelson, N. W. (2010). Language and literacy disorders. *Infancy through adolescence*. Boston, MA: Allyn and Bacon.

Nelson, H. D., Nygren, M., Walker, M., and Panoscha, R. (2006). Screening for speech and language delay in preschool children: Systematic evidence review for the US Preventive Service Task Force. *Pediatrics*, 117(2), e298-e319.

No Child Left Behind (NCLB) *Act of 2001, Pub. L. No. 107-110, § 115, Stat. 1425 (2002).*

Paul, R., Spangle-Looney, S. and Dahm, P. (1991). Communication and socialization skills at age 2 and 3 in "late talking" young children. *Journal of Speech and Hearing Research*, 34, 858 –865.

Powell, T. W., Elbert, M. and Dinnsen, D. A. (1991). Stimulability as a factor in the phonological generalization of misarticulating preschool children. *Journal of Speech and Hearing Research,* 34, 1318-1328.

Renfrew, C. E. (1997). *The Renfrew Language Scales Action Picture Test*. Bicester, UK: Speechmark.

Rescorla, L., Dahlsgaard, K. and Roberts J. (2000). Late-talking toddlers: MLU and IPSyn outcomes at 3;0 and 4;0. *Journal of Child Language*, 27, 643–664.

Reilly, S. Wake, M., Bavin, E. L., Prior, M., Williams, J., Bretherton, L., Eadie, P., Barret, Y., Ukoumunne, O. C. (2007). Predicting language at 2 years of age: A prospective community study. *Pediatrics*, 120, e1441-1449.

Rice, M. L., (2004). Growth models of developmental language disorders. In: M. L. Rice and S. F. Warren (Eds.), *Developmental language disorders: From phenotypes to etiologies* (pp. 207-240). Mahwah, NJ: Lawrence Erlbaum.

Robinson, W. (2012). Curriculum-based assessment of oral language and listening comprehension: A tool for intervention and progress monitoring in the common core state standards. *Seminars in Speech and Language*, 33(2), 160-172.

Ruben, R. J. (2000). *Redefining the survival of the fittest: Communication disorders in the 21st century*. Laryngoscope, 110, 241-245.

Semel, E., Wiig, E. H. and Secord, W. A. (2003). *Clinical Evaluation of Language Fundamentals* (4th ed.) (CELF-4). Toronto: The Psychological Corporation.

Semel, E., Wiig, E. H. and Secord, W. A. (2004). *Clinical Evaluation of Language Fundamentals* (4th ed.) – Screening Test (CELF-4 Screening Test). Toronto: The Psychological Corporation.

Shriberg, L. D., Kwiatkowski, J. and Gruber, F. A. (1994). Developmental phonological disorders II: Short-term speech-sound normalization. *Journal of Speech and Hearing Research,* 37, 1127-1150.

Skarynski, H. and Piotrowska, A. (2012). Prevention of communication disorders - screening pre-school and school-age children for problems with hearing, vision and speech: European Consensus Statement. *Medical Science Monitor: International Journal of Experimental and Clinical Research,* 18(4), SR17-21.

Smith, L. (1998). Predicting communicative competence at 2 and 3 years from pragmatic skills at 10 months. *International Journal of Language and Communication Disorders,* 33, 127 –148.

Snowling, M. J., Adams, J. W., Bishop, D. V. M., and Stothard, S. E. (2001). Educational attainments of school leavers with a preschool history of speech-language impairments. *International Journal of Language and Communication Disorders*, 36, 173-183.

Staskowski, M. and Rivera, E. A. (2005). Speech-language pathologists' involvement in Responsiveness to Intervention activities. *Topics in Language Disorders*, 25(2), 132-147.

Stothard, S. E., Snowling, M. J., Bishop, D. V., Chipchase, B. B., and Kaplan, C. A. (1998). Language-impaired preschoolers: A follow up into adolescence. *Journal of Speech, Language, and Hearing Research,* 41, 407 –418.

Tomblin, J. B., Hardy, J. and Hein, H. (1991). Predicting poor communication status in preschool children using risk factors present at birth. *Journal of Speech and Hearing Research*, 34, 1096-1105.

Tomblin, J. B., Smith, E. and Zhang, X. (1997). Epidemiology of specific language impairment: Prenatal and perinatal risk factors. *Journal of Communication Disorders*, 30, 325-344.

Troia, G. A. (2005). Responsiveness to Intervention. Roles for speech-language pathologists in the prevention and identification of learning disabilities. *Topics in Language Disorders,* 25(2), 106-119.

University of Oregon Center on Teaching and Learning. (2012). 2012-2013 DIBELS Data System Update Part II: DIBELS Next Benchmark Goals (Technical Brief No. 1203). Eugene, OR: University of Oregon.

Van der Lely, H. K. J. and Marshall, C. R. (2010). Assessing component language deficits in the early detection of reading difficulty risk. *Journal of Learning Disabilities*, 43(4), 357-368.

Weindrich, D., Jennen-Steinmetz, C., Laucht, M., Esser, G., and Schmidt, M. H. (2000). Epidemiology and prognosis of specific disorders of language and scholastic skills. *European Child and Adolescent Psychiatry*, 90, 186-194.

Williams, A. L., McLeod, S. and McCauley, R. J., (2010). *Interventions for speech sound disorders in children*. Baltimore, MD: Paul H. Brookes.

Yliherva, A., Olsén, P, Mäki-Torkko, E., and Järvelin, M. R. (2001). Linguistic and motor abilities of low birthweight children as assessed by parents and teachers at 8 years of age. *Acta Paediatrics*, 90, 1440-1449.

Yoshinaga-Itano, C., Sedey, A. L., Coulter, D. K., and Mehl, A. L. (1998). Language of early- and later-identified children with hearing loss. *Pediatrics*, 102, 1161-1171.

Young, A. R., Beitchman, J. H., Johnson, C., Doughlas, L., Atkinson, L., Escobar, M., and Wilson, B. (2002). Young adult academic outcomes in a longitudinal sample of early identified language impaired and control children. *Journal of Child Psychology and Psychiatry,* 43, 635-645.

In: School Health Screening Systems
Editors: Bradley McPherson and Carlie J. Driscoll
ISBN: 978-1-63117-942-6

Chapter 6

DENTAL SCREENING FOR SCHOOL CHILDREN

Colman McGrath*
The University of Hong Kong, China

ABSTRACT

Oral disease and disorders remain the most common health problems encountered in childhood. Screening for schoolchildren's oral health is described, focusing on assessments of dental caries experience and periodontal disease (including various oral hygiene indices and gingival health indices). In addition, consideration is given to the assessment of dental fluorosis/ enamel defect, which is important to monitor, especially in areas with fluoridated water supplies. For completeness, key indices of orthodontic treatment needs are outlined.

The aim is to provide a useful resource of 'what to' and 'how to' screen for schoolchildren's oral health.

INTRODUCTION

Oral disease and disorders remain the most common health problems of childhood. Moreover, oral health has considerable impact on children's day-to-day lives and quality of life, and that of their families (McGrath, Broder, &Wilson-Genderson, 2004). In addition, oral health problems can impact on general (or systemic) health and the dental management of children with specific systemic health problems requires special consideration (Meechan & Welbury, 1996).

To this end, numerous countries around the world offer some form of 'dental services' for children which vary in terms of types of services offered and their comprehensiveness. Most often this relates to school-aged children, typically at least primary school but some extend services to secondary school children as well. Oral health screening of pre-school (or kindergarten) children is typically not conducted despite evidence that dental diseases and disorders occur in young children. Oral health screening services are usually provided

* Email: mcgrathc@hku.hk.

through public health services and are 'free' to service users or at a nominal charge. An important underlying component is screening for dental diseases and disorders – oral health screening for schoolchildren.

This chapter outlines important and commonly employed assessment measures (or indices) of screening for oral health among schoolchildren. While attempts were made to cover the range of common oral health problems, it is acknowledged that within a single chapter some limitations in the breath of screening tools covered within some aspects of oral health exist. Nonetheless, this chapter is intended to be a useful resource when considering the particulars of screening schoolchildren's oral health.

Dental Caries Status

In assessing dental carries status among children, the most widely used approach is to determine the number of decayed (D), missing (M), and filled (F) teeth (DMFT) among permanent teeth to provide an assessment of dental caries experience (Klein, Palmer, & Knutson, 1938). DMFT quantifies a person's lifetime experience of dental caries in the permanent dentition. It is calculated either for 28 (permanent) teeth excluding third molars (18, 28, 38, and 48) or for 32 teeth.

The third edition of "Oral Health Surveys - Basic methods" recommends 32 teeth (WHO, 1987). In calculating DMFT, teeth not counted are unerupted teeth, congenitally missing teeth, supernumerary teeth, teeth removed for reasons other than dental caries, or retained primary teeth (refer to Table 1). When a carious lesion(s) exists or both carious lesion(s) and a restoration are present, the tooth is listed as decayed (D). When a tooth has been extracted due to caries, it is listed as an M (missing).

When a permanent or temporary filling is present, or when a filling is defective but not decayed, this is counted as filled (F). Teeth restored for reasons other than caries are not counted as filled. Various descriptive statistics can be produced from the DMFT index, such as percentage of children with a dental caries experience (%DMFT >0), mean DMFT and, likewise, descriptive statistics for individual components, that is, %D, mean D, %F, mean F, et cetera. In 2000, the World Health Organization (WHO) developed the significant caries index (SiC) to be used when studying DMFT scores on a global basis (Bratthall, 2000). A single population may include a number of individuals with low DMFT scores, as well as those with high scores.

Thus, a mean DMFT value may not accurately reflect the status of the population as a large proportion may be caries free. The SiC Index isolates and highlights those individuals with the highest caries values in a particular population. To calculate a SiC Index, individuals are sorted according to DMFT values and the third of the population with highest caries scores is isolated, and a mean DMFT for this subgroup is calculated which is the resulting value for the SiC Index. A more detailed index is a count of the number of decayed, missing, and filled tooth surfaces, DMFS. This considers five surfaces on the posterior teeth: buccal, lingual, mesial, distal, and occlusal; and four surfaces on anterior teeth: buccal, lingual, mesial, and distal.

Table 1. Codes and descriptors for DMFT system

Code	Description
0	A zero indicates a sound crown or root, showing no evidence of either treated or untreated caries. A crown may have defects and still be recorded as 0. Defects that can be disregarded include: white or chalky spots; discolored or rough spots that are not soft; stained enamel pits or fissures; dark, shiny, hard, pitted areas of moderate to severe fluorosis; or abraded areas.
1	One indicates a tooth with caries. A tooth with a definite cavity, undermined enamel is designated a 1. A tooth with a temporary filling, and teeth that are sealed but decayed, are also termed 1. A 1 is not assigned to any tooth in which caries is only suspected.
2	Filled teeth, with additional decay, are termed 2. No distinction is made between primary caries which is not associated with a previous filling, and secondary caries, adjacent to an existing restoration.
3	A 3 indicates a filled tooth with no decay. If a tooth has been crowned because of previous decay, that tooth is judged a 3. When a tooth has been crowned for another reason such as aesthetics or for use as a bridge abutment, a 7 is used.
4	A 4 indicates a tooth that is missing as a result of caries. When primary teeth are missing, the score should be used only if the tooth is missing prematurely. Primary teeth missing because of normal exfoliation need no recording.
5	A permanent tooth missing for any other reason than decay is given a 5. Examples are teeth extracted for orthodontia, teeth that are congenitally missing, or teeth missing because of trauma.
6	A 6 is assigned to teeth on which sealants have been placed. Teeth on which the occlusal fissure has been enlarged and a composite material placed should also be termed 6.
7	A 7 is used to indicate that the tooth is part of a fixed bridge. When a tooth has been crowned for a reason other than decay, this code is also used. Teeth that have veneers or laminates covering the facial surface are also termed 7 when there is no evidence of caries or restoration. A 7 is also used to indicate a root replaced by an implant. Teeth that have been replaced by bridge pontics are scored 4 or 5.
8	This code is used for a space with an unerupted permanent tooth where no primary tooth is present. The category does not include missing teeth. Code 8 teeth are excluded from calculations of caries.
9	Erupted teeth that cannot be examined, for example, because of orthodontic appliances.

Source: WHO Oral Health Survey Basic Methods (1997).

The list of teeth not counted is the same as for DMFT calculations, and coding of D, M, and F is also conducted in a similar way. When a carious lesion or both a carious lesion and a restoration are present, the surface is listed as decayed (D). When a tooth has been extracted due to caries, it is listed as missing (M). When a permanent or temporary filling is present, or when a filling is defective but not decayed, this surface is counted as filled (F). Surfaces restored for reasons other than caries are not counted as filled. The total count is 128 or 148 surfaces.

The 'dmf' index is a variation that is applied to the primary dentition - written in *lowercase* letters. The caries experience for a child is expressed as the total number of teeth or surfaces that are decayed (d), missing (m), or filled (f). The dmft index expresses the number of affected teeth in *primary dentition*, with scores ranging from 0 to 20 for children. The dmfs index expresses the number of affected surfaces in primary dentition (five per posterior tooth and four per anterior tooth), with a score range of 0 to 88 surfaces. A variation of this is to use the corresponding designations of 'deft' or 'defs', where 'e' indicates extracted tooth/teeth due to caries. Because of the difficulty in distinguishing between teeth extracted due to caries and those that have naturally exfoliated, missing teeth may be ignored according to some protocols. In this case, it is called the df index.

Table 2. Codes and descriptors for caries in pits and fissures

Code	Description
0	Sound
1	First visual change in enamel (seen only after prolonged air drying or restricted to within the confines of a pit or fissure)
2	Distinct visual change in enamel
3	Localized enamel breakdown (without clinical visual signs of dentinal involvement)
4	Underlying dark shadow from dentine
5	Distinct cavity with visible dentine
6	Extensive distinct cavity with visible dentine

Source: www.icdas.org.

Table 3. Codes and descriptors for caries-associated with restorations and sealants

Code	Description
0	Sound, i.e., surface not restored or sealed (use with the codes for primary caries)
1	Sealant, partial
2	Sealant, full
3	Tooth colored restoration
4	Amalgam restoration
5	Stainless steel crown
6	Porcelain or gold or PFM crown or veneer
7	Lost or broken restoration
8	Temporary restoration
9	Used for the following conditions:
	96 Tooth surface cannot be examined: surface excluded
	97 Tooth missing because of caries (tooth surfaces will be coded 97)
	98 Tooth missing for reasons other than caries (all tooth surfaces will be coded 98)
	99 Unerupted (tooth surfaces coded 99)

Source: www.icdas.org

While DMFT/DMFS/dmf/dmfs indices can provide powerful data and perspectives on dental caries, they can also present some limitations (Broadbent & Thomson, 2005). For one, researchers have noted a significant amount of inter-observer bias and variability. Other criticisms include that the values do not provide any indication as to the number of teeth at risk or data that is useful in estimating treatment needs, in that: the indices give equal weight to missing, untreated decay, or well-restored teeth; the indices do not account for teeth lost for reasons other than decay (such as periodontal disease); and they do not account for sealed teeth owing to the fact that sealants and other cosmetic restorations did not exist when this method of assessing dental caries was devised. A more recent development has been the International Caries Detection and Assessment System (ICDAS). This new paradigm for measurement of dental caries employs an evidence-based and preventively oriented approach to caries assessment, a detection and assessment system that can classify the stages of the caries process, and can be employed to support decision-making at both individual and public health levels (Ismail et al., 2007). The ICDAS detection codes for coronal caries range from 0 to 6 depending on the severity of the lesion (see Table 2). There are minor variations between the visual signs associated with each code depending on a number of factors including the surface characteristics (pits and fissures versus free smooth surfaces), whether there are adjacent teeth present (mesial and distal surfaces), and whether or not the caries is associated with a restoration or sealant.

A full description of what constitutes each code can be found on the ICDAS website (www. icdas.org). Various reporting systems can be used including the basic reporting system: no obvious decay – code 0 to 2, obvious decay – code 5 and 6, or the merged code reporting system: sound – code 0, initial stage decay – code 1 and 2, moderate decay – code 3 and 4, extensive decay 4 and 5. For caries-associated with restorations and sealants (CARS), specific detection criteria (a two-number coding system) is employed to identify restorations/sealants with the first digit, followed by the appropriate caries code (see Table 3).

ICDAS codes and descriptors described relate to clinical visual assessments. Additionally, ICDAS can be used with lesion detecting devices, such as radiographs, fiberoptic transillumination, and electronic caries monitors. Further developments on ICDAS are being considered, such as its use in detecting and assessing caries in primary teeth.

PERIODONTAL HEALTH STATUS

In assessing periodontal health status, the most widely used index is the Community Periodontal Index – CPI (Ainamo et al., 1982). Using a specially designed lightweight probe with a 0.5-mm ball tip bearing a black band between 3.5 and 5.5 mm from the ball tip, assessments on index teeth from various sextants of the mouth are examined (refer to Table 4). The mouth is divided into sextants defined by teeth numbers 18-14, 13-23, 24-28, 38-34, 33-43, and 44-48. A sextant should be examined only if there are two or more teeth present and not indicated for extraction. When only one tooth remains in a sextant, it is included in the adjacent sextant. In the case of children, this is an unlikely event. For young people up to the age of 19 years, only six teeth - 16, 11, 26, 36, 31, and 46 - are examined. This modification is made in order to avoid classifying the deepened crevices associated with eruption as periodontal pockets. For the same reason, when examining children under the age of 15, recording for pockets should not be attempted, that is, only bleeding and calculus should be considered. If no index tooth is present in a sextant qualifying for examination, single fully erupted incisors or premolars may be substituted.

An index tooth should be probed, using the probe as a "sensing" instrument to determine pocket depth and to detect subgingival calculus and bleeding response. The sensing force used should be no more than 20 grams. A practical test for establishing this force is to place the probe point under the thumb nail and press until blanching occurs. For sensing subgingival calculus, the lightest possible force that will allow movement of the probe ballpoint along the tooth surface should be used. When inserting the probe, the ballpoint should follow the anatomical configuration of the surface of the tooth root. If the child feels pain during probing, this is indicative of the use of too much force.

Table 4. Codes and descriptors for the Community Periodontal Index

Code	Description*
4	pocket > 6 mm (black area of probe not visible)
3	pocket 4 or 5 mm (gingival margin situated on black area of probe)
2	calculus felt during probing but all the black area visible
1	bleeding observed, directly or by using mouth mirror, after sensing
0	healthy

*Note: For children under the age of 15, recording of pockets should not be attempted, i.e., only bleeding and calculus should be considered.

Table 5. Codes and descriptors for the Periodontal Index (PI)

Code	Description
0	Negative. Neither overt inflammation nor loss of function caused by the destruction of supporting tissue is noted.
1	Mild Gingivitis. Overt inflammation in the free gingiva is present, but does not circumscribe the tooth.
2	Gingivitis. Inflammation surrounds the tooth, but there is no apparent break in the epithelial attachment.
6	Gingivitis with pocket formation. The epithelial attachment of gum to tooth is broken. There is no interference with normal function. The tooth is not loose or drifting.
8	Advanced destruction with loss of function. The tooth may be loose or drifting. It may sound dull on percussion and may be depressible in the socket.

Source: O'Heir & Suvan (1997).

The probe tip should be inserted gently into the gingival pocket and the depth of insertion read against the color coding. The total extent of the pocket should be explored. At least six points on each tooth should be examined: mesio-buccal, mid-buccal, disto-buccal, and the corresponding lingual sites. The incisor and either the first molars (up to 19 years) should be sensed (six sites per tooth) and the highest score recorded. A single CPI score is used to define the periodontal health status of the child/young person, that is, the highest CPI score at any site from and index teeth from all sextants (i.e., if even at only one site calculus was detected then the child's CPI score is 2).

The Periodontal Index (PI) was developed by Russell (1956) specifically to determine the periodontal disease status of populations in epidemiologic studies. Each tooth is scored according to the condition of the surrounding tissues and assigned a score using the following criteria noted in Table 5. Scores for each tooth are added, and the total divided by the number of teeth examined. Scores can be interpreted as follows: 0-0.2 clinically normal supportive tissues; 0.3-0.9 simple gingivitis; 0.7-1.9 beginning destructive periodontal disease; 1.6-5.0 established destructive periodontal disease; and 3.8-8.0 terminal periodontal disease.

There are a plethora of other periodontal indices that are used to varying degrees in screening children's periodontal conditions but in reality they are proxy assessments as they are more concerned with assessment of oral hygiene and plaque deposition than periodontal health status per se. Nonetheless, a description of commonly used indices is provided for comprehensiveness.

Oral Hygiene Indices

The Oral Hygiene Index (OHI), developed by Greene and Vermillion (1960), has two components, the debris index (DI) and the calculus index (CI), and is an assessment of oral cleanliness. For DI, debris is defined as soft, foreign matter consisting of bacterial plaque and food debris. The criteria include: 0 - no debris or stain present; 1 - debris covering not more than one-third of the tooth surface or extrinsic stain without debris; 2 - debris covering between one- and two-thirds of the tooth surface; and 3 - debris covering more than two-thirds of the tooth surface. For the CI component, four criteria are considered in recoding calculus: 0 - no calculus present; 1 - supragingival calculus present covering not more than one third of the tooth surface; 2 - supragingival calculus covering between one- and two-thirds of the tooth surface, or scattered subgingival calculus; and 3 - supragingival calculus covering more than two-thirds of the tooth surface, or a continuous heavy band of subgingival calculus around the tooth. The DI and CI can be used singly or in combination.

The dentition is considered by individual sextant; and the tooth that is covered with the greatest amount of debris and calculus on the buccal and lingual tooth surface is examined (12 surfaces in total) - a surface includes half the circumference of the tooth. The DI and CI scores are derived by dividing the total scores for each tooth by the number of sextants. The OHI score is comprised of the DI added to the CI score which can range from 0 -12. Green and Vermillion (1964) developed a simplified OHI index (OHI-S) in which assessments are conducted only on one tooth surface in each sextant: buccal surface of 16, 11, 26, 31, and lingual surface of 36 and 46. In the OHI-S, scores can range from 0 to 6.

The Plaque Index (PLI) was developed by Silness and Löe (1964) and assesses the thickness of plaque at the cervical margin of the tooth closest to the gum. Four areas, distal, buccal, mesial, and lingual, are examined on six index teeth 16, 12, 24, 36, 32, and 44. Each tooth is dried and examined visually using a mirror and explorer probe with adequate light. The explorer is passed over the cervical third to test for the presence of plaque. Four different scores are possible: 0 indicates no plaque present; 1 indicates a film of plaque present on the tooth; 2 represents moderate accumulation of soft deposits in the gingival pocket or on the tooth that can be seen by the naked eye; and 3 represents an abundance of soft matter within the pocket or on the tooth. Each area of each tooth is assigned a score from 0 to 3. Scores for each tooth are summated and divided by the four surfaces scored. To determine a total PLI score for an individual, the scores for each tooth are summated and divided by the number of teeth examined. Scores can be interpreted as follows: 'excellent' (score 0), 'good' (score 0.1-0.9), 'fair' (score 1.0-1.9), or 'poor' (score 2.0-3.0).

A similar system for measuring plaque has been described by O'Leary, Drake, and Naylor (1972). This system measures plaque present but no attempt is made to differentiate the quantity of plaque seen on each surface. The number of surfaces examined can be four or six. The four-surface format considers three buccal sites (disto-buccal, mid-buccal, and mesio-buccal) and one lingual site (mid-lingual). When using the six-surface format, the buccal, mesio-buccal, mesio-lingual, lingual, disto-lingual, and disto-buccal are assessed. To determine an individual's score, the number of surfaces with plaque is divided by the number of tooth surfaces examined and multiplied by 100. A score under 10% is considered good.

Other plaque indices include the Quigley-Hein index (1962) with subsequent modification (Turesky, Gilmore, & Glickman, 1970) to assess the quantity of plaque at each site - buccal and lingual of all teeth. Each site is scored: 0 = no plaque; 1 = separate flecks of plaque; 2 = continuous band to 1 mm; 3 = >1mm and <1/3 of tooth surface; 4 = >1/3 and <2/3; 5 = >2/3 of tooth covered with plaque.

Gingival Indices

A widely used measure is the Gingival Index (GI, Löe & Silness, 1963) that assesses the severity of gingivitis based on color, consistency, and bleeding. The mesial, distal, buccal, and lingual surfaces on each tooth are considered separately. Full mouth or selected teeth (index teeth) can be assessed and scoring is: 0 - healthy (normal); 1 - inflamed appearances but no bleeding on probing (mild inflammation, slight color change and edema, no bleeding); 2 - appears inflamed and bleeds when pressure applied on gingival margin with a periodontal probe (moderate inflammation, redness, edema, bleeds on probing); 3 - spontaneous bleeding upon application of pressure with periodontal probe (severe inflammation, marked redness and edema, ulceration, spontaneous bleeding).

A modified version of the Gingival Index (mGI) was developed subsequently (Löe, 1967) to be more sensitive in the lower portion of the scale, and to be non-invasive as it excludes the bleeding on probing component. Scores include: 0 - healthy (absence of inflammation); 1 - mild inflammation (slight change in color, little change in texture of the marginal or papillary gingival unit); 2 - moderate inflammation (glazing, redness, edema, and/or hypertrophy of the marginal or papillary gingivae); and 4 - severe inflammation (marked redness, edema and/or hypertrophy of the marginal or papillary gingivae, spontaneous bleeding, congestion or ulceration).

Another used measure is the Papilla, Marginal and Attached Gingival Index, which was designed to measure gingivitis among children (Schour & Massler, 1947). The papilla (P) is rated on a 0 to 5 point scale: 0 - no inflammation to 5 - atrophy and loss of papilla through inflammation; margin (M) is rated on a 0 to 5 point scale: 0 - no inflammation to 5 - recession of the free marginal gingivae below the cemento-enamel junction due to inflammatory changes; attached gingivae (A) is rated on a 0 to 3 point scale: 0 - normal (pale, pink, scalloped) to 3 - advanced periodontitis (deep pockets evident).

A number of gingival bleeding indices exist. The Sulcus Bleed Index (SBI, Mühlemann & Son, 1971) considers bleeding from sulcus after probing and four sites per tooth are scored: 0 - no bleeding on probing; 1 - bleeding on probing but no change in color or contour; 2 - bleeding on probing and erythema; 3- bleeding on probing with erythema and mild edema; 4 - bleeding on probing with erythema and severe edema; and 5 - spontaneous bleeding on probing, severe edema with or without ulceration. The Papilla Bleeding Index (PBI, Mühlemann, 1977) assesses only the interdental papilla and scoring is 1 - a single point of bleeding is observed 20-30 seconds after probing; 2 - shortly after probing a fine line of blood or several bleeding points are visible at the gingival margin; 3 - shortly after probing the interdental triangle becomes basically filled with blood; and 4 - profuse bleeding immediately after probing filling the interdental area.

The Gingival Bleeding Index Floss (GBI floss) assesses interproximal bleeding using floss (Carter & Barnes, 1974). Score 0 represent absence of bleeding within 10 seconds of passing floss through gingival crevice; score 1 represents presence of bleeding within 10 seconds of passing floss into gingival crevice.

The Gingival Bleeding Index Probe (GBI probe) assesses bleeding on probing at four or six surfaces on all or index teeth (Ainamo & Bay, 1975). A score 0 is assigned when there is no bleeding within 10 seconds of gentle probing of the gingival crevice with a periodontal probe; and a score of 1 is given when bleeding is seen within 10 seconds of gentle probing of the gingival crevice with a periodontal probe. The Eastman Interdental Bleeding Index (EIBI; Caton & Folson, 1985) utilizes triangular shaped toothpicks of soft pliable wood and they are inserted four times horizontally between teeth from the buccal surface, depressing the interproximal tissue up to 2mm. A score of 0 is given if no bleeding is observed within 15 seconds of interproximal toothpick insertion; a score of 1 if interdental bleeding is seen within 15 seconds of toothpick insertion.

FLUOROSIS AND ENAMEL DEFECTS

Dental fluorosis is a developmental disturbance of dental enamel caused by excessive exposure to high concentrations of fluoride during tooth development. The risk of fluoride overexposure occurs between the ages of 3 months and 8 years. The appearance can vary from hardly noticeable white specks/ spots/ lines to brown markings or pitted enamel.

Dean (1934) developed a fluorosis index which classified individuals into five categories, depending on the degree of enamel alteration, and which is based on the identification of the two most severely affected teeth. This index was subsequently modified over time to its current format, shown in Table 6.

To determine the severity of dental fluorosis as a public health problem, Dean et al. (1935) subsequently devised a method of calculating the prevalence and severity of fluorosis in a group or community, referred to as the Community Fluorosis Index, by applying a weighting to components: 0 - normal, 0.5 - questionable, 1.0 - very mild, 2.0 - mild, 3.0 - moderate, and 4.0 - severe.

Thylstrup and Fejerskov (1978) developed an index (T-F) based on the biological aspects of dental fluorosis, classifying individuals into 10 categories characterizing the macroscopic degree of fluorosis in relation to histological aspects, and shown in Table 7. In the original classification, buccal, occlusal and lingual surfaces of all teeth are examined.

Table 6. Codes and descriptors for Dean's Index of Fluorosis

Code	Description
Normal (0)	Smooth, glossy, pale creamy-white translucent surface
Questionable (1)	A few white flecks or white spots
Very Mild (2)	Small opaque, paper white areas covering less than 25% of the tooth surface
Mild (3)	Opaque white areas covering less than 50% of the tooth surface
Moderate (4)	All tooth surfaces affected; marked wear on biting surfaces; brown stain may be present
Severe (5)	All tooth surfaces affected; discrete or confluent pitting; brown stain present

Table 7. Codes and descriptors for Thylstrup and Fejerskov Index of Fluorosis

Code	Description
0	Normal translucency of enamel remains after prolonged air-drying.
1	Narrow white lines corresponding to the perikymata.
2	*Smooth surfaces:* More pronounced lines of opacity that follow the perikymata. Occasionally confluence of adjacent lines. *Occlusal surfaces:* Scattered areas of opacity <2 mm in diameter and pronounced opacity of cuspal ridges.
3	*Smooth surfaces:* Merging and irregular cloudy areas of opacity. Accentuated drawing of perikymata often visible between opacities. *Occlusal surfaces:* Confluent areas of marked opacity. Worn areas appear almost normal but usually circumscribed by a rim of opaque enamel.
4	*Smooth surfaces:* The entire surface exhibits marked opacity or appears chalky white. Parts of surface exposed to attrition appear less affected. *Occlusal surfaces:* Entire surface exhibits marked opacity. Attrition is often pronounced shortly after eruption.
5	*Smooth surfaces and occlusal surfaces:* Entire surface displays marked opacity with focal loss of outermost enamel (pits) <2 mm in diameter.
6	*Smooth surfaces:* Pits are regularly arranged in horizontal bands <2 mm in vertical extension. *Occlusal surfaces:* Confluent areas <3 mm in diameter exhibit loss of enamel. Marked attrition.
7	*Smooth surfaces:* Loss of outermost enamel in irregular areas involving <1/2 of entire surface. *Occlusal surfaces:* Changes in the morphology caused by merging pits and marked attrition.
8	*Smooth and occlusal surfaces:* Loss of outermost enamel involving >1/2 of surface.
9	*Smooth and occlusal surfaces:* Loss of main part of enamel with change in anatomic appearance of surface. Cervical rim of almost unaffected enamel is often noted.

Table 8. Codes and descriptors for Tooth Surface Index of Fluorosis

Code	Description
0	Enamel shows no evidence of fluorosis.
1	Enamel shows definite evidence of fluorosis, namely areas with parchment-white color-that total less than one-third of the visible enamel surface. This category includes fluorosis confined only to incisal edges of anterior teeth and cusp tips of posterior teeth ("snowcapping").
2	Parchment-white fluorosis totals at least one-third of the visible surface, but less than two-thirds.
3	Parchment-white fluorosis totals at least two-thirds of the visible surface.
4	Enamel shows staining in conjunction with any of the preceding levels of fluorosis. Staining is defined as an area of definite discoloration that may range from light to very dark brown.
5	Discrete pitting of the enamel exists, unaccompanied by evidence of staining of intact enamel. A pit is defined as a definite physical defect in the enamel surface with a rough floor that is surrounded by a wall of intact enamel. The pitted area is usually stained or differs in color from the surrounding enamel.
6	Both discrete pitting and staining of the intact enamel exist.
7	Confluent pitting of the enamel surface exists. Large areas of enamel may be missing and the anatomy of the tooth may be altered. Dark-brown stain is usually present.

Source: Horowitz et al. (1984).

Horowitz, Driscoll, Meyers, Heifetz, and Kingsman (1984) developed a fluorosis index based on aesthetic aspects of tooth surfaces, the Tooth Surface Index of Fluorosis (TSIF), which classifies individuals into eight categories (as seen in Table 8). In this index, a value is given for each anterior tooth surface not restored (buccal and lingual) and three values for posterior tooth surfaces (buccal, lingual, and occlusal). The highest code is ascribed to the individual.

After reviewing previous studies and classifications of developmental defects of enamel, the working group of the World Dental Federation (FDI) Commission on Oral Health, Research and Epidemiology, proposed a descriptive index, known as the Index of Developmental Defects of Enamel (FDI DDE Index, 1982). Subsequently, a modified version of the index was developed (FDI, 1992). Although the system was designed for full-mouth assessment, it can also be adapted for partial mouth examinations. As the classification is based on descriptive criteria it can record any enamel defect on a person, tooth, or tooth surface basis, as outlined in Table 9.

Moreover, the recording system allows investigators to record the information on the type, number, extent, and location of the enamel defects. The use of a set of color prints which demonstrate each type of defect recognized by the classification can be used to aid screening.

Table 9. Codes and descriptors for the modified FDI Index of Developmental Defects of Enamel

Score	Category	Description
0	Normal	
1	Demarcated opacity	A defect which involves an alteration in the translucency. The defective enamel is of normal thickness with a smooth surface. It has a distinct and clear boundary with the adjacent normal enamel. Some maintain a surface translucency while others are dull in appearance.
2	Diffuse opacity	An abnormality which involves an alteration in the translucency of the enamel. The defective enamel is of normal thickness and at eruption has a relative smooth surface and is white in color. It has no clear boundary with the adjacent normal enamel.
3	Hypoplasia	A defect which involves the surface of the enamel and is associated with a reduced localized thickness of enamel. The enamel of reduced thickness could be translucent or opaque.
4	Other defects	

Source: World Health Organization (1997).

Malocclusion and Orthodontic Treatment Need

In the assessment of malocclusion, occlusal indices can be categorized according to (i) diagnostic indices, (ii) epidemiological indices, (iii) orthodontic treatment indices, (iv) orthodontic treatment outcome indices, and (v) orthodontic treatment complexity indices (Borzabadi-Farahani, 2011). Since a key concern in screening is ability to identify 'treatment need', the following section will focus on orthodontic treatment indices.

The Handicapping Labio-lingual Deviation index (HLD) was developed in the 1960s with several subsequent modifications. Various attributes of malocclusion are considered along with prescribed weightings in deriving an overall score with defined cut-off points indicating treatment need.

The most recent version, referred to as the California HLD or HLD (CalMod), was derived by Parker (1998) and considers 12 factors: overjet, overbite, open bite, cleft lip-palate, anterior crowding, mandibular protrusion, labio-lingual spread, deep impinging overbite, severe traumatic deviations, crossbite of individual anterior teeth, ectopic eruption of anterior teeth, and posterior unilateral crossbite (Table 10).

Conditions 1 to 6 are qualifying attributes and, if present, further scoring is not needed and subjects are deemed to have a treatment need. Otherwise, the sum of other conditions (7-14) must be 26 or above to be considered as a "handicapping malocclusion"; although there are variations as to cut-off value..

Table 10. Codes and descriptors of the Handicapping Labio-lingual Deviation Index

Code	Description	Score
1	Cleft palate deformity	Qualifying attribute
2	Cranio-facial anomaly	Qualifying attribute
3	Deep impinging overbite When the lower incisors are destroying the soft tissue of the palate. Tissue laceration and/or clinical attachment loss must be present.	Qualifying attribute
4	Crossbite of individual anterior teeth when clinical attachment loss and recession of the gingival margin are present.	Qualifying attribute
5	Severe traumatic deviations Attach a description of condition, i.e., loss of a premaxilla by burn, trauma, or pathology.	Qualifying attribute
6	Overjet greater than 9 mm Reverse overjet greater than 3.5 mm	Qualifying attribute
7	Overjet ($\leq$9 mm)	__(mm)
8	Overbite including the reverse overbite	__(mm)
9	Mandibular protrusion (reverse overjet $\leq$ 3.5 mm)	__(mm) x 5
10	Open bite	__(mm) x 4
11	Ectopic eruption: Count each tooth, excluding third molars	(count) x 3
12	Anterior crowding: Score one point for the maxilla, and/or one point for mandible; two points maximum for anterior crowding.	(1,or 2) x 5
13	Labio-Lingual spread, Arch length insufficiency must exceed 3.5 mm excluding mild rotations that may react favorably to stripping or mild expansion procedures.	__(mm)
14	Posterior unilateral crossbite Must involve two or more adjacent teeth, one of which must be a molar and not including the posterior bilateral crossbite.	+4
		Total score =

All measurements are recorded in the order given and rounded off to the nearest millimeter (mm). If both anterior crowding and ectopic eruption are present in the anterior portion of the mouth, the most severe condition will be scored, not both conditions. Overjet is recorded with the patient's teeth in centric occlusion and measured from the labial portion of the lower incisors to the labial of the upper incisors. The Dental Aesthetic Index (DAI; Cons, Jenny, & Kohout, 1986) assesses malocclusion severity from which various cut-off points have been suggested to be indicative of treatment need (refer to Table 11). Widely used cut off values are: ≤ 25 normal / minor - no treatment need / slight need; 26-30 definite - treatment elective; 31-35 severe - treatment highly desirable; ≥ 36 very severe / handicapping - treatment mandatory. The WHO Oral Health Survey Methods recognized the DAI as a cross-cultural index (1997).

The Index of Orthodontic Treatment Need (IOTN) and The Swedish Medical Board Index (SMBI) have many similarities in that the former was developed based on the latter. The IOTN is one of the most commonly used occlusal indices that assess orthodontic treatment need among children and adults.

The IOTN has two separate components, a clinical component called the Dental Health Component (DHC) and an Aesthetic Component (AC). AC consists of a 10-point scale illustrated by a series of photographs arranged from the most attractive to the least attractive (judged to be equidistantly spaced on the scale). In its original form: Grades 1-4 represent no or little need, grades 5, 6, and 7 represent borderline need, and grades 8, 9, and 10 represent a clear need for treatment on aesthetic grounds. However, different cut-off points have been suggested in different settings.

Table 11. Descriptors and scoring of Dental Aesthetic Index

Description	Score
No. of visibly missing teeth: incisors, canines, and premolars in the maxillary and mandibular arches	x 6
Assessment of incisal segment crowding (0, 1, or 2): 0 = no segment crowded; 1 = 1 segment crowded; 2 = 2 segments crowded	x 2
Assessment of incisal segment spacing (0, 1, or 2): 0 = no segment spaced; 1 = 1 segment spaced; 2 = 2 segments spaced	x 1
Diastema (mm)*	x 3
Largest anterior maxillary irregularity (mm)**	x 1
Largest anterior mandibular irregularity (mm)**	x 1
Anterior maxillary overjet (mm)***	x 2
Anterior mandibular overjet (mm)***	x 4
Vertical anterior open bite (mm)***	x 4
Assessment of antero-posterior molar relation:*** Largest deviation from normal either left or right: 0 = normal; 1 = ½ cusp either mesial or distal; 2 = full cusp or more either mesial or distal	x 3
Constant	13
Total DAI Score =	

* Largest measurement; ** Site of greatest rotations or displacement from normal arch alignment; *** Measured with teeth in centric occlusion.

Table 12. Scoring and descriptors of the Index of Orthodontic Treatment Need

Grade 5 Very great need	
5i:	Impeded eruption of teeth (with the exception of third molars) due to crowding, displacement, the presence of supernumerary teeth, retained deciduous teeth, and any pathological cause.
5h:	Extensive hypodontia with restorative implications (more than one tooth missing in any quadrant) requiring pre-restorative orthodontics.
5a:	Increased overjet > 9 mm.
5m:	Reverse overjet greater than 3.5 mm with reported masticatory and speech difficulties.
5p:	Defect of cleft lip and palate/craniofacial anomalies.
5s:	Submerged deciduous teeth.
Grade 4 Great need	
4h:	Less extensive hypodontia requiring pre-restorative orthodontics or orthodontic space closure to obviate the need for a prosthesis.
4a:	Increased overjet > 6 mm but ≤ 9 mm.
4b:	Reverse overjet > 3.5 mm with no masticatory or speech difficulties.
4m:	Reverse overjet greater than 1 mm but ≤ 3.5 mm with recorded masticatory and speech difficulties.
4c:	Anterior or posterior crossbites with > 2 mm discrepancy between retruded contact position and intercuspal position.
4l:	Posterior lingual crossbite (scissors bite) with no functional occlusal contact in one or both buccal segments.
4d:	Severe contact point displacements of teeth > 4 mm.
4e:	Extreme lateral or anterior open bites > 4 mm.
4f:	Increased and complete overbite with gingival or palatal trauma.
4t:	Partially erupted teeth, tipped and impacted against adjacent teeth.
4x:	Presence of supernumerary (e.g., supplemental teeth).
Grade 3 Borderline need	
3a:	Increased overjet > 3.5 mm but ≤ 6 mm with incompetent lips.
3b:	Reverse overjet greater than 1 mm but ≤ 3.5 mm.
3c:	Anterior or posterior crossbites with >1 mm but ≤ 2 mm discrepancy between retruded contact position and intercuspal position.
3d:	Contact point displacement of teeth > 2 mm but ≤ 4 mm.
3e:	Lateral or anterior open bite greater than 2 mm but ≤ 4 mm.
3f:	Increased and complete overbite without gingival or palatal trauma.
Grade 2 Little need	
2a:	Increased overjet > 3.5 mm ≤ 6mm with competent lips.
2b:	Reverse overjet > 0 mm but ≤ 1mm.
2c:	Anterior or posterior crossbite with ≤ 1 mm discrepancy between retruded contact position and intercuspal position.
2d:	Contact point displacement of teeth >1 mm but ≤ 2 mm.
2e:	Anterior or posterior open bite > 1 mm but ≤ 2mm.
2f:	Increased overbite ≥ 3.5 mm without gingival contact.
2g:	Pre-normal or post-normal occlusions with no other anomalies. Includes up to half a unit discrepancy.
Grade 1 No need.	Extremely minor malocclusions including displacements ≤ 1 mm.

Table 13. Scoring and descriptors of the Swedish Medical Board Index

Grade	Description
4	Very urgent need Aesthetically and/or functionally handicapping anomalies, such as cleft lip and palate, extreme post-normal or pre-normal occlusion, retained upper incisors, extensive aplasia.
3	Urgent need Pre-normal forced bite, deep bite with gingival irritation not only on papilla incisiva, large overjet with lower lip behind upper centrals, extremely open bite, crossbite causing transverse forced bite, scissors bite interfering with articulation, severe frontal crowding or spacing, retained canines, aesthetically and/or functionally disturbing rotations.
2	Moderate need Aesthetically and/or functionally disturbing proclined or retroclined incisors, deep bite with gingival contact but without gingival irritation, severe crowding or spacing, infraocclusion of deciduous molars and permanent teeth, moderate frontal rotations.
1	Little need Mild deviations from normal (ideal) occlusion, such as prenormal occlusion with little negative overjet, post-normal occlusion without other anomalies, deep bite without gingival contact, open bite with little frontal opening, crossbite without a forced bite, mild crowding or spacing, mild rotations of only little aesthetic and/or functional significance.
0	No need Normal (ideal) occlusion without deviations.

Source: Swedish Medical Health Board, 1966.

The DHC is a hierarchical scale that assesses missing teeth, overjet, crossbite, displacement, and overbite to derive a five-grade scale with 30 subcategories (Table 12). If two or more occlusal anomalies achieve the same DHC grade, the occlusal anomaly with higher rank is recoded for the subject. There are discrepancies sometimes between the DHC and AC grading of treatment need. The DHC and AC can be applied clinically and on study casts, although the protocol of assessment differs and assumes the worst case scenario (Richmond, Roberts & Andrews, 1994).

A modified version of the IOTN (Burden, Pine, & Burnside, 2001) has been proposed to simplify scoring into a two-grade scale: need or no definite need; every case with IOTN DHC ≥4 and/or IOTN AC ≥ 8 is classified as treatment need. This has obvious advantages for epidemiological and screening studies.

The Swedish Medical Board Index (SMBI, Linder-Aronson, 1974; Swedish Medical Health Board, 1966) considers similar attributes to the IOTN (given that the latter was developed based on the former). The SMBI calls for the subjective views (patient's perceptions) to be considered when deciding on the treatment need (Mockbil & Huggare, 2009). See Table 13 for scoring details.

The Index of Complexity, Outcome, and Need (ICON) is a single assessment method to measure the orthodontic treatment complexity, outcome, and need (Daniels & Richmond, 2000). The ICON is unique in incorporating an aesthetic score (refer to Table 14) as an integral part of the treatment need evaluation. Assessment of upper arch crowding/spacing is considered as well as crossbite, openbite/overbite, and buccal segment relationship.

Table 14. Scoring and descriptors of the Index of Complexity, Outcome and Need (ICON)

	Component	Score						Weight
1	Aesthetic Component	AC score 1-10						x 7
2*		0	1	2	3	4	5	
	Upper arch Crowding	<2mm	2.1-5mm	5.1-9mm	9.1-13mm	13.1-17mm	>17mm	x 5
	Upper arch Spacing	<2mm	2.1-5mm	5.1-9mm	>9mm		Impacted tooth	x 5
3								
	Crossbite	no	yes					x 5
4**								
	Incisor open bite	Edge to edge	<1mm	1.1-2mm	2.1-4mm	>4mm		x 4
	Incisor overbite	< 1/3 lower incisor coverage	1/3 to 2/3 incisor coverage	2/3 incisor coverage	Fully covered			x 4
5***								
	Buccal segment	Cusp to embrasure, Class I-III	Any cusp relationship up to cusp to cusp	Cusp to cusp				x 3

*The difference between the sum of the mesio-distal tooth diameters and the available arch circumference in the upper arch is recorded on a 5-point score. Impacted teeth (score 5) must be unerupted and either ectopic or have less than 4 mm of space between adjacent permanent teeth. Retained deciduous teeth (without permanent successor), erupted supernumerary teeth, or lost teeth due to trauma are counted as space, unless they are to be maintained and obviate the need for prosthetic replacement or space is maintained for a prosthetic replacement (i.e., tooth lost in trauma).

** If both anterior open bite and deep bite are present only the highest score is counted.

***Quality of buccal segment interdigitation, not the Angle Classification, is measured on both sides then added together.

Source: Daniels & Richmond (2000).

Conclusion

A description of the key clinical indices used in screening oral health among schoolchildren has been outlined. The focus has been on the key clinical parameters and 'how to' use the indices. It should be borne in mind that the decision to employ specific screening indices will depend on the local context and specific aims of the screening. In addition, while clinical assessments of oral health status are of key importance to screening children's oral health, it is acknowledged that the subjective measures of oral health to assess the impact of oral health on children's lives are also important but it is beyond the scope of this chapter to consider these in depth.

References

Ainamo, J., Barmes, D., Beagrie, G., Cutress, T., Martin, J., & Sardo-Infirri, J. (1982). Development of the World Health Organization (WHO) community periodontal index of treatment needs (CPITN). *International Dental Journal,* 32(3), 281-291.

Ainamo, J., & Bay, I. (1975). Problems and proposals for recording gingivitis and plaque. *International Dental Journal,* 25, 229-235.

Borzabadi-Farahani, A. (2011). An insight into four orthodontic treatment need indices. *Progress in Orthodontics*, 12(2), 132-142.

Bratthall, D. (2000). Introducing the Significant Caries Index together with a proposal for a new global oral health goal for 12-year-olds. *International Dental Journal*, 50(6), 378-384.

Broadbent, J. M., & Thomson, W. M. (2005). For debate: Problems with the DMF index pertinent to dental caries data analysis. *Community Dentistry Oral Epidemiology,* 33(6), 400-409.

Burden, D. J., Pine, C. M., & Burnside, G. (2001). Modified IOTN: An orthodontic treatment need index for use in oral health surveys. *Community Dentistry Oral Epidemiology*, 29, 220-225.

Carter, H. G., & Barnes, G. P. (1974). The Gingival Bleeding Index. *Journal of Periodontology,* 45, 801-805.

Caton, J. G., & Polson, A. M. (1985). The interdental bleeding index: A simplified procedure for monitoring gingival health. *Compendium Continuing Education in Dentistry,* 88, 90-92.

Cons, N. C., Jenny, J., & Kohout, F. J. (1986). *DAI:* The dental aesthetic index. College of Dentistry, Iowa City, IA: University of Iowa.

Daniels, C., & Richmond, S. (2000). The development of the index of complexity, outcome and need (ICON). *Journal of Orthodontics,* 27, 149-162.

Dean, H.T. (1934). Classification of mottled enamel diagnosis. *Journal of the American Dental Association*, 21, 1421-1426.

Dean H.T., & Elvove, E. (1935). Studies on the minimal threshold of the dental sign of chronic endemic fluorosis (mottled enamel). *Public Health Reports*, 50, 1719-1721.

FDI Commission on Oral Health, Research and Epidemiology. (1982). An epidemiological index of development defects of dental enamel (DDE Index). *International Dental Journal*, 32, 159-167.

FDI Commission on Oral Health, Research and Epidemiology. (1992). A review of the developmental defects of enamel index (DDE Index). *International Dental Journal,* 42, 411-426.

Greene, J. C., & Vermillion, J. R. (1960). Oral Hygiene Index. *Journal of the American Dental Association,* 61, 172-179.

Greene, J. C., & Vermillion, J. R. (1964). The simplified oral hygiene index. *Journal of the American Dental Association,* 68, 7-13.

Horowitz, H. S., Driscoll, W. S., Meyers, R. J., Heifetz, S. B., & Kingman, A. (1984). A new method for assessing the prevalence of dental fluorosis-the Tooth Surface Index of Fluorosis. *Journal of American Dental Association,* 109, 37-41.

Ismail, A. I., Sohn, W., Tellez, M., Amaya, A., Sen, A., Hasson, H., & Pitts, N.B. (2007). The International Caries Detection and Assessment System (ICDAS): An integrated system for measuring dental caries. *Community Dentistry Oral Epidemiology,* 35(3), 170-178.

Klein, H., Palmer, C. E., & Knutson, J. W. (1938). Dental status and dental needs of elementary school children. *Public Health Reports*, 53, 751-765.

Linder-Aronson, S. (1974). Orthodontics in the Swedish Public Dental Health Service. *Transactions of the European Orthodontic Society*, 1974: 233-240.

Löe, H. (1967). The Gingival Index, the Plaque Index and the Retention Index Systems. *Journal of Periodontology,* 38 (Suppl), 610-616.

Löe, H., & Silness, J. (1963). Periodontal disease in pregnancy I. Prevalence and severity. *Acta Odontologica Scandinavica*, 21, 533-551.

McGrath, C., Broder, H., & Wilson-Genderson, M. (2004). Assessing the impact of oral health on the life quality of children: Implications for research and practice. *Community Dentistry Oral Epidemiology*, 32(2), 81-85.

McGrath, C., Broder, H., & Wilson-Genderson, M. (2004). Assessing the impact of oral health on the life quality of children: Implications for research and practice. *Community Dentistry Oral Epidemiology*, 32(2), 81-85.

Meechan, J. G., & Welbury, R. R. (1996). Medical problems affecting the management of children in dentistry. *Dental Update,* 23(6), 242-245.

Mockbil, N., & Huggare, J. (2009). Uniformity in selection for subsidized orthodontic care-focus on borderline treatment need. *Swedish Dental Journal,* 33, 19-25.

Mühlemann, H. R. (1977). Psychological and chemical mediators of gingival health. *Journal of Preventive Dentistry,* 4, 6-17.

Mühlemann, H. R., & Son, S. (1971). Gingival sulcus bleeding - a leading symptom in initial gingivitis. *Helvetica Odontologica Acta,* 15, 107-113.

O'Heir, T. E., & Suvan, J. (1997). Perio reports: Compendium of current research. Arizona: Modern Press.

O'Leary, T. J., Drake, R. B., & Naylor, J. E. (1972). The plaque control record. *Journal of Periodontology*, 43, 38.

Parker, W. S. (1998). The HLD (CalMod) index and the index question. *American Journal of Orthodontics and Dentofacial Orthopedics,* 114, 134-141.

Quigley, G. A., & Hein, J. W. (1962). Comparative cleansing efficiency of manual and power brushing. *Journal of American Dental Association,* 65, 26-29.

Richmond, S., Roberts, C. T., & Andrews, M. (1994). Use of the Index of Orthodontic Treatment Need (IOTN) in assessing the need for orthodontic treatment pre- and post-appliance therapy. *British Journal of Orthodontics,* 21(2), 175-184.

Russell, A. (1956). A system of classification and scoring for prevalence surveys of periodontal disease. *Journal of Dental Research,* 35, 350-359.

Schour, I., & Massler, M. (1947). Gingival disease in postwar Italy (1945) prevalence of gingivitis in various age groups. *Journal of American Dental Association,* 35, 475-482.

Silness, J., & Löe, H. (1964). Periodontal disease in pregnancy. II. Correlation between oral hygiene and periodontal condition. *Acta Odontologica Scandinavica,* 22, 121-135.

Swedish Medical Health Board. (1966). Socialstyrelsen Kungl Medicinalstyrelsens circular den 21 februari 1966 angående anvisningarna för journalföring inom folktandvårdens tandregleringsvård. [National Board of the Royal Medical Board, Circular 21 February

1966 regarding guidelines for record keeping in the public dental orthodontic care system]. Stockholm, Swedish Medical Health Board.

Thylstrup, A., & Fejerskov, O. (1978). Clinical appearance of dental fluorosis in permanent teeth in relation to histologic changes. *Community Dentistry Oral Epidemiology,* 6, 315-328.

Turesky, S., Gilmore, N. D., & Glickman, I. (1970). Reduced plaque formation by the chloromethyl analogue of vitamin C. *Journal of Periodontology,* 41, 41-43.

World Health Organization (WHO). (1987). Oral health surveys: Basic methods (3rd ed.). Geneva, WHO.

World Health Organization (WHO). (1997). Oral health surveys: Basic methods (4th ed.). Geneva, WHO.

In: School Health Screening Systems
Editors: Bradley McPherson and Carlie J. Driscoll

ISBN: 978-1-63117-942-6

Chapter 7

MENTAL HEALTH SCREENING FOR SCHOOL CHILDREN

Joni Williams Splett[1*], Maura Mulloy[2], Ashley Jones Philp[3] and Mark D. Weist[4]
[1]University of South Carolina School Mental Health Team
[2]Independent Scholar, Ethiopia
[3]Richland Two School District, Columbia, SC, US
[4]University of South Carolina School Mental Health Team, US

ABSTRACT

Screening for mental health and behavioral problems in elementary schools has only recently been recommended and implementation is limited to less than 10 percent of schools. However, in the United States current multi-tiered improvement efforts in schools, including School-Wide Positive Behavior Supports (SWPBS) and Response to Intervention (RtI), have created systems that align well with principles of universal screening for mental health concerns. Both systems are based on a public health continuum model of prevention, early intervention, and treatment, and rely on ongoing data collection to monitor progress and identify students in need of additional academic and behavioral supports. As SWPBS and RtI are increasingly implemented, the use of universal screening mechanisms to identify students with emerging and identifiable mental health concerns should also increase. Therefore, the purpose of this chapter is to raise awareness of the need for mental health screening in schools, describe available screening tools, and provide a real-life, school-based example. The chapter reviews recommendations and current systems (i.e., SWPBS and RtI) for universal mental health screening in schools and identifies several factors that should be considered when selecting a screening tool, including: school and community buy-in; parental concerns and consent; selecting an appropriate tool (e.g., psychometric properties, staff resources and training, and cost); and effective administration and usage procedures (e.g., feasibility to administer, staff resources and training to score and interpret, staff resources to provide intervention). Psychometric, feasibility, and usability factors are described for

---

* splett@mailbox.sc.edu.

eight universal screening tools currently available. A case example describes how one elementary school with an ongoing behavior intervention program for students with an elevated number of office discipline referrals selected a screening tool to more accurately and comprehensively identify students in need of additional behavioral supports and monitor progress. Finally, limitations and ethical concerns for universal screening of mental health concerns in schools are discussed. As the case example illustrates, universal screening of mental health and behavioral concerns in elementary schools is most effective when utilized as part of a multi-tiered system of prevention, early intervention, and treatment services.

INTRODUCTION

Mental health screening for youth is increasingly recommended but rarely implemented (Romer & McIntosh, 2005). Research has documented a range of negative outcomes resulting from failure to identify and effectively treat mental health problems early, when they usually first manifest in childhood and adolescence (O'Connell, Boat, & Werner, 2009). In fact, data indicate that less than 50% of children presenting with mental health concerns receive treatment (Merikangas et al., 2010). Without effective treatment, youth are at an increased risk to experience multiple mental health concerns and negative life events such as academic failure, substance use, delinquency, unemployment, and incarceration across the lifespan (Moffit, 1993). At the same time, knowledge and access to effective prevention and early intervention strategies have increased, seemingly making it more likely for youth to receive needed mental health services (Greenberg, Domitrovich, & Bumbarger, 2001; for practice examples, see McIntosh, Filter, Bennett, Ryan, & Sugai, 2010 and Weist, Stiegler, Stephan, Cox, & Vaughan, 2010). However, effective identification of youth with or at-risk of developing mental health problems is crucial to achieving these results (Glover & Albers, 2007). Schools are a prime location for effectively implementing universal mental health screenings for youth given their unparalleled access advantages and current educational initiatives that align well with a public health approach to prevention and intervention (Doll & Cummings, 2008).

Recent recommendations for universal mental health screening practices have come from several professional and governmental organizations. In the U.S., over the past decade, prevention strategies including school-based universal mental health screenings were recommended in the President's New Freedom Commission (President's New Freedom Commission on Mental Health, 2003) and the President's Commission on Excellence in Special Education (U.S. Department of Education Office of Special Education and Rehabilitative Services, 2002). The Institute of Medicine (O'Connell et al., 2009), American Academy of Pediatrics (AAP; AAP, Committee on Children with Disabilities, 2001), and National Research Council (Donovan & Cross, 2002) have also recommended universal mental health screenings for youth across multiple settings, while recent legislation has more specifically called for early prevention and intervention strategies such as universal screening in schools (Individuals with Disabilities Education Act, IDEA, 2004; U.S. Department of Education, 2001).

As mentioned, mental health screening practices align well with current prevention-based, multi-tiered, public health initiatives being widely implemented in schools, including Response to Intervention (RtI; National Center on Response to Intervention, 2010) and

School-Wide Positive Behavior Supports (SWPBS; Horner, Sugai & Anderson, 2010). These models are based on a public health approach and promote a continuum of support across three tiers commonly called universal, selective, and indicated; primary, secondary, and tertiary; or Tier 1, Tier 2, and Tier 3 (Gordon, 1983; Horner et al., 2010; National Center on Response to Intervention, 2010). Given that some have argued that the terms primary, secondary, and tertiary, as well as Tiers 1, 2, and 3, suggest an ordinal value for each level which may be interpreted as one level being more important than another (Gordon, 1983), the terms universal, selective, and indicated will be used in the remainder of this chapter.

In the public health model on which SWPBS and RtI are based, all students have access to universal services and practices, and the majority of students (e.g., 80%) will only need this level of support. At this level, universal screening is used for systemic evaluation (e.g., program evaluation, population monitoring) and identifies youth in need of further evaluation and supports (Ikeda, Neesen, & Witt, 2008). Students demonstrating emerging difficulties (e.g., about 15%) should be identified through universal screening procedures and provided selective level evaluation and intervention supports. Screening at the selective level should also target children who present risk for adjustment problems, such as those with identified learning problems, transient youth, minority status, of low socioeconomic status, and/or involved in the child welfare or juvenile justice systems (Lane, Kalberg, Bruhn, Mahoney, & Driscoll, 2008; U.S. Surgeon General, 2001; Wasserman et al., 2003). At the indicated level, an even smaller percentage of students (e.g., about 5%) will need treatments such as comprehensive assessment and frequent screening of crisis events such as sudden mood changes, suicidality, substance use, and violent intentions (Ikeda et al., 2008; Lane et al., 2008).

Despite the convergence of these multiple factors that should, theoretically, be increasing the use of universal screenings to identify early mental health concerns in school children, implementation of such recommendations has been isolated and insufficient (Romer & McIntosh, 2005). In fact, estimates suggest less than two percent of school systems implement a universal screening system to identify children with or at-risk of developing mental health concerns (Romer & McIntosh, 2005). In the following sections, several factors that should be considered when selecting a screening tool will be detailed and then universal screening tools currently available will be identified. A case example will then illustrate how these factors were considered and a universal screening practice was implemented to inform a targeted intervention program. Finally, limitations and ethical concerns for universal screening of mental health concerns in schools will be discussed.

Selecting and Implementing a Mental Health Screening Tool

This section will address the key issues that schools should consider in order to effectively integrate behavioral screening measures into their overall school improvement efforts. It is important to plan for all aspects of the screening process in order to ensure beneficial results, including how to build support for mental health screening among relevant stakeholders, communicate effectively with parents/students during all aspects of the process, select appropriate screening tools, and connect positive screens with appropriate follow-up supports and services. A checklist including key steps and considerations when adopting and implementing a school mental health screening process is provided in Figure 7.1 at the end of this section.

Increasing Buy-In Across the School Community

The first step in ensuring an effective behavioral screening process is to build a broad foundation of support for doing so across multiple stakeholders (school personnel, parents, students). Using the term "behavioral screening" instead of "mental health screening" may help to bolster more widespread acceptance. The term "behavioral screening" takes into account the full continuum of mental, social, emotional, and behavioral needs being assessed, while also avoiding the societal stigma unfortunately associated with the "mental health" term (Chafouleas, Kilgus, & Wallach, 2010).

Because the issues identified by behavioral screenings may point to the need for school-wide changes, it is especially important for staff to understand the value of assessing and proactively addressing students' social-emotional-behavioral needs in order to build a key foundation for academic success (Sugai & Horner, 2002). Support can be increased by clearly laying out the importance of assessing behavioral issues within a school context – including the integral relationship between mental health/behavioral issues and academic outcomes (see Mulloy & Weist, 2012; O'Connell et al., 2009) – as well as of the advantages of taking a more proactive approach to preventing and treating issues early instead of a "wait to fail" one (Glovers & Abers, 2007; Mulloy & Weist, 2012). Due to the close relationship between behavioral and academic issues, the integration of academic and behavioral screening approaches complement each other and strengthen a school's overall efforts to improve students' capacity for school success.

In a related vein, behavioral screening efforts can be easily aligned with multi-tiered school improvement efforts such as RtI or SWPBS. By building in behavioral screening tools at multiple levels of intervention as described previously, schools can effectively identify school-wide issues that need more preventative attention (universal level), highlight groups of at-risk students to receive more targeted support and skill development (selective level), and identify students whose more serious issues call for intensive supports and/or individual treatment (indicated level; Ikeda et al., 2008; Mulloy & Weist, 2012). The integration of comprehensive academic and behavioral screening thus helps schools move towards a strengths-based preventive approach that better supports all levels of student need, from the system to the individual level (Dowdy, Ritchie, & Kamphaus, 2010; Mulloy & Weist, 2012).

Finally, staff are more likely to support and be involved in screening efforts if processes are clear – including selecting behavioral screening instruments to align with school-wide efforts to bolster student success and to assess issues that the community agrees upon as important (Ikeda et al., 2008), training staff on how to administer and interpret selected screening measures, and setting forth clear guidelines for how positive screens will lead to further action. Procedures should include information on how to communicate with students' parents during all phases of the process, from informing them of the purpose of screening and gaining their consent (as indicated in the following section), ensuring student confidentiality, and following up with parents of students who screen positively *before* implementing any selective or indicated interventions.

Addressing Parental Concerns and Gaining Consent

Schools do not necessarily have to obtain parental consent for certain types of universal screenings – for example, IDEA (2004), a major education policy in the U.S., dictates that no consent is required if screening efforts are used to determine instruction or are part of regular school activities. For example, a universal screening measure such as the direct behavior rating (DBR) may be used with the primary intention of gauging students' classroom behaviors in order to plan more effective classroom instruction and, therefore, would not necessarily require previous parental notification or consent (Chafouleas et al., 2010). Whether obtaining formal parental consent or not, it is important for schools to contact parents in advance to explain the purpose of behavioral screening processes (e.g., to identify problems early and link students with supports), and to proactively address and resolve any concerns that parents may have. If schools clearly communicate with parents about the purpose and value behind comprehensive screening efforts and their link to increased supports for students, they "will find that parents are far more likely to be supportive rather than alarmed by it" (Walker, 2010, p. 109).

Parents should also be made aware that they will be contacted in the event of a positive screen in order to discuss the results and to collaboratively determine next steps, and that no interventions will be initiated without their involvement and clear consent (Kahlberg, Lane, & Menzies, 2010; Walker, 2010). Best practice guidelines also suggest that schools should provide parents/eligible-age students the option to refuse to participate (National Association of School Psychologists, 2000; O'Connell et al., 2009). Maintaining student and family privacy during all aspects of the screening process should be of utmost concern, and procedures for doing so should be clearly communicated to parents (Chafouleas et al., 2010; Friedman, 2006).

Selecting the Appropriate Screening Tools

Before selecting screening tools, schools should interact with community stakeholders about key emotional/behavioral constructs to be included in screening (Ikeda et al., 2008); how screening tools can be aligned with current multi-tiered efforts such as RtI or SWPBS (Chafouleas et al., 2010); the validity, reliability, usability, and cost of certain tools under consideration (Glover & Abers, 2007), and personnel available to score and analyze screening measures and provide follow-up services to students in need (Weist, Rubin, Moore, Adelsheim, & Wrobel, 2007). Best practice suggests organizing a committee of key stakeholders, including administrators, school and community mental health practitioners, key educators and support staff, parents, students and relevant community members, to identify the issues that are important for the community to assess, and to evaluate the merits of particular instruments in regards to doing so (Ikeda et al., 2008).

Select Screening Tool Aligned with Relevant Level of Intervention

Schools are advised to implement a multi-tiered or "multigate" screening process that provides both overall risk assessment to guide school-wide prevention efforts, as well as more intensive diagnostic assessments to guide the implementation of appropriate interventions

(Chafouleas et al., 2010; Doll & Cummings, 2008). SWPBS and RtI represent overarching frameworks that can guide this work (Severson, Walker, Hope-Doolittle, Kratochwill, & Gresham, 2007). For example, within the SWPBS and RtI frameworks, broad-based screeners at the universal level can be used to quickly screen an entire student population for a variety of academic and psychosocial issues, and, at the selective and indicated levels, more focused, narrow-banded tools can be used to identify the existence and severity of a problem and help to connect students with relevant interventions (Dowdy et al., 2010; Levitt, Saka, Romanelli, & Hoagwood, 2007).

Validity, Reliability, and Usability of Tools

Screening tools should be cost-efficient, accurate, practical and easy to use, valid for the intended purpose, and incorporate multiple methods of assessment including rating scales, checklists, teacher and/or parent nominations, and focused interviews (Elliott, Gresham, Frank, & Beddow, 2008). Screening instruments should also be standardized and reliable, and appropriate for the population being assessed. Because internalizing symptoms (e.g., depression, anxiety, trauma symptoms) are harder for staff to assess, it is also important to consider using tools that have multiple informants – including students, parents, and teachers. In most cases when conducting universal and/or large-scale screenings, the student should be the primary informant (Levitt et al., 2007). However, in regards to externalizing problems (e.g., impulsivity, conduct problems, noncompliance), teachers and caregivers often provide more accurate and reliable information than self-reports (Mulloy, Evangelista, Betkowski, & Weist, 2011).

Resource Issues

One of the key advantages of many screening tools is that they can be administered quickly, and provide a relatively time- and cost-efficient means of assessing the overall health of the school as well as of the students within in order to guide a more efficient use of school resources. For students who score positively on certain areas of a brief and cost-effective universal screening measure, more specific tools can then be used to follow up to determine specific problem areas and to match students in need with relevant school supports (e.g., targeted social skills, counseling; Walker, 2010).

However, it should be noted that financial issues can be a major factor in ability to conduct effective screenings (Weist et al., 2007). Although some tools are free of charge and can be administered by untrained staff, others are more costly and require more extensive levels of training and support. In addition to the cost of screening instruments and related training, staff resources will be required to score, interpret, and follow through with parent discussion, referrals, and intervention plans. This must be a clear part of the planning process in regards to selecting instruments that make sense for the identified purpose, and to correspond with the level of intervention (i.e., universal, selected, indicated).

Schools should also carefully consider the fact that screenings will likely result in more students being identified for support, and may strain the resource capacity of the school mental health delivery system. The adoption of universal screening measures will also shift resource use towards more preventative, broad-based support measures instead of interventions that target only the highest-need students. Schools should plan in advance regarding how to adjust resources accordingly, and how to connect with additional outside sources of support as needed. If their mental health staff is already strained to capacity, then schools need to be clear about how they can assist in efforts to connect students to additional sources of help in the community (Chafouleas et al., 2010). Schools can also integrate these community-based agencies within schools to ensure a broader continuum of care (see Expanded School Mental Health models, Weist & Albus, 2004).

Establishing Procedures to Ensure Effective Administration, Evaluation, and Next Steps

Staff Training, Timing, and Locale

Staff should be trained in how to effectively administer screening measures, including how to assess for both externalizing (e.g., impulsivity, acting-out behaviors) and harder-to-recognize internalizing symptoms (e.g., depression, anxiety, and withdrawal). It is also important to train staff in logistical matters to do with student confidentiality and strict adherence to screening procedures, in order to maintain privacy and ensure accurate screening results (Chafouleas et al., 2010).

Because screenings allow schools to identify problems early and build in supports, they should take place early in the school year after key staff has time to become acquainted with students, at the mid-point of the school year, and at key transition points (e.g., move from elementary to middle school, transfer student's entry into school setting). Screening tools are quickly administered, and can also be used at regular intervals to monitor progress (i.e., to determine how resources are impacting students and to identify students who may need further supports). Screenings should take place in confidential spaces and, in the case of self-report tools, include alternative activities for non-participating students (Weist et al., 2007).

Establishing Decision Trees and Memoranda of Understanding

Schools should establish clear decision trees or flow charts to guide procedural steps at all stages of the behavioral screening process, and to ensure that students in need are connected with appropriate levels of support (Mulloy et al., 2011). These decision trees should clearly illustrate next steps in the case of positive screens including follow-up with parents and teachers, suggested interventions appropriate for the level of need, and referral procedures. Developed memoranda of understanding between schools and collaborating mental health agencies who offer additional support can also help to clarify staff responsibilities at each step of the process, and ensure that students in need will be appropriately matched with school and/or community supports (Weist et al., 2007).

Staff should be assigned appropriately (e.g., school mental health professionals, student support team) to analyze screening results, and to recommend next steps and any needed interventions at the school or student-level (Walker, 2010). In the case of positive screens, schools should establish clear referral and care coordination procedures ahead of time, in order to connect students with identified needs with clear supports – whether within the school (e.g., school mental health team) or through a collaborating agency (e.g., community-based mental health agencies). By embedding individuals within a comprehensive "continuum of care", decision tree models help to ensure beneficial results of screening (Kessler, 2009). Indeed, without clear planning for next steps, behavioral screenings have little value and can do more harm than good (Kessler, 2009).

Checklist: Planning For And Implementing Behavioral Screening Measures

- **Increase Support for Behavioral Screening Across School Community**
  - Communicate the integral connection between mental health/behavioral issues and academic achievement.
  - Convey the value of identifying problems early in order to connect students in need with supports, thereby greatly improving their chances for school success.
  - Communicate that behavioral screening approaches can be easily aligned with school improvement efforts (e.g., SWPBS and RtI), and can complement and strengthen such efforts.
  - Gather community input regarding constructs that are important to assess.
  - Address any staff and/or parental concerns related to behavioral screening, and set out clear procedures for communicating with parents and maintaining student privacy during all phases of the process.
- **Address Parental/Student Concerns and Gain Consent/Assent (as Needed)**
  - Contact parents (or eligible-age students) in advance to explain the purpose of the behavioral screening process (i.e., to identify potential problems early and link students with supports), and to address and resolve any concerns.
  - Communicate school procedures in the event of a positive screen, including contacting parents/students to discuss results and collaborate regarding next steps. Emphasize that no individual interventions will be implemented without first discussing with parents/students.
  - Provide parents and eligible-age students with the option to refuse to participate, if relevant.
  - Communicate plans regarding the maintenance of student privacy during all aspects of the screening process.
- **Select Appropriate Screening Tools**
  - Convene a representative group of interested stakeholders (e.g., administrators, teachers, school mental health personnel, parents, students) to select behavioral screening measures and plan for implementation and follow-up.
  - Select screening tools to align with issues that the community agrees upon as important.
  - Choose tools to align with multi-tiered school improvement efforts and/or school plans to prevent problems and intervene early:
    - Universal: Identify school-wide issues in need of preventative interventions; flag students in need of further follow-up.
    - Selective: Highlight groups of at-risk students to receive more targeted support and skill development.
    - Indicated: Identify students with more serious needs who would benefit from more intensive supports and/or treatment.
  - Determine validity, reliability, ease of use, and cost of tools under consideration.
- **Establish Procedures Regarding Administration, Evaluation, and Next Steps**
  - Determine availability of school personnel to screen, score, evaluate, and provide follow-up as needed.
  - Plan the timing and locale of screenings.
  - Train staff (as needed) on how to administer and interpret screening measures.

- Set forth clear guidelines on how to communicate with parents during all phases of the screening process.
- Establish decision trees to guide next steps, including plans to contact parents/students in the event of positive screens, potential interventions for various levels of need, and referral procedures to school mental health personnel and/or community agencies.
- Establish memoranda of understanding between schools and outside sources of community support (e.g., community mental health agencies, pediatricians) as needed.

Figure 7.1. Key steps and considerations when adopting and implementing a school mental health screening process.

SCHOOL MENTAL HEALTH SCREENING INSTRUMENTS

In this section, universal mental health screening tools currently available for use in schools are reviewed, including brief descriptions of areas assessed, administration procedures, cost, and psychometric properties. Table 7.1, at the end of this section, provides a brief overview of each tool and can be used to more easily compare important dimensions and considerations when selecting a universal school mental health screening instrument.

Behavior Assessment Scale for Children Two (BASC-2): Behavioral and Emotional Screening System (BESS)

Based upon the popular *Behavioral Assessment Scale for Children*, the BASC-2: BESS is intended for use as a brief, universal screener to identify students with needs in both academic and social-emotional domains (i.e., internalizing, externalizing, school problems), so it is ideal for integration into a school's comprehensive screening and assessment system. The BESS also allows for multiple informants, including a parent (Dowdy, Chin, Twyford, & Dever, 2011), teacher (Dever, Mays, Kamphaus, & Dowdy, 2012), and student (Grades 3 through 12; Dowdy et al., 2011) form that can be used individually or in combination. The forms can be quickly and easily filled out, no training is required for administration, and scoring is done via computer. Individual or group reports can be generated, thus enabling the BESS to function as both a universal and selective/indicated-level screener. The BASC-2: BESS has been normed on a sample that aligns with the U.S. Census population characteristics. The initial test kit costs approximately US$100, the scoring/reporting software prices in at over US$600, and additional reporting forms cost around US$25 per pack.

Direct Behavior Rating – Single Item Scale (DBR-SIS)

The DBR-SIS comprises direct teacher observation ratings on academic engagement (student's active or passive participation in classroom activity), disruptive behavior (student action that interrupts regular school or classroom activity), and compliance (student's socially acceptable initiation and execution of adult requested behaviors; Chafouleas, Riley-Tillman, & Christ, 2009; Kilgus, Chafouleas, Riley-Tillman, & Welsh, 2012). The DBR-SIS is free, time-efficient, and can be regularly administered to monitor student progress and establish a useable data stream. The DBR-SIS website (http://directbehaviorratings.org/cms/) includes a free online training module to improve the accuracy of teachers' direct observation ratings by including practice, feedback, and examples. The DBR-SIS does not include any internalizing behavior ratings or strengths-based rating scales.

Resiliency Scales for Children and Adolescents (RSCA)

The RSCA (Prince-Embury, 2006, 2007) are designed to measure the extent to which students possess personal resiliency factors that contribute to success in school (e.g., sense of mastery or self-efficacy, sense of relatedness, and capacity for emotional regulation). The full RSCA measure includes 64 Likert-type items and yields two Index scores: Resource (combination of Sense of Mastery and Sense of Relatedness) and Vulnerability (difference between the Emotional Reactivity factor and the Resource Index score). Students with low vulnerability scores are likely to be more resilient in the face of adversity and stress than those with high vulnerability scores (i.e., those who tend to be more emotionally reactive and have fewer personal resources to draw upon in times of adversity). The RSCA can be easily incorporated into multi-tiered frameworks to monitor the effects of school-wide improvement efforts and identify students whose lower resiliency/greater vulnerability scores highlight their need for additional assistance (Prince-Embury, 2011). The RSCA has high validity across gender and race/ethnicity and high interrater and test-retest reliability scores suggesting that it can also be used as a progress monitoring tool over time (Prince-Embury, 2011).

Deveurux Student Strengths Assessment (DESSA) System

The DESSA is a strengths-based system of screening measures designed to assess kindergarten through eighth grade students' social-emotional competency and resiliency (LeBuffe, Shapiro, & Naglieri, 2009; Naglieri, LeBuffe, & Shapiro, 2011a). The DESSA system includes the DESSA-mini (eight items) and the DESSA (72 items), each of which can be completed by teachers, parents, and/or after-school staff in regular contact with children (LeBuffe et al., 2009; Naglieri, et al., 2011a). The DESSA-mini includes four, 8-item forms with adequate psychometric qualities and can be used for broader screening and progress monitoring (Naglieri et al., 2011a; Naglieri, LeBuffe, & Shapiro, 2011b). One form is completed by a teacher for each child requiring approximately 45 minutes to complete an entire classroom (Naglieri et al., 2011b). The DESSA is psychometrically sound and includes 72-items across eight protective factor subscales, including Optimistic Thinking, Self-Management, Goal-Directed Behavior, Self-Awareness, Social-Awareness, Personal Responsibility, Decision Making, and Relationship Skills (LeBuffe et al., 2009). In the DESSA system, it is suggested that when concerns are indicated on the DESSA-mini, further assessment should include the 72-item DESSA completed by teachers and parents (Naglieri et al., 2011a). Both the DESSA and DESSA-mini can be hand-scored and online administration, scoring, and interpretation are also available, including student, class, and school level reports. Both rating scales are available in English and Spanish.

System Systematic Screening for Behavior Disorders (SSBD)

The SSBD (Walker & Severson, 1992) is a universal screening tool for use with grades K to six to identify students with, or at-risk, of developing externalizing and internalizing behavior problems. SSBD is implemented in a multiple-gating process including three steps where meeting a certain criteria is required at each step to pass on to the next step with each successive stage becoming more focused (Walker & Severson, 1992). In stage 1, teachers rank order, from most likely (1) to least likely (10), students in their class on each behavioral domain (e.g., externalizing and internalizing). In stage 2, teachers complete the Critical Events Index rating scale for each student ranked as first, second, or third on the externalizing and/or internalizing domains. The Critical Events Index is a 33-item rating scale measuring adaptive and maladaptive skills on a Likert scale (Walker & Severson, 1992). Stage 3 is optional and only completed for those students who exceed national, normative cutoffs on the Critical Events Index. Schools who decide to implement stage 3 conduct classroom and playground observations of identified students using a prescribed direct observation technique of academic engaged time and peer social behavior (Walker & Severson, 1992). At stages 2 and 3, students exceeding cutoffs are referred to intervention teams for further evaluation and support. Estimates suggest that stages 1 and 2 take approximately 1.5 hours or less for teachers to complete and the developers suggest using the SSBD twice each year in fall and spring (Walker et al., 2009). The SSBD has been found to have acceptable psychometric properties (Walker & Severson, 1992; Walker et al., 1994) and is low cost. It has been implemented in research and practice settings with success (Walker et al., 2009).

Student Risk Screening Scale (SSRS)

The SSRS (Drummond, 1994) is a one-step, seven-item screening scale used to identify students with behavior problems. Teachers rate each student in their class on a four-point Likert scale on seven items, including: (a) steals; (b) lies, cheats, sneaks; (c) behavior problems; (d) peer rejection; (e) low academic achievement; (f) negative attitude; and (g) aggressive behavior. A total score is computed for each student and classified into three risk levels established by Drummond (1994), including low, moderate, and high. The SSRS is available free online through several initiatives, including Michigan's Integrated Behavior and Learning Support Initiative (http://miblsi.cenmi.org/MiBLSiModel/Evaluation/Measures/StudentRiskScreeningScale.aspx) and reportedly only takes elementary classroom teachers approximately 10 minutes to complete for their entire roster (Menzies & Lane, 2011). Although validity and reliability estimates are within acceptable ranges, the SSRS has not demonstrated acceptable psychometric properties for the detection of internalizing behaviors. As the seven items included on the SRSS suggest, the SRSS was developed to detect antisocial behaviors more closely aligned with overt, externalizing behaviors than internalizing symptoms such as anxiety or depression (Lane et al., 2009). However, the SRSS was recently adapted in the SSRS-Internalizing and Externalizing (SSRS-IE; Lane et al.,

2012) including seven additional items reflecting common internalizing behavioral characteristics, including: (a) emotionally flat; (b) shy, withdrawn; (c) sad, depressed; (d) anxious; (e) obsessive-compulsive behavior; (f) lonely; and (g) self-inflicts pain. While research has only begun to examine the psychometric properties and feasibility of the SSRS-IE, initial exploratory evidence supports the use of only five of the seven additional internalizing items (Lane et al., 2012).

Strengths and Difficulties Questionnaire (SDQ)

The SDQ is a one-page, 25-item questionnaire completed by teachers, parents, and youth (ages 11-16) designed to assess psychological adjustment including prosocial and maladaptive behaviors of youth ages four to 16 (Goodman, 1997). The SDQ teacher and parent report forms are very similar and each include five items on each of the five domains, including (a) Hyperactivity, (b) Emotional Symptoms, (c) Conduct Problems, (d) Peer Problems, and (e) Prosocial Behavior. Teachers and parents rate their agreement with each item on a three-point scale. Rating scales and additional resources are available online for free at http://www.sdqinfo.com. Scoring instructions and resources are available online at www.sdqscore.org. Total scores are divided into ranges of normal, borderline, and abnormal across reporters to identify children in need of further assessment and intervention. The SDQ requires approximately five minutes per child for teachers and parents to complete (Goodman & Scott, 1999) and research has demonstrated adequate psychometric properties across nearly 50 studies (Stone, Otten, Engels, Vermulst, & Janssens, 2010).

Social Skills Improvement System (SSIS) Performance Screening Guide

The SSIS Performance Screening Guide (Elliott & Gresham, 2007b) is a mass screener used to evaluate four skill areas (prosocial behaviors, motivation to learn, reading skills, math skills). Items were selected by the developers based on “an assumption that a balanced assessment of prosocial and problem behaviors is most critical to the assessment of children’s social functioning and identification of entry points for the application of effective interventions” (Elliott et al., 2008, p. 18). A 5-point rubric is provided with criteria for rating each area. The rating is then compared to a cut score (1 = *high level of concern*, 2–3 = *moderate level of concern*, 4–5 = *at or above expected level*). Space is provided to write the names of students with ratings of 1 (*high levels of concern*) or 2–3 (*moderate level of concern*) and the action to be taken. A strength of this screener is that it has strong intervention validity, or the capacity to inform intervention efforts (Elliott et al., 2008). The SSIS is socially valid in terms of teacher time to complete and score (about 30 minutes per class of 25 students). Nearly all teachers who participated in field testing (n = 138) indicated that the behaviors addressed were important and found the SSIS Performance Screening Guide easy to understand and useful in identifying students who needed additional assessment and interventions (Elliott & Gresham, 2007a, b). Some schools may find the tool less feasible, however, in terms of cost. Preschool protocols cost approximately US$17 for a pack of four and elementary/secondary protocols cost US$42 for a pack of 10. One protocol per classroom is needed.

Table 7.1. Comparison of Universal School Mental Health Screening Tools Currently Available

Screening Tool	Raters	Areas Assessed	Administration	Cost (US$)	Website
Behavior Assessment Scale for Children: Behavioral and Emotional Screening System (BESS)	Parents, Teachers, and Youth (Grades 3 to 12) Forms	Externalizing behaviors, internalizing behaviors, and school problems	25 to 30 items per form	$100+ Complete Kit $620 scoring and reporting software $25 per pack of 25 forms	http://www.pearsonassessments.com/HAIWEB/Cultures/en-us/Productdetail.htm?Pid=PAaBASC2bess
Direct Behavior Rating – Single Item Scale (DBR-SIS)	Teachers	Academic engagement, disruptive behavior, and compliance/ respect	Three items rated for each student following observation period across at least five days	Free	http://www.directbehaviorratings.org/cms/
Resiliency Scales for Children and Adolescents (RSCA)	Youth (ages 9-18)	Sense of Mastery, Sense of Relatedness, and Emotional Reactivity scales	64 items total (20-24 items per scale)	$115 Complete Kit $70 per pack of 25 Combination Scales $37 per pack of 25 Individual Scales $72 manual	http://www.pearsonassessments.com/HAIWEB/Cultures/en-us/Productdetail.htm?Pid=015-8006-186
Devereux Student Strengths Assessment (DESSA) System	Teachers, Parents, After-school staff	Strength of social-emotional competence	Eight items Online administration, scoring and interpretation available. When concerns are indicated, further assessment available through DESSA (72 items).	Contact authors for pricing information	http://www.devereux.org/site/PageServer?pagename=dessa_index
System Systematic Screening for Behavior Disorders (SSBD)	Teachers	Internalizing and Externalizing Behaviors	Multiple-gating procedures: 1) rank order students in class on Internalizing and Externalizing scales, 2) Critical Events Index (33 items) completed for each student rated as first, second, or third on either scale, and 3) direct observation of students surpassing national norms on Critical Events Index (optional)	$135 full kit, $17 pack of 6 forms	http://www.soprislearning.com/cs/Satellite/Systematic_Screening_for_Behavior_Disorders_SSBD_Overview?cmsid=Sopris

Table 7.1. (Continued)

Screening Tool	Raters	Areas Assessed	Administration	Cost (US$)	Website
Student Risk Screening Scale (SSRS)	Teachers	Externalizing behaviors, peer rejection, academic achievement, and attitude toward school	Seven items SSRS	Free	http://miblsi.cenmi.org/MiBLSiModel/Evaluation/Measures/StudentRiskScreeningScale.aspx
Strengths and Difficulties Questionnaire (SDQ)	Teachers, Parents, and Youth (ages 11-16)	Hyperactivity, Emotional symptoms, Conduct Problems, Peer Problems, and Prosocial Behavior	25 items	Free	http://www.sdqinfo.com
Social Skills Improvement System (SSIS) Performance Screening Guide	Teachers	Prosocial Behaviors, Motivation to Learn, Reading Skills, Math Skills	Each student rated on scale of 1 (high level of concern) to 5 (at or above expected level of concern) in four areas	$42 pack of 10 protocols, 1 protocol needed per classroom	http://www.pearsonassessments.com/pai/ca/RelatedInfo/SSISOverview.htm

CASE EXAMPLE

The case example is taken from a suburban elementary school serving a high-poverty, high-minority, moderately-transient population of approximately 630 students in kindergarten through fifth grade. The school had a history of high rates of discipline referrals and large numbers of struggling learners. In 2006-2007, 11% of the student population received six or more office discipline referrals; in the spring semester alone (i.e., a 90 day period), more than 850 office discipline referrals were submitted. In the fall of 2008, more than 40% of students in kindergarten through second grade scored in the below average range on a curriculum-based measure for reading and early literacy skills.

Beginning in 2006, as part of a State Improvement Grant, the school mandatorily implemented a School-Wide Positive Behavior Support Program. In the third year of implementation, with decreased discipline referrals overall but a subset of the population still struggling to follow school-wide expectations, the site-based School Psychologist and the school's full-time Special Education Teacher of a combination disability resource class launched an initiative to address these struggling students. They lobbied the school's administration and gained permission to implement a targeted behavior intervention program beginning in the 2008 school year. In the first year, only students in the third through fifth grades were included; this was expanded to the second and then first grades in subsequent years as the staffs' skills developed and demand for the program increased.

The Behavior Education Program (BEP; Crone, Hawken, & Horner, 2010) was chosen as the targeted intervention program, primarily because it was judged to be the most feasible of the empirically-driven targeted intervention programs available at the time. BEP is a modified check-in, check-out intervention implemented with students – with and without disabilities – who demonstrate persistent behavior problems across multiple settings and are at-risk for more severe problem behaviors. The system provides students with clearly defined expectations and goals, increased positive adult attention, feedback from teachers at regular intervals throughout the school day, increased opportunities for reinforcement of desirable behavior, and an efficient method of home-school collaboration. Research indicates that when BEP is implemented with high fidelity, it is effective in decreasing office discipline referrals for the majority of students who received the intervention (Hawken, MacLeod, & Rawlings, 2007; Filter et al., 2007). As supplemental components to the BEP, this elementary school offered a weekly social skills group with the School Psychologist and an end-of-year field trip, which provided a reality-based opportunity to practice prosocial skills in a community setting and to celebrate student progress.

In the first year of the program, students were identified for BEP solely on discipline referrals and staff recommendation, and progress monitoring data was limited to daily Behavior Report Card points and discipline data collected by office staff. Recognizing the limitations of the data available, the BEP leadership team (i.e., the School Psychologist, the Special Education Teacher, a General Education Teaching Assistant, and a School Psychology graduate student) moved towards a more data-driven decision making process by utilizing the SSIS Performance Screening Guide (Elliott & Gresham, 2007a).

In choosing a universal behavioral screening tool, the BEP leadership team considered a number of factors, with technical soundness, feasibility, efficiency, and progress monitoring capabilities being most important. Relative to other screeners reviewed, the SSIS

Performance Screening Guide (Elliott & Gresham, 2007a) was low in cost and quick and easy to prepare and complete. The psychometric properties were sound and, as part of an integrated system, the SSIS offered a standardized assessment at the targeted level. The SSIS Rating Scales can be used up to four times per year as a progress monitoring tool for students in targeted interventions. The multi-rater Rating Scales broadly assess students' social behaviors, problem behaviors (i.e., those that can affect relationships with peers and school staff), and academic performance; the parent-, teacher-, and self-reports have the option of computerized scoring.

At the case example school, the SSIS Performance Screening Guide was prepared by leadership team members and provided to all teachers in grades selected for intervention. Teachers independently completed the screeners after receiving a written introduction with directions. They were informed that completion of the screener was required for their students to be considered for inclusion. They were given approximately two weeks to complete and return the screener. Unresponsive teachers were contacted via email and personal contact to encourage participation.

Upon receipt of completed screeners, the data were reviewed and summarized by leadership team members. The names of students receiving "at-risk" ratings (e.g., a score of 1 or 2 in the "prosocial behaviors" domain) were presented to the school's Intervention Assistance Team (IAT) at the first meeting of the school year. IAT considered other data (e.g., discipline referrals and history, anecdotal records, other services currently in place) in addition to screener data when determining students appropriate for inclusion in the program. Students moving into the school and those with emergent behavior problems were considered at subsequent monthly IAT meetings.

Following recommendation by the IAT team, students' parents were provided with a passive consent letter from the school's principal and completion of baseline SSIS Rating Scales was requested of parents and teachers. The Rating Scales were requested again at mid-year and end-of-year. Obtaining these from parents proved difficult, with a maximum of 30% of parents returning the forms at each benchmark period. Although the majority of teachers returned the forms, much follow-up was necessary. The leadership team logged many hours making phone calls, sending emails, and preparing written communication in an attempt to collect the Rating Scales data.

"Jessica" was a student referred to BEP during the 2010-2011 school year when she was in the fourth grade. She was retained in the third grade, had attended six schools since enrolling in kindergarten, and had spent time in foster care. Jessica attended the case example school for the second half of her first year of third grade and her entire second year of third grade, but was not referred to BEP. At the beginning of her fourth grade year, Jessica's teacher indicated on the SSIS Performance Screening Guide that Jessica was struggling in all areas and was in need of additional intervention. Between August and March, Jessica earned 11 office discipline referrals and was academically functioning below grade level. Her baseline SSIS Teacher Rating Scale, obtained in September, indicated social skills in the "well-below average" range and problem behaviors in the "well-above average" range. Parent ratings were sought, but were not obtained. In November, after participating in BEP for approximately eight weeks with little progress, Jessica was referred for a Functional Behavior Assessment and Behavior Intervention Plan. As part of this plan, she began to receive individualized counseling, her BEP Daily Report Card was modified to increase opportunities for reinforcement, and the rewards available through BEP were individualized to increase saliency. The charts below summarize the ratings of Jessica's performance over two administrations of the SSIS Teacher Rating Scale. R1 is the September 2010 rating and R2 is the January 2011 rating. These progress charts indicate that Jessica's social skills changed very little in the four months that targeted interventions were in place, staying in the "well-below" average range, and that her problem behaviors worsened, moving higher within the "well-above average" range. Following review of this and other data by the IAT, permission was sought to conduct a comprehensive evaluation for special education services. Following her comprehensive evaluation in March 2011, Jessica was found eligible for special services as a student with an Emotional Disability. Jessica continued to participate in BEP as a supplement to her special education services for the remainder of the school year, which supported her participation in the general education classroom.

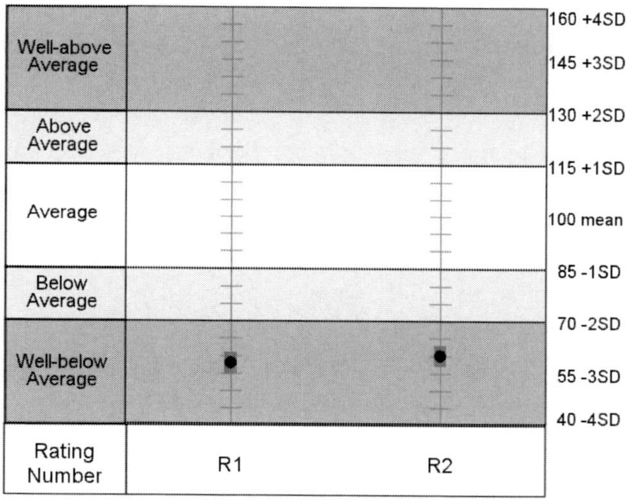

Figure 7.1. SSIS Social Skills Progress Chart.

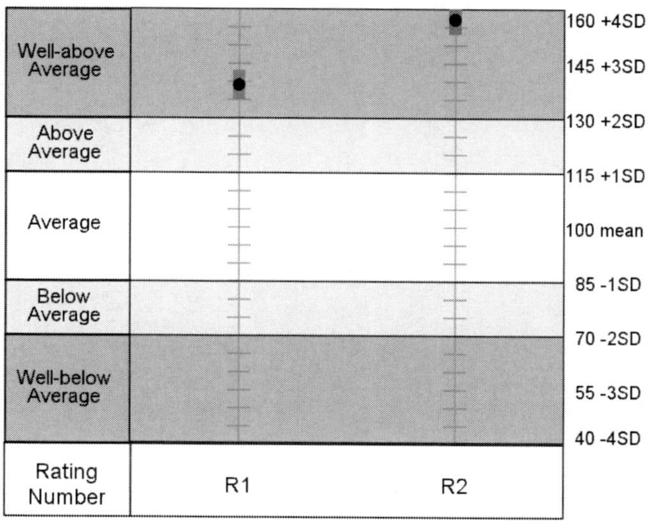

Figure 7.2. SSIS Problem Behaviors Progress Chart.

A total of 50 students have been served through BEP over four years at the case example school, with several receiving services over multiple years. Thirteen of these students were referred to the Special Services Department for evaluation while participating in the program, nine of whom were identified as having a behavioral disability such as an Emotional Disability or an Other Health Impairment (for Attention Deficit Hyperactivity Disorder). Another 21 students were already receiving special services as students with disabilities prior to beginning the BEP, ranging from Hearing and Speech/Language Impairments to behavioral disabilities. Many of these special education students were able to access through BEP a valuable general education intervention that supported their participation in lesser restrictive special education programs. One student, “Rodney,” moved into the district from an out-of-state Residential Treatment Center (RTC) and was initially served through a self-contained program at another school. In less than a semester, Rodney had earned his way out of self-contained and was being served in a less-restrictive resource model, spending half of his school day in general education at the case example school. BEP was instituted as a general education support and, by the end of the school year, Rodney was the school’s first BEP “graduate.”

Implementation of BEP in the case example school has led to decreases in discipline referrals for the majority of students participating in the program. Many of the students who were not successful in the program were eventually placed in more intensive special education programs, as the example of Jessica illustrates. Figure 7.3 illustrates the drop in number of office discipline referrals (ODR) for students participating in BEP in the first year of implementation. Four students (students E-H) were transfer students from other schools or districts with an unknown referral history; these students were referred for BEP based on records indicating a history of behavioral troubles or the receipt of behavioral interventions.

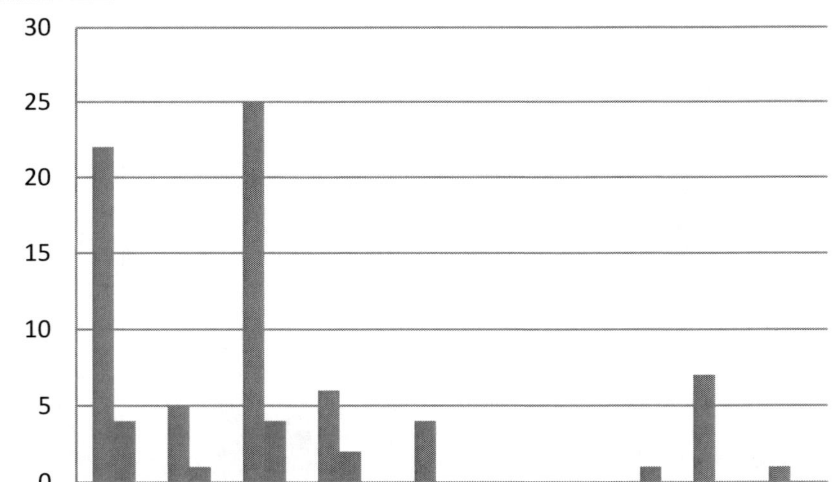

	A	B	C	D	E	F	G	H	J	K
ODR 2007-8	22	5	25	6					7	1
ODR 2008-9	4	1	4	2	4	0	0	1	0	0

Figure 7.3. Office Discipline Referrals (ODR) for students (A-K) in BEP.

LIMITATIONS AND ETHICAL CONCERNS

Some limitations and ethical concerns regarding screening – as well as potential resolutions – are addressed below, including privacy issues, misidentification, and cultural sensitivity.

ADDRESSING CONCERNS RELATED TO PRIVACY AND INTERVENTIONS

When implementing behavioral screening measures, schools must be prepared to address concerns related to student and family privacy as well as fears that screens may result in forced interventions or a push towards medication. First, schools must have clear procedures in place to protect student and family privacy (Friedman, 2006), including training staff to maintain student confidentiality and adhere strictly to screening guidelines (Chafouleas et al., 2010). Schools should also respect parents' and eligibility-age students' rights, including the right to "opt out" of screening (O'Connell et al., 2009). Moreover, in the event of a positive screen, it must be clear policy that parents will be contacted to discuss potential next steps, and that no individual interventions will be undertaken without clear parent consent and student assent. It is also important to note that the goal of screening is to determine the need for further assessment, and not to directly guide the use of medications or other treatments.

Schools must also have very clear guidelines in place regarding how to handle positive screens in order to ensure that students receive appropriate follow-up (with the consent of their parents, of course) – screenings without such clear directives on next steps may do more harm than good (Kessler, 2009).

POTENTIAL MISIDENTIFICATION OF STUDENTS

No screening tool is 100 percent accurate, and there is always a chance for misidentification – whether in the case of false positives (i.e., pointing to the existence of a problem where there is none) or false negatives (i.e., overlooking a student that does have problems). Large-scale screening instruments that measure for overlapping disorders are especially susceptible to these errors, yet researchers argue that it may be preferable to use sensitive instruments that risk over-identifying students in order to ensure that students in need are not overlooked (Glover & Albers, 2007). The risks involved with over-identification include spending valuable school resources on follow-up evaluations that may not be truly necessary, or in worrying students or families unnecessarily that a problem exists when that is not necessarily the case. However, the risks involved with under-identification and overlooking students in need constitute a more serious problem. Ikeda and colleagues (2008) suggest that it is best to follow the "least dangerous assumption" (p. 3) – that is, that it is better to identify a student as at-risk for failure and build in supports rather than to miss identifying a student in need altogether. Of course, a positive result on a screen should not be used to initiate any individual interventions – rather, it should simply point to the need for further follow-up evaluations to determine whether a problem is truly present. Using tools that have adequate psychometric qualities as well as those that require multiple methods for assessment and/or multiple informants will also help to minimize false positives and negatives (Elliott et al., 2008).

NEED FOR CULTURALLY SENSITIVE INSTRUMENTS

Another issue related to validity concerns the fact that many behavioral screening tools are not validated for use across diverse populations and/or are not culturally sensitive (Dembo et al., 2005). This can increase the odds that minority students will be disproportionately and, perhaps, erroneously flagged as having behavioral issues when in truth there may be more subtle cultural issues at play (Donovan & Cross, 2002) – particularly in regards to culturally different patterns of symptom presentation and help-seeking (Dembo et al., 2005). This is a topic in urgent need of attention – both in research (e.g., to create an evidence base of screening tools that are validated and standardized for use across various populations), and in practice in schools. To ensure that screening processes are culturally sensitive, schools should carefully consider the characteristics of their student population and monitor inappropriate disproportionality (Skiba, Eaton, & Sotoo, 2004). Schools should obtain family and student perspectives regarding all aspects of the screening process, from planning to intervention, in order to develop culturally competent protocols/decision trees and to consider the impact of culture upon certain behaviors instead of rushing to label or diagnose. Again, screening results should comprise only a part of the decision-making process regarding how to provide additional supports and/or classify students– carefully done with family and staff input.

CONCLUSION

Mental health screening in elementary schools is a critically important agenda for schools to ensure that students who are struggling with emotional-behavioral problems are identified and receive appropriate and evidence-based supports and services. Students' mental health problems impair their learning and academic achievement, but well done, evidence-based school mental health services reduce barriers to student learning and lead to improvements in school behavior and achievement (Durlak & Dupre, 2008; Hoagwood & Erwin, 1997). However, there are many factors to consider before beginning a mental health screening system in schools. Most schools do not have the infrastructure or staff resources to adequately conduct screening and ensure that students in need actually receive appropriate supports or services in a timely manner. Other issues related to community and parental buy-in, and confidentiality must also be resolved before mental health screenings in schools can be conducted. These concerns underscore the need for increased priority on building capacity, infrastructure, and collaboration in schools and communities to better meet the mental health needs of all students. In addition to schools increasing resources for this agenda, partnerships with collaborating community agencies, as in expanded school mental health programs, both bolster available services to conduct and follow-up on screening and increase student and family connections to relevant community programs and resources (Andis et al., 2002; Weist, Evans, & Lever, 2003). Our hope is that this chapter provides guidance on how to proceed with mental health screening in schools, and serves as an impetus for increased research and practice.

References

AAP, Committee on Children with Disabilities. (2001). Developmental surveillance and screening of infants and young children. *Pediatrics, 101,* 192-195.

Andis, P., Cashman, J., Oglesby, D., Praschil, R., Adelman, H., Taylor, L., & Weist, M. (2002). A strategic and shared agenda to advance mental health in schools through family and system partnerships. *International Journal of Mental Health Promotion, 4,* 28-35, doi: 10.1080/14623730.2002.9721886.

Chafouleas, S. M., Kilgus, S. P., & Wallach, N. (2010). Ethical dilemmas in school-based behavioral screening. *Assessment for Effective Intervention, 35,* 245- 252. doi: 10.1177/1534508410379002.

Chafouleas, S.M., Riley-Tillman, T.C., & Christ, T.J. (2009). Direct Behavior Rating (DBR): An emerging method for assessing social behavior within a tiered intervention system. *Assessment for Effective Intervention, 34,* 195-200.

Crone, D. A., Hawken, L. S., & Horner, R. H. (2010). *Responding to problem behavior in schools: The Behavior Education Program* (2nd ed.). NY: Guilford.

Dembo, R., Walters, W., & Meyers, K. (2005). A practice/research collaborative: An innovative approach to identifying and responding to psychosocial functioning problems and recidivism risk among juvenile arrestees. *Journal of Offender Rehabilitation, 41*, 39-66. doi: 10.1300/J076v41n01_02.

Dever, B. V., Mays, K. L., Kamphaus R. W., & Dowdy, E. (2012). The factor structure of the BASC-2 Behavioral and Emotional Screening System Teacher Form, Child/Adolescent. *Journal of Psychoeducational Assessment, 30,* 488- 495 doi: 10.1177/0734282912438869.

Doll, B., & Cummings, J. (2008). Why population-based services are essential for school mental health, and how to make them happen in your school. In B. Doll, & J. Cummings (Eds.), *Transforming school mental health services: Population-based approaches to promoting the competency and wellness of children* (pp. 1-20). Thousand Oaks, CA: Corwin Press.

Donovan, M. S., & Cross, C. T. (2002). *Minority students in special and gifted education.* Washington, DC: National Academy Press.

Dowdy, E., Chin, J. K., Twyford, J. M., & Dever, B. V. (2011). A factor analytic investigation of the BASC-2 Behavioral and Emotional Screening System parent form: Psychometric properties, practical implications, and future directions. *Journal of School Psychology, 49,* 265-280. doi: 10.1016/j.jsp.2011.03.005.

Dowdy, E., Ritchey, K., & Kamphaus, R. W. (2010). School-based screening: A population-based approach to inform and monitor children's mental health needs. *School Mental Health, 2,* 166-176. doi: 10.1007/s12310-010-9036-3.

Dowdy, E., Twyford, J., Chin, J., DiStefano, C. A., Kamphaus, R., & Mays, K. (2011). Factor structure of the BASC2 Behavioral and Emotional Screening System student form. *Psychological Assessment, 23*, 379-387. doi:10.1037/a0021843.

Drummond, T. (1994). *The Student Risk Screening Scale (SRSS)*. Grants Pass, OR: Josephine County Mental Health Program.

Durlak, J. A., & DuPre, E. P. (2008). Implementation matters: A review of research on the influence of implementation on program outcomes and the factors affecting implementation. *American Journal of Community Psychology, 41,* 327-350. doi: 10.1007/s10464-008-9165-0.

Elliott, S. N., & Gresham, F. M. (2007a). *Social Skills Improvement System: Classwide intervention program guide*. Bloomington, MN: Pearson Assessments.

Elliott, S. N., & Gresham, F. M. (2007b). *Social Skills Improvement System: Performance Screening Guides.* Bloomington, MN: Pearson Assessments.

Elliott, S. N., Gresham, F. M., Frank, J. L., & Beddow, P. A. (2008). Intervention validity of social behavior rating scales. *Assessment for Effective Intervention, 34,* 15–24.

Filter, K. J., McKenna, M. K., Benedict, E. A., Horner, R. H., Todd, A. W., & Watson, J. (2007). Check in/ check out: A post-hoc evaluation of an efficient, secondary-level targeted intervention for reducing problem behaviors in schools. *Education and Treatment of Children, 30*, 69-84. doi: 10.1353/etc.2007.0000.

Friedman, R.A. (2006). Uncovering an epidemic: Screening for mental illness in teens. *New England Journal of Medicine, 355*, 2717-2719.

Glover, T. A., & Albers, C. A. (2007). Considerations for evaluating universal screening assessments. *Journal of School Psychology, 45,* 117-135. doi: 10.1016/j.jsp.2006.05.005.

Goodman, R. (1997). The Strengths and Difficulties Questionnaire: A research note. *Journal of Child Psychology and Psychiatry, 38,* 581-586. doi: 0021-9630/97.

Goodman, R., & Scott, S. (1999). Comparing the Strengths and Difficulties Questionnaire and the Child Behavior Checklist: Is small beautiful? *Journal of Abnormal Child Psychology, 27,* 17-24.

Gordon, R. S. (1983). An operational classification of disease prevention. *Public Health Reports, 98,* 107-109.

Greenberg, M. T., Domitrovich, C., & Bumbarger, B. (2001). The prevention of mental disorders in school-aged children: Current state of the field. *Prevention and Treatment, 4.* doi: 10.1037/1522-3736.4.1.41a.

Hawken, L., MacLeod, K., & Rawlings, L. (2007). Effects of the Behavior Education Program (BEP) on problem behavior with elementary school students. *Journal of Positive Behavior Interventions, 9,* 94-101. doi: 10.1177/10983007070090020601.

Hoagwood, K., & Erwin, H. D. (1997). Effectiveness of school-based mental health services for children: A 10-year research review. *Journal of Child and Family Studies, 6,* 435-451. doi: 10.1023/A:1025045412689.

Horner, R.H., Sugai, G., & Anderson, C.M. (2010). Examining the evidence base for school-wide positive behavior support. *Focus On Exceptional Children, 42*, 1-16.

Ikeda, M. J., Neessen, E., & Witt, J. C. (2008). Best practices in universal screening. In A. Thomas, & J. Grimes (Eds.), *Best practices in school psychology* (5th ed., Vol.2, pp. 103-114). Bethesda, MD: National Association of School Psychologists.

Individuals with Disabilities Education Improvement Act of 2004. (2004). Pub. L., 108–446, 118 Stat. 2647.

Kahlberg, J. R., Lane, K. L., & Menzies, H. M. (2010). Using systematic screening procedures to identify students who are nonresponsive to primary prevention efforts:

Integrating academic and behavioral measures. *Education and Treatment of Children, 33,* 561-584.

Kessler, R. (2009). Identifying and screening for psychological and comorbid medical and psychological disorders in medical settings. *Journal of Clinical Psychology, 65*, 253-267.

Kilgus, S. P., Chafouleas, S. M., Riley-Tillman, T. C., & Welsh, M. E. (2012). Direct behavior rating scales as screeners: A preliminary investigation of diagnostic accuracy in elementary school. *School Psychology Quarterly, 27,* 41-50. doi: 10.1037/a0027150.

Lane, K. L., Kalberg, J. R., Bruhn, A. L., Mahoney, M. E., & Driscoll, S. A. (2008). Primary prevention programs at the elementary level: Issues of treatment integrity, systematic screening, and reinforcement. *Education and Treatment of Children, 31,* 465-494. doi: 10.1353/etc.0.0033.

Lane, K. L., Little, A. M., Casey, A. M., Lambert, W., Wehby, J. H., Weisenbach, J. L., & Phillips, A. (2009). A comparison of systematic screening tools for emotional and behavioral disorders: How do they compare? *Journal of Emotional and Behavioral Disorders, 17,* 93–105.

Lane, K. L., Oakes, W. P., Harris, P. J., Menzies, H. M., Cox, M., & Lambert, W. (2012). Initial evidence for the reliability and validity of the Student Risk Screening Scale for Internalizing and Externalizing behaviors at the elementary level. *Behavioral Disorders, 37,* 99-122.

LeBuffe, P. A., Shapiro, V. B., & Naglieri, J. A. (2009). *The Devereux Student Strengths Assessment.* Lewisville, NC: Kaplan.

Levitt, J. M., Saka, N., Romanelli, L. H., & Hoagwood, K. (2007). Early identification of mental health problems in schools: The status of instrumentation. *Journal of School Psychology, 45,* 163-191. doi: 10.1016/j.jsp.2006.11.005.

McIntosh, K., Filter, K. J., Bennett, J. L., Ryan, C. & Sugai, G. (2010). Principles of sustainable prevention: Designing scale-up of school-wide positive behavior support to promote durable systems. *Psychology in the Schools, 47,*5-21. doi: 10.1002/pits.20448.

Menzies, H. M. & Lane, K. L. (2011). Validity of the Student Risk Screening Scale: Evidence of predictive validity in a diverse, suburban elementary setting. *Journal of Emotional and Behavioral Disorders, 20,* 82-91. doi: 10.1177/1063426610389613.

Merikangas, K. R., He, J. P., Brody, D., Fisher, P. W., Bourdon, K., & Koretz, D. S. (2010). Prevalence and treatment of mental disorders among US children in the 2001-2004 NHANES. *Pediatrics, 125,* 75-81. doi: 10.1542/peds.2008-2598.

Moffitt, T. E. (1993). Adolescence-limited and life-course-persistent antisocial behavior: A developmental taxonomy. *Psychological Review, 100*, 674 – 701.

Mulloy, M., Evangelista, N., Betkowski, J., & Weist, M. (2011). Mental health screening for adolescents. In R. Levesque (Ed.), *Encyclopedia of Adolescence*. NY: Springer.

Mulloy, M., & Weist, M. (2012). Implementing a public mental health framework within schools. In N. Quinn, & L. Knifton (Eds.), *Public mental health: An international perspective*. NY: McGraw Hill.

Naglieri, J. A., LeBuffe, P. A., & Shapiro, V. (2011a). Devereux Student Strengths Assessment-mini. Lewisville, NC: Kaplan Press.

Naglieri, J. A., LeBuffe, P., & Shapiro, V. B. (2011b). Universal screening for social-emotional competencies: A study of the reliability and validity of the DESSA-MINI. *Psychology in the Schools, 48,* 660-671. doi: 10.1002/pits.20586.

National Association of School Psychologists. (2000). *Principles for professional ethics guidelines for the provision of school psychological services.* Bethesda, MD: Author. Retrieved from http://www.nasponline.org/standards/ProfessionalCond.pdf

National Center on Response to Intervention. (2010, March). *Essential Components of RTI – A Closer Look at Response to Intervention.* Washington, DC: U.S. Department of Education, Office of Special Education Programs, National Center on Response to Intervention.

O'Connell, M. E., Boat, T., & Warner, K. E. (Eds.). (2009). *Preventing mental, emotional and behavioral disorders among young people: Progress and possibilities.* Washington, DC: National Academies Press.

President's New Freedom Commission on Mental Health. (2003). Achieving the promise: Transforming mental health care in America. Final report. (U.S. DHHS Pub. No. SMA-03-3832). Rockville, MD: U.S. Department of Health and Human Services.

Prince-Embury, S. (2006). *Resiliency Scales for Adolescents: Profiles of personal strengths.* San Antonio, TX: Harcourt Assessments.

Prince-Embury, S. (2007). *Resiliency Scales for Children and Adolescents: Profiles of personal strengths.* San Antonio, TX: Harcourt Assessments.

Prince-Embury, S. (2011). Assessing personal resiliency in the context of school settings: Using the Resiliency Scales for Children and Adolescents. *Psychology in the Schools, 48,* 672-685. doi: 10.1002/pits.20581.

Romer, D. & McIntosh, M. (2005). The role and perspectives of school mental health professionals in promoting adolescent mental health. In D. L. Evans, E. B. Foa, R. E. Gur, H. Hendin, C. P. O'Brien, M. E. P. Seligman, & T. Walsh (Eds.), *Treating and preventing adolescent mental health disorders: What we know and what we don't know: A research agenda for improving the mental health of our youth* (pp. 597-615). NY: Oxford University Press, Annenberg Foundation Trust at Sunnyland.

Severson, H. H., Walker, H. M., Hope-Doolittle, J., Kratochwill, T. R., & Gresham, F. M. (2007). Proactive, early screening to detect behaviorally at-risk students: Issues, approaches, emerging innovations, and professional practices. *Journal of School Psychology, 45,* 193-223. doi: 10.1016/j.jsp.2006.11.003.

Skiba, R.J., Eaton, J., & Sotoo, N. (2004). Factors associated with state rates of out-of- school suspension and expulsion. Bloomington, IN: Center for Evaluation and Education Policy. Retrieved from http://www.iub.edu/~safeschl/ChildrenLeftBehind/pdf/2b.pdf

Stone, L. L., Otten, R., Engels, R. C. M. E., Vermulst, A. A., & Janssens, J. M. A. M. (2010). Psychometric properties of the parent and teacher versions of the Strengths and Difficulties questionnaire for 4-to 12-year-olds: A review. *Clinical Child and Family Psychology Review, 13,* 254-274. doi: 10.1007/s10567-010-0071-2.

Sugai, G., & Horner, R.H. (2002). The evolution of discipline practices: School-wide positive behavior supports. *Child and Family Behavior Therapy, 24*, 23-25. doi: 10.1300/J019v24n01_03.

U.S. Department of Education. (2001). *No child left behind.* Retrieved September 17, 2012, from http://www.ed.gov/nclb

U.S. Department of Education Office of Special Education and Rehabilitative Services. (2002). *A new era: Revitalizing special education for children and their families.* Washington, DC: Author.

U.S. Surgeon General. (2001, April 11). *Youth violence: A report of the surgeon general.* Washington, DC: Author.

Walker, B. A. (2010). Effective schoolwide screening to identify students at risk for social and behavioral problems. *Intervention in School and Clinic, 46,* 104-110. doi: 10.1177/1053451210374989.

Walker, H. M., & Severson, H. (1992). *Systematic screening for behavioral disorders (SSBD): Technical manual.* Longmont, CO: Sopris West.

Walker, H. M., Severson, H. H., Naquin, G., D'Atrio, C., Feil, E. G., Hawken, L., & Sabey, C. (2009). Implementing universal screening systems within an RtI-PBS context. In B. Doll, W. Pfohl, & J. Yoon (Eds.), *Handbook of Prevention Science* (pp. 96-120). NY: Routledge.

Walker, H. M., Severson, H., Nicholson, F., Kehle, T., Jenson, W., & Clark, E. (1994). Replication of the Systematic Screening for Behavior Disorders (SSBD) procedure for the identification of at-risk children. *Journal of Emotional and Behavioral Disorders, 2,* 66-77

Wasserman, G. A., Jensen, P. S., Ko, S. J., Cocozza, J., Trupin, E., Angold, A.....Grisso, T. (2003). Mental health assessments in juvenile justice: Report on the consensus conference. *Journal of the American Academy of Child and Adolescent Psychiatry, 42,* 752-761. doi: 10.1097/01.CHI.0000046873.56865.4B.

Weist, M.D., & Albus, K.E. (2004). Expanded school mental health: Exploring program details and developing the research base. *Behavior Modification, 28*, 463-471.

Weist, M. D., Evans, S. W., & Lever, N. (2003). *Handbook of school mental health: Advancing practice and research.* NY: Springer

Weist, M.D., Rubin, M., Moore, E., Adelsheim, S., & Wrobel, G. (2007). Mental health screening in schools. *Journal of School Health, 77*, 53-58.

Weist, M. D., Stiegler, K., Stephan, S., Cox, J., & Vaughan, C. (2010). School mental health and prevention science in Baltimore City schools. *Psychology in the Schools, 47,* 89-100. doi: 10.1002/pits.20453.

In: School Health Screening Systems
Editors: Bradley McPherson and Carlie J. Driscoll ISBN: 978-1-63117-942-6

Chapter 8

PEDICULOSIS SCREENING FOR SCHOOL CHILDREN

Rick Speare[1*], Helen Weld[2], Megan Counahan[3] and Deon V. Canyon[4]
[1]Tropical Health Solutions Pty Ltd, Australia
James Cook University
[2]Public health nurse consultant, Australia
[3]AusAID, Samoa
[4]University of Hawai'i at Manoa

ABSTRACT

While head lice can be dealt with on an individual basis, lone action makes it more difficult to control. Infection with head lice often means the loss of class time for children and teachers, the loss of work time for parents and the unnecessary use and occasional misuse of potentially harmful pesticide treatments. Because head lice transmission commonly occurs within the classroom, schools have a duty of care to their pupils and staff. Working together within local communities is arguably the best strategy and school programs are well-placed to launch community efforts. These programs empower parents to deal with what too often is thought to be a hopeless reoccurring or persistent problem. Prior to the 1990s, school nurses employed by local or state governments were often responsible for screening students for head lice. The label "nit nurses" was applied to these health professionals. Formal government screening reduced or ceased in many developed countries during the 1990s and head lice control became a responsibility of parents and guardians. Local screening programs run by the school community became more common towards the end of the 1990s and early 2000s. The role of government has changed from in former years running head lice screening programs using nit nurses to currently providing educational and health promotional material, as well as logistical material such as templates for letters, results slips, et cetera, for schools to run their own screening programs. The typical practice is now for screening in individual schools to be conducted by a local collaboration of school administration, parents, teachers and the local parent association. Occasionally, private schools will only accept pupils if parents formally agree to their child participating in a school-based pediculosis screening

* Email: rickspeare@gmail.com.

program. Hence, head lice screening programs in schools depart from standard health screening programs since the screening is usually not done by health professionals, and the school community, rather than an official organization, conducts the screening. The change from a screening program driven by outside experts to screening driven by the school community raises challenges, but also offers opportunities for building capacity within the school community to better understand and manage health issues.

INTRODUCTION

Definitions and Terminology

Pediculosis is the term ascribed to an infection with *Pediculus humanus* var. *capitis*, the head louse. This is actually the narrow definition since there is another sucking louse of humans in the genus *Pediculus* called the body louse, *P. humanus* var. *corporis*. This is a rare ectoparasite even in developing countries and only seen in the homeless and in displaced populations in mass disasters. So, in medical jargon, infection with head lice is called pediculosis capitis and infection with body lice is called pediculosis corporis. In this chapter, we will use pediculosis to refer to the former only. We use "infection" with head lice rather than the more commonly used "infestation". While both terms describe a micro-organism invading a body, "infestation" is typically reserved for micro-organisms that are visible and superficial. However, since "infestation" is a term that comes with more emotional baggage than "infection" and since we do not wish to reinforce stigma with pediculosis, in this chapter we have chosen to use the more neutral term. In this chapter we use the term "nits" to mean eggs of head lice, hatched, unhatched or dead.

- "Viable egg or nit" means an egg that contains a live embryo (eggs hatch between 6 and 11 days after being laid).
- "Hatched egg or nit" is an egg in which the embryo has fully developed and emerged.
- "Dead egg or nit" is one in which the embryo has died in the egg. An aim of all insecticidal treatments is to kill the embryos in their eggs, but few achieve it. A product that kills eggs is an ovicide.
- What to call live lice? We like the term "climbers"; quite unscientific, but certainly descriptive!
- Climbers come in four stages: first, second, and third stage nymphs and adults. Adults are easily separated into two sexes, male and female, while determining the sex of the immature stages is not anatomically possible.

We also use "parents" to include a much broader group of both parents and guardians who take responsibility for the health and care of a child.

Pediculosis

Pediculosis has two forms: active pediculosis and inactive pediculosis.

- *Active pediculosis* is a current infection with lice and/or eggs containing live embryos in the hair.
- *Inactive pediculosis* is "dead" pediculosis, only egg shells or eggs with dead embryos remain in the hair. Inactive pediculosis is an historical marker of past infection; a child with inactive pediculosis is not infectious and cannot spread head lice. This latter point is very important in the school situation since children are often misdiagnosed by teachers as having pediculosis because the teacher sees hatched eggs in their hair. Hatched eggs are much easier to see on black hair than blonde hair, and dark haired children may be discriminated against since inactive pediculosis is more obvious. A case of pediculosis, which has been diagnosed by a teacher seeing eggs, shifts from the diagnostic category of inactive to active only when a live louse is found.

Children (and their families) are entitled to an accurate diagnosis that is non-discriminatory.

Impact of Pediculosis on School Children and Schools

Health professionals who deal with serious diseases (such as HIV, TB, heart disease, etc.) often regard pediculosis as a minor health issue, and some even ignore the condition. However, a minor health problem that impacts on large numbers of individuals, particularly vulnerable groups such as children, can have a significant cumulative health impact at the societal level. Researchers are only beginning to explore the mental health implications of pediculosis, which is an infection that must be taken seriously. Pruritus (itch) is an unreliable sign of head lice infection and diagnosis based on itch alone would miss most cases. Itch occurs in less than half of all cases; Mumcuoglu, Klaus, Kafka, Teiler, and Miller (1991) found pruritus in children with and without pediculosis (36% and 21%, respectively). This is an important finding since in schools pediculosis is often diagnosed when children scratch their scalps. Pediculosis causes a non-blistering rash, typically confined to the scalp and upper nape of the neck, but only in some children (Mumcuoglu et al., 1991). If children scratch, secondary bacterial infection of the scalp may occur, but this is uncommon (Mumcuoglu et al., 1991). The amount of blood ingested by head lice in the average case, and even heavy infected cases, is so low that anemia due to head lice is very unlikely (Speare, Canyon, & Melrose, 2006). However, some cases of severe anemia due to pediculosis have been reported in adults (Guss, Koenig, & Castillo, 2011).Arguably the major health impact of pediculosis in Australia and other developed market economies is on mental health. People usually react to head lice with negative emotions, some very strong (Parison, Canyon, & Speare, 2010; 2013). Parental frustration is common. We have encountered high levels of anxiety and even depression in children due to pediculosis. The negative emotions can result in children with pediculosis becoming isolated and stigmatized as dirty or unclean. However, the major mental health impact is arguably on individuals caring for the person with the problem; that is, parents rather than children. Treatment of pediculosis by parents involves time and resources and is viewed negatively (Parison, Speare, & Canyon, 2008). Despite only 5% of parents spending more than $150 a year on treatment products, the cost of treatment is often the major issue among Australian parents (Counahan, Andrews, Weld, Walsh, and Speare, 2007). In Norway, direct monetary costs were low for most parents, but increased with number of children (Rukke, Birkemoe, Soleng, Lindstedt, & Ottesen, 2012). Single parents were more concerned about the direct cost of pediculosis (Rukke et al., 2012). The major cost is time, including time taken shopping for treatments, application of treatments, repeated checking, and time absent from work when parents are asked to retrieve children from school after being diagnosed with pediculosis (Parison et al., 2008). In addition to these direct effects, pediculosis has an indirect impact on schooling. A high proportion of children (14%) in Victoria, Australia missed school due to pediculosis (Counahan et al., 2007) and, in Norway, a third of households had kept an infected child away from school (Rukke et al., 2012). Teachers are arguably at a higher risk of acquiring head lice than non-teachers due to their higher level of contact with potentially infected students. Pediculosis may legitimately thus be considered an occupational health and safety issue. In a questionnaire study of 275 primary school teachers from 16 schools in Victoria and 23 in North Queensland, almost three-quarters of participants felt that head lice posed a risk to them, and this risk concerned over 81% (Counahan, Walsh, & Speare, 2009). Work absenteeism due to pediculosis was reported by 14% of teachers in North Queensland and 4% in Victoria. In Victoria, the number of days absent from school ranged from one to three (median = one day) and for all North Queensland teachers it was one day. Over half of the teachers used preventative methods designed to minimize the chance of acquiring head lice at school. Finally, an unreported impact of pediculosis in schools is to increase stress on school executives and front-office staff who deal directly with parents (Figure 1). Parents complain to the school when they think their children acquire head lice at school. Complaints about pediculosis are very common. When we were conducting screening in Australian schools, principals frequently reported how relieved they felt since parental complaints would decrease as the school could be seen as “tackling the head lice problem”.

Figure 1. Collage of headlines from Australian newspapers highlighting how schools are drawn into the issue of pediculosis.

Biology of Head Lice

Head lice are insects that are highly specialized to live a parasitic existence on humans (Figure 2). Adult females are the largest, being 2.3-3.3 mm in length; males are smaller at 2.1-2.6 mm (Buxton, 1947). The newly hatched first stage nymph is the smallest at 1.5 mm. Eggs are 0.8 mm in length. All stages of the life cycle are visible to the unaided eye, including the eyes of parents. Hence, it is an unusual affliction since it is obvious to the lay person, unlike many other conditions screened for at school.

Figure 2. Adult male head louse on hair (from http://en.wikipedia.org/wiki/File:Male_human_head_louse.jpg. Licensed under Creative Commons Attribution-Share Alike 2.0 Generic license).

Head lice have no other host; an important point in control strategies. Head lice feed and hydrate by sucking blood. They are very efficient, being able to puncture a scalp capillary and fill up within 5 minutes. Feeding changes the color of the louse, giving it a dark red tinge, owing to the gut containing deoxygenated blood. Head lice cannot absorb water from the environment and so are very susceptible to dehydration (Figure 3). They also have to get rid of water from a blood meal and can die if this is prevented. The dimethicones (a common silicone compound in conditioners) appear to kill lice by preventing transpiration.

Each of the louse's six legs ends in a claw, highly specialized for attaching to hairs (Figure 4). Head lice are so specialized that they are unable to live for any length of time off a human host. A head louse off the host will face a very high likelihood of dying within a few hours from dehydration. Again, this is another absolutely critical point for control strategies. Head lice are not found in the environment (see section on transmission below). Time and effort spent "spring cleaning" is wasted in terms of head lice control. Concentrate on the head!

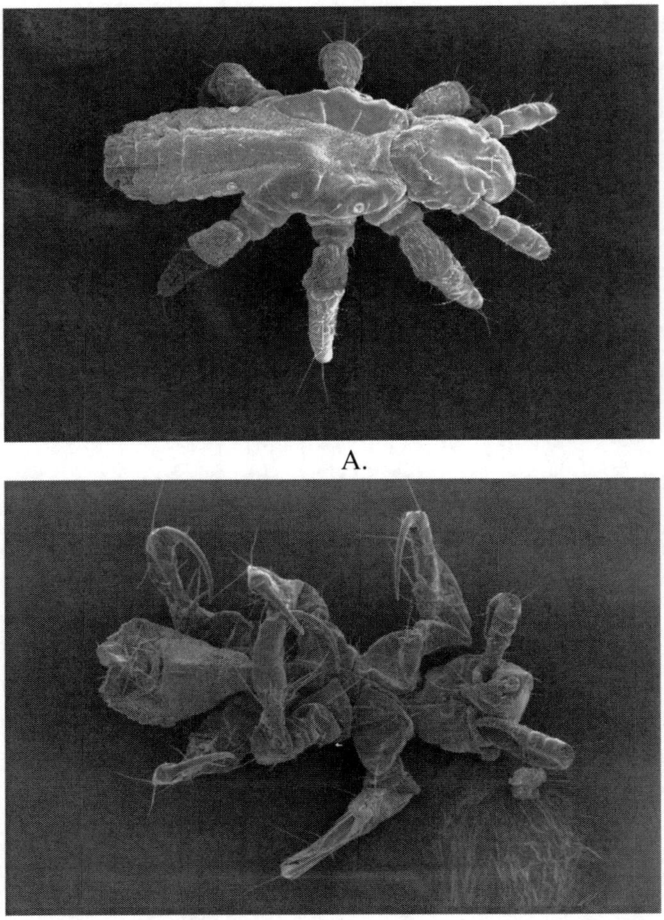

A.

B.

Figure 3. First stage nymph. A. Nymph just after emerging from the egg; B. Nymph that has died from dehydration after failing to obtain a blood meal (scanning electron micrographs).

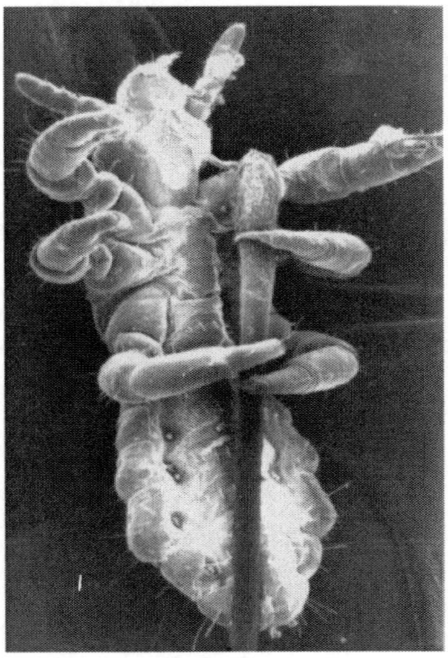

Figure 4. A head lice nymph grasping a hair with three of its six claws (scanning electron micrograph).

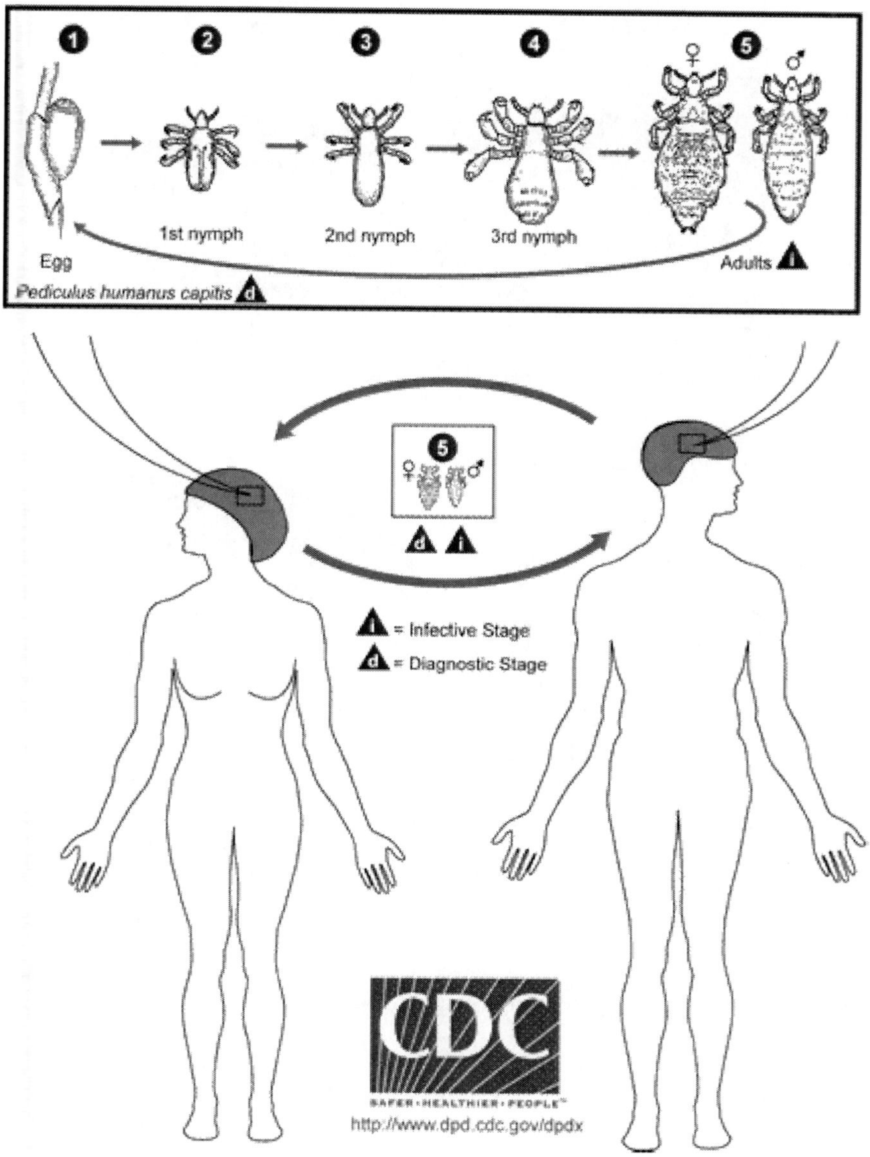

Figure 5. Life cycle of head lice (from Centers for Disease Control - http://www.dpd.cdc.gov/dpdx/HTML/Headlice.htm).

Understanding the life cycle of head lice is absolutely essential in designing control strategies (Figure 5).

Eggs are laid by the adult female and are firmly attached to hair shafts by an elegant mechanism that makes them difficult to remove (Figure 6A). Eggs are, thus, unlikely to fall off a head into the environment.

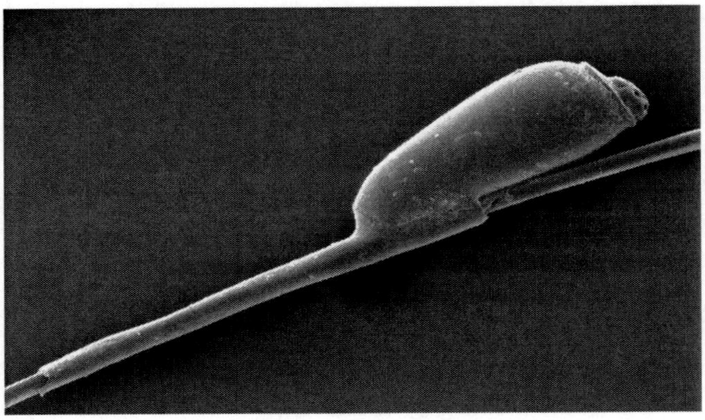

A.

B.

Figure 6. Egg of the head louse is firmly attached to the hair shaft by encircling tube. A. Unhatched egg (scanning electron microscopy); B. Appearance of eggs on hairs during examination (Image by Prof. Jorg Heukelbach).

Eggs are 0.8 mm long by 0.3 mm wide, pale brown, and typically attached about 1 cm from the scalp. The eggs hatch in 5 to 11 days, but the empty egg shell remains strongly fastened to the hair shaft (Figure 6B). Since hair grows about 1 cm per month (Myers & Hamilton, 1951), hatched eggs are typically present for many months; for example, for a girl with medium length hair (15 cm) hatched eggs may be visible for over a year. Eggs with an embryo (viable eggs) are brown; hatched and dead eggs are tan in color. If pediculosis is diagnosed visually, it is typically through teachers seeing hatched eggs (inactive pediculosis). If a child has no climbers (active pediculosis), they may be diagnosed as having pediculosis for an historical event that occurred many months previously. First stage nymphs hatch from the egg, undergo three molts while passing through two additional nymphal stages (second, third) to reach the adult male or adult female (Figure 7). From hatching to adult is about 8 days. Females are larger than males and have a V-shaped posterior end while males have a rounded end (Figure 8). Males and females mate and females start laying eggs about 15 hours after mating (Burgess, 2004). Females lay about 6 eggs per day. Time from an egg being laid to the next generation of eggs being laid is about 14 days. Females live about 32 days.

Figure 7. Adult males, females and nymphs under the microscope embedded in glycerin jelly.

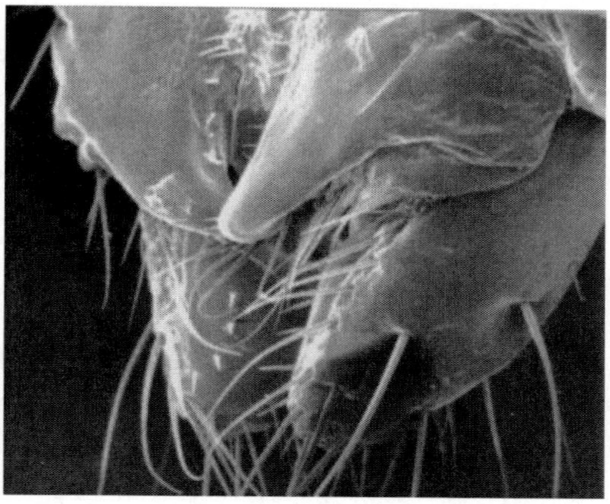

A.

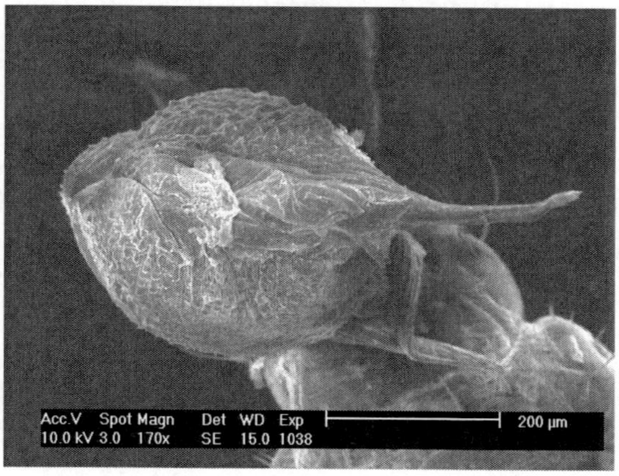

B.

Figure 8. A. Adult female louse has a V-shaped notch at posterior end with bilateral gonopods to enable hair to be grasped and egg laid; B. Adult male louse has an aedeagus (penis) with the tip protruding from the louse's posterior end when detumescent (see Figure 2). This expands immensely and emerges to sit over the back of the louse prior to mating with female (as in scanning electron micrograph above).

All stages suck blood by inserting a tube formed from stylets into a capillary on the scalp. Feeding takes about 5 minutes and only very small amounts of blood are imbibed per feed: an adult female ingests 0.0005 ml blood per day (Speare et al., 2006). We have set up a blood loss page online to allow parents to calculate in theory how much blood their child could lose from pediculosis (see http://www.tropicalhealthsolutions.com/headlice/bloodlosscalculator).

Transmission

Head lice are very active and can move rapidly forwards and backwards along hairs, using their claws to grasp the shaft, at a maximum speed of 2.5 cm/second. They can also transfer hair to hair on the head and between heads. Head lice use very specific cues to transfer, being more likely to move across to a hair that is above them and moving at right angles to the hair they are standing on (Canyon, Speare, & Müller, 2002). Transfer to another host occurs when hairs touch. It is important to understand this and its relevance to head-to-head lice transmission. The concept of head-to-head contact groups is essential to controlling pediculosis in schools.

Epidemiology of Pediculosis in Schools

Pediculosis can occur at any age so long as some hair longer than 0.5 cm is on the head. In developed market economies pediculosis is rare under two years of age, common in pre-schools and primary schools, uncommon in secondary schools, and uncommon in adults. However, pediculosis may become a problem in the elderly in nursing homes (Speare & Ahn, 1999). In developing countries, the prevalence of head lice varies with the society. In South Africa, for example, pediculosis was so uncommon among black Africans that even experienced nurses had not seen head lice (Govere, Speare, & Durrheim, 2003). Ethnicity and/or hair type has some protective effect against head lice. African Americans have a much lower prevalence of pediculosis than Caucasians in the USA (Juranek, 1977). Similarly, in a mixed race primary school in South Africa pediculosis was found only in children of European and Indian ancestry and not in "black" African children (Govere et al., 2003). Having pediculosis in the past is a risk factor for being currently infected with head lice (Değerli, Malatyalı, & Mumcuoğlu, 2013; Ortega-Marín, Márquez-Serrano, Lara-López, Moncada, & Idrovo, 2013). For a child with pediculosis, the most common relative with pediculosis is the mother (Casstex, Suarez, & De la Cruz, 2000).

Seasonality

Pediculosis in southern Australia (Tasmania) had a lower prevalence at the start of the school year in January and increased as the year progressed (Goldsmid, Crowther, Doering, & Wilkinson, 1981). However, Counahan (2006) in an analysis of "nit-nurse" school screening data from Victoria, Australia found prevalence in primary school children higher in the winter months (mid-school year) and lowest at the end of the school year. In general, prevalence appears to be higher in warmer climates (Counahan et al., 2007) and warmer months (Bauer,

Jahnke, & Feldmeier, 2009; Mimouni, Ankol, Gdalevich, Grotto, Davidovitch, & Zangvil, 2002), but there will be local exceptions of course.

Intensity of Infection

Most infected children have less than 10 climbers on their heads at any one time. In a study in Townsville primary schools, Speare, Thomas, and Cahill (2002) found that 57.7% of infected children had less than 10 lice, 34.5% had 10-99 lice, 7.5% had 100-499 lice and one child had 1,623 lice. The average number of lice per infected child was 30 (median 6) with an average of 130 lice per class. Examples of head lice numbers in classrooms are shown in Figures 9, 11 and 12. It is very useful to count head lice in individual children, particularly if they have recurrent pediculosis. The reason is that parents can see a quantitative improvement (lower numbers of lice on their child's head) even if head lice persist. This gives them some encouragement that their efforts are making a difference!

Gender Effects

Pediculosis in primary schools in both developed and developing countries has a higher prevalence in girls (sometimes up to six times that in boys) (Bachok, Nordin, Awang, Ibrahim, & Naing, 2006; Counahan, Andrews, Büttner, Byrnes, & Speare, 2004; Değerli et al., 2013; Gulgun, Balci, Karaoğlu, Babacan, & Türker, 2013; Heukelbach, Wilcke, Winter, & Feldmeier, 2005; Mohammed, 2012; Motovali-Emami, Aflatoonian, Fekri, & Yazdi, 2008; Ortega-Marín et al., 2013; Speare & Buttner, 1999). This is related to gender, not hair length (Counahan et al., 2004; Speare & Buttner, 1999). It is most likely due to gender-related behavioral factors that result in more head-to-head contact rather than gender per se (Speare & Buttner, 1999).

Hair Length

Prevalence of pediculosis is related to hair length in some studies, but not in others (Bachok et al., 2006; Counahan et al., 2004; Değerli et al., 2013; Mumcuoglu, Friger, Ioffe-Uspensky, Ben-Ishai, & Miller, 2001; Ortega-Marín et al., 2013; Willems, Lapeere, Haedens, Pasteels, Naeyaert & De Maeseneer, 2005; Speare & Buttner, 1999). Active pediculosis is more difficult to cure in children with long hair because it is difficult to get 100% coverage with treatments and fine-tooth combing can be painful, which may terminate a treatment session early. Reducing the length of hair will make eliminating head lice easier in children with long hair, but it is not necessary. Shaving heads is definitely not required to cure pediculosis! Any hair cuts should make the child feel valued, not stigmatized.

Personal Susceptibility

Some children are highly prone to acquiring pediculosis while others appear to be unsuitable hosts. Unfortunately, individual susceptibility has not been documented. However, it should be borne in mind since parents of highly susceptible children may invest a great amount of time and effort in dealing with pediculosis, much more than a parent with a less susceptible child. Yet, the parents with the susceptible children may have to suffer accusations of laziness and incompetence if they cannot eradicate infection and their children are seen as a perpetual source or reservoir of infection. Expert assistance from the school community, not blame, is needed for parents having difficulties with recurrent pediculosis.

Class Effects

Pediculosis in schools clusters by class, supporting the hypothesis that head lice frequently transmit within school classrooms (Speare & Buttner, 1999). In a typical primary school in Australia, some classes will have a high prevalence of pediculosis (e.g., >50%) while others have a low prevalence or even no head lice (Figure 9). This variation may distort parents' perceptions of a head lice "problem" in their child's school. Some may think that pediculosis is not an issue (child in a class with low prevalence) while others may regard pediculosis as out of control (child in a class with high prevalence). Clustering by class and family was also a significant risk factor for pediculosis in a Belgium study (Willems et al., 2005).

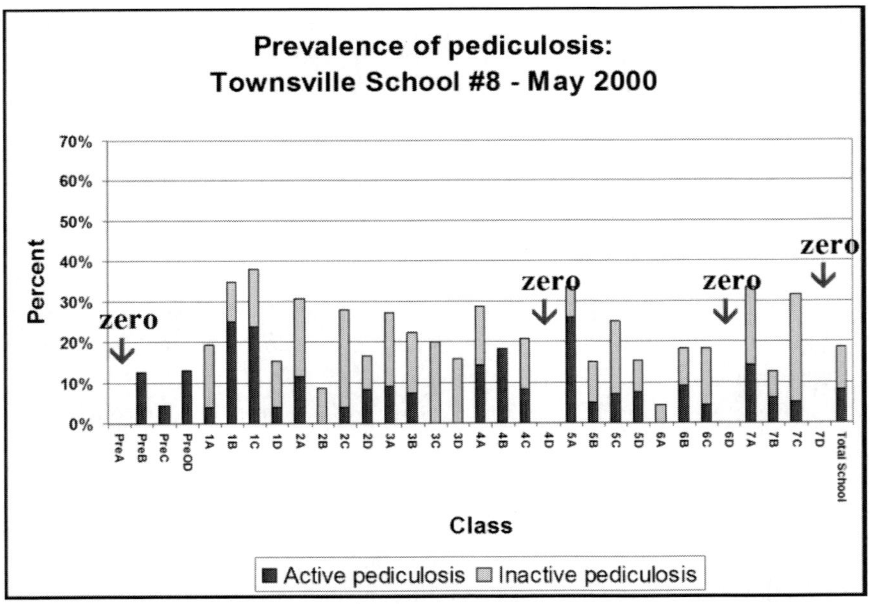

Figure 9. Prevalence of pediculosis across classes in a primary school in Townsville, Australia. Although the overall school prevalence of active pediculosis is 8%, some classes have prevalences of over 20% while others have no active pediculosis. Note that if pediculosis is diagnosed only by finding eggs (inactive pediculosis) the prevalence of pediculosis is doubled, giving a misleading impression of the severity of the problem.

Just as the number of lice on a child's head is an important indicator of the intensity of pediculosis, it is useful to calculate how many lice are actually present in a school classroom (Figures 11 & 12). In a Townsville study, we found the average number of climbers per infected class with an average of 25 students was 130 (Speare et al., 2002).

Environmental Reservoirs: Dispelling a Myth

To test whether the environment is a source of head lice we examined the heads of 2,230 primary school children in Townsville, Australia and at the same time the floors of their classrooms (Speare et al., 2002). We found a prevalence of 21% active pediculosis with an average of 130 lice per infected class. We collected a total of 14,033 head lice from the children's hair. While the children were out of their classrooms, we vacuumed the classroom floors using a filter to trap head lice. On the floors we found no lice at all. Cleaning the environment in which infected people live, work, and play is, thus, not supported by data and control should focus on eliminating lice from people's heads.To explore this issue further, we wondered if a high risk situation for transmission might be bedding. We did a study examining the pillow cases of children with head lice to test the hypothesis that head lice actively detach from a child's head onto the pillow case overnight (Speare, Cahill, & Thomas, 2003). We did find lice on the pillow cases, but in small numbers. Only four percent of the pillow cases had head lice and these made up 0.1% of the total head lice numbers on heads and pillow cases combined. Also, a third of the lice on pillow cases were dead. Our conclusion was the pillow cases may act as a very small reservoir for head lice. So, putting pillow cases in hot water, a hot wash or a hot clothes dryer or even ironing them to kill any possible lice is advisable when treating pediculosis (Izri & Chosidow, 2006; Speare et al., 2003).

Diagnosis of Pediculosis

Pediculosis is diagnosed by direct observation of climbers. Clinical signs and symptoms (e.g., itch) are non-specific and should not be used to make a diagnosis of pediculosis. They quite validly can be used to raise suspicion of pediculosis, but active pediculosis should only be diagnosed when a climber is found. The accuracy of parents in diagnosing pediculosis in their children varies with the location. In Australia, it is low. We found that parents in Victoria missed a large proportion of cases (sensitivity 16%), but did not have a large proportion of false positives (specificity 94%) (Counahan, Andrews, & Speare, 2005). Pediculosis was more liable to be missed in boys (Speare & Buttner, 1999). In Nigeria, parents were much more accurate in diagnosing head lice (sensitivity 74% and specificity 99%), failing to detect pediculosis mainly when children had less than five lice (Ugbomoiko, Speare, & Heukelbach, 2008). In contrast to these findings, parents in an urban slum in Brazil were highly accurate in correctly diagnosing active pediculosis in their children, leading to the recommendation that in this community, a treatment program could be based on parental self-diagnosis of active pediculosis (Heukelbach, Kuenzer, Counahan, Feldmeier, & Speare, 2006). In Australia and Norway, the majority of parents will treat their child if they think they have pediculosis (Speare & Buttner, 1999; Rukke et al., 2012). This also applies in developing countries. In Nigeria, for example, 79% of people had attempted to treat pediculosis when diagnosed, but only 5% had applied an insecticidal treatment (Heukelbach & Ugbomoiko, 2011). Questionable parental diagnostic skills in most locations, plus the high rate of treatment once a diagnosis is made result in children being unnecessarily exposed to treatments. It highlights that screening programs at school do have an important role. Diagnostic techniques used in school-based screening must have a high sensitivity and specificity and parents must be advised to use effective treatments when children go home with positive results.

- Visual inspection: Hair is examined visually by the unaided eye, being searched in an organized sequence either by hand or by use of wooden spatulas. Eggs and climbers can be detected. However, climbers tend to run away from mechanical disturbances in the hair and they may be missed. The sensitivity of this technique is low; for example, in German schools visual inspection detected 29% of cases of active pediculosis (Jahnke, Bauer, Hengge, & Feldmeier, 2009).
- Dry combing: Hair is combed with a nit comb in an organized sequence with the comb being examined after each sweep from roots to tip. Eggs and climbers can be detected. Climbers can run away from the comb, but if captured, the comb makes them obvious. This technique detects more cases of pediculosis (x4) than visual inspection (Mumcuoglu et al., 2001). Dry combing is also faster than visual inspection: time to detection of first louse was 57 seconds by dry combing and 116 seconds by visual inspection (Mumcuoglu et al., 2001).
- Wet combing: Hair is made wet with water or even washed. It is then combed with a nit comb in an organized sequence with the comb being examined after each sweep from roots to tip. Eggs and climbers can be detected. Immersion immobilizes head lice, but they quickly recover in less than a minute (Canyon & Speare, 2007). Climbers can run away from the comb, but if captured, the comb makes them obvious. Wet combing is probably equivalent to dry combing, but more effort is involved.
- Conditioner and nit comb: Conditioner is combed through the hair using a standard comb with the aim of coating each hair from root to tip. Hair is then combed with a nit comb in an organized sequence with the comb being examined after each sweep from roots to tip. Best done by wiping the conditioner and any captures onto white tissue paper or toilet paper and examining this for climbers and eggs (Figure 10). Conditioner stuns head lice and they cease moving for up to 20 minutes (Canyon & Speare, 2007). It also helps detangle hair and allows the nit comb to slide over hairs more freely. This is the most sensitive diagnostic technique, detecting up to 3.5 times the prevalence of active pediculosis than visual inspection. Surprisingly, visual inspection in German schools had a higher sensitivity in detecting inactive pediculosis than conditioner and nit comb (Jahnke et al., 2009).

Some people apply conditioner to wet hair; others apply it to dry hair. Conditioner can also be washed off or left on the hair. Bug Busting, a school-based program in UK, applies conditioner after washing the child's hair with shampoo (Ibarra, Fry, Wickenden, Jenner, &

Franks, 2009). The authors state that washing the hair with shampoo before applying conditioner is more effective than applying conditioner to dry hair (Fry, Ibarra, Smith, & Wickenden, 2002). However, no evidence for this statement is provided. In our school-based programs, we take the minimal effort route and apply conditioner to dry hair and do not wash it off after assessment is complete unless the child requests this.

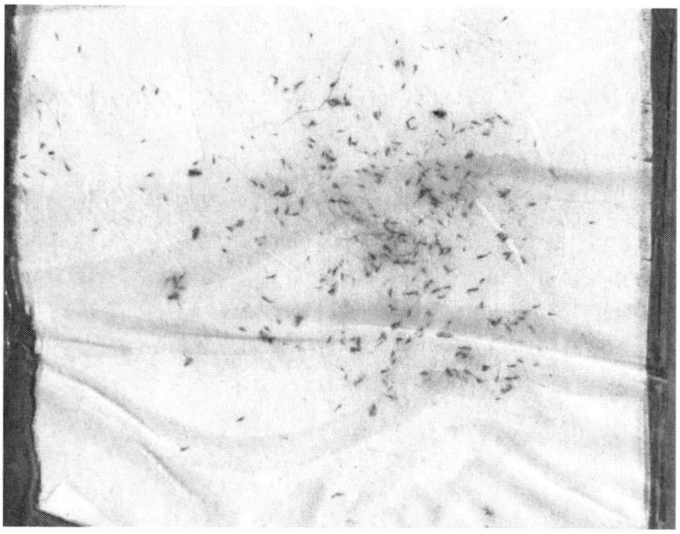

Figure 10. Head lice and eggs collected from hair after application of white conditioner by a fine tooth comb and wiped onto white tissue paper.

Which Nit Comb?

Humans have been using fine tooth combs or nit combs to remove head lice from antiquity (Mumcuoglu & Zias, 1988). The teeth are spaced closer than a standard comb (0.09-0.3 mm vs. 0.7-1 mm) and allow a hair to just pass between the teeth, but not climbers. Hair has an average diameter of 0.07 mm (Lapeere et al., 2005). Most combs are made of plastic; some of metal and others of both plastic and metal. The Bug Busting comb has been most extensively trialed (Ibarra et al., 2009). A trial comparing the effectiveness of a cheap plastic comb with flat teeth (Lady Jayne™) against a more expensive comb with metal cylindrical teeth (Lice Meister™) showed that both were equally effective in removing climbers, but the Lice Meister removed about four times the number of eggs (Speare, Canyon, Cahill, & Thomas, 2007). Similarly, a study of two metal combs showed no difference with climbers (Kurt et al., 2009). However, a study in Argentina showed differences in number of climbers removed by different combs (Gallardo, Toloza, Vassena, Picollo, & Mougabure-Cueto, 2012). Combs with more closely spaced teeth appeared more effective; metal was better than plastic, but other less well defined design factors appeared to have an impact. Since school screening programs only need to detect climbers to confirm diagnosis, fine-toothed plastic combs that are cheap and disposable are sufficient. Bug Busting uses a purpose built plastic comb as part of a kit that can be prescribed in the UK by doctors (Ibarra et al., 2007).

Options for Detecting Pediculosis in Screening at School

Diagnosis of pediculosis does not require sophisticated implements and readily lends itself to school-based screening programs. Since active pediculosis requires treatment and inactive pediculosis does not, it is important to use a technique that differentiates between the two states. Visual inspection alone should not be used as it will miss a high proportion of cases of active pediculosis. Dry combing increases detection of cases of active pediculosis by a factor of four and is twice as fast as visual inspection. Hence, for a minimal program, dry combing is better. For a comprehensive program, the use of conditioner and plastic nit combs is recommended. The only technique that has been evaluated extensively is the Bug Busting approach (see Evaluation section below in this chapter). This involves shampooing hair prior to application of conditioner. However, our preferred method is to use conditioner liberally on dry hair with a nit comb (see below in this chapter). Although a combination of visual inspection followed by conditioner and nit comb gives a more accurate prevalence of pediculosis (Janke et al., 2009), the minimal number of additional cases detected by adding visual inspection may not justify the additional time and effort required. Of more importance are those children and parents who do not take any action to treat pediculosis once a positive diagnosis has been made.

TREATMENT

We will not discuss treatment of pediculosis in detail since the focus in most school based programs is on diagnosis of pediculosis with treatment left to parents at home. To summarize, there are four general treatment modalities:

1. Physical removal of lice by:
    - hand
    - fine tooth comb (nit comb) with or without application of a liquid to the hair;

2. Killing of lice by local physical means:
    - electrocution of lice using a purpose designed comb
    - hot air applied to the hair using purpose designed equipment
    - application of silicon based compounds (dimeticones and cyclomethicones);

3. Killing of lice by locally applied chemicals:
    - insecticides that act on the nervous system (pyrethrins, permethrin, bioallethrin, malathion, carbaryl, ivermectin)
    - insecticides with site of action unknown (herbal products, spinosad);

4. Killing of lice by orally administered chemicals (ivermectin; Currie, Reynolds, Glasgow, & Bowden, 2010).

A comprehensive review on treatments for head lice is given by Heukelbach (2010, pp.73-87). The most effective treatment approach is application to the hair of compounds that include the silicones dimethicone and/or cyclomethicone (Heukelbach, Speare, & Ramos, 2010). Some of these have an ovicidal effect (Heukelbach , Sonnberg, Becher, Melo, Speare, & Oliveira, 2011). Killing is by physical means since the dimethicones either asphyxiate lice or stop them transpiring water (Burgess, 2009). If the ovidical effect is 100%, a single application is adequate (Burgess, Brunton, & Burgess, 2013; Burgess & Burgess, 2011). Resistance to chemicals can occur when the killing action is mediated by damage to key biochemical systems within the lice; for example, those that kill by interfering with the function of the louse's nervous system. Resistance to pyrethrins and permethrin is most common and less so for the organophosphates (malathion, carbaryl) (Durand et al., 2012). Resistance to permethrin is so prevalent in developed countries that some authors have queried whether it should be still marketed (Burgess et al., 2013). Insecticide resistance can be a reason for treatment failure, but other factors must be considered. Hair conditioner does not kill lice and is ineffective when used alone without physical removal of lice. Active pediculosis can be cured by use of conditioner and nit comb alone. Practical clinical trials have shown that Bug Busting using a fine-toothed comb is comparable or better than insecticides (Ibarra et al., 2009) (see Evaluation section below in this chapter). Conditioner and nit comb used frequently can cure active pediculosis by removing climbers initially and then nymphs as they hatch from viable eggs. Bug Busting uses combing on days 1, 5, 9 and 13. Regular use of fine-toothed combing is recommended where reinfection is ongoing. However, the best strategy in this case is simultaneous screening of the index case's head to head contact group. Ask the child who their friends are! If conditioner and nit comb is used to detect active pediculosis in a school screening program and the hair is thoroughly combed, then treatment can be said to have already started. Typically, more than 95% of climbers will be removed if combing is thorough. Parents just need to continue treatment at home. This is a major advantage over using visual census or dry combing to make a diagnosis. However, if the purpose of a screening program is diagnosis and parents are responsible for treatment, then parents must not be under any illusion that their infected children have "received" a treatment at school.

IMPORTANCE OF SCREENING FOR PEDICULOSIS IN SCHOOLS

Policies on Pediculosis

Most schools and education departments have policies on pediculosis. In the 20th Century, these were more likely to be punitive and children with pediculosis were typically sent home before the end of the school day. We make two important points here: i) the official definition of pediculosis did not specify that a child could only be excluded for *active* pediculosis; hence, most children were excluded on the basis of nits being seen and may not have been an infection risk; and ii) most exclusions were based on a teacher suspecting an individual child had pediculosis and conducting a no-touch visual inspection. Since visual inspection is highly likely to result in misdiagnosis and if other children in the class are not examined at the same time, this approach is subject to marked selection bias and could even be discriminatory. Hatched eggs stand out in children with black hair, but are almost invisible in children with blonde hair. The action expected of parents varies according to official policy and micro-policies adopted by schools. In some jurisdictions, parents were expected to administer an effective treatment only and proof of freedom from lice was not required. In other jurisdictions, parents were required to treat and for their child to be lice-free (climbers gone) before entry back to school. In others, children could only be readmitted to school if they were free of all climbers and all head lice eggs. The latter approach was labeled the "no nit policy" (Pontius, 2011). This approach is promoted in the USA by the National Pediculosis Association (http://www.headlice.org/index.html). Since there is no effective and time-efficient way to remove all head lice eggs and since nits alone are not an infection risk, the no nit policy has been criticized strongly by parasitologists, pediatricians, and public health groups (Mumcuoglu, Meinking, Burkhart, & Burkhart, 2006). Some products claim to assist in removal of nits from hair. However, the only products tested showed no effect (Burgess, 2010). School exclusion because of pediculosis is a bad policy because there is no evidence to justify it. Nothing has been published in the peer-reviewed literature to demonstrate that the incidence of pediculosis in schools falls when children with pediculosis detected by teachers are excluded. Enlightenment has arrived in the 21st Century! In most developed countries, children are not excluded from school for pediculosis by macro-policies. In Australia, the official policy at state and territory level is that school children suspected of having pediculosis stay at school. They are not isolated and the school informs their parents that they appear to have pediculosis and asks the parents to manage the infection. To support this, a health promoting schools approach is used to create a supportive environment that assists parents and the school community to manage pediculosis. Various programs now support this policy: for example, Scratching for Answers (Victoria), Nitbusters (NSW), Head Lice in Primary Schools (Queensland), Healthy Heads without Head Lice (South Australia). Even in the USA, the home of the "no-nit" policy, similar changes have been implemented in some districts (Pontius, 2011). Current policy in USA from a school nurse perspective is that i) screening will be conducted at the school nurse's discretion, but widespread school screening is no longer recommended; ii) the presence of nits or live lice do not warrant exclusion from school; and iii) treatment education should be provided by the school nurse (Andresen & McCarthy, 2009). For schools who wish to develop their own local policies or guidelines, the document *Steps for developing headlice guidelines for your early childhood centre or school* may assist in making the process all inclusive (South Australia Department of Health, 2002).

APPROACHES TO SCHOOL BASED SCREENING: LESSONS LEARNED

In Australia, parents regard pediculosis as an issue they are responsible for in their own children (Counahan et al., 2007). However, they think that schools should play a strong supportive role in assisting them in controlling pediculosis. This attitude is probably indicative of the situation in most other countries.

Getting Started

To reach the target of 100% participation of students, garnering support within the school community is vital. Identifying a motivated core group of volunteer "leader" parents who are committed is essential. These parents can coordinate consents, provisions, and volunteer help on screening days, as well as liaise with the school administration. Once parents resolve to deal with the lice problem, the school administration needs to be approached and convinced of parental commitment. Most administrators are relieved that there are proactive individuals willing to take this on and are supportive of parental action. Although teachers cannot necessarily deal with head lice "hands on", they should be encouraged to reinforce the education about head lice. Teachers can also be involved as recorders during the screening process. Another possibility for screeners is that school districts could employ an "outside" trained team of 2-5 people available within communities to augment programs. Each team would cover a district and go to schools on a rotating basis once per term to assist parents. However, since involvement of the school community is a key factor, the role of outsiders should be to provide support, guidance, and expert assistance to the school community, not to do the screening by themselves.

Mobilizing the School Community

These suggestions and guidelines can be applied to any social group including families, neighborhoods, playgroups, classrooms, schools, communities-at-large, and even individuals.

Education Is Paramount

Ensuring that all involved children, parents, teachers, and administrators have current and relevant training on head lice is the foundation of head lice control. Ignorance and misinformation are big hurdles to overcome and significant stigma issues are associated with misinformation. Once all stakeholders have the correct information and public awareness has been raised, people tend to talk amongst themselves much more openly. Collaborative action is the only way to win! A sample teaching guide, which can be adapted in content and duration depending on the target audience, is provided at http://www.tropicalhealthsolutions.com/headlice/schools.

Children

Educational sessions should be offered to students prior to screening sessions, so that children have a good understanding of the process. Teachers or trained volunteer parents can do this presentation. Age appropriate material can be supplied to teachers after each session. A coloring activity for younger students and a crossword for older children are provided at http://www tropicalhealthsolutions.com/headlice/schools. Lice photos for display and identification and posters depicting the life cycle help the educational process. Giving people the opportunity to view lice under a dissecting microscope is a very popular teaching tool and promotes lively discussions. Education sessions for students should be done annually. Further education can be delivered during the combing and conditioning process.

Parents

Scheduling educational sessions for parents is vital. Offering these at different times depending on work schedules (e.g., AM after school drop off; PM before school pick up; lunch hour; after hours in evening) ensures the best attendance possible. School newsletter articles including key messages and "tips" each week are another good strategy. To reach some parents it might take active one-on-one communication initiated by the parent coordinators. These efforts serve to stimulate discussions wherever parents convene. Parents on the sidelines of sporting events often engage in discussing head lice challenges. As with children, the process of education is ongoing, primarily on an informal basis during screening sessions. "New" preschool parents should be educated at the beginning of the year about head lice. For most of them, it will be their first experience with head lice and it is important to get them involved early.

Teachers and Administrators

Request to have time to present during a teacher/staff meeting. People always learn something new! This is an opportunity to explain the teachers' role on the day of school screening. Work closely with administrators with general organization and scheduling, as well as keeping communication open.

How to Run a Parent-Managed School Screening Program

Once people are "on board" with the idea of a school screening process, the organizational gears begin to churn. Anticipating problems early and getting as much as possible done ahead of the screening day will alleviate stress.

Obtaining Consent

It is a legal requirement to obtain written parental consent for screening or treatment before any volunteers have contact with a child. In many jurisdictions in developed countries, official clearance may now be required for volunteers (even parents) in the form of a card that certifies that the volunteer is cleared to work with children. This is obtained from particular government bodies and involves screening of official records by the police. Parental permission is easier to obtain if treatment is not being administered since treatment at school is unpopular with many parents (in Australia). Start off by sending consent forms home (see http://www.tropicalhealthsolutions.com/headlice/schools) with the children, following up with calls to those who don't respond, explaining the issue thoroughly and having a "compassionate ear" to listen to the frustrations that parents experience. If some parents are reluctant to have their children participate, suggest that they come on the day and screen their own children. A program with a low participation rate is futile. Aim for at least 60%. An alternative strategy is an opt-out approach in which parents are asked to sign a form if they do NOT want their child to be screened. This indicates that it is "normal" practice and reduces associated stigma. At some schools, parents are asked to consent for their children to be screened for head lice as part of the enrolment process.

Scheduling Screening Days

Screening days should be coordinated for the beginning of each term, usually in the second week, so volunteers can be given a reminder during the first week. Screening sessions once-a-term seems adequate for control and do not create parent "burn out".

Recruiting Parents to Volunteer

Parent-managed, school-based programs can certainly work to control head lice. The biggest factor affecting sustainability of school programs is maintaining a steady group of support from a core group of parents who are willing to assist. Not knowing if there will be enough parental help on a screening day is always stressful!

Through trial and error, we found breaking the school up into class group times was much more acceptable to potential volunteers. This also prevents parent "burn out" which can happen when parents have been screening all day. For example, screen the Preschool-Grade 2 group from the beginning of school to Morning Tea; Grades 3, 4, 5 from Morning Tea to Lunch; Grade 6 and 7 after lunch. This enables parent volunteers to attend when their child will be screened. A sample letter of invitation to parent volunteers is provided at http://www.tropicalhealthsolutions.com/headlice/schools.This is usually combined with the consent form.

General Logistics

Parental Roles

- A team of six experienced helpers can usually screen/treat (comb and condition) a class of 30 children in 30 minutes. This anticipates having children with long hair/short hair and some active cases. Even if one person gets "stuck" with a child with particularly heavy infection, the routine can be paced quite smoothly.
- An "extra" parent to keep combs clean. Some parents are very willing to help, but feel squeamish about touching hair; so this is a useful and vital role for them.
- Having an overall coordinator to "float" is good too. This person can oversee the whole process, facilitating good flow of students, troubleshooting, and communicating throughout the day with the principal and the teachers.

- Parents can be trained to be excellent diagnosticians.
- Good organization, leadership, and teamwork pays off; in one school 750 children were successfully screened (conditioner and nit combing) in one day with three teams in action simultaneously! The more efficient the process, the less disruptive it will be for the school day.
- Follow up with "thank you" notes in the school newsletter after screenings and provide basic follow up information.
- Letter of confidentiality to be signed by all parent volunteers is provided at http://www.tropicalhealthsolutions.com/headlice/schools.

Teachers' Roles

- Teachers can do the record keeping on their class list and hand out letters to be sent home (See http://www.tropicalhealthsolutions.com/headlice/schools for an example). All children receive a letter, regardless of their head lice status. Having teachers involved definitely helps with accurate record keeping and helps with time management.
- This also frees up a "worker" to just "do" heads and not get the record lists wet!
- Another advantage of having the teachers involved is that they become aware of the incidence and prevalence of cases in their classroom. Most teachers are more than happy to assist and tally the cases at the end of their stint. This makes it much easier on coordinators at the end of a long day.
- Instructions on what details workers should record need to be visible at each work station.

Supplies and Funding

- Conditioner (cheap, plain, white) is the best. Two bottles per class should be sufficient, but amounts will vary according to hair length since long hair needs more than short hair..
- Wide tooth combs for detangling (10-15).
- Tissues (10 boxes, but again depends on length of hair and level of infestations).
- Quality head lice combs with long stainless steel rounded "teeth" combs. Bug Buster combs are robust and designed for a long life. The number of combs required for use will depend on the numbers of volunteers available, with at least two combs per volunteer to ensure time efficiency. If funds are short, cheap plastic combs are adequate.
- Towels (small) to cover shoulders (children can bring their own from home).
- Disinfectant.
- Dental floss, old tooth brushes or long pins to remove eggs from head lice combs.
- Gloves for helpers (small, medium and large).

There are many businesses that are empathetic to the head lice problem and are happy to make donations or give discounts for supplies. Offering creative fundraisers will help augment funding from the school or PTA budget. We ran a "Scary Nitpickers Disco" on Friday the 13th, which proved to be the most popular fundraiser with the students.

Infection Control

- All volunteers are required to wear gloves. The gloves do not need to be taken off or changed between children as long as they are rinsed in disinfectant if lice are found. Wearing gloves ensures that the volunteer and the child are protected from each other in case of any open wounds from any source.
- All combs should soak in hot water and disinfectant after use. Lice die in hot water at 60°C in less than 30 seconds (Speare, 2000). The head lice comb will need to be scrubbed with an old hard toothbrush and perhaps a pin or dental floss used to remove eggs caught in the base of the comb. Check in good light that the job is done properly.
- Volunteers should tie their hair back.

Helpful Tips on Screening Day

- Organize supplies.
- Request volunteers to arrive 15 minutes before first class for orientation and general preparedness.
- Ensure that there is a hot water supply accessible.
- Set up comb cleaning stations (two plastic basins for each station).
- Line up rows of chairs and benches.
- Provide plastic bags for tissue disposal.
- Set up table for teacher to record, tape instructions to desk.
- Organize class lists in sequential order, in a manila folder or using software, according to schedule. Provide columns for recording. (MS Excel spreadsheet works well.)
- Set up a TV monitor and have an educational video showing (nature videos work for all ages) for entertainment.

METHOD OF SCREENING AND TREATMENT AT SCHOOL

1. Apply plain white conditioner liberally to dry hair.
2. Cover scalp to the ends of the hair.
3. De-tangle hair with large, sturdy comb (Do not detangle with the nit comb).
4. Leave conditioner in hair for 5 minutes (conditioner stuns lice up to 20 minutes and makes combing easier).
5. Separate the hair into sections.
6. Comb through with the head lice comb.
7. Wipe the conditioner from the comb onto a tissue and look for lice and eggs (nits).
8. Remove all nits to assure total lice treatment.
9. Rinse conditioner from hair. Leaving conditioner in hair during school screenings causes no harm.
10. Clean the head lice comb in accordance with infection control (see above).
11. Record findings accurately.
12. Active cases of head lice are retreated in 7 days.
13. Provide every child who participates with a fun stamp on his/her hand.

14. Send every child home with a follow up letter, even if clear (See example at http://www.tropicalhealthsolutions.com/headlice/schools).

Record Keeping

Keep accurate records for each class, including the pediculosis status of each child. Keep all records strictly confidential and use a simple code to indicate the child's status: LL = Live Lice; EGGS = Live eggs or dead eggs / CL=Clear; AB=Absent / NC=No Consent. The definitions of pediculosis used are:

- Active pediculosis: Climbers found (LL).
- Inactive pediculosis: No climbers found. Eggs found on hair shafts. These can be hatched or dead. Some may be alive, but confirming viability is difficult and only possible using a microscope. Parents should be informed that eggs have been detected.

Observational Notes

- Live lice, climbers, are best captured with the conditioner and nit combing method. "Dry" checking is not adequate since it is less sensitive as head lice can move quickly away. When dry checking is done due to lack of time and parental help, some children are deemed "clear" when in fact they are probably not.
- Findings from each class are evaluated and children with heavy infections are assessed.
- Identify if some particularly heavily infected classes had one or two children who had high numbers of lice on their head and then try to assist them and their parents more intensely (loan a comb to take home). Bug Busting in schools often provides children with head lice with a Bug Buster kit.
- Identify patterns and clusters of active cases. One particularly memorable situation was a mother of five who had been extremely vigilant about head lice control, combing and conditioning, but was still dealing with repeated infections. Finally, she realized that the grandmother who lived with her family was the source of lice (the adult day care centre). Assistance was subsequently provided to the centre with lice education and control. Pediculosis in the elderly can be missed and has even caused problems in nursing homes (Speare & Ahn, 1999).

Evaluating the Impact of Pediculosis Screening Programs

What type of screening program is best? The options to be considered are:

1. School screening program: a) run by an external agent (e.g., government, contractor); b) run by the school community; or

2. School detection and treatment program.

A pediculosis screening and treatment program, using topical treatment, will reduce the prevalence and intensity of pediculosis at primary schools, but not to zero (Figure 11). Overall, prevalence in this example fell from 29% to 10% and intensity from 27 lice per infected child to 4 lice. This is a typical result for such a program. It illustrates that a school-based detection and treatment program can reduce pediculosis, but the costs in time and money have to be seriously considered against the benefits.

The effectiveness of screening by an external agent such as "nit nurses" with no or minimal involvement from the school community appears to have minimal effect on prevalence of head lice. After analyzing local government data from school screening in Victoria, Australia, Counahan (2006) concluded that there is no evidence to suggest that traditional inspection programmes (which do not remove lice) have any influence on parental treatment regimes, re-infection risk or effect on controlling the prevalence of head lice. The average cost per case detected was estimated at between AUD32-50 in the 1990s (Counahan, 2006).

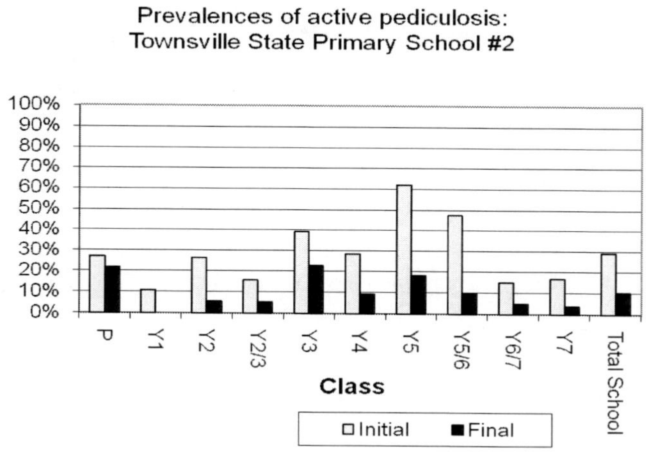

A.

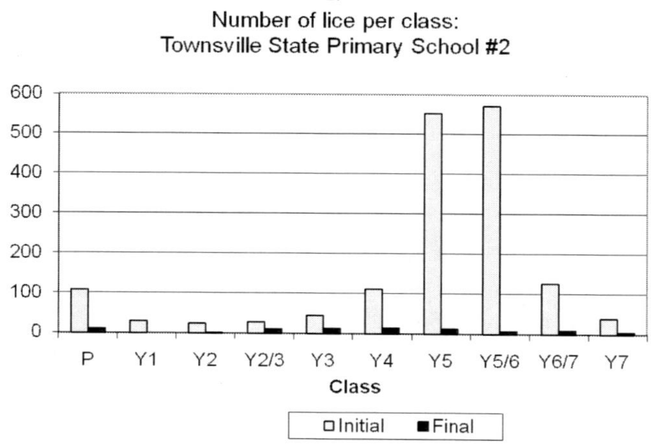

B.

Figure 11. (Continued).

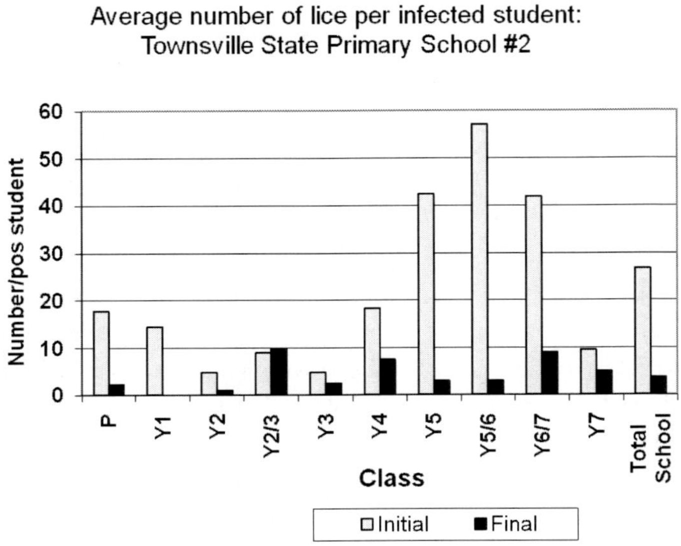

C.

Figure 11. Changes in pediculosis 14 days after screening at a small primary school with 209 students and an opt-out program in Townsville, Australia. Two treatments were given at school on days 0 and 7: A) prevalence of pediculosis; B) number of lice per class; C) average number of lice per infected student.

Although the evidence is not strong, it would seem that routine screening programs done by government nit nurses or other external agents that do not involve the school community are not effective. Are screening programs owned by the school community more effective? The only whole school approach evaluated appears to be Bug Busting in UK (Ibara et al., 2007). Parents find it acceptable in the UK, Belgium, and Denmark (Ibara et al., 2007).

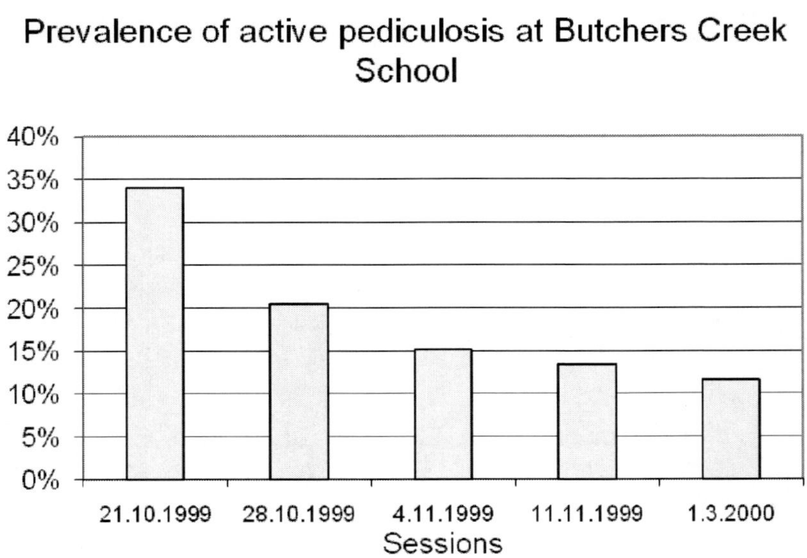

A.

Figure 12. (Continued).

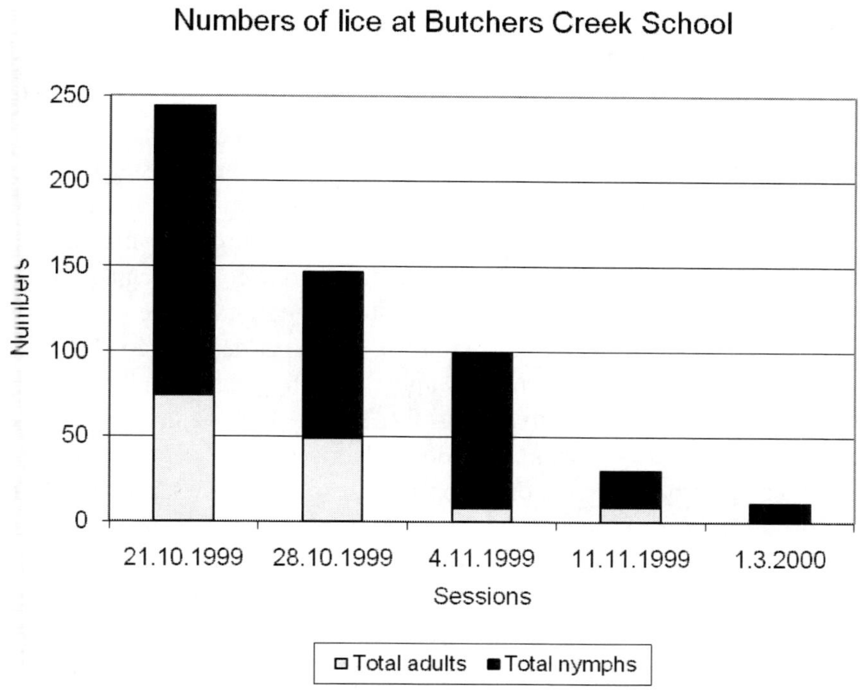

B.

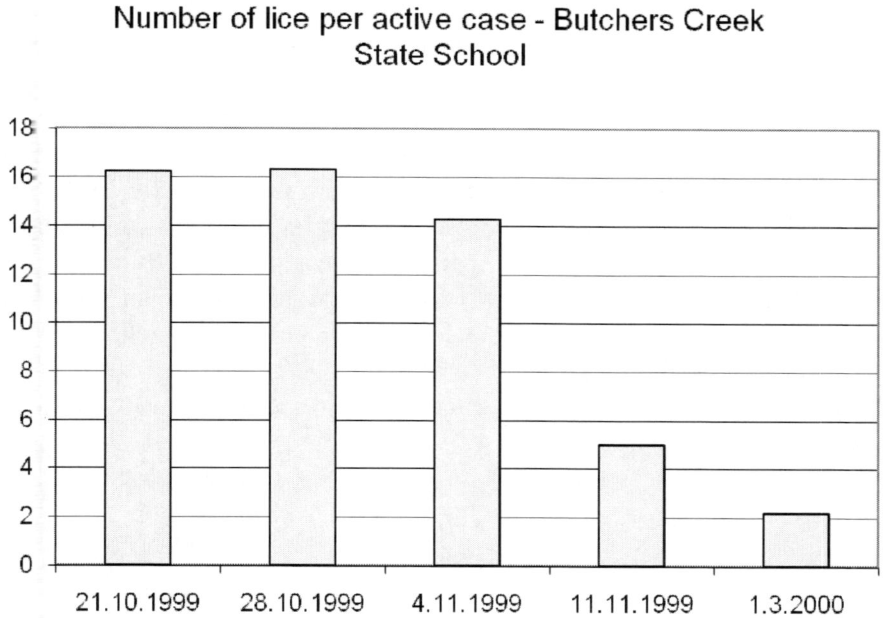

C.

Figure 12. Change in pediculosis with a whole school detection program using conditioner and fine tooth comb (Far North Queensland, Australia). Rural school with total enrolment of 50 pupils. A) prevalence; B) number of lice found; C) average number of lice per infected child. Repeat sessions indicated by dates.

This approach which uses conditioner and a specific fine tooth comb to diagnose and remove head lice and trains parents and children in the Bug Busting method is comparable to insecticides; in some trials insecticide was more effective (Roberts, Casey, Morgan, & Petrovic, 2000) while in others Bug Busting was more effective (Plastow, Luthra, Powell, Wright, Russell, & Marshall, 2001). The latest version of the Bug Buster kit proved more effective than insecticides when parents managed treatment at home (Hill, Moor, Cameron, Butlin, Preston, Williamson, & Bass, 2005). For a school screening program, the Bug Busting approach (as an example of the conditioner and fine tooth comb technique) is the best approach since it combines a sensitive detection technique, starts the control process at school, and provides practical health education. In our experience, if conditioner and fine tooth comb are used in a whole of school screening program, combined with education about control, the reduction is generally equivalent to that expected with a detection and treatment program. For example, a study in a rural school in North Queensland showed that a whole school program using conditioner for detection with parental follow-up reduced prevalence and intensity of pediculosis (Figure 12). Bug Busting used in a primary school in the UK resulted in a marked decline in prevalence (Ibarra et al., 2007).

The education component is important. Shirvani, Shokravi, and Ardestani (2013) found that in Iran a screening program combined with practical education of children about head lice significantly improved knowledge, favorable attitudes to head lice control, behavior about personal hygiene, and reduced the prevalence of pediculosis. The test group prevalence fell from 69% to 27%; prevalence in the control group fell from 82% to 74%.

CONCLUSION

The best school-based screening program for head lice is a whole school program run by the school and parents, includes practical education about pediculosis for teachers, parents and children, and offers advice on feasible control strategies for families and schools. It is based on combing with conditioner using a fine tooth comb, with treatment managed by parents with assistance in difficult cases from experts in the school community. Commencing early in the school year will ensure that the school community is knowledgeable and has feasible management strategies for pediculosis throughout the school year. If possible, an opt-out system should be implemented with permission for pupils to be involved in head lice screening given at the time of enrolment.

REFERENCES

Andresen, K., & McCarthy, A. M. (2009). A policy change strategy for head lice management. *Journal of School Nursing*, *25*(6), 407-416. doi:10.1177/1059840509347316.

Bachok, N., Nordin, R.B., Awang, C.W., Ibrahim, N.A., & Naing, L. (2006). Prevalence and associated factors of head lice infestation among primary schoolchildren in Kelantan, Malaysia. *Southeast Asian Journal of Tropical Medicine and Public Health*, *37*(3), 536-543. doi: 10.1016/S2221-1691(12)60250-0.

Bauer, E., Jahnke, C., & Feldmeier, H. (2009) Seasonal fluctuations of head lice infestation in Germany. *Parasitology Research*, *104*(3), 677-681. doi: 10.1007/s00436-008-1245-4.

Burgess, I. F. (2009). The mode of action of dimeticone 4% lotion against head lice, *Pediculus capitis*. *BMC Pharmacology*, *20*(9), 3. doi: 10.1186/1471-2210-9-3.

Burgess, I. F. (2010). Do nit removal formulations and other treatments loosen head louse eggs and nits from hair? *Medical and Veterinary Entomology*, *24*(1), 55-61. doi: 10.1111/j.1365-2915.2009.00845.x.

Burgess, I. F., Brunton, E. R., & Burgess, N. A. (2013). Single application of 4% dimeticone liquid gel versus two applications of 1% permethrin creme rinse for treatment of head louse infestation: A randomised controlled trial. *BMC Dermatology*, *13*, 5. doi: 10.1186/1471-5945-13-5.

Burgess, I. F., & Burgess, N.A. (2011). Dimeticone 4% liquid gel found to kill all ice and eggs with a single 15 minute application. *BMC Research Notes*, *4*, 15. doi: 10.1186/1756-0500-4-15.

Buxton, P. A. (1947). *The Louse. An account of the lice which infest man, their medical importance and control*. London: Edward Arnold & Co.

Canyon, D., Podger, D., & Speare, R. (2005). *How much blood do head lice drink and are they a danger?* Retrieved from http://www.tropicalhealthsolutions.com/headlice/bloodlosscalculator

Canyon, D. V., & Speare, R. (2007). Do head lice spread in swimming pools? *International Journal of Dermatology*, *46*(11), 1211-1213.

Canyon, D.V., Speare, R., & Müller, R. (2002). Spatial and kinetic factors for the transfer of head lice (Pediculus capitis) between hairs. *Journal of Investigative Dermatology, 119,* 629-31.

Casstex, L., Suarez, S., & De la Cruz, A. M. (2000). Presencia de pediculosis en convivientes con ninos positives a *Pediculus capitis* (Anoplura: Pediculidae). *Revista Cubana de Medicina Tropical*, *52*, 225-227.

Counahan, M. (2006). *Scratching for Answers? The public health aspects of head lice control*. Doctor of Public Health thesis. James Cook University; Townsville, Australia.

Counahan, M., Andrews, R., Büttner, P., Byrnes, G., & Speare, R. (2004). Head lice prevalence in primary schools in Victoria, Australia. *Journal of Pediatrics and Child Health*, *40*(11), 616-619.

Counahan, M., Andrews, R., & Speare, R. (2005). Reliability of written parental reports of head lice in their children. *Medical Journal of Australia*, *182*(3), 137-138.

Counahan, M., Andrews, R., Weld, H., Walsh, W., & Speare, R. (2007). What parents in Australia know and do about pediculosis. *Rural and Remote Health*, *7*, 687.

Counahan, M., Walsh, H., & Speare, R. (2009). Head lice as an OHS risk to primary school teachers in Australia. *Journal of Occupational Health and Safety*, *25*(6), 477-481.

Currie, M. J., Reynolds, G. J., Glasgow, N. J., & Bowden, F. J. (2010). A pilot study of the use of oral ivermectin to treat head lice in primary school students in Australia. *Pediatric Dermatology*, *27*(6), 595-599. doi: 10.1111/j.1525-1470.2010.01317.x.

Değerli, S., Malatyalı, E., & Mumcuoğlu, K. Y. (2013). Head lice prevalence and associated factors in two boarding schools in Sivas. *Türkiye Parazitoloji Derneği*, *37*(1), 32-35. doi: 10.5152/tpd.2013.08.

Durand, R., Bouvresse, S., Berdjane, Z., Izri, A., Chosidow, O., & Clark, J. M. (2012). Insecticide resistance in head lice: Clinical, parasitological and genetic aspects. *Clinical Microbiology and Infection*, *18*(4), 338-344. doi: 10.1111/j.1469-0691.2012.03806.x.

Fry, F., Ibarra, J., Smith, J., & Wickenden, C. (2002). Wet combing to eradicate head lice. *Journal of the Royal Society of Medicine*, *95*(12), 630-631.

Gallardo, A., Toloza, A., Vassena, C., Picollo, M. I., & Mougabure-Cueto, G. (2012). Comparative efficacy of commercial combs in removing head lice (*Pediculus humanus capitis*) (Phthiraptera: Pediculidae). *Parasitology Research*, *112*(3), 1363-1366. doi: 10.1007/s00436-012-3208-z

Goldsmid. J. M., Crowther, W. E. L., Doering, M. J., & Wilkinson, A. M. (1981). Head louse infestation in Tasmanian schoolchildren. *Australian Family Physician*, *10*(10), 784-792.

Goldsmid, J. M., Langley, J. G., Naylor, P., & Bashford, P. (1989). Further studies on head lice and their control in Tasmania. *Australian Family Physician*, *18*(3), 253-255.

Govere, J. M., Speare, R., & Durrheim, D. N. (2003). The prevalence of pediculosis in rural South African schoolchildren. *South African Journal of Science*, *99*, 21-23.

Gulgun, M., Balci, E., Karaoğlu, A., Babacan, O., & Türker, T. (2013). Pediculosis capitis: Prevalence and its associated factors in primary school children living in rural and urban areas in Kayseri, Turkey. *Central European Journal of Public Health*, *21*(2), 104-108.

Guss, D. A., Koenig, M., & Castillo, E. M. (2011). Severe iron deficiency anemia and lice infestation. *Journal of Emergency Medicine*, *41*(4), 362-365. doi: 10.1016/j.jemermed.2010.05.030

Heukelbach, J. (Ed). (2010). *Management and control of head lice infestations*. Bremen: Uni-Med Science.

Heukelbach, J., Kuenzer, M., Counahan, M., Feldmeier, H., & Speare, R. (2006). Correct diagnosis of current head lice infestation made by affected individuals from a hyperendemic area. *International Journal of Dermatology*, *45*, 1437-1438. doi: 10.1111/j.1365-4632.2006.03097.x

Heukelbach, J., Sonnberg, S., Becher, H., Melo, I., Speare, R., & Oliveira, F. A. (2011). Ovicidal efficacy of high concentration dimeticone: A new era of head lice treatment. *Journal of the American Academy of Dermatology*, *64*(4), e61-2. doi: 10.1016/j.jaad.2010.04.003.

Heukelbach, J., Speare, R., & Ramos, A. N. (2010). General considerations on treatments and treatment schemes. In J. Heukelbach (Ed.), *Management and control of head lice infestations* (pp. 97-101). Bremen: UNI-MED Verlag AG.

Heukelbach, J., & Ugbomoiko, U. S. (2011). Knowledge, attitudes and practices regarding head lice infestations in rural Nigeria. *Journal of Infection in Developing* Countries, *5*(9), 652-657. doi:10.3855/jidc.1746

Heukelbach, J., Wilcke, T., Winter, B., & Feldmeier, H. (2005). Epidemiology and morbidity of scabies and pediculosis capitis in resource-poor communities in Brazil. *British Journal of Dermatology*, *153*, 150–156.

Hill, N., Moor, G., Cameron, M. M., Butlin, A., Preston, S., Williamson, M. S., & Bass, C. (2005). Single blind, randomised, comparative study of the Bug Buster kit and over the counter pediculicide treatments against head lice in the United Kingdom. *British Medical Journal*, *331*(7513), 384-387.

Ibarra, J., Fry, F., Clarice, W., Olsen, A., Vander Stichele, R.H., Lapeere, H., … Smith, J. L. (2007). Overcoming health inequalities by using the Bug Busting 'whole-school approach' to eradicate head lice. *Journal of Clinical Nursing, 16*(10), 1955-1965. doi: 10.1111/j.1365-2702.2007.01795.x

Ibarra, J., Fry, F., Wickenden, C., Jenner, M., & Franks, A. (2009). The impact of well-developed preventative strategies on the eradication of head lice. *Perspectives in Public Health, 129*(4), 165-173. doi: 10.1177/1466424008094804

Izri, A., & Chosidow, O. (2006). Efficacy of machine laundering to eradicate head lice: Recommendations to decontaminate washable clothes, linens, and fomites. *Clinical Infectious Diseases, 42*(2), e9-10. doi: 10.1086/499105

Jahnke, C., Bauer, E., Hengge, U.R., & Feldmeier, H. (2009). Accuracy of diagnosis of pediculosis capitis: Visual inspection vs wet combing. *Archives of Dermatology, 145*(3), 309-313. doi: 10.1001/archdermatol.2008.587.

Juranek, D. D. (1977). Epidemiology of lice. *Journal of School Health, 47*, 352–355.

Kurt, O., Tabak, T., Kavur, H., Muslu, H., Limoncu, E, Bilac, C.,,& Larsen, K. (2009). Comparison of two combs in the detection of head lice in school children. *Turkiye Parazitoloji Dergisi, 33*, 50-53.

Lapeere, H., Brochez, L., Haeghen, Y. V., Mabilde, C., Vander Stichele, R., Leybaert, L., & Naeyaert, J-M. 2005). Method to measure force required to remove *Pediculus humanus capitis* (Phthiraptera: Pediculidae) eggs from human hair. *Journal of Medical Entomology, 42*(1), 89-93.

Mimouni, D., Ankol, O. E., Gdalevich, M., Grotto, I., Davidovitch, N., & Zangvil, E. (2002). Seasonality trends of Pediculosis capitis and Phthirus pubis in a young adult population: Follow-up of 20 years. *Journal of the European Academy of Dermatology and Venereology, 16*(3), 257-259.

Mohammed, A. L. (2012). Head lice infestation in schoolchildren and related factors in Mafraq governorate, Jordan. *International Journal of Dermatology, 51*(2), 168-172. doi: 10.1111/j.1365-4632.2011.04972.x

Motovali-Emami, M., Aflatoonian, M. R., Fekri, A., & Yazdi, M. (2008). Epidemiological aspects of pediculosis capitis and treatment evaluation in primary-school children in Iran. *Pakistan Journal of Biological Science, 11*(2), 260-264.

Mumcuoglu, K. Y., Friger, M., Ioffe-Uspensky, I., Ben-Ishai, F., & Miller, J. (2001). Louse comb versus direct visual examination for the diagnosis of head louse infestations. *Pediatric Dermatology, 18*(1), 9-12.

Mumcuoglu, K. Y., Klaus, S., Kafka, D., Teiler, M., & Miller, J. (1991). Clinical observations related to head lice infestation. *Journal of the American Academy of Dermatology, 25*(2 Pt 1), 248-251.

Mumcuoglu, K. Y., Meinking, T. A., Burkhart, C. N., & Burkhart, C. G. (2006). Head louse infestations: The "no nit" policy and its consequences. *International Journal of Dermatology*, 2006, *45*(8), 891-896.

Mumcuoglu, Y. K., & Zias, J. (1988). Head lice, *Pediculus humanus capitis* (Anoplura: Pediculidae) from hair combs excavated in Israel and dated from the first century B.C. to the eighth century A.D. *Journal of Medical Entomology, 25*(6), 545-547.

Myers, R. J., & Hamilton, J. B. (1951). Regeneration and rate of growth of hairs in man. *Annals of the New York Academy of Sciences, 53*, 562-568.

Ortega-Marín, L., Márquez-Serrano, M., Lara-López, L M., Moncada, L. I., & Idrovo, A. J. (2013). Effect of households' social networks on lice infestation among vulnerable

Mexican children: A qualitative comparative analysis. *Journal of Tropical Pediatrics*, *59*(5), 413-418. doi: 10.1093/tropej/fmt041

Parison, J., Canyon, D., & Speare, R. (2010). Head lice and the impact of knowledge, attitudes and practices - a social science overview. In J. Heukelbach (Ed.), *Management and control of head lice infestations* (pp. 104-109). Bremen: UNI-MED Verlag AG.

Parison, J., Canyon, D., & Speare, R. (2013). Head lice: The feelings people have. *International Journal of Dermatology*, *52*(1), 169-171. doi: 10.1111/j.1365-4632.2011.05300.x.

Parison, J., Speare, R., & Canyon, D. V. (2008). Uncovering family experiences with head lice: The difficulties of eradication. *Open Dermatology Journal*, *2*, 9-17.

Plastow, L., Luthra, M., Powell, R., Wright, J., Russell, D., & Marshall, M. N. (2001). Head lice infestation: Bug busting vs. traditional treatment. *Journal of Clinical Nursing*, *10*(6), 775-783.

Pontius, D. J. (2011). Hats off to success: Changing head lice policy. *NASN School Nurse*, *26*(6), 356-362. doi: 10.1177/1942602X11421349

Roberts, R. J., Casey, D., Morgan, D. A., & Petrovic, M. (2000). Comparison of wet combing with malathion for treatment of head lice in the UK: A pragmatic randomised controlled trial. *Lancet*, *356*(9229), 540-544.

Rukke, B.A., Birkemoe, T., Soleng, A., Lindstedt, H.H., & Ottesen, P. (2012). Head lice in Norwegian households: Actions taken, costs and knowledge. *PLoS One*, *7*(2), e32686. doi: 10.1371/journal.pone.0032686

Shirvani, G.Z., Shokravi, A. F., & Ardestani, M. S. (2013). Evaluation of a health education program for head lice infestation in female primary school students in Chabahar city, Iran. *Archives of Iranian Medicine*, *16*(1), 42-45. doi: 013161/AIM.0013

South Australia Department of Health. (2004). *Steps for developing headlice guidelines for your early childhood centre or school*. Adelaide: South Australia Department of Health. Retrieved from http://www.health.sa.gov.au/pehs/branches/headlice/headlice-guidelines.pdf

Speare, R. (2000). Hot water kills head lice experimentally placed on brushes. *International Journal of Dermatology*, *39*, 954-956.

Speare, R., & Ahn, S. (1999). Eradicating head lice in a nursing home. *Australian Family Physician*, *28*, 915-917.

Speare, R., & Buttner, P. (1999). Prevalence of head lice in a primary school in Australia and implications for control. *International Journal of Dermatology*, *38*, 285-290.

Speare, R., Cahill, C., & Thomas, G. (2003). Head lice on pillows and strategies to make a small risk even less. *International Journal of Dermatology*, *42*, 626-629.

Speare, R., Canyon, D. V., Cahill, C., & Thomas, G. (2007). Comparative efficacy of two nit combs in removing head lice (*Pediculus humanus* var. *capitis*) and their eggs. *International Journal of Dermatology*, *46*(12), 1275–1278. doi: 10.1111/j.1365-4632.2007.03410.x.

Speare, R., Canyon, D., & Melrose, W. (2006). Quantification of blood intake of the head louse, *Pediculus humanus capitis*. *International Journal of Dermatology*, *45*, 543-546.

Speare, R., Thomas, G., & Cahill, C. (2002). Head lice are not found on floors in primary school classrooms. *Australian and New Zealand Journal of Public Health*, *26*(3), 208-211.

Ugbomoiko, U. S., Speare, R., & Heukelbach, J. (2008). Self-diagnosis of head lice infestation in rural Nigeria as a reliable rapid assessment tool for pediculosis. *Open Dermatology Journal*, *3*, 95-97.

Willems, S., Lapeere, H., Haedens, N., Pasteels, I., Naeyaert, J. M., & De Maeseneer, J. (2005). The importance of socio-economic status and individual characteristics on the prevalence of head lice in schoolchildren. *European Journal of Dermatology*, *15*(5), 387-392.

In: School Health Screening Systems
Editors: Bradley McPherson and Carlie J. Driscoll

ISBN: 978-1-63117-942-6

Chapter 9

SCOLIOSIS SCREENING FOR SCHOOL CHILDREN

Daniel Y. T. Fong*[•], *Keith D. K. Luk*, *Kenneth M. C. Cheung* and *Yat-Wa Wong
The University of Hong Kong, China

ABSTRACT

Scoliosis refers to the side-to-side or lateral curvature of the spine, which may cause both physical and cosmetic concerns. Around 80% or more of patients with the disorder have unknown etiology; of which around 80% have scoliosis manifested during adolescence. Scoliosis, if untreated, may progress and eventually require corrective but invasive spinal fusion surgery. Hence, scoliosis screening has been advocated for identifying adolescent idiopathic scoliosis (AIS) when non-invasive conservative treatment, such as bracing, can be applied; thus, minimizing the need for surgery. However, the United States Preventive Services Task Force first recommended neither support nor opposition for scoliosis screening in 1996, later changing the recommendation to against screening in 2004. Their main concerns were the lack of screening tests, lack of efficacious conservative treatments, and that most patients identified by screening will not progress to a clinically significant form of scoliosis.

Tests that have been used in scoliosis screening are the forward bending test (FBT), the measurement of the angle of trunk rotation (ATR) by a scoliometer, moiré topography, and low-dose roentgenography. Most scoliosis screening programs have utilized the FBT only because of its ease of use and simplicity. However, its use alone has been shown to be inadequate and a tandem use with other additional screening tests may increase the accuracy of identifying AIS patients. In particular, the use of FBT, measurement of ATR, and moiré topography in tiers has been shown to be accurate and predictive in identifying AIS patients with Cobb angle ≥20°, a curvature that deserves clinical observation or even treatment. Commencing screening when children are 10 years of age has been shown to achieve satisfactory screening accuracy.

Bracing has been the traditionally used conservative treatment for controlling curve progression of AIS patients; but its efficacy has not been established. Recent efforts have been made and results are yet to be revealed. Nevertheless, the implementation of

[•] E-mail: dytfong@hku.hk.

scoliosis screening has made the data available for study of a disorder with poorly known etiology and has increased public awareness of the disorder.

INTRODUCTION

Scoliosis

Scoliosis refers to a lateral or side-to-side curvature of the spine (Figure 9.1). It is the most common form of spinal deformity, with a very long history dating back to the Stone Age when there were cave drawings of people with scoliosis (Cotton, 1991). The term "scoliosis" was derived from a Homeric word used by Hippocrates in 460 BC and was first used by Galen in 131–201 AD (Machida, 1999). A patient with scoliosis can have a single curve in the form of a "C" shape, or multiple curves in the form of an "S" shape. A curve may occur at any part of the spine depending on the location of the apex, which can lead to cervical, thoracic, or lumbar curves.

Scoliosis can also be classified based on the known etiology, for example, congenital when the spinal deformity is caused by vertebral anomalies (Goldberg, Moore, Fogarty, and Dowling, 2008). Other causes include neuromuscular diseases, neurofibromatosis, Marfan syndrome, or other inherited syndromal disorders of connective tissue (Goldberg et al., 2008; Reamy and Slakey, 2001).

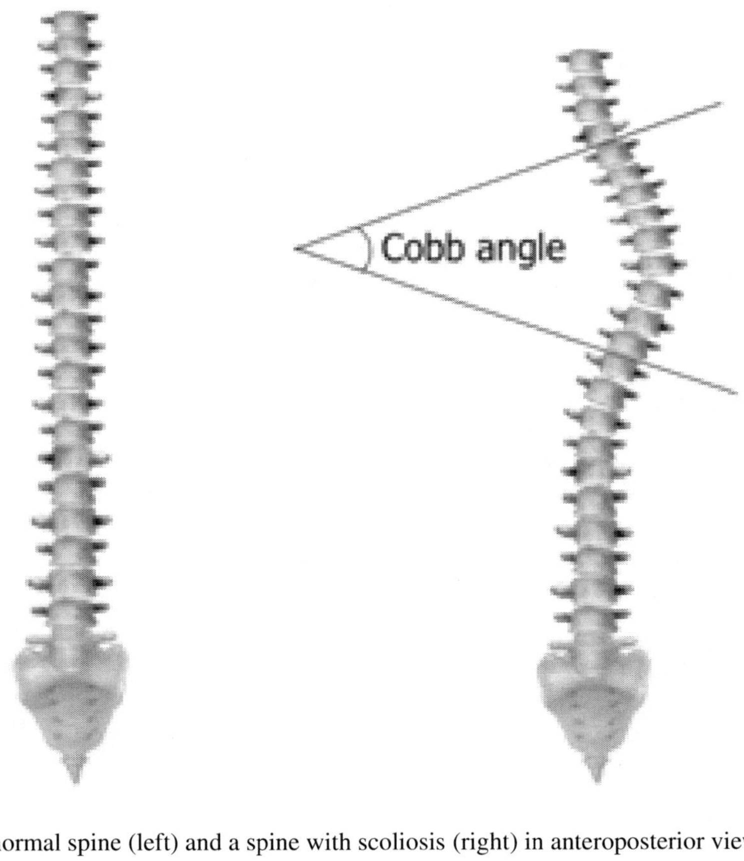

Figure 9.1. A normal spine (left) and a spine with scoliosis (right) in anteroposterior view.

However, the etiology of 80% or more cases cannot be determined and is classified as idiopathic (Reamy and Slakey, 2001). Idiopathic scoliosis can be further sub-divided according to the age at onset. Idiopathic scoliosis developed between 0 to 3 years of age is infantile, that between 3 to 10 years is juvenile, that between 10 years to skeletal maturity is adolescent, and after skeletal maturity is termed adult. Infantile and juvenile idiopathic scoliosis account for only less than 1% and 10% of all cases, respectively. In contrast, adolescent idiopathic scoliosis (AIS) is by far the most common, representing 80% of cases (Asher and Burton, 2006; Reamy and Slakey, 2001).

Diagnosis

The current gold standard method of diagnosing scoliosis is the measurement of Cobb angle on a radiograph of the spine (Leaver, Alvik, and Warren, 1982; Reamy and Slakey, 2001). Specifically, a standing radiograph of the whole spine is taken, from which the apex of the curvature is located. The two most tilted vertebrae, above and below the apex, are then identified. The intersecting angle of two lines, one drawn from the upper endplate of the superior rostral vertebra and the other from the lower endplate of the inferior caudal vertebra, forms the Cobb angle (Figure 9.1). A larger Cobb angle indicates a more severe spinal deformity. The Scoliosis Research Society (SRS) defined the diagnosis of scoliosis as a Cobb angle larger than 10° (SRS, 2012).

Prevalence of Adolescent Idiopathic Scoliosis

The prevalence of AIS reported in the literature varied with the defining Cobb angle used. The prevalence of curves with a Cobb angle of at least 5° ranged from 5% to 15%, but that with a Cobb angle of at least 10° was only 0.1% to 7% (Fong et al., 2010; Karachalios, Roidis, Papagelopoulos, and Karachalios, 2000; Rinsky and Gamble, 1988). Moreover, there were 0.1% to 0.3% of curves exceeding 20°, and 0.03% to 0.1% of curves greater than 40° (Karachalios et al., 2000; Reamy and Slakey, 2001). In a more recent meta-analysis of 36 cohort studies from 17 countries that evaluated school scoliosis screening, the pooled prevalence of curves with a Cobb angle ≥ 10° was 1.3% (range = 0.1% to 7.5%), whereas that with a Cobb angle ≥ 20° was 0.2% (range = 0.02% to 0.91%) (Fong et al., 2010). In Mainland China, there has not been much epidemiological information reported on scoliosis. This may be due to the lack of a regular scoliosis screening program in China, with only Beijing, Changsha, Shanxi, and Shanghai having an *ad hoc* screening program for scoliosis evaluated for research purposes (Liu and Huang, 1996; Ma, Zhao, and Lin, 1995; Pin et al., 1985; Zhang, Li, Wei, Cao, and Cui, 1988). These studies reported 1.0% to 12.1% of children had a Cobb angle > 10°. In Hong Kong, a large retrospective cohort study of 115,190 adolescents reported that the prevalence of ≥10° curves during adolescence was 2.5% and that of ≥20° curves during adolescence was 1.4% (Luk et al., 2010).

The prevalence of AIS may also vary with gender and geographical location. Small curves under 10° are equally likely to be found in boys and in girls, whereas curves larger than 30° are nine times more likely to occur in girls than in boys (Reamy and Slakey, 2001;

Rinsky and Gamble, 1988). On the other hand, the prevalence of idiopathic scoliosis was reported to increase from the area around the equator to the north (Grivas, Vasiliadis, Mouzakis, Mihas, and Koufopoulos, 2006).

Complications of Adolescent Idiopathic Scoliosis

Scoliosis hinders the movement of the ribs and may displace the muscles to a position of mechanical disadvantage, which causes back pain. AIS patients may be 21% to 26% more likely to experience back pain than normal subjects (Mayo, Goldberg, Poitras, Scott, and Hanley, 1994; Weinstein et al., 2003). Moreover, a deformed curve may also restrict and distort the skeletal structure of the spine which impairs respiratory movements of the ribs. Severe deformity may lead to impairment of cardiopulmonary function (Asher and Burton, 2006; Iwahara, Imai, and Atsuta, 1998; Koumbourlis, 2006; Theologis, Jefferson, Simpson, Turner-Smith, and Fairbank, 1993). More seriously, premature death can also occur (Nilsonne and Lundgren, 1968).

In addition, AIS patients may have significantly poorer self-image because of the cosmetic deformity (Asher and Burton, 2006). This may be developed to an extent that leads to handicap in social functions, such as marriage, especially for females (Nilsonne and Lundgren, 1968).

Natural History of Adolescent Idiopathic Scoliosis

AIS may progress if it is left untreated. The rate of progression can be as fast as 2° per month, and the progression may go beyond 100° (Asher and Burton, 2006). The natural history of idiopathic scoliosis has been discussed in many studies, but still it is not fully understood (Ascani et al., 1986; Asher and Burton, 2006; Bunnell, 1986; Goldberg, Dowling, Hall, and Emans, 1993; Weinstein et al., 2003; Wong and Tan, 2010).

In general, curves < 30° seldom progress and curves > 30° have a higher chance of progression. Single thoracic curves between 50° and 75° may progress for an average of 29° in an average of 40.5 years (Ascani et al., 1986; Weinstein and Ponseti, 1983). For a double major curve, the lumbar component is more likely to progress than the thoracic component. Additionally, right lumbar apex curves are twice as likely to progress as left lumbar apex curves.

Apart from curve severity and curve pattern, patients who are still under spinal growth are more likely to progress (Reamy and Slakey, 2001). Spinal growth continues from infancy until skeletal maturity. Assessment of skeletal maturity can be made by the Risser sign, a grading that ranges from 1 to 5 with a higher grade indicating a higher degree of skeletal maturity (Risser, 1958). The grading is made by assessing the radiograph of the iliac apophysis for the amount of ossification, and a Risser sign of 5 indicates the iliac apophysis has completely fused to the iliac crest. Skeletal maturity is often reached by 2 years after menarche for girls or at latest by the age of 19 years (Greulich and Pyle, 1959; Richards, Bernstein, D'Amato, and Thompson, 2005). Patients who take a longer time before they are skeletally matured are more likely to show progression of the disorder (Reamy and Slakey,

2001). In general, curves > 30° with a low Risser sign are highly likely to progress. Furthermore, curve progression is highly related to the skeletal growth velocity which is different across genders owing to the different periods of growth spurt. A higher curve progression velocity was found in 12- to 15-year-old boys, and 9- to 13-year-old girls (Ylikoski 2005; Yrjonen and Ylikoski, 2006).

A more recent study developed a more refined risk classification rule for AIS in a southern Chinese population of differing risks of progressing to 30° (Lee et al., 2012). Based on 2,308 untreated AIS patients with a curvature < 30° at presentation, four risk groups of curve progression were identified. Patients with a curvature ≥ 26° and < 18° constituted the highest and lowest risk groups, respectively. The two intermediate groups were identified by the age of 11.3 years, menarche status, and body height of 154 cm. The risk classification rule only uses information obtained at the first presentation and may aid physicians in deriving efficient management.

MANAGEMENT OF ADOLESCENT IDIOPATHIC SCOLIOSIS

Not all AIS patients require treatment. Only 10% of AIS patients require some form of medical intervention (Reamy and Slakey, 2001). In general, there are currently three common options for managing AIS, namely, observation, bracing, and spinal fusion. The selection of these options is mainly determined by the curve size and the risk of curve progression (Canavese and Kaelin, 2011).

Bracing is the most common conservative, that is, non-operative, treatment for AIS, which has been utilized in practice for more than 60 years (Blount, Schmidt, and Bidwell, 1958; Blount, Schmidt, Keever, and Leonard, 1958; Maruyama, Takeshita, and Kitagawa, 2008; Watts, Hall, and Stanish, 1977). A brace is often made of rigid material tailored specifically to the body contour of individual patients (Figure 9.2). It aims to control curve progression by applying corrective forces on the curve from the bracing frame (D'Amato, Griggs, and McCoy, 2001). There are several types of brace, and their use depends on the apex position of the curve. The Milwaukee brace was the first brace developed by Blount and Schmidt in 1946 and was used for upper thoracic curves (Blount, Schmidt, and Bidwell, 1958; Blount, Schmidt, Keever, et al., 1958; Fayssoux, Cho, and Herman, 2010). Then, in 1977, Hall and his colleagues developed the Boston brace, also known as the underarm brace, for lower thoracic, thoraco-lumbar, or lumbar curves (Fayssoux et al., 2010; Watts et al., 1977). A Boston brace extends from the chest down to the beginning of the pelvic area in the front and from below the shoulder blades to the tail bone in the back (Figure 9.2). Bracing is often considered for skeletally immature curves of Cobb angles between 25° and 30° or those of Cobb angles below 25° but showing significant progression (Kim, Blanco, and Widmann, 2009). Patients prescribed to be braced are often required to wear the brace for at least 20 hours each day until they become skeletally matured. However, bracing cannot correct curvature; thus, it is no longer helpful or recommended once a curve has deteriorated to a severe level, or the patient has been skeletally matured.

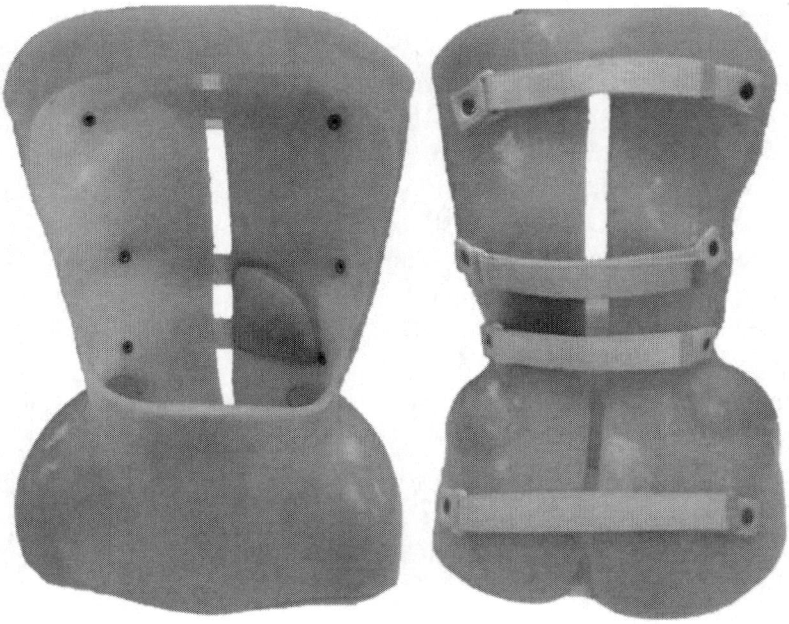

Figure 9.2. An under-arm brace with the front (left) and back (right) sides.

Spinal fusion surgery has been used to treat scoliosis since 1914 (Hibbs, 1911). It corrects spinal curvature by fixing the spine in a balanced position with metallic rods and fusing the affected segment with onlay bone grafts (Koumbourlis, 2006). Despite the known efficacy of spinal fusion in correcting curvature, the procedure limits the movement of ribs and the growth in length of the fused segment. Moreover, spinal fusion surgery usually requires a long operating time and a lengthy hospital stay of around five to seven days. It may also induce risk of complications during and after surgery, such as worsening lung function and pain (Maruyama, Kitagawa, Takeshita, Mochizuki, and Nakamura, 2003). In addition, the surgery leaves a long scar on the back, which may bring cosmetic concern. Therefore, recommendation of spinal fusion surgery is often made only for skeletally matured patients who have reached a Cobb angle of 45° or more or have a highly progressive curve (Little, Song, Katz, and Herring, 2000).

Scoliosis Screening: The Controversy

As surgical treatment for AIS is invasive and may lead to undesirable complications, it is advantageous to detect AIS early so that conservative treatments can be applied for preventing progression. Unfortunately, the presence of scoliosis, especially when it is mild, is often unnoticeable until it has become so severe that it leads to cosmetic concern or morbidity problems. Consequently, by the time an individual proactively seeks help from an orthopedist, the curvature may have already progressed to such a level that conservative treatments are no longer effective. Therefore, early detection of AIS is better achieved by mass screening of individuals at risk of AIS.

Scoliosis screening was first started in the late 1950s in Delaware, in the United States. Since then, scoliosis screening programs have been implemented in Canada, followed by some European and Asian countries (Fong et al., 2010; Grivas et al., 2007). However, there have been different opinions on the use of mass scoliosis screening for identifying AIS patients (Karachalios et al., 2000).

Many orthopedic organizations, including the American Academy of Orthopedic Surgeons, the SRS, the Pediatric Orthopedic Society of North America, and the American Academy of Pediatrics, support the use of scoliosis screening. In 1996, the US Preventive Services Task Force (USPSTF) made its first recommendation of neither support nor opposition to scoliosis screening because of the lack of sufficient evidence (USPSTF, 1996). However, in 2004, the USPSTF changed the recommendation to one that is against screening (Grivas et al., 2007; USPSTF, 2004b). The change of recommendation was made from their conclusions that: 1) there is a lack of good evidence that screening asymptomatic adolescents detects idiopathic scoliosis at an earlier stage than detection without screening; 2) there is a lack of efficacious conservative treatments, and; 3) most patients identified by screening will not progress to a clinically significant form of scoliosis (USPSTF, 2004a). However, this recommendation was criticized as a change of position in the absence of a change in evidence (Richards and Vitale, 2008), and it has been recently given the lowest grade, D, of recommendation using the Scottish Intercollegiate Guideline Network (SIGN) criteria (Plaszewski, Nowobilski, Kowalski, and Cieslinski, 2012).

Following the recommendations from various authorities, a number of high quality studies and systematic reviews on the use of scoliosis screening have been published. The effectiveness of scoliosis screening will be assessed in more detail later in this chapter.

Approaches to Scoliosis Screening

Tests for Screening Scoliosis

Although radiography is the gold standard for diagnosing scoliosis, it is not a desirable screening tool for mass screening because of both the concerns of high cost and increased risk of cancer from radiation exposure (Cote, Kreitz, Cassidy, Dzus, and Martel, 1998). In particular, it has been shown that the excess lifetime risk of cancer was about 1 to 2% among female AIS patients (Karachalios et al., 1999; Levy, Goldberg, Hanley, Mayo, and Poitras, 1994). Therefore, screening for AIS should be performed by using other more rapid, simple, safe, and less costly tests. By which, only those children who are likely to have AIS would be identified and referred for diagnostic radiography.

The Adam's Forward Bending Test (FBT) is the most common test for scoliosis screening (Karachalios et al., 1999). In a FBT, a child, who is bare-backed or in tight clothes, stands with feet together and bends forward at the waist with legs straight, arms dangling and palms opposed (Figure 9.3). A screener then inspects the child's back, from behind and from the side, for the presence of asymmetry or rib hump on the child's back (Lonstein, 1989; Reamy and Slakey, 2001). This screening test is simple, fast, and inexpensive (Lonstein, Bjorklund, Wanninger, and Nelson, 1982). However, it is purely subjective and may produce many false positive and false negative cases (Grossman, Mazur, and Cummings, 1995).

Therefore, FBT is not recommended as the only screening test in a scoliosis screening program (Karachalios et al., 1999).

The Scoliometer, also known as an inclinometer, was developed to complement the subjectivity of FBT (Bonagamba, Coelho, and Oliveira, 2010). It measures the angle of inclination of the child's back in the forward bending position, called the angle of trunk rotation (ATR) (Figure 9.3). Specifically, a scoliometer is placed by a screener at the apex of a spinal curvature, perpendicular to the long axis of the body, in order to measure the ATR. Common cutoff values of ATR for indicating AIS range from 4° to 7°, with 5° being more widely used (Grivas, Samelis, Polyzois, Giourelis, and Polyzois, 2002; Ma et al., 1995; Pruijs, van der Meer, Hageman, Keessen, and van Wieringen, 1996; Stirling et al., 1996; Wang, Ye, and Wu, 1996; Wong, Hui, Rajan, and Chia, 2005; Yawn et al., 1999). However, an optimal cutoff for ATR has not been determined (Huang, 1997). The Scoliometer is another simple, quick, and inexpensive screening test for scoliosis, and its measured ATR has been shown to be highly correlated with the Cobb angle (Bunnell, 1984). However, the main criticism of using a scoliometer is its inadequacy to consider the body size of patients before determining the significance of the rib deformity (Bunnell, 1984). Moreover, there are other causes of back asymmetry besides scoliosis.

Moiré topography is another screening test for scoliosis which has gained popularity (Bunnell, 1984). It makes use of a biostereometric technique to three-dimensionally describe the shape of the back of a subject (Willner, 1979).

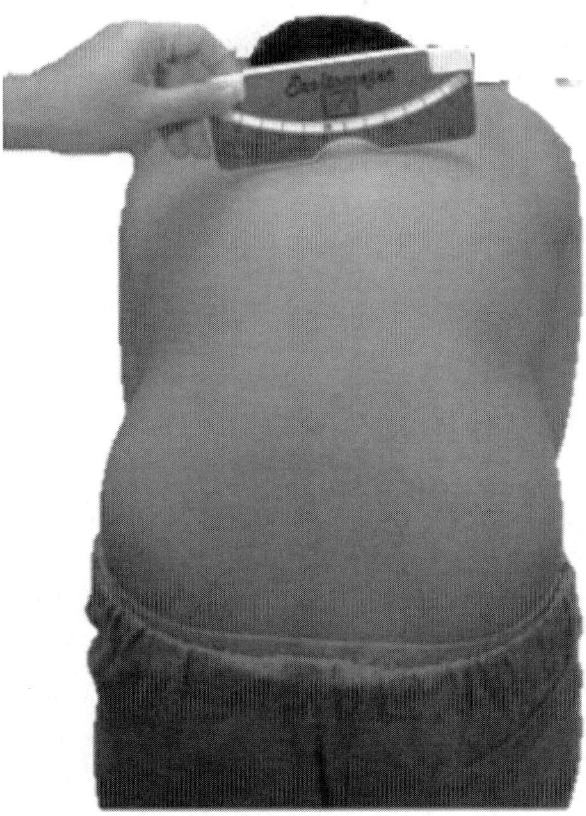

Figure 9.3. Forward bending test with measurement of the angle of trunk rotation by a scoliometer.

The technique consists of three components: a light source, a screen filter with grids of fixed width, and a camera (Figure 9.4a). The light source projects contour lines, called moiré fringes, through the screen filter onto the child's back (Figure 9.4b). The camera captures the moiré fringes and a photograph is used to assess the overall body shape.

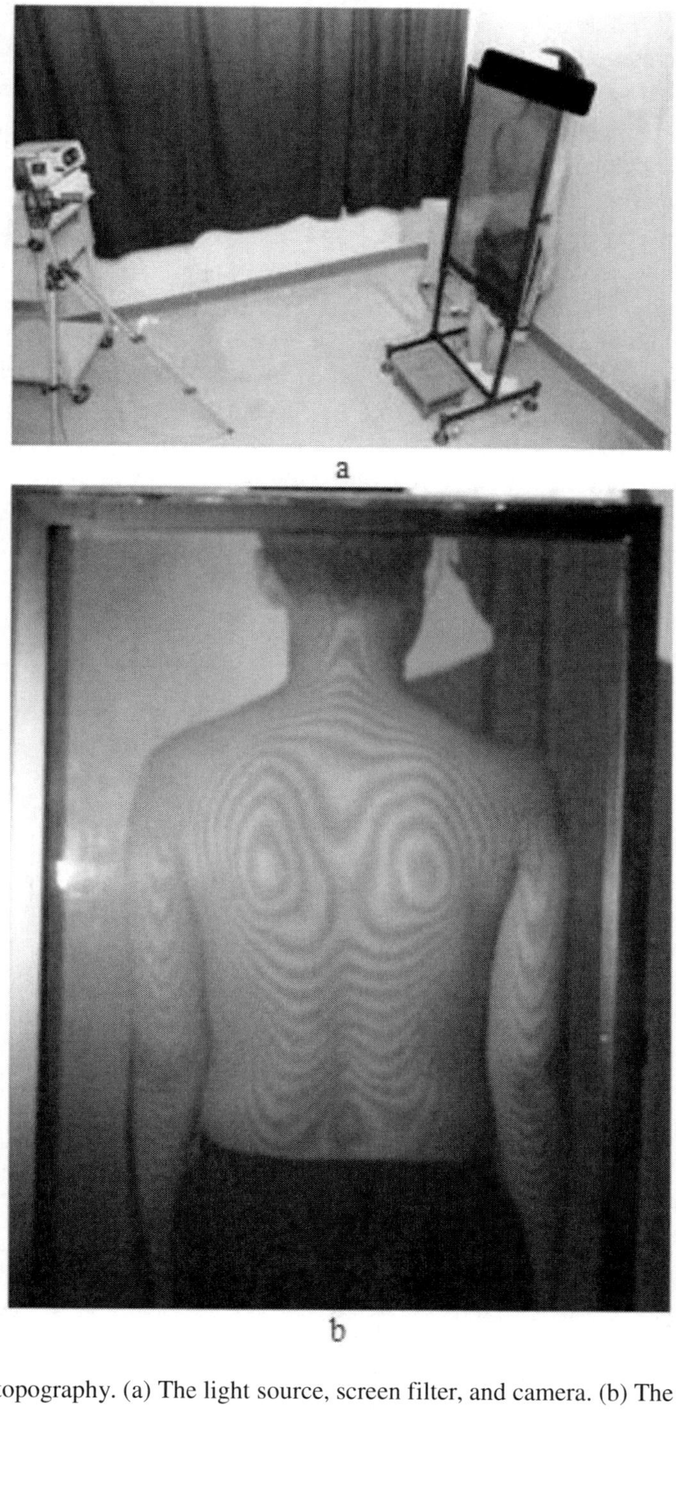

Figure 9.4. Moiré topography. (a) The light source, screen filter, and camera. (b) The projected moiré fringe lines.

The asymmetry of the body surface is measured by comparing the deviation of moiré fringes on the two halves of the back. A deviation of two or more fringe lines is an indication of scoliosis (Pruijs, Keessen, van der Meer, and van Wieringen, 1995). The width of moiré fringes depends on the width of grids on the screen filter and the distance between screen filter and light source. Thus, technicians are required to ensure proper operation of the devices and measurement of the deviation of moiré fringes. The whole process of moiré topography, including the interpretation of results, may take around 20 minutes (Lee et al., 2010a). Moiré topography utilizes three-dimensional information of a subject's body and is sensitive enough to detect AIS cases (Karachalios et al., 1999). However, it requires more resources, including financial expenses, technicians, and time. Therefore, it is often used only in subjects who have shown an initial indication of AIS by FBT and/or ATR.

There are other screening tests that are less common but have been used for scoliosis screening. The Humpometer is a device that assesses spinal deformity by measuring the height of the rib hump (H) and rib depression (D) on the two halves of the back, respectively, in the forward bending position (Karachalios et al., 1999). The total of these two measurements (H+D) indicates the degree of asymmetry. While it is similar to a scoliometer in that it also provides an objective measure of curvature, it is time-consuming and more costly, making it less desirable for mass scoliosis screening (Bunnell, 2005). Another test is low-dose roentgenography which is radiography with reduced radiation dose when compared with the diagnostic full-spinal radiography. Although it is predictive for scoliosis, there is still an undesirable excess risk of cancer (Dickman and Caspi, 2001). Therefore, low-dose roentgenography is not a common screening test. Other tests, such as ultrasound, thermography, magnetic resonance imaging (MRI), and computerized surface mapping systems can also be used to describe the shape of back in detail (Schwend, Hennrikus, Hall, and Emans, 1995). However, they are also time-consuming and costly, which does not render them as a practical test for mass scoliosis screening (Bunnell, 2005).

Scoliosis Screening Programs

The first scoliosis screening program, initiated in Delaware in the late 1950s, utilized the FBT for screening scoliosis (Karachalios et al., 2000). Indeed, many early screening programs utilized FBT as the only screening test. However, the FBT relies on subjective clinical observation and its accuracy in identifying AIS can be variable, depending on screeners' experience. Since the late 1970s, there have been scoliosis screening programs considering a tandem use of screening tests.

A review identified 36 cohort studies that evaluated scoliosis screening (Fong et al., 2010). The screening tests considered by these studies together with a more recent study in Hong Kong are summarized in Table 9.1. A total of 62% of screening programs used the FBT only, whereas 22% additionally utilized a scoliometer to measure the ATR, and 8% further used moiré topography. Moreover, one program used the FBT and moiré topography, and two programs did not screen children with either the FBT or the measurement of ATR but only utilized both moiré topography and low-dose roentgenography. Moiré topography was not used in screening programs implemented in North America and it was only considered in the Netherlands, Denmark, Beijing, Hong Kong, and Japan (Fong et al., 2010).

Table 9.1. A summary of screening tests utilized in scoliosis screening programs

Screening test(s) utilized[1]	N (%)
FBT	23 (62)
FBT + ATR	8 (22)
FBT + ATR + Moiré topography	3 (8)
FBT + Moiré topography	1 (3)
Moiré topography + Low-dose roentgenography	2 (5)

[1] FBT = Forward bending test, ATR = Angle of trunk rotation.

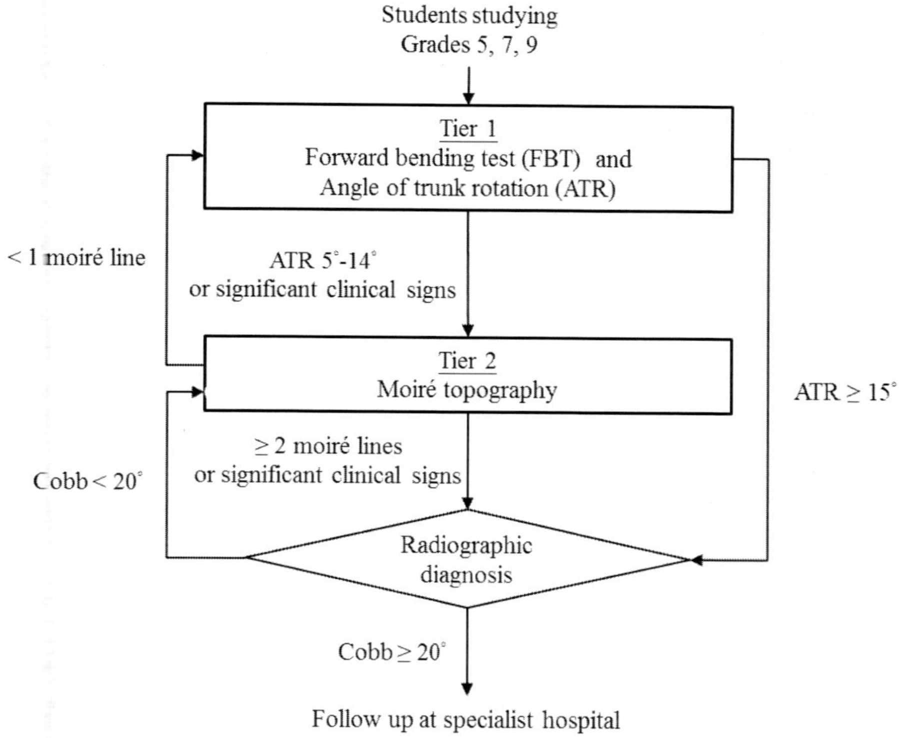

Figure 9.5. The two-tier scoliosis screening program in Hong Kong.

The starting age of scoliosis screening also varies across programs (Fong et al., 2010). Some scoliosis screening programs start screening children as soon as they reach 6 years of age—when they are in Grade 1—whereas some programs start at a later age—14 years, when children are in Grade 9. There has been no general consensus on the optimal age of screening but screening children at 10 years of age has been shown to achieve satisfactory accuracy in a large retrospective cohort (Lee et al., 2010).

In particular, the scoliosis screening program in Hong Kong has received much attention because of its more reliable evaluation and high effectiveness in identifying AIS patients (Lee et al., 2010a; Luk et al., 2010). It is a two-tier, voluntary, school-based screening program that utilizes the FBT and the measurement of ATR in tier 1 and moiré topography in tier 2 (Figure 9.5). The criteria of referring children to tier 2 and radiographic diagnosis are summarized in

Figure 9.5. More details of the screening schedule can be found in the original evaluation study (Luk et al., 2010).

There has been diversity across screening programs in the target group of children, and the screening frequency. Most existing screening programs start screening children at the age of 6 to 13 years, while some screen girls only (Fong et al., 2010). Moreover, the screening frequency of a child may be only once or at intervals depending on the screening results.

FOLLOW-UP AND COMPLIANCE WITH SCOLIOSIS SCREENING

Scoliosis screening is often incorporated as part of an existing national health assessment service. Many routine scoliosis screening programs are voluntary, but there are some mandatory programs, such as those in Japan and in some States in the US (Grivas et al., 2007). The participation rate may vary from 51% in Singapore to around 80% in the Netherlands (Luk et al., 2010).

In a community setting, children undergoing the screening procedures may be referred for further assessments or radiographic diagnosis but not attend as scheduled. There is a scarcity of reports on the compliance of children in scoliosis screening programs. In 10 routine scoliosis screening programs identified in a review and another later published routine screening program in Hong Kong, numbers of children referred for radiographic diagnosis along with 'did-not-attend/lost to follow-up' rates were reported (as summarized in Table 9.2). With the exception of the screening program in Wisconsin of the US, which had a did-not-attend rate of 7%, US programs reported considerable rates of 26-65% of referred children failing to proceed to the diagnostic stage. In contrast, screening programs in Asia reported did-not-attend rates of only 4-10% in referred children. In programs conducted in two tiers, that is, those in Hong Kong, Japan, and the Netherlands, did-not-attend rates were 24%, < 5%, and 27%, respectively.

Did-not-attend cases may be due to incomplete records in a retrospective evaluation, ignorance of scheduled appointments, or the seeking of other medical treatment or follow-up by the parents of the children. Children not complying with the screening procedures, although an inevitability in a community setting, may reduce the estimated accuracy of a screening program. Adequate follow-up is essential for the success of a screening program and further evaluation of student compliance is desirable.

EVALUATING SCOLIOSIS SCREENING PROGRAM PERFORMANCE

Clinical Effectiveness

Since the first evaluation of scoliosis screening in 1977, there has been a continued interest in evaluating program performance (Fong et al., 2010). Such investigations encompass the estimation of different measures of clinical effectiveness of screening for a certain condition, such as a curvature of ≥10° or ≥20°. The measures include: sensitivity, specificity, positive and negative predictive values (PPV and NPV, respectively); and referral rates for diagnostic radiography.

Table 9.2. Referred and did-not-attend rates for radiography in various scoliosis screening programs

Author, year, Location	Screening tests[1]	Follow-up	Number (rate) of children referred for radiography	Number of children did-not-attend (rate) for radiography
Rogala, 1978, Montreal/Canada	FBT	On scoliotic cases only	Not reported	Not reported
Gore, 1981, Wisconsin/US	FBT	On scoliotic cases only	629 (7.5%)	45 (7%)
Ohtsuka, 1988, Chiba/Japan	Moiré ≥ 5mm, Low-dose roentgenography	Varied from none to school completion	9652 (1%)	Not specifically reported but there were some
Juma, 1989, Jeddah/Saudi Arabia	FBT	On scoliotic cases only	202 (4.1%)	64 (32%)
Pruijs, 1996, Central Netherlands	FBT, rib hump height, ATR ≥ 5°, Moiré ≥ 2 lines	3 years	1931 (6.3%)	1260 (65%)
Koukourakis, 1997, Crete/Greece	FBT	On scoliotic cases only (6-12 months)	2049 (9.7%)	Not reported
Yawn, 1999, Rochester/US	FBT/ATR ≥ 7° (yearly in Grade 5-9)	Up to age 19 years	92 (4.1%)	24 (26%)
Velezis, 2002, Columbia/US	FBT	Varied from none to 1 year	1218 (2.3%)	Not reported (30%)
Nussinovitch, 2002, Israel	FBT	On scoliotic cases only	Not reported	Not reported
Wong, 2005, Singapore	FBT/ATR ≥ 5°	None	759 (0.4%)	30 (4%)
Luk, 2010, Hong Kong	FBT/ATR ≥ 5°, Moiré ≥ 2 lines	Up to age 19 years	3228 (2.8%)	334 (10%)

[1] FBT = Forward bending test, ATR = Angle of trunk rotation.

A good scoliosis screening program should be highly sensitive, specific, and predictive, with a minimal referral rate. A suggested standard for considering a screening program to be worthy of implementation is a sensitivity of at least 70% to 80% and a PPV from 30% to 50% (Glascoe, 2005). Specificity and NPV are less of a concern for scoliosis screening because they are often very high, at least 90%, due to the low prevalence of AIS. Most evaluation studies have been integrated in a systematic review and a meta-analysis.

A systematic review by Sabirin, Bakri, Buang, Abdullah, and Shapie (2010) integrated 28 studies obtained from searching eight electronic databases. These studies were published between 1977 and 2004, with 16 having evaluated the effectiveness, seven having assessed the cost, and seven having reported the diagnostic accuracy of scoliosis screening tests. Moreover, they utilized different designs which ranged from cross-sectional to randomized controlled trial (RCT). The review concluded that a fair level of evidence could be found confirming that school scoliosis screening is safe, reduces the need for surgery, and is cost-effective. In addition, screening only girls at 12 years of age due to the higher prevalence in girls than boys, and the use of a combination of screening tests to increase screening accuracy were suggested.

Fong et al.'s (2010) meta-analysis analyzed 36 cohort studies identified from searching three complementary electronic databases without any language restriction. The cohort studies were published between 1977 and 2005. The meta-analysis was graded as 2++, the highest grade of evidence among non-randomized control trial reviews according to the SIGN checklist for meta-analysis of cohort studies (Plaszewski et al., 2012). The highest grade 1 level is not attained because it requires the inclusion of RCTs (Obremskey, Pappas, Attallah-Wasif, Tornetta, and Bhandari, 2005). The RCT design is not applicable for evaluating the effectiveness of a scoliosis program because the program should have been implemented as a community-based program to allow realistic assessment in the presence of various compliance issues, and randomization is not necessary to obtain the different accuracy measures such as the sensitivity, specificity, and predictive values (Fong et al., 2010). Therefore, the cohort design, although it is one grade below the RCT design in terms of the level of evidence, is the best applicable design for evaluating a scoliosis screening program.

Based on the 36 cohort studies, the pooled referral rate for radiography was 5%. The pooled estimated percentage of referred students with a Cobb angle ≥10° detected was 28% and that with a Cobb angle ≥20° was 5.6%. These PPVs are clearly low, indicating that many students were unnecessarily referred. However, there was substantial heterogeneity across the studies in terms of their reported prevalence rates of AIS, referral rates for radiographic diagnosis, and PPVs.

One contributing factor in the studies' heterogeneity was the use of different screening tests. Specifically, the sole use of the FBT has been meta-analytically shown to be an inadequate screening test. It increased the odds of referral for radiography by almost 200% and, at the same time, it also reduced the PPV for detecting ≥10° curves by around 50% and that for detecting ≥20° curves by 66%. Thus, using the FBT alone would unnecessarily refer children to receive radiographic assessment. This echoes the concern of the USPSTF that the reported effectiveness of the FBT was highly variable.

Another contributing factor in the studies' heterogeneity was the diversity of follow-up rates of children after screening. Only 20 (66%) of studies provided follow-up information for the screened children; of which, only four studies had taken follow-up information for 1 to 3 years on the screened children, and only one study had followed all screened children until they had reached skeletal maturity. It is well known that idiopathic scoliosis commonly presents during the few years of adolescent growth spurt but the exact time of onset remains uncertain. A young girl screened negative for scoliosis at the age of 10 years may develop scoliosis during her adolescence. Thus, follow-up information of screened students until skeletal maturity is desirable. The only such study published before 2010 had only screened 2,242 students and referred 92 for radiographic assessment. Therefore, there is a need for larger scale studies with sufficient follow-up information of students to obtain more reliable and representative estimates of screening accuracy. In response to this, a series of evaluations on the Hong Kong scoliosis screening program has been reported.

A large, retrospective, cohort study that assessed the clinical effectiveness of the Hong Kong scoliosis screening program collected the screening and medical history of 115,190 children up to 19 years of age (Luk et al., 2010). Based on these data, the referral rate for diagnostic radiography was estimated as 2.8%, with a very reliable 95% confidence interval (CI) of (2.7 - 2.9%). For identifying curves of a Cobb angle ≥20°, a curvature deserving at least clinical observation, the screening sensitivity was 88.1% (95% CI = 86.4 - 89.6%) and the PPV was 43.6% (95% CI = 41.8 - 45.3%). The corresponding specificity and NPV were over 95% With reference to the suggested standard for considering a screening program as worthwhile, the Hong Kong scoliosis screening program can be considered as predictive and sensitive with a low referral rate (Glascoe, 2005; Luk et al., 2010).

In addition, the accuracy of using different screening eligibility, referral criteria, and use of screening tests was also examined (Lee et al., 2010b). Screening children at grades 5, 7, and 9 (approximately at 10, 12, and 14 years of age, respectively) appeared to be adequate in early detection of significant curves. The tandem use of ATR, moiré topography, and observation of clinical signs outperformed the use of only a subset of them. Note the use of at least one moiré line as an indication of AIS has previously been shown to have no significant improvement over the FBT only (Wong, Balasubramaniam, Rajan, and Chng, 1997). Thus, the use of at least two moiré lines appears to be essential. The use of ATR ≥15° for referring children to receive radiography without the need to conduct moiré topography optimized the screening performance. However, if not all the tests were used, the cutoff for ATR could be lowered to 9° or 10°. Moreover, re-screening of students with an initial indication of AIS at regular intervals is also important.

Cost

Cost is another important consideration, especially to policy makers, concerning whether scoliosis screening should be implemented. The cost of scoliosis screening has also been reported in the literature. However, the reported cost varied across studies, mainly due to the variation in the cost items included. In general, it has been suggested that the costs spent on screening, diagnosis, and treatment should all be accounted (Lonstein and Morrissy, 1989). Some studies only reported the cost spent on the screening staff and materials (Lonstein et al., 1982), whereas some studies included also costs of diagnostics and treatment (Thilagaratnam, 2007). In addition, the children considered in most cost evaluation studies were not followed for the whole period of adolescence. This would not fully consider the costs for any repeated screening or treatment and, thus, these studies would not provide a realistic cost estimate for scoliosis screening.

There were only two studies that fully accounted for all costs of school screening based on students with follow-up information until they have been skeletally matured. One was conducted in Rochester, United States of America, and reported that the cost, including screening, diagnosis, and treatment, per student screened was US$54 (in the year of 2005, after adjusting for inflation) based on 2,197 screened students (Yawn and Yawn, 2000). The other, Hong Kong study assessed a larger group of 115,190 students and reported the total cost of US$55 (in the year of 2005) (Lee et al., 2010a). The two programs differed in that the Rochester study only used FBT and ATR for screening, whereas the Hong Kong program additionally used moiré topography. Despite the differences, the costs of the two programs are very close. Considering also the higher predictive power, the Hong Kong school scoliosis screening program appears to be more cost-effective.

Alternative Approaches to Scoliosis Screening

Most, if not all, current scoliosis screening approaches are based on measurements of body surface topography that are fully non-invasive and do not induce any additional risks. An alternative approach that has received much attention is the use of genetic tests. Genetic markers have been searched and more than 300 single nucleotide polymorphisms have been identified to be associated with the curve development and progression in AIS patients (Chan et al., 2002; Ogilvie, 2011; Ogilvie et al., 2006). After a statistical selection procedure, 53 markers that most predicted curve progression were selected and they, together with the patient's Cobb angle at the time of the test, formed a 1-200 score, known as the ScoliScore™, for assessing the risk of curve progression (Ward et al., 2010). A score of 50 or below indicates less than a 1% chance of progression to a severe curve of Cobb >45°, while a score larger than 180 indicates a high risk of curve progression. Patients with a score between 51 and 180 are considered at intermediate risk of progression and they would need close monitoring or treatments. The ScoliScore™ is a salvia-based genetic test and has been shown to predict progression to a severe curve on independent Caucasian samples (Ward et al., 2010). In 2011, the test cost US$2950 per application, which was comparable with other genetic tests such those for breast cancer genes (Ogilvie, 2011). Despite the genetic test being available in the Western market, it is yet to be assessed in other ethnic groups and, therefore, its effectiveness for mass scoliosis screening cannot be fully ascertained.

Conclusion

Scoliosis, if not properly managed, can be a life-long disorder. Current corrective treatment is the invasive spinal fusion surgery which may be avoided if scoliosis can be detected early when conservative treatments, such as bracing, are applicable. Scoliosis screening can effectively identify AIS patients requiring clinical follow-up despite the varied effectiveness of different scoliosis screening protocols. Although the FBT has been the most common screening test because of its simplicity and ease of use, it should not be used alone for screening and the use of additional screening tests is desirable. The scoliosis screening protocol in Hong Kong, which utilizes the FBT, measurement of ATR, and moiré topography in tiers, has been carefully planned and maintained, serving as a potential model for effective detection of AIS patients with a Cobb angle ≥20°, a curvature that deserves at least clinical monitoring.

To justify the importance of early detection by screening, we still need evidence on the efficacy of conservative treatments such as bracing (Labelle et al., 2013). Despite bracing having been a standard practice in many places for treating mild to moderate curves, there have not been any well-conducted RCTs to establish its efficacy. There were two planned RCTs, one in The Netherlands and the other in North America. However, because of the low acceptance of randomization, the RCT in North America was revised to be a preference study in which patients were allowed to choose the treatment they desired (Weinstein, Dolan, Wright, and Dobbs, 2013). The Dutch study has been discontinued (Bunge, Habbema, and de Koning, 2010). The low recruitment rate and strong treatment preference in AIS patients might largely limit the generalizability of the results. Indeed, a RCT design can generally assess efficacy but not, necessarily, effectiveness. In view of this, a new design consisting of both a RCT and a preference component has been proposed to assess both the efficacy and effectiveness of bracing for AIS patients. A feasibility study has just been completed for proper planning of a future large scale study. The results will be important for determining future health policy guidelines.

Scoliosis screening has developed a platform to collect the medical history of AIS patients. These data have enabled the development of research to study the natural history of scoliosis, such as the development of a new classification rule for AIS patients at different risks of curve progression (Lee et al., 2012). In addition, having scoliosis screening as part of a national health assessment would increase the public awareness of this disorder which, if neglected, is life-long. Hence, scoliosis screening should be introduced or continued, as far as resources allow.

REFERENCES

Ascani, E., Bartolozzi, P., Logroscino, C. A., Marchetti, P. G., Ponte, A., Savini, R.,. Di Silvestre, M. (1986). Natural history of untreated idiopathic scoliosis after skeletal maturity. *Spine,* 11(8), 784-789.

Asher, M. A., and Burton, D. C. (2006). Adolescent idiopathic scoliosis: Natural history and long term treatment effects. *Scoliosis,* 1(1), 2. doi: 10.1186/1748-7161-1-2

Blount, W. P., Schmidt, A. C., and Bidwell, R. G. (1958). Making the Milwaukee brace. *Journal of Bone and Joint Surgery,* 40-A(3), 526-528.

Blount, W. P., Schmidt, A. C., Keever, E. D., and Leonard, E. T. (1958). The Milwaukee brace in the operative treatment of scoliosis. *J. Bone Joint Surg. Am.,* 40-A(3), 511-525.

Bonagamba, G. H., Coelho, D. M., and Oliveira, A. S. (2010). Inter and intra-rater reliability of the scoliometer. *Revista brasileira de fisioterapia,* 14(5), 432-438.

Bunge, E. M., Habbema, J. D. F., and de Koning, H. J. (2010). A randomised controlled trial on the effectiveness of bracing patients with idiopathic scoliosis: Failure to include patients and lessons to be learnt. *European Spine Journal,* 19(5), 747-753. doi: DOI 10.1007/s00586-010-1337-6

Bunnell, W. P. (1984). An objective criterion for scoliosis screening. *Journal of Bone and Joint Surgery,* 66(9), 1381-1387.

Bunnell, W. P. (1986). The natural history of idiopathic scoliosis before skeletal maturity. *Spine,* 11(8), 773-776.

Bunnell, W. P. (2005). Selective screening for scoliosis. *Clinical Orthopaedics and Related Research,* (434), 40-45.

Canavese, F., and Kaelin, A. (2011). Adolescent idiopathic scoliosis: Indications and efficacy of nonoperative treatment. *Indian Journal of Orthopaedics,* 45(1), 7-14. doi: 10.4103/0019-5413.73655

Chan, V., Fong, G. C., Luk, K. D., Yip, B., Lee, M. K., Wong, M. S., Chan, T. K. (2002). A genetic locus for adolescent idiopathic scoliosis linked to chromosome 19p13.3. *American Journal of Human Genetics,* 71(2), 401-406. doi: 10.1086/341607

Cote, P., Kreitz, B. G., Cassidy, J. D., Dzus, A. K., and Martel, J. (1998). A study of the diagnostic accuracy and reliability of the Scoliometer and Adam's forward bend test. *Spine,* 23(7), 796-802.

Cotton, L. A. (1991). Unit rod segmental spinal instrumentation for the treatment of neuromuscular scoliosis. *Orthopaedic Nursing / National Association of Orthopaedic Nurses,* 10(5), 17-23.

D'Amato, C. R., Griggs, S., and McCoy, B. (2001). Nighttime bracing with the Providence brace in adolescent girls with idiopathic scoliosis. *Spine,* 26(18), 2006-2012.

Dickman, D., and Caspi, O. (2001). Diagnosis and monitoring of idiopathic scoliosis: Overview and technological advances. *Clinical Application Notes, February*, 1-7.

Fayssoux, R. S., Cho, R. H., and Herman, M. J. (2010). A history of bracing for idiopathic scoliosis in North America. *Clinical Orthopaedics and Related Research,* 468(3), 654-664. doi: 10.1007/s11999-009-0888-5

Fong, D. Y., Lee, C. F., Cheung, K. M., Cheng, J. C., Ng, B. K., Lam, T. P., Luk, K. D. (2010). A meta-analysis of the clinical effectiveness of school scoliosis screening. *Spine,* 35(10), 1061-1071. doi: 10.1097/BRS.0b013e3181bcc835

Glascoe, F. P. (2005). Standards for screening test construction. Retrieved 3rd March, 2011, from www.dbpeds.org

Goldberg, C. J., Dowling, F. E., Hall, J. E., and Emans, J. B. (1993). A statistical comparison between natural history of idiopathic scoliosis and brace treatment in skeletally immature adolescent girls. *Spine,* 18(7), 902-908.

Goldberg, C. J., Moore, D. P., Fogarty, E. E., and Dowling, F. E. (2008). Scoliosis: A review. *Pediatric Surgery International,* 24(2), 129-144. doi: 10.1007/s00383-007-2016-5

Gore, D. R., Passehl, R., Sepic, S., and Dalton, A. (1981). Scoliosis screening: Results of a community project. *Pediatrics,* 67(2), 196-200.

Greulich, W. W., and Pyle, S. I. (1959). Radiographic atlas of skeletal development of the hand and wrist (2nd ed.). Stanford, Calif.: Stanford University Press.

Grivas, T. B., Samelis, P., Polyzois, B. D., Giourelis, B., and Polyzois, D. (2002). School screening in the heavily industrialized area--Is there any role of industrial environmental factors in idiopathic scoliosis prevalence? *Studies in Health Technology Information,* 91, 76-80.

Grivas, T. B., Vasiliadis, E., Mouzakis, V., Mihas, C., and Koufopoulos, G. (2006). Association between adolescent idiopathic scoliosis prevalence and age at menarche in different geographic latitudes. *Scoliosis*, 1-9. doi: 10.1186/1748-7161-1-9

Grivas, T. B., Wade, M. H., Negrini, S., O'Brien, J. P., Maruyama, T., Hawes, M. C., Neuhous, T. (2007). SOSORT consensus paper: School screening for scoliosis. Where are we today? *Scoliosis,* 2, 17.

Grossman, T. W., Mazur, J. M., and Cummings, R. J. (1995). An evaluation of the Adams forward bend test and the scoliometer in a scoliosis school screening setting. *Journal of Pediatric Orthopedics,* 15(4), 535-538.

Hibbs, R. A. (1911). An operation for progressive spinal deformity. *New York Medical Journal,* 93, 1013-1017.

Huang, S. C. (1997). Cut-off point of the Scoliometer in school scoliosis screening. *Spine,* 22(17), 1985-1989.

Iwahara, T., Imai, M., and Atsuta, Y. (1998). Quantification of cosmesis for patients affected by adolescent idiopathic scoliosis. *European Spine Journal,* 7(1), 12-15.

Juma, A. H. A., Mursal, A. M., Mangoud, A. M., and Ibrahim, M. A. (1989). Adolescent idiopathic scoliosis in school-children. *Saudi Medical Journal,* 10(3), 213-215.

Karachalios, T., Roidis, N., Papagelopoulos, P. J., and Karachalios, G. G. (2000). The efficacy of school screening for scoliosis. *Orthopedics,* 23(4), 386-391.

Karachalios, T., Sofianos, J., Roidis, N., Sapkas, G., Korres, D., and Nikolopoulos, K. (1999). Ten-year follow-up evaluation of a school screening program for scoliosis. Is the forward-bending test an accurate diagnostic criterion for the screening of scoliosis? *Spine,* 24(22), 2318-2324.

Kim, H. J., Blanco, J. S., and Widmann, R. F. (2009). Update on the management of idiopathic scoliosis. *Current opinion in pediatrics,* 21(1), 55-64. doi: 10.1097/MOP.0b013e328320a929

Koukourakis, I., Giaourakis, G., Kouvidis, G., Kivernitakis, E., Blazos, J., and Koukourakis, M. (1997). Screening school children for scoliosis on the island of Crete. *Journal of Spinal Disorders,* 10(6), 527-531.

Koumbourlis, A. C. (2006). Scoliosis and the respiratory system. *Paediatric Respiratory Reviews,* 7(2), 152-160. doi: 10.1016/j.prrv.2006.04.009

Labelle, H., Richards, S. B., De Kleuver, M., Grivas, T. B., Luk K. D. K., Wong, H. K., Thometz, J., Beausejour, M., Turgeon, I., and Fong D. Y. T. (2013). Screening for adolescent idiopathic scoliosis: an information statement by the scoliosis research society international task force. *Scoliosis*, 8, 17. doi:10.1186/1748-7161-8-17

Leaver, J. M., Alvik, A., and Warren, M. D. (1982). Prescriptive screening for adolescent idiopathic scoliosis: A review of the evidence. *International Journal of Epidemiology,* 11(2), 101-111.

Lee, C. F. Fong, D. Y., Cheung, K. M., Cheng, J. C., Ng, B. K., Lam, T. P., Luk, K. D. (2010a). Costs of school scoliosis screening: A large, population-based study. *Spine,* 35(26), 2266-2272. doi: 10.1097/BRS.0b013e3181cbcc10

Lee, C. F. Fong, D. Y., Cheung, K. M., Cheng, J. C., Ng, B. K., Lam, T. P., Luk, K. D. (2010b). Referral criteria for school scoliosis screening: Assessment and recommendations based on a large longitudinally followed cohort. *Spine,* 35(25), E1492-1498. doi: 10.1097/BRS.0b013e3181ecf3fe

Lee, C. F., Fong, D. Y., Cheung, K. M., Cheng, J. C., Ng, B. K., Lam, T. P., Luk, K. D. (2012). A new risk classification rule for curve progression in adolescent idiopathic scoliosis. *Spine Journal*, 12(11), 989-995.

Levy, A. R., Goldberg, M. S., Hanley, J. A., Mayo, N. E., and Poitras, B. (1994). Projecting the lifetime risk of cancer from exposure to diagnostic ionizing radiation for adolescent idiopathic scoliosis. *Health Physics,* 66(6), 621-633.

Little, D. G., Song, K. M., Katz, D., and Herring, J. A. (2000). Relationship of peak height velocity to other maturity indicators in idiopathic scoliosis in girls. *Journal of Bone and Joint Surgery,* 82(5), 685-693.

Liu, S. L., and Huang, D. S. (1996). Scoliosis in China. A general review. *Clinical Orthopaedics and Related Research,* 323, 113-118.

Lonstein, J E. (1989). Adolescent idiopathic scoliosis: Screening and diagnosis. *Instructional Course Lectures,* 38, 105-113.

Lonstein, J E., Bjorklund, S., Wanninger, M. H., and Nelson, R. P. (1982). Voluntary school screening for scoliosis in Minnesota. *Journal of Bone and Joint Surgery,* 64(4), 481-488.

Lonstein, J. E., and Morrissy, R. T. (1989). Scoliosis school screening: Is it of value? *Orthopedics,* 12(12), 1589-1593.

Luk, K. D., Lee, C. F., Cheung, K. M., Cheng, J. C., Ng, B. K., Lam, T. P., Fong, D. Y. (2010). Clinical effectiveness of school screening for adolescent idiopathic scoliosis: A large population-based retrospective cohort study. *Spine,* 35(17), 1607-1614. doi: 10.1097/BRS.0b013e3181c7cb8c

Ma, X., Zhao, B., and Lin, Q. K. (1995). [Investigation on scoliosis incidence among 24,130 school children]. *Zhonghua Liu Xing Bing Xue Za Zhi,* 16(2), 109-110.

Machida, M. (1999). Cause of idiopathic scoliosis. *Spine,* 24(24), 2576-2583.

Maruyama, T., Kitagawa, T., Takeshita, K., Mochizuki, K., and Nakamura, K. (2003). Conservative treatment for adolescent idiopathic scoliosis: Can it reduce the incidence of surgical treatment? *Pediatric Rehabilitation,* 6(3-4), 215-219. doi: 10.1080/1363849031000 1642748

Maruyama, T., Takeshita, K., and Kitagawa, T. (2008). Milwaukee brace today. *Disability and Rehabilitation. Assistive technology,* 3(3), 136-138. doi: 10.1080/17483100801904036

Mayo, N. E., Goldberg, M. S., Poitras, B., Scott, S., and Hanley, J. (1994). The Ste-Justine Adolescent Idiopathic Scoliosis Cohort Study. Part III: Back pain. *Spine,* 19(14), 1573-1581.

Nilsonne, U., and Lundgren, K. D. (1968). Long-term prognosis in idiopathic scoliosis. *Acta Orthopaedica Scandinavica,* 39(4), 456-465.

Nussinovitch, M., Finkelstein, Y., Amir, J., Greenbaum, E., and Volovitz, B. (2002). Adolescent screening for orthopedic problems in high school. *Public Health,* 116(1), 30-32.

Obremskey, W. T., Pappas, N., Attallah-Wasif, E., Tornetta, P., III, and Bhandari, M. (2005). Level of evidence in orthopaedic journals. *Journal of Bone and Joint Surgery,* 87(12), 2632-2638.

Ogilvie, J. W. (2011). Update on prognostic genetic testing in adolescent idiopathic scoliosis (AIS). *Journal of Pediatric Orthopedics,* 31(1 Suppl), S46-48. doi: 10.1097/BPO.0b013e3181fd87eb

Ogilvie, J. W., Braun, J., Argyle, V., Nelson, L., Meade, M., and Ward, K. (2006). The search for idiopathic scoliosis genes. *Spine, 31*(6), 679-681. doi: 10.1097/01.brs.0000202527.25356.90

Ohtsuka, Y., Yamagata, M., Arai, S., Kitahara, H., and Minami, S. (1988). School screening for scoliosis by the Chiba University Medical School screening program. Results of 1.24 million students over an 8-year period. *Spine,* 13(11), 1251-1257.

Pin, L. H., Mo, L. Y., Lin, L., Hua, L. K., Hui, H. P., Hui, D. S., Yuan, L. (1985). Early diagnosis of scoliosis based on school-screening. *Journal of Bone and Joint Surgery,* 67(8), 1202-1205.

Plaszewski, M., Nowobilski, R., Kowalski, P., and Cieslinski, M. (2012). Screening for scoliosis: Different countries' perspectives and evidence-based health care. *International Journal of Rehabilitation Research,* 35(1), 13-19.

Pruijs, J. E., Keessen, W., van der Meer, R., and van Wieringen, J. C. (1995). School screening for scoliosis: The value of quantitative measurement. *European Spine Journal,* 4(4), 226-230.

Pruijs, J. E., van der Meer, R., Hageman, M. A., Keessen, W., and van Wieringen, J. C. (1996). The benefits of school screening for scoliosis in the central part of The Netherlands. *European Spine Journal,* 5(6), 374-379.

Reamy, B. V., and Slakey, J. B. (2001). Adolescent idiopathic scoliosis: Review and current concepts. *American Family Physician,* 64(1), 111-116.

Richards, B. S., Bernstein, R. M., D'Amato, C. R., and Thompson, G. H. (2005). Standardization of criteria for adolescent idiopathic scoliosis brace studies: SRS Committee on Bracing and Nonoperative Management. *Spine,* 30(18), 2068-2075.

Richards, B. S., and Vitale, M. G. (2008). Screening for idiopathic scoliosis in adolescents. An information statement. *Journal of Bone and Joint Surgery,* 90(1), 195-198.

Rinsky, L. A., and Gamble, J. G. (1988). Adolescent idiopathic scoliosis. *West Journal of Medicine,* 148(2), 182-191.

Risser, J. C. (1958). The Iliac apophysis: An invaluable sign in the management of scoliosis. *Clinical Orthopaedics,* 11, 111-119.

Rogala, E. J., Drummond, D. S., and Gurr, J. (1978). Scoliosis: Incidence and natural history. A prospective epidemiological study. *Journal of Bone and Joint Surgery,* 60(2), 173-176.

Sabirin, J., Bakri, R., Buang, S. N., Abdullah, A. T., and Shapie, A. (2010). School scoliosis screening programme-a systematic review. *Medical Journal of Malaysia,* 65(4), 261-267.

Schwend, R. M., Hennrikus, W., Hall, J. E., and Emans, J. B. (1995). Childhood scoliosis: Clinical indications for magnetic resonance imaging. *Journal of Bone and Joint Surgery,* 77(1), 46-53.

Scoliosis Research Society (SRS). (2012). Scoliosis Research Society, 2012. Retrieved from http://www.srs.org/professionals/glossary/glossary.asp

Stirling, A. J., Howel, D., Millner, P. A., Sadiq, S., Sharples, D., and Dickson, R. A. (1996). Late-onset idiopathic scoliosis in children six to fourteen years old. A cross-sectional prevalence study. *Journal of Bone and Joint Surgery,* 78(9), 1330-1336.

Theologis, T. N., Jefferson, R. J., Simpson, A. H., Turner-Smith, A. R., and Fairbank, J. C. (1993). Quantifying the cosmetic defect of adolescent idiopathic scoliosis. *Spine,* 18(7), 909-912.

Thilagaratnam, S. (2007). School-based screening for scoliosis: Is it cost-effective? *Singapore medical journal,* 48(11), 1012-1017.

USPSTF. (1996). Guide to Clinical Preventive Services (2nd ed.). Washington, DC: Office of Disease Prevention and Health Promotion.

USPSTF. (2004a). Screening for idiopathic scoliosis in adolescents: A brief evidence update. Retrieved from http://www.uspreventiveservicestaskforce.org/3rduspstf/scoliosis/scolioup.htm

USPSTF. (2004b). Screening for idiopathic scoliosis in adolescents: Recommendation statement. Retrieved 4th March, 2011, from http://www.uspreventiveservices taskforce.org

Velezis, M. J., Sturm, P. F., and Cobey, J. (2002). Scoliosis screening revisited: Findings from the District of Columbia. *Journal of Pediatric Orthopedics,* 22(6), 788-791.

Wang, Y. P., Ye, Q. B., and Wu, B. (1996). [Result on the screening of scoliosis among school students in Beijing area]. *Zhonghua Liu Xing Bing Xue Za Zhi,* 17(3), 160-162.

Ward, K., Ogilvie, J. W., Singleton, M. V., Chettier, R., Engler, G., and Nelson, L. M. (2010). Validation of DNA-based prognostic testing to predict spinal curve progression in adolescent idiopathic scoliosis. *Spine,* 35(25), E1455-1464. doi: 10.1097/BRS.0b013e3181ed2de1

Watts, H. G., Hall, J. E., and Stanish, W. (1977). The Boston brace system for the treatment of low thoracic and lumbar scoliosis by the use of a girdle without superstructure. *Clinical Orthopaedics and Related Research,* 126, 87-92.

Weinstein, S. L., Dolan, L. A., Spratt, K. F., Peterson, K. K., Spoonamore, M. J., and Ponseti, I. V. (2003). Health and function of patients with untreated idiopathic scoliosis: A 50-year natural history study. *Journal of the American Medical Association,* 289(5), 559-567.

Weinstein, S. L., and Ponseti, I. V. (1983). Curve progression in idiopathic scoliosis. *Journal of Bone and Joint Surgery,* 65(4), 447-455.

Weinstein, S. L., Dolan, L. A., Wright, M. D., and Dobbs, M. B. (2013). Effects of bracing in adolescents with idiopathic scoliosis. *New England Journal of Medicine*, 369, 1512-1521.

Willner, S. (1979). Moire topography--a method for school screening of scoliosis. *Archives of Orthopedic Trauma Surgery,* 95(3), 181-185.

Wong, H. K., Balasubramaniam, P., Rajan, U., and Chng, S. Y. (1997). Direct spinal curvature digitization in scoliosis screening: A comparative study with Moire contourgraphy. *Journal of Spinal Disorders,* 10(3), 185-192.

Wong, H. K., Hui, J. H., Rajan, U., and Chia, H. P. (2005). Idiopathic scoliosis in Singapore schoolchildren: A prevalence study 15 years into the screening program. *Spine,* 30(10), 1188-1196. doi: 00007632-200505150-00014

Wong, H. K., and Tan, K. J. (2010). The natural history of adolescent idiopathic scoliosis. *Indian Journal of Orthopaedics,* 44(1), 9-13. doi: 10.4103/0019-5413.58601

Yawn, B. P., and Yawn, R. A. (2000). The estimated cost of school scoliosis screening. *Spine,* 25(18), 2387-2391.

Yawn, B. P., Yawn, R. A., Hodge, D., Kurland, M., Shaughnessy, W. J., Ilstrup, D., and Jacobsen, S. J. (1999). A population-based study of school scoliosis screening. *Journal of the American Medical Association,* 282(15), 1427-1432. doi: joc80146 [pii]

Ylikoski, M. (2005). Growth and progression of adolescent idiopathic scoliosis in girls. *Journal of Pediatric Orthopaedics Part B / European Paediatric Orthopaedic Society, Pediatric Orthopaedic Society of North America,* 14(5), 320-324.

Yrjonen, T., and Ylikoski, M. (2006). Effect of growth velocity on the progression of adolescent idiopathic scoliosis in boys. *Journal of Pediatric Orthopaedics Part B,* 15(5), 311-315.

Zhang, G. P., Li, Z. R., Wei, X. R., Cao, Y. L., and Cui, Q. L. (1988). Screening for scoliosis among school children in Beijing. *Chinese Medical Journal (English),* 101(2), 151-154.

PART III: BEYOND THE SCREENING TEST

In: School Health Screening Systems
Editors: Bradley McPherson and Carlie J. Driscoll
ISBN: 978-1-63117-942-6

Chapter 10

COMMUNICATING SCHOOL HEALTH SCREENING RESULTS TO PARENTS AND CHILDREN

Tammy Hoffmann,[1,2,*] Rae Thomas[1] and Chris Del Mar[1]
[1]Centre for Research in Evidence-Based Practice,
Faculty of Health Sciences and Medicine, Bond University
[2] School of Health and Rehabilitation Sciences, University of Queensland

ABSTRACT

Conducting a screening program is one thing, communicating the results to individuals is another altogether. We believe effective communication to be the nexus of health decision-making. How you convey screening choices and results to parents, teachers, and children may have both positive and negative consequences to parental and teacher perceptions of the child's behavior, expectations of his/her future development, and the child's view of themselves. In this chapter, we address the challenges and necessity of informed consent, the importance of understanding the implications of false positive and false negative results, and the potential consequences of communicating screening results. We also discuss what should be communicated and how it should be communicated and provide some practical suggestions about possible formats and strategies for conveying complex statistical information.

INTRODUCTION

Receiving screening results often means that there is a wealth of information that needs to be communicated to parents, the child, and teachers. The volume of information is even greater if the screening process identifies a difficulty, which subsequently leads to a diagnosis, or a need for repeated screening, or further assessment. Professionals who are involved in the screening process need to give consideration to the way in which the screening results are communicated to others (this may be the parents, the child, teachers, or

* thoffmann@bond.edu.au.

others). This consideration should include both the content (what is said) and the presentation (how it is said).

Communicating screening results to parents, regardless of screening outcome, can be a confronting topic. In the same way that conducting a screening test and interpreting its result requires specialised knowledge and skills, and often technical skills, so too does communicating the results of the screening test. Unfortunately, this part of the process is sometimes not given the same level of attention, consideration, or planning. Communicating results is often seen as "just telling them" and the last step in the process. However, poor communication can have many negative consequences. These can include distress, mistrust, misunderstanding, misinterpretation of advice, and ill-informed decisions about what to do next (National Health and Medical Research Council, NHMRC, 2006).

Why Communicate Screening Results?

Screening is designed to detect a likely disease or condition of which a child (or family, or teacher) is unaware. However, implicit to the screening process, and often not discussed, is the decision to intervene if a condition is detected so that the condition can be corrected to minimize its effects. Therefore, screening may only be helpful if effective treatment is available (Cadman et al., 1987). Clearly then, some form of communication has to precede the intervention step and, ideally, also before the screening step. Providing individuals with enough information to make an informed decision about whether or not to screen is the essential first step in the communication process. Also, the parents and the child (and perhaps, teacher, depending on the sensitivity of the diagnosis and the nature of the intervention/s) need to be told what happens once the screening has been completed. However, it is not that simple. One of the first considerations is how to discuss the screening information so that a parent (or older child) can make an "informed consent".

Informed Consent: Communication Before the Screening Occurs

Every participant in a screening program should, with few exceptions, be offered the choice of whether or not to participate, with information presented in a way that enables the decision to be properly informed. This is a challenge, not only because screening programs involve large numbers of participants, but also because it can be difficult to clearly communicate some of the involved concepts.

Unlike diagnostic tests, screening programs are offered to healthy individuals who have no symptoms of disorder or disease. Screening healthy individuals has potential to do harm. Therefore, it is essential for potential "screenees" to understand the ramifications of the screening process. Although one of the outcomes of screening can be that an individual does not have the condition for which they were tested, the other outcome (and the purpose of screening) is to pick up abnormalities and direct the "screenee" to effective intervention. It is, therefore, important that the professional provides enough information to the potential participant for them to understand the risk of screening. However, results from screening studies have reported inadequate informed consent processes (Hoffman et al., 2010; Stefanek, 2011).

As a professional, you need to be familiar with the statistical information of your screening test. This is obviously different for all tests and so beyond the scope of this chapter. The parent should be provided with information about the likelihood of false positive and false negative results (see below) of the test and information about the effectiveness of the intervention. This information has to be non-biased and can be provided in written form to allow time for the parent to consider whether they wish their child to participate in screening. This process should be an "opt in" process where parents actively decide to participate and contact the screening organization. This is different to the "opt out" process where the children would be automatically screened unless the parents contact the screening organization to decline.

WHICH SCREENING RESULTS SHOULD BE COMMUNICATED?

Most of this chapter focuses on communicating a 'positive' result, but some less obvious questions about communicating screening results are: 1) should we communicate negative results? and 2) how do we explain the possibility of false positives and false negatives?

Starting with the possibility of false positive and false negative results: not many parents (or professionals!) find Bayesian reasoning intuitive. That is, they are unlikely to appreciate that a positive screening result for a rare condition is most likely to be a false positive. This means that even though the child has a positive result from the first test, another (and more sensitive) test will indicate the child does not have the condition. This means that professionals need to be careful to explain this when delivering the results of any positive screening test. Also, the professionals involved in conducting the screening should take the trouble to investigate the specific characteristics of the test, including its sensitivity and specificity (see Chapter 1 for further detail).

It is also important to know the underlying prevalence of the condition being tested for in the population (for example, of children in that age group). Knowing this prevalence will allow estimation of two very important pieces of information: the positive posterior probability, and its companion, the negative posterior probability, which is the probability of the condition if the test is positive, and of the child not having the condition if the test is negative, respectively.

A similar approach should be taken with negative results. Although Bayesian reasoning means that the chance of there being a condition is even smaller after a negative screening test, it is not zero.

In other words, there is still a chance the child has the condition despite the normal test. Again, it can be worth providing an estimate of this chance, so that the parents have some idea of the amount of risk. Although this may seem somewhat overwhelming, by knowing this information you can provide parents with accurate information.

POTENTIAL CONSEQUENCES OF COMMUNICATING SCREENING RESULTS

All screening does harm (Gray & Austoker, 1998). This bold statement encompasses a great truth that we may easily forget in the stampede to detect a "stitch in time". As professionals, we are often led to believe that identifying psychological, biological, or physical disorders in children will always lead to positive outcomes for the child but this is not the case. Regardless of the screening outcome, there can be both positive and negative consequences to children, parents, and teachers. In this section, we will explore some of the potential positive and negative consequences of communicating unfavorable screening results to parents and children.

The Achilles' heel of any parent is the health of their child. Informing a parent that their child may have health or developmental problems will result in a continuum of emotional responses. Be prepared that parents may display feelings of sadness, anger, disbelief, or even relief. These are all okay. Parent responses to hearing unfavorable screening results can depend on parental perception of acceptability of the screening process, the extent to which effective treatments are available for the condition, and the recognition that not treating the condition could result in severe developmental consequences for the child (Al-Qabandi, Gorter, & Rosenbaum, 2011). For example, telling a parent that their child has a biological, physical, or developmental disability such as phenylketonuria, hearing or visual deficits, or Downs syndrome can result in feelings of grief, loss, and anxiety for the parent. However, early intervention for these conditions may positively impact the child's developmental course. With clear information and effective and available interventions, parents are able to assume the role of advocate for their children. They may actively seek information and follow professional recommendations.

In contrast, if the screening test is less robust and if the screen is for conditions which are seen as subjective (for example, obesity, pervasive developmental disorder, behavioural disorders, or anxiety), parents may respond differently. A parent may deny the screening results, withdraw the child from health services, or become hypervigilant to the child's health to the extent that the child is prevented from participating in normal childhood experiences. There are many opportunities within the communication process that have the potential to help or hinder how a parent reacts to unfavorable information. There can be both positive and negative consequences of the screening process for parents, and a professional's communication strategies play an important role in how these consequences may or may not manifest. It is also important to realize that positive and negative consequences can also occur for the child and their teacher.

Positive and Negative Consequences of Unfavorable Screening Results

Parent. Sometimes parents are aware that their child is not achieving developmental milestones as easily as their peers. Childhood birthday parties often serve as exercises in developmental comparisons and parents of children with developmental delays are often alerted to them at these times. This can be very upsetting and cause anxiety. However, when this occurs, screening results may confirm a parent's suspicion or concern and provide relief.

This can help parents form realistic expectations of their child's future developmental progress and achievements, and provide explanations to family members and friends as to the reason their child performs differently to others.

In addition, parents may assume the role of advocate and seek out information and potential interventions. These are effective, problem-focused coping strategies (Graungaard & Skov, 2006). Having access to effective interventions enables parents to focus on their child's future capabilities and possibilities rather than on disabilities, therefore, providing emotion-focused coping strategies (Graungaard & Skov, 2006).

Possibly the most overwhelming positive consequence for parents is the opportunity to be an active participant in the remediation of, or intervention for, the problem. Positive collaborations between professionals and parents strongly predict parent satisfaction in the screening process and outcomes (Galil et al., 2006). This is essential for future engagement within the school and health setting and for future, positive child development.

In contrast, for some parents the communication of unfavorable screening results can result in negative consequences. Studies have shown that parents may initially feel grief or injustice about unfavorable screening outcomes and believe that their actions caused the problem (Bratt, Östmann-Smith, Sparud-Lundin, & Axelsson, 2011). Depending on the screening outcome, some parents may experience the "loss of an expected future". Most parents have dreams and aspirations for their children. Sometimes screening results alter these dramatically. For example, a diagnosis of Asperger's syndrome, severe learning disabilities, or intellectual impairment may require parents to re-evaluate their aspirations for their child, potentially causing grief and depression. Perseveration of guilt and sense of loss may create an inability on the parent's part to look to the future and hinder effective coping strategies.

If results of a screen are unexpected, the first time a parent is informed about a problem with their child's development may result in confusion, misinterpretation of screening results, or denial. For example, in a study about child weight status (Perrin, Skinner, & Steiner, 2012), less than one-quarter of parents informed that their child was overweight remembered being told. Positive communication strategies and provisions of support by the professional when discussing screening results have been shown to influence a parent's perception of provided information (Rahi, Manaras, Tuomainen, & Hundt, 2004).

Even when parents are informed of unfavorable screening results, have access to, and then implement interventions, they can remain more anxious and hypervigilant of their child's development than parents of children with developmental problems who were informed but had no intervention (Cadman et al., 1987). Therefore, access to intervention does not necessarily improve the likelihood of positive consequences. Finally, one of the most challenging and disheartening of negative consequences to unfavorable screening results is when a parent disengages from the child, school, and health professionals due to the belief that the child has deficits that cannot be altered. Even when an unfavorable screening outcome is subsequently reversed, mothers have been documented as having ongoing psychological and parenting difficulties. A recent study (Viaux-Savelon et al., 2012) reported mothers who participated in a pre-natal ultrasound, and who were informed their child had abnormalities which a later, more specific test refuted (remember this is a "false positive" screening result), had more anxiety, depression, and intrusive parenting practices when the child was 2 months old compared to mothers with a normal initial screening result. Screening results can have both positive and negative parental consequences that can continue for many months, sometimes years, after the screening results are communicated.

Child. Results of a screening test may facilitate greater understanding of a child's condition and his/her subsequent behavior by parents, siblings, extended family, teachers, and peers. The child's behavior may be viewed in a more understanding and favorable light and may help frame the expectations of others. Further, it could provide necessary information to assist applications for ongoing support by appropriate education and/or disability services. A diagnosis may also steer families toward interventions specific to certain conditions. However, although a diagnosis can help others to understand a child's behavior and point towards effective interventions for specific disorders, and even reduce some problematic behaviors, this does not take away the underlying symptoms and ongoing challenges faced by the child and the family.

Children grow up within family narratives. Most adults have stories about themselves as children that were told time and again in family circles about events that either epitomized their personality or helped shape their character. Children with disabilities also have narratives. A positive consequence to an unfavorable screening result may result in a narrative with the overarching theme of overcoming adversity. In these situations, children will be characterized by their ability to succeed even though they have a diagnosis that limits their ability. Unfortunately, some children will develop a narrative of being limited by their diagnosis. They will develop expectations about their personality and potential as being constrained by adversity rather than enhanced by it. In addition to the family narrative, children diagnosed with certain conditions are often stigmatized by the label of the diagnosis.

Results of screening programs that identify problems for the child are often recorded in health and education files. Consequently, they become a permanent record of events following the child throughout their time in primary and secondary education and, sometimes, indefinitely if electronic health records are used. Psychological disorders are often used to explain and justify behaviors, and knowledge about a child's diagnosis has the potential to lower teacher expectations of academic achievement creating a self-fulfilling prophecy (Katzenstein, Fastenau, Dunn, & Austin, 2007). Psychological diagnoses can also be used as taunts by peers.

Adverse psychological consequences (for example, thinking your behavior and emotions are beyond your control) can also result from an unfavorable screening outcome. In a qualitative study with a group of incarcerated adolescent boys diagnosed with Attention Deficit Hyperactivity Disorder (ADHD), the boys described symptoms of their disorder as making them commit offences and absolved themselves of wrong-doings because events were seen to be out of their control (Tidefors & Strand, 2012). The long-term consequences of an ADHD diagnosis for these adolescents and how they view their behavior remains to be seen.

As discussed, an essential ingredient of an effective screening program is effective interventions. But not all treatment is effective. A 10-year follow-up of a school-based screening and intervention program for children diagnosed with ADHD determined that none of the interventions were associated with improvements in children's ADHD symptoms or classroom learning problems (Sayal et al., 2010). Medication is sometimes an effective intervention. However, although short-term benefits for some medications have been found for certain diagnoses, little is known of long-term medication outcomes for many disorders. These unknowns constitute considerable potential harm for the child.

Teachers. Screening outcomes can provide teachers with many positive consequences. Guidance can be provided to teachers regarding appropriate training and development. Appropriate strategies could enhance their teaching and facilitate constructive outcomes for the child to reach their full potential. With new knowledge, a teacher could form realistic expectations about a child's behavior, achievements, and rate of progress. He or she could advocate for appropriate resources and develop practical classroom strategies they could implement on a daily basis. Knowledge could help teachers facilitate classroom discussions with peers to assist with overcoming barriers to inclusion and reduce marginalization of children with disabilities.

However, teacher knowledge of screening results may also produce negative consequences. Studies have demonstrated that when teachers were aware of students with heightened scores on behavior inventories they were more likely to treat these children differently (such as lowered expectations and increased negative judgments) perpetuating the labelling effect (Sayal et al., 2010; Silver & Harkins, 2007). In a study using vignettes to describe children with a history of difficult, ambiguous, or no behavior problems, teachers were more likely to use negative labelling to describe the child with a known history of difficult behavior problems or an ambiguous history compared to a child with no known history of behavior problems (Silver & Harkins, 2007).

Case Examples

Positive Consequences: An Empowered Parent

As a young boy, Shane always came across as a little odd. His mother noticed his behavior was difficult to manage when things happened unexpectedly and how he often preferred to play by himself. When he did play with other children, it often didn't end well. Shane's mother wanted to learn more effective ways to manage his challenging behavior before he stared school next year so she enrolled them both in an intensive behavior management intervention. Early in the intervention, Shane was diagnosed with Asperger's syndrome. His mother was both distraught and relieved. She had always suspected there was something wrong with the way Shane interacted with others and now she felt she had some answers. Shane's mother continued to engage in the behavior management program as she recognized that not all his behaviors were beyond his control and she wanted to ensure she knew the difference. In addition, she began reading about Asperger's syndrome and asked the psychologist to assist with an education plan for Shane when he commenced school in a few months' time. When it came time for Shane to commence school, his mother was ready to assist the teachers with Shane's behaviors.

Negative Consequences: A Disengaged Parent

Mrs Smith presented at a psychological intervention service with her six-year-old son John at the suggestion of John's school. The school reported John's behavior to be very challenging to manage. He was non-compliant in the classroom, and would swear, run away from the teacher, and routinely end up in the deputy principal's office for some "thinking time". Mrs Smith was exasperated and reported that "nothing worked" at home; not time out, washing his mouth out with soap, or removal of all his toys for a month. Mrs Smith agreed to attend an intensive behavior management intervention. At each attendance, Mrs Smith would express her annoyance at her son's behavior and struggle to identify positive exchanges between them throughout the week. During the behavioural intervention, John's pediatrician diagnosed him with Attention Deficit Hyperactivity Disorder and prescribed medication. At this time, Mrs Smith withdrew from the intervention because she had an "ADHD child" and believed that she didn't need alternative behavior management techniques when it was an innate problem with John and medication would remedy this.

Practical Considerations When Communicating Screening Results

There are a number of practical decisions that need to be made before communicating screening results. Some of the basic decisions that need to be made are: when will the results be communicated; to whom will they be communicated; how will they be communicated, and what are the health literacy levels of those who are receiving the screening results.

When Will the Results Be Communicated?

As discussed earlier in this chapter, there are many emotional reactions that can be experienced after receiving screening results. Appointments with parents should be scheduled so that: where possible, both parents can attend; parents can attend without the child being present (depending on the child's age and other circumstances, a separate time to meet with the parents and the child together to explain the results to the child may be required); an adequate amount of time is scheduled for the discussion; and an appropriately quiet and private location is available to hold the discussion. If the parents are being advised of an unfavorable screening result, it may not be possible or wise to communicate all the information in one session. Individuals who are experiencing an emotional reaction to information are sometimes not able to fully comprehend or remember subsequent information that is shared (Theis & Johnson, 1995). People often have questions that arise after the consultation. Therefore, scheduling another session for further questions and discussion is important. If this is not possible, at the minimum, providing a telephone number that parents can call when further questions arise can help parents to feel supported and less overwhelmed.

To Whom Will the Results Be Communicated?

Ideally, the results should be communicated to both parents, although it may be that only one parent is available for the initial meeting. Depending on the age of the child, a simplified version of the results (along with age-appropriate information about what this means for the child), should be explained to the child. Parent/s may wish to do this on their own, in a familiar environment, and at a time and in a way that is most appropriate for their child. Sometimes parents request support in discussing unfavorable screening outcomes with their child. As a professional, you must support the parents in this process and either be prepared to assist in the actual conversation or at minimum, provide helpful information. In many cases, the child's teacher, and sometimes other key school staff, may also need to be told the results of the screening test. This depends on the nature and sensitivity of the condition and its likely impact on the child at school. If the screening process is one that happened external to the school environment, it may be that the child's parent/s arranges a meeting with the teacher to discuss the screening results and implications for the child while at school. Alternatively, if the screening process was conducted in conjunction with the school, it may be possible for the parent/s (once they have already been told) and the professional to meet together with the child's teacher.

How Will the Results Be Communicated (i.e., in What Format)?

Will communication of the results occur in a face-to-face appointment, a telephone call, or via a letter? Ideally, communication of results should be done in a face-to-face consultation. However, for various logistical reasons, this may not always be possible. Using a letter to communicate results should be reserved for communicating results of a screen that did not identify any difficulties and requires no further action.

A combination of verbal and written information should be used to communicate screening results. Verbal education is the format used most frequently by health professionals for communicating with parents about the health of their child. However, one of the major problems with verbal communication and education is that individuals frequently forget the information that is provided to them (Kitching 1990). It has been estimated that most individuals remember less than a quarter of what they have been told (Boundouki, Humphris, & Field, 2004). For this reason, written information is a particularly valuable format that should ideally be used to supplement or reinforce information that is presented verbally (Hill, 1997). Written materials have the advantage of being available to refresh one's memory as needed (Ley, 1988).

As mentioned earlier, many individuals will formulate questions after the consultation with the professional, not during it (Tang & Newcomb, 1998). To some extent, written materials may be able to assist individuals in answering the questions that occur when they are not interacting with a professional. Written materials have a number of advantages such as: message consistency, reusability, portability, flexibility of delivery, permanence of information, and they are economical to produce and update. A further benefit of written materials is that individuals can choose the level and amount of information that best suits them as their level of coping changes (Weinman, 1990).

Consider the Health Literacy Levels of Those Receiving Screening Results

Of course, prior to deciding to use written materials with an individual, the professional needs to consider factors such as the individual's reading ability, health literacy level, primary language, and other abilities that can impact on processing written information such as vision. Health literacy refers to the "…cognitive and social skills which determine the motivation and ability of individuals to gain access to, understand and use information in ways which promote and maintain good health" (World Health Organization, 1998, p. 10). Professionals should be aware of the literacy skills of individuals so they can alter the educational intervention accordingly (Weiss, Reid, & Kleigman, 1995). People with poor literacy often use a range of strategies to hide literacy problems (Weiss et al., 1995) and are often reluctant to ask questions for fear of appearing ignorant. Written materials will not benefit individuals if they are unable to understand it. If a professional chooses to use written materials with an individual, it is essential that appropriate attention is given to the design of the written materials, particularly its readability and suitability.

Readability of written materials: The reading level, or readability, of a written material refers to how easy it is to read. Written materials should be written simply, at the lowest level that conveys the information accurately (Hoffmann & Worrall, 2004). Unfortunately, it is quite common for health education materials to be written at a reading level that is higher than the reading ability of the majority of the clients who received the materials (Beaver & Luker, 1997: Griffin, McKenna, & Tooth, 2006; Hoffmann & McKenna, 2006). In general, a 5th- 6th grade reading level (typically equivalent to 10-11 years of age in the Australian education system) is recommended (Doak, Doak, & Root, 1996; Weiss et al., 1998).

There are a number of readability formulas that allow the calculation of an estimate of the reading grade level of the material. Two well-known readability formulas are the SMOG (McLaughlin, 1969) and the Flesch Reading Ease formula (Flesch, 1948). The latter is available through some word processing programs such as Microsoft Word. The SMOG is fast and simple to use, widely used in health research, and has been recommended as one of the best readability formulas for assessing health education materials (Meade & Smith, 1991). Other than in the original reference, there are many websites which provide instructions and scoring for the SMOG, as well as some online calculators (e.g., www.niace.org.uk/misc/SMOG-calculator/smogcalc.php#).

However, readability is only one element that contributes to the appropriateness of written health education materials. When designing new written materials or evaluating existing materials, there are a number of features that should be considered in addition to readability. Appropriate written health education materials contain content and design features intended to maximize the effectiveness of the written material. The following categorization system can be a way of grouping the content and design features that should be used in written health education materials: content, language, organization, layout and typography, illustrations, and learning and motivation (Doak et al., 1996). Although it is beyond the scope of this chapter to elaborate on each of these features, a list of recommended content and design features that should be followed when designing written materials has been compiled by Hoffmann and Worrall (2004). There are also checklists available that professionals can use to evaluate the suitability of written materials that they have developed or those that have come from other sources and they are considering using them. Two of these checklists are the Suitability of Assessment of Materials (SAM) (Doak et al., 1996) and a checklist of content and design characteristics that was developed by Paul, Redman, and Sanson-Fisher (1997).

A word about Internet-informed parents: Professionals may find that parents, teachers, or even children will come to them with information that they have found on the Internet and wish to discuss. The Internet can be a valuable source of information for individuals and health information is one of the most frequently searched topics on the Internet (McMullan, 2006). Active consumers of health information will have a need to seek out their own information either before and/or after they have seen the professional and received results of the screening test (McMullan, 2006). Professionals need to be aware that "Internet-informed" individuals can affect the traditional professional-client relationship and professionals should acknowledge parents' search for information, answer questions they have about information that they have found, and assist parents by directing them to reliable and accurate Internet sites (McMullan, 2006).

An additional topic that needs to be thought through before communicating screening results to the parent, child, or teacher is how will the statistical information (the numbers) involved with screening results be communicated. This is a complex topic that is elaborated on in the section below.

Communicating Statistical Information

Screening results typically produce quantitative results. For example, results may be expressed in means, percentiles, or as a risk statistic. Additional associated quantitative information that may also be communicated to those who receive the screening results (such as parents or teachers) may include prevalence information (such as 3 in 1000 children of this age experience this condition) or prognostic information (e.g., over the next 5 years, there is a 80% chance that the child will be able to demonstrate age-appropriate development milestones).

Communicating statistical information well can be tricky. Often, professionals do not understand the information themselves (Gigerenzer, Gaissmaier, Kurz-Milcke, Schwartz, & Woloshin, 2007). However, it is important that the communication of this information is done well. If those who are receiving screening results do not receive accurate information that is conveyed to them in a manner in which they can understand, then their ability to participate in informed and shared decision-making is hampered.

There are often differences between how professionals and patients understand probability and risk. Many health professionals have been trained to understand these as mathematical probabilities of an event happening within a whole population. Health professionals subsequently tend to view these statistics as objective and impersonal. Conversely, patients' views and understanding of these concepts are commonly influenced by emotions, anxieties, concerns about the future, what they have seen and heard reported in the media, and by the views of their social networks. Indeed, individuals (such as parents, patients, etc.) often personalize risk and are less interested in what happens to 'populations' (NHRMC, 2006). Information about risks can also be hard for individuals to understand when they do not have previous experience to compare the numbers to; for example, if the risk of an event is 20%, patients may not know whether this is relatively high or low (NHMRC, 2006). It is beyond the scope of this chapter to cover this topic in detail. Readers who are interested in learning about this topic in more detail may wish to read additional resources on this matter (e.g., Hoffmann & Tooth, 2013). However, some basic principles about how to present statistical information to individuals are (Hoffmann & Tooth, 2013):

- Be open about uncertainties surrounding benefits and risks.
- Give information in terms of both positive and negative outcomes to avoid bias.

    - Framing of information refers to whether the information is presented in a positive or negative manner. If information is positively framed it is presented in terms of who will benefit. Conversely, information that is presented in terms of harms (such as side-effects) is negatively framed. How information is framed has been found to influence patients' perceptions of test or treatment options and confidence in medical decision-making (Gigerenzer & Edwards, 2003).
- Present natural frequencies (that is, plain numbers) rather than percentages or relative risks.
    - Risk of a condition refers to the probability of developing the condition in a certain time frame. Relative risk gives an indication of the degree of risk and is the ratio of two risks: the risk in the population exposed to a factor (such as a treatment), divided by the risk of those not exposed. Many research articles report their results in terms of relative risk (or relative risk reduction or relative risk increase). However, using relative risks to communicate findings can be misleading (as they make benefits appear larger and harms appear smaller than they really are). Instead, we know, from numerous research studies that individuals prefer to receive and better understand natural frequencies. For example, 12 of 100 children will develop a side-effect from undergoing a particular intervention.
- Use multiple formats: for example, verbal and written descriptions. Where possible, use simple visual aids such as graphs, pictures or perspective charts to aid understanding.
    - For people who are facing decisions about the best way to manage their health, whether it is a decision about treatment or screening, decision aids are a communication tool that may be of some assistance in certain situations. Decision aids are interventions designed to help patients make decisions by providing them with information about the options, the personal importance of possible benefits and harms, and encouraging their active participation in the decision-making process together with their health professional (Stacey et al., 2011).
    - Decision aids are not available for many conditions though. Instead, professionals should consider using simple, readily available visual aids such as pictographs or bar charts. For example, a pictograph of a population of 1000 people (represented by circles) which you can color in to show how many will benefit (or be harmed) by a particular intervention is one way of showing data in an absolute manner.
- Avoid using descriptors, for example, "high" "low", "rare" and "frequent". These words are vague and can be interpreted differently by different people.
- Avoid presenting too much information, particularly in the first session. Only present the key statistics that are useful for helping individuals to make informed decisions.

Questions That Parents Should Be Encouraged to Ask

After receiving a screening result which indicates that a child has the condition that was being screened for, one of the most common questions that parents will ask is "what can be done?" If it is a face-to-face or telephone discussion that is being conducted, this question will naturally lead into a discussion about intervention options. While a detailed discussion about how to communicate information about interventions (and their associated benefits and harms) is beyond the scope of this chapter, in the section below we have listed some of the broad questions that parents should be encouraged to ask when initially considering their intervention options. These questions come from a very useful book, aimed at consumers, by Irwig and colleagues (2007) which can be downloaded for free at: www.sensiblehealt hadvice.org.

1. What will happen if I do nothing?

What happens if you just watch and wait? "No treatment" is nearly always an option, but often one that people do not consider because they feel they should do something. Many conditions get better on their own. Many get better just, or almost, as quickly without treatment as with treatment. But with treatment, there is usually expense (of seeing a health professional and of the treatment, such as medication), inconvenience, and sometimes side-effects.

2. What are my test or treatment options?

For many conditions, there are a few treatment options (and as explained above, "no treatment" is one of them). So first, make sure you are aware of all the options.

3. What are the benefits and harms of each option?

Each option has benefits and harms. Some treatments will be more effective than others (some may even not help at all). Some treatments might be more convenient or acceptable to you. Treatment harms do not mean just the side-effects (although these are important). There is also the expense, inconvenience, or level of discomfort of a treatment.

4. How do the benefits and harms weigh up for me?

Everyone has different preferences and values. Decisions about your health are a personal choice. What may be an acceptable option for one person may not be for another. Only you can make a decision that is right for you and your family.

5. Do I have enough information to make a choice?

Before you can make an informed decision, you need good quality information about each of these questions. Asking your health professional the above questions is a good place to start. If you are not satisfied or convinced with their answers, consider seeking another opinion. The Internet is a popular place to look for health information – before or after seeing a health professional. However, a lot of the information on websites is not accurate or reliable. Being able to work out which websites are reputable providers of health information, and which are not, is a worthwhile skill. For example, websites that display the Health on the Net (HON) code (www.hon.ch) have been assessed as providing reliable health information.

For those that do not, you can assess their quality yourself with a short checklist called DISCERN (www.discern.org.uk).

Conclusion

"All screening programmes do harm. Some do good as well..." (Gray & Austoker, 1998, p.983). The potential positive and negative consequences of communicating screening results that were discussed in this chapter are based on the assumption that the screening result was accurate and the child does have a difficulty of some description. However, as this chapter also discussed, all screening tests produce false positive and false negative results. A false positive is when a family is told the child has a difficulty and he/she does not, and a false negative is when a family is told a child does not have a difficulty and he/she does. There are limitations to all screening tests and these must be communicated to all concerned.

As a professional, you have a duty of care to the individuals and groups you service. Good communication of screening results is an exceptionally important task and should never be something that is just tacked on to the end of a screening program. Some of the topics raised in this chapter may be daunting, but careful preparation and considered communication strategies will ensure parents and teachers will be better informed about screening, better educated about results and, ultimately, children will be better serviced by you and your peers.

References

Al-Qabandi, M., Gorter, J. W., & Rosenbaum, P. (2011). Early autism detection: Are we ready for routine screening? *Pediatrics, 13,* e211-e217.

Beaver, K., & Luker, K. (1997). Readability of patient information booklets for women with breast cancer. *Patient Education and Counselling, 31*, 95-102.

Bratt, E., Östman-Smith, I., Sparud-Lundin, C., & Axelsson, B. Ä. (2011). Parents' experiences of having an asymptomatic child diagnosed with hypertrophic cardiomyopathy through family screening. *Cardiology in the Young, 21,* 8–14.

Boundouki, G., Humphris, G., & Field, A. (2004). Knowledge of oral cancer, distress and screening intentions: Longer term effects of a patient information leaflet. *Patient Education and Counselling, 53*, 71-77.

Cadman, D., Chambers, L. W., Walter, S. D., Ferguson, R., Johnston, N., & McNamee, J. (1987). Evaluation of public health preschool child developmental screening: The process and outcomes of a community program. *American Journal of Public Health, 77,* 45-51.

Doak, C., Doak, L., & Root, J. (1996). Teaching patients with low literacy skills (2nd ed.). Philadelphia PA: Lippincott.

Flesch, R. (1948). A new readability yardstick. *Journal of Applied Psychology, 32,* 221-233.

Galil, A., Bachner, Y. G., Merrick, J., Flusser, H., Lubetzky, H., Heiman, N., & Carmel, S. (2006). Physician-parent communication as predictor of parent satisfaction with child development services. *Research in Developmental Disabilities, 27,* 233-242.

Gigerenzer, G., & Edwards A. (2003). Simple tools for understanding risks: From innumeracy to insight. *British Medical Journal, 327*, 741–744.

Gigerenzer, G., Gaissmaier, W., Kurz-Milcke, E., Schwartz, L.M., & Woloshin, S. (2007). Helping doctors and patients make sense of health statistics. *Psychological Science in the Public Interest, 8, 53–96.*

Graugaard, A. H., & Skov, L. (2006). Why do we need a diagnosis? A qualitative study of parents' experiences, coping and needs, when the newborn child is severely disabled. *Child. Care, Health and Development, 33,* 296-307.

Gray, M. J. A., & Austoker, J. (1998). Quality assurance in screening programmes. *British Medical Bulletin, 54,* 983-992.

Griffin, J., McKenna, K., & Tooth, L. (2006). Discrepancy between older clients' ability to read and comprehend and the reading level of written educational materials used by occupational therapists. *American Journal of Occupational Therapy, 60,* 70-80.

Hill, J. (1997). A practical guide to patient education and information giving. *Baillieres Clinical Rheumatology, 11,* 109-127.

Hoffman, R. M., Lewis, C. L., Pignone, M. P., Couper, M. P., Barry, M. J., Elmore, J G., Levin, C. A., Van Hoewyk, J., & Zikmund-Fisher, B. J. (2010). Decision-making processes for breast, colorectal, and prostate cancer screening: Results from the DECISIONS study. *Medical Decision Making, 30 (5 Suppl),* 53S-64S. doi: 10.1177/0272989X10378701.

Hoffmann, T., & McKenna, K. (2006). Analysis of stroke patients' and carers' reading ability and the content and design of written materials: Recommendations for improving written stroke information. *Patient Education and Counselling, 60*, 286-293.

Hoffmann, T., & Worrall, L. (2004). Designing effective written health education materials: Considerations for health professionals. *Disability and Rehabilitation, 26*, 1166-1173.

Hoffmann, T., & Tooth, L. (2013). Talking with patients about evidence. In T. Hoffmann, S. Bennett, & C. Del Mar (Eds), *Evidence-based practice across the health professions (2nd ed) (pp.328-352).* Sydney: Elsevier.

Irwig, L., Irwig, J., Trevena, L., & Sweet, M. (2008). *Smart health choices: Making sense of health advice.* London: Hammersmith Press.

Katzenstein, J. M., Fastenau, P. S., Dunn, D. W., & Austin, J. K. (2007). Teachers' ratings of the academic performance of children with epilepsy. *Epilepsy and Behavior, 10*, 426–431.

Kitching, J. (1990). Patient information leaflets: The state of the art. *Journal of the Royal Society of Medicine, 83*, 298-300.

Ley, P. (1988). The use of written information. In P. Ley (Ed.), *Communicating with patients* (pp.125-140). London: Chapman & Hall.

McLaughlin, H. (1969). SMOG grading: A new readability formula. *Journal of Reading, 12*, 639-646.

McMullan, M. (2006). Patients using the Internet to obtain health information: How this affects the patient–health professional relationship. *Patient Education and Counselling, 63*, 24-28.

Meade, C. D., & Smith, C. F. (1991). Readability formulas: Cautions and criteria. *Patient Education and Counselling, 17*, 153–158.

National Health and Medical Research Council of Australia (NHMRC). (2006). *Making decisions about tests and treatments: Principles for better communication between healthcare consumers and healthcare professionals.* Canberra: Australian Government Printer.

Paul, C., Redman, S., & Sanson-Fisher, R. (1997). The development of a checklist of content and design characteristics for printed health education materials. *Health Promotion Journal of Australia, 7*, 153-159.

Perrin, E. M., Skinner, A. C., & Steiner, M. J. (2012). Parental recall of doctor communication of weight status: National trends from 1999 through 2008. *Archives of Pediatric and Adolescent Medicine, 166,* 317-322.

Rahi, J. S., Manaras, I., Tuomainen, H., & Hundt, G. L. (2004). Meeting the needs of parents around the time of diagnosis of disability among their children: Evaluation of a novel program for information, support, and liaison by key workers. *Pediatrics, 114,* e477-e483.

Sayal, K., Owen, V., White, K., Merrell, C., Tymms, P., & Taylor, E. (2010). Impact of early school-based screening and intervention programs for ADHD on children's outcomes and access to services: Follow-up of a school-based trial at age 10 years. *Archives of Pediatric and Adolescent Medicine, 164,* 462-469.

Silver, C., & Harkins, D. (2007). Labeling, affect, and teachers' hypothetical approaches to conflict resolution: An exploratory study. *Early Education and Development, 18,* 625-645.

Stacey, D., Bennet, C.L., Barry, M.J., Col, N. F., Eden, K. B., Holmes-Rovner, M., ... Thomson, R. (2011). Decision aids for people facing health treatment or screening decisions. Cochrane Database of Systematic Reviews; Art No.: CD001431. doi: 10.1002/14651858.CD001431.pub3.

Stefanek, M. E. (2011). Uniformed compliance or informed choice? A needed shift in our approach to cancer screening. *Journal of the National Cancer Institute, 103,* 1-6. doi: 10.1093/jnci/djr474

Tang, P., & Newcomb, C. (1998). Informing patients: A guide for providing patient health information. *Journal of the American Medical Informatics Association, 5*, 563-570.

Theis, S., & Johnson, J. (1995). Strategies for teaching patients: A meta-analysis. *Clinical Nurse Specialist, 9,* 100-105.

Tidefors, I., & Strand, J. (2012). Life history interviews with 11 boys diagnosed with Attention-Deficit/Hyperactivity Disorder who had sexually offended: A sad storyline. *Journal of Trauma & Dissociation, 13,* 421-434.

Viaux-Savelon, S., Dommergues, M., Rosenblum, O., Bodeau, N., Aidane, E., Philippon, O., ... Cohen, D. (2012). Prenatal ultrasound screening: False positive soft markers may alter maternal representations and mother-infant interactions. *Plos One, 7,* e30935, doi:10.1371/journal.pone.0030935

Weinman, J. (1990). Providing written information for patients: Psychological considerations. *Journal of the Royal Society of Medicine, 83*, 303-305.

Weiss, B., Coyne, C., Michielutte, R., Davis, T. C., Meade, C. D., Doak, L. G., et al. (1998). Communicating with patients who have limited literacy skills: Report of the National Work Group on Literacy and Health. *Journal of Family Practice, 46*, 168-175.

Weiss, B., Reed, R., & Kligman, E. (1995). Literacy skills and communication methods of low income older persons. *Patient Education and Counselling, 25*, 109-119.

World Health Organization (WHO). (1998). *Health promotion glossary*. Geneva: WHO.

In: School Health Screening Systems
Editors: Bradley McPherson and Carlie J. Driscoll

ISBN: 978-1-63117-942-6

Chapter 11

DATA MANAGEMENT IN SCHOOL HEALTH CARE SYSTEMS

K. Todd Houston*, Tali R. Weinberg, Anne M. Fleming and Kelly J. Brown
University of Akron, US

ABSTRACT

In the United States, millions of public school students with disabilities and other health conditions receive health care and related services that support their academic success in the educational setting. Fortunately, public laws have evolved over the past half-century that ensure these children receive a free and appropriate education, regardless of disability or health condition. Often, these students receive screening and other health care services from school-based health care centers and the school nurse, but barriers have prevented the sharing of a student's health information with local service providers, health care systems, and other practitioners. New federal laws and Health Information Exchanges (HIEs) are creating opportunities for improved coordination of health care services for all students, which, in turn, promotes better long-term health, wellness, and academic success.

INTRODUCTION

Students with disabilities and other health conditions are routinely educated in public school systems in the United States. In 2008, for example, there were 49.3 million students enrolled in public elementary and secondary schools, and 6.48 million of these students had disabilities that required some degree of health management and tracking (Snyder & Dillow, 2011). As a matter of public policy, the Individuals with Disabilities Education Improvement Act of 2004 (IDEA) mandates that all children with disabilities have available to them a free appropriate public education that emphasizes special education and related services designed

* Email: houston@uakron.edu.

to meet their unique needs and prepare them for further education, employment, and independent living (U.S. Congress, 2004). Thus, as Snyder and Dillow (2011) acknowledge, in 2008, 13.2% of students in public schools were supported by federally supported special education programs. The emphasis on public education for all children has led to an increase in the number of students with disabilities and a range of health conditions being served.

ESTABLISHING A PRECEDENT FOR SERVING CHILDREN WITH DISABILITIES IN PUBLIC SCHOOLS

Prior to the enactment of the Education for All Handicapped Children Act of 1975, several federal laws were in place supporting the improvement of education programs and services for children with disabilities. For example, the Teachers of the Deaf Act of 1961 (PL 87-276) trained individuals to work with deaf or hard of hearing children and was later expanded in 1965 to include the training of instructors across all disability areas. In 1965, the Elementary and Secondary Education Act (PL 89-10) and the State Schools Act (PL 89-313) were established to assist the education of children with disabilities by providing direct grant assistance to states (U.S. Office of Special Education Programs, 2007).

Unfortunately, even with these federal laws, the educational needs of students with disabilities were still not being met. In 1970, only one in five students with disabilities was appropriately educated in public schools (U.S. Office of Special Education Programs, 2007) and many states had laws excluding certain students, including children who were deaf, blind, emotionally disturbed, or cognitively impaired. When they were in the public schools, students with disabilities often were either not served or grossly underserved. These students failed to receive appropriate educational services, due to the lack of adequate resources to serve children who had a range of disabilities and other health conditions, and were frequently segregated from other typically developing children (IDEA, U.S. Congress, 2004).

The public education system needed federal legislation statutes that set strict precedents for educating students, regardless of disability or medical need. The Education for All Handicapped Children Act of 1975, which was later amended in 2004 to become the Individuals with Disabilities Education Improvement Act or IDEA (Wright & Wright, 2010), was one of the most significant federal educational laws enacted to protect the educational rights of students with disabilities. Outlining the guidelines for providing appropriate services to students with disabilities, the Education for All Handicapped Children Act required that all children with disabilities were to be provided with a free and appropriate public education. Rather than transporting students with disabilities or other health conditions to specialized institutions, the law supported the education of these students in their neighborhood schools with same aged peers.

While not all children with disabilities or health conditions receive special education or related services under IDEA, all children with disabilities are protected under Section 504 of the Rehabilitation Act of 1973. Section 504 is a civil rights law that mandates school districts to provide a "free appropriate public education" (FAPE) to each qualified student with a disability who resides in the school district's jurisdiction, regardless of the nature or severity of the disability (U.S. Department of Education Office for Civil Rights, 2011). Under Section 504, qualifying students are to be provided with regular or special education and related services that meet their needs as adequately as those of their typical peers. While it does not provide extra funding, Section 504 does require the elimination of all barriers preventing a student with disabilities from participating fully within the educational setting. To ensure it is upheld, an enforcement mandate is included in the law that could lead to a loss of federal funding if violations are determined by the U.S. Department of Education Office of Civil Rights (Council for Exceptional Children, 2002).

To determine if a child is a qualified disabled student under Section 504, an evaluation must be conducted. Section 504 requires the use of evaluation procedures that ensure that children are not misclassified, unnecessarily labeled as having a disability, or incorrectly placed based on inappropriate selection, administration, or interpretation of evaluation materials (U.S. Department of Education Office for Civil Rights, 2011). The evaluation process, which may be the same as the plan used to assess the needs of those under IDEA, includes items such as a medical diagnosis from a physician, aptitude and achievement tests, teacher recommendations, physical condition, social and cultural background, and adaptive behavior (U.S. Department of Education Office for Civil Rights, 2011). The medically diagnosed illness must greatly limit the student's ability to learn or partake in another major life activity to qualify under Section 504. In addition, those that qualify under both IDEA and Section 504 are only required to have a single individualized education plan (IEP) for IDEA, which meets the requirement for a free appropriate public education. (U.S. Department of Education Office for Civil Rights, 2011).

Today, because of IDEA, early intervention services are provided to almost 200,000 eligible infants and toddlers and their families, while nearly 6 million students receive special education and related services at public schools to meet their individual needs. Not only has IDEA allowed for the education of more children in their neighborhood schools, rather than in separate schools and institutions, but the law has also contributed to improvements in the rate of high school graduation, post-secondary school enrollment, and post-school employment of youth with disabilities (U.S. Office of Special Education Programs, 2007).

As well, IDEA has led to an increase in the identification of students with health or medical needs. In 1980, only 98,000 students in the public schools were documented as having conditions that limited strength, vitality, or alertness due to chronic or acute health problems (e.g., heart conditions, tuberculosis, rheumatic fever, nephritis, asthma, sickle cell anemia, hemophilia, epilepsy, lead poisoning, leukemia, or diabetes). As more students with these conditions are being educated in public schools, this number has increased significantly. In 2008 alone, 659,000 students were identified as having health impairments (Snyder & Dillow, 2011). With this rise in numbers came the need for the management of students' individual health needs.

School Based Health Care Systems

Origins and Statistics of School Based Health Care Systems

With the increase in the identification of children with disabilities, schools began to seek methods for managing students' individual health needs. In the late 1970's, school based health centers (SBHC) were developed to increase and improve student's access to health care. Much more than a typical school nurse's office, SBHC, also located in school buildings (Holmes, 2010), offer on-site services such as immunizations, physical examinations, or on-site therapy for children with special mental health needs (Committee on School Health, 2001). Through various forms of funding, including mainstream health care institutions and community hospitals (32 percent), public health departments (17 percent), community health centers (17 percent), and academic medical centers (5 percent) (Lear, 2007), more than 1,700 SBHCs have been established in 48 states and U.S. territories as of 2005. Found predominantly in urban communities, SBHCs are located among various grade levels, including 33% in high schools, 24% in elementary or middle schools, and 43% in alternative schools or schools with combinations of grade levels (Council on School Health, 2012). Thus, SBHCs offer a range of critical healthcare services, resulting in significant benefits to the students who are under their care.

Relevance of Integrated Health Care

While clinics vary based upon the needs of the communities, SBHCs provide a range of services to meet the various health and medical needs of students. Therefore, SBHCs are comprised of multidisciplinary teams including members such as nurse practitioners, physicians, clinical social workers, psychologists, nutritionists, dentists, dental hygienists, and administrators (Holmes, 2010). These clinicians collaborate with school faculty to ensure the SBHC is working as a fundamental component of the school (Holmes, 2010). In turn, SBHCs assist students, families, health professionals, and society in general with improved coordination of healthcare services.

It comes as no surprise that students not only accomplish more academically when they are present in class, but also when they are healthy. By making health care services available at school where the students are located, SBHCs reduce absences due to illness or doctor appointments and address health problems that may be hampering students' learning processes. SBHCs, which primarily serve uninsured or underserved students, may also provide mental health services to students (Holmes, 2010). In a supportive and safe environment, students are more willing to talk about personal or family issues, and mental health clinicians are better able to provide continuous preventive support to address major causes of youth mortality, such as suicide and homicide (Committee on School Health, 2001). Finally, SBHCs are increasingly focusing on wellness and prevention. Students are being exposed to more information and raising of their health awareness, which leads to better health care consumers (Holmes, 2010).

Parents and caregivers of students also benefit from SBHC services. First, free of the burden of driving children to doctors' appointments, family members are able to save time and income by remaining at work while their children's health care needs are being met. Second, families unfamiliar with preventive medicine in traditional settings can be taught how to use these services at schools (Committee on School Health, 2001, p. 198). As well, families can save personal income by avoiding hospital and emergency room visits (Holmes, 2010).

Broader health care interests and scientific research are being met through SBHCs. For example, follow-up compliance among patients is better as clinicians are able to be in contact with students more easily (Committee on School Health, 2001). And, with increased interest in prevention and chronic disease management (Lear, 2007), health concerns among children, such as obesity, are better suited to be addressed directly with students. Due to their direct work with children, government agencies and professional organizations have called on SBHC clinicians and professionals to monitor or treat chronic conditions including asthma, diabetes, and other disabling conditions (Lear, 2007). This, in turn, facilitates easier tracking of health care outcomes and promotes increased compliance among the students served.

Finally, local communities benefit from SBHCs. SBHCs strengthen communication and connections between schools and local communities (Holmes, 2010) and reduce emergency room visits for underserved minority students by providing them with better access to high-quality health care. In a retrospective cohort study of Denver health patients, SBHC users had more primary care visits and less emergency room visits than those who used non-SBHC clinics. In addition, students utilizing SBHCs were more likely to have received advised vaccinations (Allison, Crane, Beaty, Davidson, Melinkovich, & Kempe, 2007).

SBHCs have provided an excellent health care resource for students, most prominently the uninsured and underserved, and have positively impacted students' families, health professionals, and society. With the management of students' individual health needs through SBHCs has come the need for an effective and safe way to share health information between the SBHCs, schools, primary care physicians, health departments, and, most importantly, the students and their families.

Data Sharing and Health Privacy Legislation

Two pieces of legislation play major roles in the sharing of private identifiable health information, the Family Educational Rights and Privacy Act (FERPA) and the Health Insurance Portability and Accountability Act (HIPAA). FERPA, also known as the Buckley Amendment, was passed by the United States Congress in 1974 to protect the storage and transfer of public school students' private educational records, both paper and computerized. Under FERPA, parents of students enrolled in federally funded schools, which includes almost all public schools and postsecondary schools, and eligible students, those 18 years and older or enrolled in postsecondary school, are granted certain rights of access to education records and disclosure of information from those records without their consent is restricted (Cheung, Clements, and Pechman, 1997). Contrary to a common misconception, FERPA does not protect the confidentiality of information in general. Instead, FERPA prohibits the improper disclosure of information contained in the education record, and the law does not apply to one's opinions or observations unless it is entered into the record (New Hampshire Department of Education, 2012).

In addition, FERPA enables parents and some eligible students to request corrections be made to their records if they feel an error has been made (Cheung, Clements, and Pechman, 1997). Like FERPA, HIPAA, which was passed by the U.S. Congress in 1996 (Nass, Levit & Gostin, 2009), protects the transfer and storage of personal identifiable information. The primary difference between the two laws is that HIPAA pertains to private patient information in healthcare settings. Therefore, HIPAA oversees the transfer of identifiable medical information through computers and between health care providers (Cheung, Clements, and Pechman, 1997).

FERPA vs. HIPAA: Which Rules Are Followed?

With the advent of SBHCs comes the difficulty of discerning which piece of legislation, either FERPA or HIPAA, is to be followed when sharing students' records between clinicians and staff members at and outside of the educational setting. Unfortunately, the distribution of public school students' health records and policies often vary by state. Simply put, in most states, for children who are in public schools that receive federal funding, their health records are protected by FERPA. That is, the HIPAA final rule explains that records that are subject to FERPA are not subject to HIPAA (Ohio Department of Education, 2009). In addition, the Ohio Department of Education states that all documentation, treatment plans, and IEP medically related information in the hands of school district employees and their contractors fall under the provisions that require FERPA, not HIPAA, to be followed (Ohio Department of Education, 2009). Often, FERPA supersedes HIPAA. Many schools, even those that are HIPAA covered entities, are not required to comply with the HIPAA Privacy Rule, because the only health records maintained by the school are education records or treatment records of eligible students under FERPA, both of which are excluded from coverage under the HIPAA Privacy Rule (U.S. Department of Health and Human Services & U.S. Department of Education, 2008).

However, in some situations, only HIPAA is to be utilized. For example, if the school is not subject to FERPA (i.e., does not receive federal funding, but maintains medical records and is a HIPAA covered entity), the HIPAA Privacy Rule must be followed. In addition, if the treatment records are disclosed to a third-party health care provider who is a HIPAA covered entity, which almost all medical practitioners are, the records would be subject to the HIPAA Privacy Rule (U.S. Department of Health and Human Services & U.S. Department of Education, 2008).

Where FERPA and HIPAA May Intersect

When a school provides health care to students as part of typical operations, such as through its health clinic, it is also a "health care provider" as defined by HIPAA. If a school also conducts any covered transactions electronically in connection with that health care, it could be considered a covered entity under HIPAA. However, as stated earlier, many schools, even those that are HIPAA covered entities, are not required to comply with the HIPAA Privacy Rule, because the only health records maintained by the school are "education records" or "treatment records" of eligible students under FERPA, both of which are excluded from coverage under the HIPAA Privacy Rule. As Hinman and Davidson (2009) report, interpretation of FERPA vary among the states, and the exchange of health-related information has often been in one direction, with schools receiving health information about students from the public health and health care systems but not providing health information to those systems without previous parental consent.

According to one study of school nurses (Hinman & Davidson, 2009), 5.6% of students require medications at school. Although 98% of nurses reported having medication guidelines, nearly one half (48.5%) reported a medication error in the preceding year; only 20.7% documented adverse effects. Whether health care providers received information about the medication errors or adverse effects (and whether they had direct health effects) is not known. What is clear is that the current interpretations of FERPA make it difficult to achieve ready exchange of health information between the educational system and the public health/health care systems, and this could have negative effects on the health of children (Hinman & Davidson, 2009).

EDUCATION AND SCHOOL HEALTH RECORDS

Education Records

An education record is comprised of educational information about an individual student, including in writing, computer-based, and video. According to the Institute of Education Sciences (IES), the research branch of the U.S. Department of Education, an education record contains information such as date and place of birth, parents/guardians biographical information, grades, test scores, special education records, disciplinary records, medical and health records that the school creates or collects and maintains, documentation of attendance, schools attended, and personal information such as the student's social security number and picture (IES, 1997).

Education records do not solely contain information regarding students' academics. At the elementary or secondary level, a student's health records, including immunization records, maintained by an educational agency or institution subject to FERPA, as well as records maintained by a school nurse, are 'education records' subject to FERPA. In addition, records that schools maintain on special education students, including records on services provided to students under the Individuals with Disabilities Education Act (IDEA), are 'education records' under FERPA. This is because these records are (1) directly related to a student, (2) maintained by the school or a party acting for the school, and (3) not excluded from the definition of 'education records' (U.S. Department of Health and Human Services & U.S. Department of Education, 2008).

However, at postsecondary institutions, medical and psychological treatment records of eligible students are excluded from the definition of 'education records' if they are made, maintained, and used only in connection with treatment of the student and disclosed only to individuals providing the treatment. These records are commonly called 'treatment records.' An eligible student's treatment records may be disclosed for purposes other than the student's treatment, provided the records are disclosed under written consent. If a school discloses an eligible student's treatment records for purposes other than treatment, the records are no longer excluded from the definition of 'education records' and are subject to all other FERPA requirements (U.S. Department of Health and Human Services & U.S. Department of Education, 2008).

School Health Records

The school health record is the compilation of health information concerning an individual student. According to the National Association of School Nurses (2004), school health records, usually kept in paper and/or electronic format, provide the mechanism for a school nurse to communicate information to students, families, the school multidisciplinary team, emergency personnel, other health care providers, and school nurse substitutes

(National Association of School Nurses, 2004). School health records are used to indicate that a student's health problems need to be addressed, to assess the quality of SBHCs, and to evaluate program outcomes. When a student moves schools, either to a new site within the district or out of the district, school health records are transferred (National Association of School Nurses, 2004).

Information Contained in School Health Records

While schools will vary based upon policy, most school health records will contain similar information. According to the Maine School Health Advisory Committee (2002), school health records should be comprised of identifying information, health history, assessment data and narratives, and some additional paperwork. The items commonly found in each section include:

Identifying information:

- Student name
- Date of birth
- Gender
- Grade level
- Parent/Guardian name and address
- Current phone number
- Emergency contacts

Health history:

- Communicable Diseases, including dates and supporting documentation when available
- Medical Conditions, including supporting documentation
- Food/Drug Allergies, including anecdotal information
- Immunization Dates

Assessment data and narrative:

- Health Appraisal/assessment
- Health Screening
- Physical Exam
- Accident/Injury Reports
- Narrative Notes
- Physician Notes (pertinent to student's education)
- Alcohol/Drug Use in School
- IDEA/504 documentation that include health issues

Inserts to the Folder:

- Documented proof of immunization/waiver
- Staffing minutes, if pertinent
- In school medications, including physician's order, parental permission, daily record sheet
- In school emergency care plans
- **Individual Health Plans (IHP's)**
- IEP's that include pertinent health planning

(Maine School Health Advisory Committee, 2002)

Information Excluded from School Health Records

School nurses often keep personal notes and logs in order to remember encounters with students. While some schools require all health related office visit information to be officially documented in the student's educational record, some permit personal notes and do not consider them to be part of the education records. This information will not be subject to FERPA regulations if all of the following criteria are true: 1) they are kept as a memory aid, 2) they are only in possession of writer, 3) they are not shared with any other professionals, and 4) the notes are not used in place of normal documentation procedures (New Hampshire Department of Education, 2012). If shared with other professionals, these personal notes would automatically become part of official school records (Colorado Department of Education, 2005).

The Colorado Department of Education suggests that if personal notes are kept, they should only include the student's name and the time of arrival and departure from the school clinic. Any additional information would need to be included in the student's school health record (2005).

GUIDELINES FOR SCHOOL HEALTH RECORDS

As formal documents containing personal information, school health records should follow certain guidelines. Because there is variation among the states, the following represents one state's (Colorado) approach to maintaining student health records (Colorado Department of Education, 2005):

- Be accurate, objective, concise but thorough, timely, well organized, and legible;
- Write handwritten notes in ink;
- Write legibly and spell correctly;
- Accompany every entry by the nurse's or service provider's name, date, and time of service;
- Document any nurse or school health action taken in response to a student problem;
- Include positive and negative findings in any assessment documentation;
- Include only essential information;
- Be precise about measurements, spelling, and standard abbreviations;

- Update all records, including progress notes, Individualized Educational Plans (IEPs), Individualized Health Plans (IHPs) at least annually and when changes occur;
- Use nursing and appropriate health or medical classification language;
- Be consistent over time with regard to frequency of documentation, based on school district policy, nursing or medical protocols and standards, and as the acuteness of the student's health status demands;
- Record the student's (or parent's) own words;
- Document only objective data, relevant to the student's care– not personal judgments and opinions;
- Do not reference school district problems, such as staff shortages;
- Detail any variation from standard protocols and any unusual student circumstances of situations;
- Document in detail notifications regarding changes in a student's health status or any unusual findings;
- Document content of any telephone consultations and direction to assistive personnel;
- Include any prescriber orders and referral orders in the health record;
- Document medications given, stating when the medication was started and ended, at the end of the year, at the end of a course of medication, or when the dose changes; and
- Document the name and title of anyone to whom access to a child's health record was given (Colorado Department of Education, 2005, pp. 14-15).

Disclosure of Education and School Health Records

Information from a student's records can only be disclosed with prior written informed consent from a student's parents or guardian, which are defined by FERPA as a natural or adoptive parent, a legal guardian, or an individual acting as a parent in the absence of the parent or guardian, or from a student at least 18 years old or enrolled in postsecondary school (Cheung, Clements, & Pechman, 1997). FERPA defines informed consent as a written account of why personal information is requested and how it will be used. In general, parents should have the option, without penalty, of agreeing or declining to provide the information an education agency or school requests. Certain information, however, is required by schools, and parents must provide the information in order for their children to be enrolled. Parents' agreement must be based on an understandable explanation of how the information will be used. Once a parent's informed consent is given for a particular purpose or set of purposes, the information cannot be 'redisclosed'– used by a third party except as originally indicated. FERPA regulations require that prior consent be given by parents for the disclosure of information to persons other than school officials (Cheung, Clements, & Pechman, 1997). These rules also apply to third parties acting on behalf of schools, such as state and local education agencies, intermediate administrative units, researchers, psychologists, or medical practitioners who work for or are under contract to schools (Institute of Education Sciences, 1997).

There are certain circumstances in which prior consent from parents is not required to release records. These instances include reporting of information required by the new school a student is transferring to or applying to, conduction of audits, inspection of school records in compliance with Federal laws, responding to subpoenas or court orders, instances of abuse or neglect, mandatory reporting of communicable diseases, or during an emergency if school officials need to provide information from education records to protect the health or safety of the student or others (Institute of Education Sciences, 1997). While a school official must attempt to inform parents before complying with the subpoena, under certain circumstances, the subpoena may specifically state that parents are not to be notified (Institute of Education Sciences, 1997).

ESSENTIAL FEATURES OF INTEGRATED DATA MANAGEMENT FOR SCHOOL BASED HEALTH CLINICS

Who Maintains School Health Records?

School nurses, who are employees of the school district, are generally the person in charge of student health records, which include: immunization records, screening records, progress notes, physician orders, physical examination records, medication and treatment logs, individualized health care plans, emergency health care plans, third party medical records, consent forms, Medicaid and other insurance billing forms, and flow charts (NASN, 2004b).

However, FERPA allows for contracted employees to also maintain such records. According to the National Association of School Nurses (NASN), contracted employees include school nurses who are employed by other agencies, including public ones, such as a community's department of health, and private ones, such as school-based health center personnel when, as employees of another community agency, they are contracted by the school district to provide school health services (NASN 2004a).

Additional Roles of the School Nurse: School Health Records

If the school district does not have written policies on school health records, the school nurse is in a position to promote the development of standardized school health record systems, with clear guidelines for local policies and procedures, and adherence to standards that protect student and family privacy. The school nurse also should ensure that release of information to serve a legitimate educational interest is defined both in terms of those who need to know to benefit the student, and those who have the expertise to understand and interpret the health information and its relationship to educational needs. The school nurse also can develop mechanisms for internal communication of student health information to appropriate school staff, and external communication that encourages interagency collaboration and private partnerships as necessary to benefit the student (Colorado Department of Education, 2005). As well, the school nurse may delegate limited access rights to specific non-nursing staff, but such staff should not be granted access to records for which they do not have specific, current, assigned responsibilities (Colorado Department of Education, 2005).

Record of Access

Schools should maintain records for each request of access to and disclosure of information from a student's education and school health records. FERPA requires that each record have an access log, showing the name and title of the person receiving information, the date of access, and the legitimate interest the person had in requesting the information (Maine School Health Advisory Committee, 2002). However, a record of access is not needed if the request was from or the disclosure was to the parent, eligible student, authorized school official, a party with written consent from the parent, or a party seeking directory information (South Dakota Department of Education, 2008).

Policy for Transfer of Education and School Health Records to New Schools

When a student transfers outside a school district, the new school is responsible for obtaining the student's education records, which includes the school health record, IEP, and records relating to the provision of special education or related services to the child. Both schools are responsible for replying to one another in a punctual manner and following FERPA's privacy policies (South Dakota Department of Education, 2008). In some states, parental consent is not needed for the transfer of records. However, some states, states such as South Dakota, require all participating schools to have policies in place that outline guidelines for forwarding education records between schools (South Dakota Department of Education, 2008).

Storage of School Health Records

The storage and maintenance of active and historical school health records is very essential to protect the privacy and confidentiality of students who have received health-related services.

School health records should be stored in locked file cabinets or secure computer files with restricted access (Maine School Advisory Committee, 2002) and active school health records should be located somewhere accessible to staff, such as the school health office (Colorado Department of Education, 2005). School districts can determine their own policy and procedures regarding how long records will be kept as no regulation is provided under FERPA. The Colorado Department of Education (2005) requires school health records to be discarded after a student graduates or leaves the school district as long as a records retention policy has been established and approved by the State Archives. In addition, when information is no longer needed to provide educational services, a school is required to destroy personally identifiable information at a parent's request. This can be done by removing identifying information from the records, separating these records from active records, and filing them in a specific location with limited access (Colorado Department of Education, 2005).

Guidelines for Protecting Confidential Student Health Information

As considerable variability across states remains in terms of how student health information is protected, the following presents one state's (Maine) approach to maintaining confidential student health information (Maine School Health Advisory Committee, 2002).

- Distinguish student health information from other types of school records;
- Extend to school health records the same protections granted medical records by federal and state law;
- Establish uniform standards for collecting and recording student health information;
- Establish district policies and standard procedures for protecting confidentiality during the creation, storage, transfer, and destruction of student health records;
- Require written, informed consent from the parent and, when appropriate, the student, to release medical and psychiatric diagnoses to other school personnel;
- Limit the disclosure of confidential health information within the school to information necessary to benefit student's health or education;
- Establish policies and standard procedures for requesting needed health information from outside sources and for releasing confidential health information, with parental consent, to outside agencies and individuals; and
- Provide regular, periodic training for all new school staff, contracted service providers, substitute teachers, and school volunteers concerning the district's policies and procedures for protecting confidentiality (Maine School Health Advisory Committee, 2002).

Sharing Healthcare Information

Electronic School Health Records

With the advent of modern technology, many schools have moved from paper to electronic records. However, computerized records are at risk for several issues such as hacking or unauthorized access, natural disaster, human error, computer viruses, computer crashes, inadvertent release, and insecure transmission over the Internet (Colorado Department of Education, 2005). In turn, new protocols have been adopted to ensure the safety of electronic student health records and student confidentiality through the use of encryption software and password protection.

Individualized Healthcare Plans and Emergency Care Plans

In addition to the school health records, a certain student's education records contain two other important documents, the Individualized Healthcare Plan (IHP) and the Emergency Care Plan (ECP). An IHP, written collaboratively by professionals who work with the student and the parents compiles the student's pertinent medical diagnoses, each with student specific outcomes, interventions, and an evaluation plan (Schwab, Panettieri, Bergren, 1998). Tailored to each student's individual needs and usually included in the student's IEP, the IHP's data sets should be both observable and measureable (Board & Bushmiaer, 2011).

An ECP, usually written by the school nurse in language that can be understood by unlicensed personnel in case of an emergency (Board & Bushmiaer, 2011), identifies potential medical emergencies as well as appropriate interventions (Schwab, Panettieri, Bergren, 1998) The ECP is usually stored with the IHP in the student's educational record but may also be separated to be shared with professionals in the school (Schwab, Panettieri, Bergren, 1998, pp. 35-36).

School Health Based Clinics: Need for Integrated Data Management Systems

By providing expanded school health services, SBHCs carry inherent and unique issues of patient confidentiality, consent, compliance, and continuity that need different solutions than they would in traditional health care settings and in schools without expanded health services (Committee on School Health, 2001). As more health services are being provided at schools, increased collaboration is needed between medical personnel, health care providers, and school-based professionals. Currently, the sharing of information between these health care providers is slow or does not exist. In turn, SBHCs are looking for a means to safely and efficiently share clinical data in order to better coordinate and meet each student's needs (Holmes, 2009).

New Federal Legislation May Reduce Barriers

As Holmes (2009) reports, new federal legislation continues to shape health care and health care delivery. For example, the Patient Protection and Affordable Care Act mandates health insurance coverage to all eligible individuals and is just beginning to change how health care is provided. Likewise, the Health Information Technology for Economic and Clinical Health Act (HITECH) was passed in 2008 and promotes the adoption of health information technology (HIT) to improve the efficiency, quality, and safety of personal health information. Within HITECH, financial incentives are provided for eligible health care professionals and hospitals to adopt electronic health records and for exploring their meaningful use. The Act also supports state Health Information Exchange (HIE) projects, support for HIT extension services, demonstration projects, education and workforce training programs, and standards for information technology (IT) interoperability.

Models of Integrated Data Management Systems

One such integrated data management program being implemented by several states and by some SBHCs, is the Health Information Exchange (HIE). HIE systems electronically consolidate health care information to be shared between organizations within a region, state, community, or hospital system (Holmes, 2009). With HIE systems in place, there is much less need for printing, faxing, and mailing documents, public health authorities have access to large amounts of health related data for specific populations, error in health records is reduced, and patient involvement in their own health care is increased (U.S. Department of Health and Human Services, 2013). Of the SBHCs that are currently using HIT, more than half (56%) use electronic billing systems, and 53 percent use an information management system. A smaller number use electronic medical records (32%) and electronic prescribing (22%), and 7 percent of SHBCs have a telemedicine system (School-Based Health Centers: National Census School Year 2007-2008).

Limitations of Current Integrated Data Management Systems

The adoption of HIE systems is just beginning between states and on regional and local levels, resulting in limited outcome data on these projects. As well, several limitations of these systems have been identified. First, many statewide HIE systems are part of non-profit corporations or partnerships, and the majority are dependent upon federal, state, or independent grant funding. Therefore, schools would have to obtain funding or become incorporated within a larger organization's system (Holmes, 2009). Second, HIE systems are still growing and do not incorporate all participating health facilities. However, growth is taking place. The Colorado Regional Health Information Organization (CORHIO), established in 2007, now includes 28 hospitals, 660 office-based providers, 38 long-term and post-acute care facilities, four behavioral health centers, and two medical labs (CORHIO, 2013). The Indiana Health Information Exchange (IHIE), formed in 2004, is the largest and one of the oldest operating HIE systems in the US. Connecting more than 25,000 health care providers in 17 states, the IHIE has data on several million patients (Indiana Health Information Exchange, 2013). Finally, legislation regarding HIE systems and Health Information Technology (HIT), the overarching term used to describe the management of health information across computer systems, is still being developed (Holmes, 2010). Concerns about confidentiality and privacy can be a barrier to communication (Council on School Health, 2012) and until firm rules and regulations regarding the electronic transfer of information are established, some schools and health care providers may not join.

The Potential Impact of Health Information Technology on SBHCs

School based health centers (SBHCs) perform a unique role in the health and wellness of students enrolled in public schools. These centers use a range of health care providers and also coordinate services with other personnel, such as the school nurse, administrators, and educators. Challenges continue to plague SBHCs when student health information should be shared with external collaborators and service providers. For the typical SBHC, participating in an HIE, even if only on a local level (i.e., with the local hospital system), would significantly improve the coordination of a student's (or multiple students') health care. The challenge, however, is the availability of technology funding for SBHCs. Most SBHCs have limited staffing and financial support and would not be equipped to establish their own health information exchange (HIE) (Holmes, 2010). Thus, as mentioned, a SBHC may be perfectly positioned to join an existing HIE, such as the local hospital system, and receive significant technology support, resulting in greater information sharing among providers and improved health outcomes for the students.

CONCLUSION

Students with disabilities and other health conditions in public schools continue to receive a range of health care services, usually delivered through coordinated services provided by the school based health center and the school nurse. In the United States, numerous federal laws have ensured that children with disabilities and those with other health care needs are entitled to receive these services. Unfortunately, barriers have prevented the sharing of student health care data between public schools and local health care providers, often leading to reduced health care and academic outcomes for the students. New legislation, however, has caused some optimism that these barriers may soon be eliminated. The use of health information exchanges (HIEs), for example, provides the opportunity for improved coordination of health care services between public schools, especially school based health centers, and local health care providers. If achieved, students in public schools will be healthier, better able to perform academically, and on a path to obtain a greater quality of life.

REFERENCES

American Diabetes Association. (2012). *Living with diabetes: Written care plans.* Retrieved from http://www.diabetes.org/living-with-diabetes/parents-and-kids/diabetes-care-at-school/written-care-plans/

Board, C., & Bushmiaer, M. (2011). *Role of the school nurse: Position statement.* Retrieved from http://www.nasn.org/portals/0/positions/2011psrole.pdf

Cheung, O., Clements, B., & Pechman, E. (1997). *Protecting the privacy of student records: Guidelines for education agencies.* National Center for Education Statistics, National Forum on Education Statistics, U.S. Department of Education. Retrieved from: http://nces.ed.gov/pubs97/p97527/

Chicago Public Schools. (2012). *Diabetes management policy.* Chicago Public Schools Policy Manual Section 704.11, Retrieved from http://policy.cps.k12.il.us/download.aspx?ID=260

Colorado Department of Education. (2005, June). *School nursing: Documentation, recordkeeping & confidentiality.* Retrieved from http://www.cde.state.co.us/HealthAndWellness/download/nurDocumentationRecordKeepingConfidentiality.pdf

Colorado Regional Health Information Organization. (2013). *About Colorado regional health information organization.* Retrieved from http://www.corhio.org/

Commonwealth of Virginia Department of Education. (2004, May). *Guidelines for the management of the student's scholastic record in the public schools of Virginia.* Retrieved from http://www.doe.virginia.gov/boe/regulations/secondary_sch_transcripts/management_scholastic_records.pdf

Council for Exceptional Children (2002). Understanding the differences between IDEA and section 504. *Teaching Exceptional Children*, 34(3), 16-23.

Gibbs, J., Timothy, C., & Ward, B. (2012, January). *Education and schools.* Retrieved from http://www.medicalhomeportal.org/clinical-practice/education-and-schools

Holmes, D. (2010). *School-based health centers: Adapting to health care reform and the utilization of health information technology.* Institute for Health Care Studies: Michigan State University.

Indiana Health Information Exchange (2013). *About Indiana health information exchange.* Retrieved form http://www.ihie.org

Institute of Education Services. (1997, May). *Protecting the privacy of student education records.* Retrieved from http://nces.ed.gov/pubs97/web/97859.asp

Maine School Health Advisory Committee. (2002). *Guidelines for school nurses on confidentiality of school health information.* Retrieved from http://www.mainecshp.com /school_counseling/SHAC/DocumentationGuidelines.pdf

Nabors, L., Lehmkuhl, H., Christos, N., & Andreone, T. L. (2003). Children with diabetes: Perceptions of supports for self-management at school. *Journal of School Health,* 73(6), 216-221.

Nass, S. J., Levit, L. A., & Gostin, L. O. National Academy of Sciences, (2009). *Beyond the HIPAA privacy rule: Enhancing privacy, improving health through research.* Retrieved from http://www.ncbi.nlm.nih.gov/books/NBK9578/pdf/TOC.pdf

National Association of School Nurses, Inc. (2004a, July). *Issue brief: School health nurses' role in education: Privacy standards for student health records.* Retrieved from http://www.nasn.org/PolicyAdvocacy/PositionPapersandReports/NASNIssueBriefsFullView/tabid/445/smid/853/ArticleID/78/Default.aspx

National Association of School Nurses, Inc. (2004b, July). *Issue brief: School nurse role in education: School health records.* Retrieved from http://www.nasn.org/PolicyAdvocacy /PositionPapersandReports/NASNIssueBriefsFullView/tabid/445/ArticleId/75/Health-Records-School-2004

National Forum on Education Statistics. (2006). *Forum guide to the privacy of student information: A resource for schools (NFES 2006-805).* U.S. Department of Education. Washington, DC: National Center for Education Statistics. Retrieved from http://nces.ed.gov/pubs2006/2006805.pdf

New Hampshire Department of Education. (2012). *Confidentiality and public school health records.* Retrieved from http://www.education.nh.gov/instruction/school_health/faq_records.htm

New York State Association of School Nurses. (n.d.). *Position statement: Electronic medical records & confidentiality.* Retrieved from http://www.nysasn.org/

Ohio Department of Education, Medicaid Schools Program, (2009). *ODE fact sheet; HIPAA vs. FERPA- what regulations should I follow in MSP?* Retrieved from website: http://www.ode.state.oh.us/gd/templates/pages/ODE/ODEGoogleSearch.aspx?page=221 &query=FERPA&start=0&OriginatingURL=/GD/Templates/Pages/ODE/ODEDefaultPage.aspx?Page=1

Schwab, N. C., Panettieri, M. J., & Bergren, M. D. (1998). *Guidelines for school nursing documentation: Standards, issues, and models.* (2nd ed.). Scarborough, ME: National Association of School Nurses, Inc.

Snyder, T. D., & Dillow, S. A. National Center for Education Statistics, (2011). *Digest of education statistics, 2010 (NCES 2011015).* Retrieved from website: http://nces.ed.gov /pubs2011/2011015_2a.pdf

South Dakota Department of Education. (2008).*Maintaining student records and meeting confidentiality requirements under FERPA, HIPAA, IDEA, 504.* Retrieved from http://doe.sd.gov/oess/documents/sped_ferpa_maintainingrecords.pdf

U.S. Congress (2004). *Individuals with Disabilities Education Improvement Act of 2004 (IDEA).* Retrieved from website: http://www.gpo.gov/fdsys/pkg/PLAW-108publ446/html/PLAW-108publ446.htmS

U.S. Department of Education Office for Civil Rights. (2011, March 17). *Protecting students with disabilities.* Retrieved from http://www2.ed.gov/about/offices/list/ocr/504faq.html

U.S. Department of Education. (2011, April 08).*Family Educational Rights and Privacy Act (FERPA).* Retrieved from http://www2.ed.gov/policy/gen/guid/fpco/ferpa/index.html

U.S. Department of Health and Human Services. (2013). *Health information technology.* Retrieved from http://www.hhs.gov/ocr/privacy/hipaa/understanding/special/healthit/

U.S. Department of Health and Human Services, & U.S. Department of Education, (2008). *Joint guidance on the application of the Family Educational Right and Privacy Act (FERPA) and the Health Insurance Portability and Accountability Act of 1996 (HIPAA) to student health records.* Retrieved from http://www.hhs.gov/ocr/privacy/hipaa/understanding/coveredentities/hipaaferpajointguide.pdf

U.S. Office of Special Education Programs. (2007, July 17). *History: Twenty-five years of progress in educating children with disabilities through IDEA.* Retrieved from http://www2.ed.gov/policy/speced/leg/idea/history.html

Wright, P. W. D., & Wright, P. D. (2010). *Special education law.* (2nd ed., p. 14). Hartfield, VA: Harbor House Law Press.

GLOSSARY

The creation of this glossary has been coordinated by the Editors, with input from a variety of sources including the works of contributing authors and listed references. The definitions provided do not necessary reflect the opinions of all contributors.

Accuracy (A'): This test performance measure is also known as the area under the receiver operating characteristics curve (AUC). It establishes the probability that a randomly chosen case with the target condition will be rated with greater suspicion that a case without the target condition.

Adolescent idiopathic scoliosis: Development of idiopathic scoliosis during adolescence.

Amblyopia: A decrease in vision in at least one eye that cannot be corrected with prescriptive lenses and has no apparent structural cause. Also known as "lazy eye".

Anemia: Insufficient number of red blood cells or hemoglobin, preventing the body's cells from getting enough oxygen.

Angle of trunk rotation: The angle of inclination of a child's back in the forward bending position.

Arthritis: Inflammation of the joints which may be due to infectious, metabolic, or genetic causes.

Articulation: The production of speech sounds. Speech sounds are usually described in terms of the place of articulation, manner of articulation, and other features of the language such as voicing. See also "speech".

Asthma: A chronic disorder of the lungs which is characterized by recurring airway obstruction and resulting in labored breathing, wheezing, and coughing.

Attention deficit: Characterized by a short attention span and, often, an unusually high activity state. Can co-morbidly occur with impulsivity, learning disorders, and behavioral problems.

Audiometer: An instrument that delivers standard, calibrated pure-tone signals at known intensity levels to earphones or other output devices.

Auditory neuropathy/dys-synchrony (AN/AD): A hearing disorder whereby outer hair cell function of the cochlea is normal but neural transmission pathways are impaired (Rance, 2005). The typical audiological profile includes: normal tympanometric results, abnormal acoustic reflexes, normal otoacoustic emissions, absent or grossly abnormal auditory brainstem responses, variable pure tone audiometric results, and speech perception abilities that are poorer than expected (AAA, 2011, p. 41).

Autism: A developmental disorder that is characterized by inability to form normal social relationships, impaired communicative function, and variable but stereotyped behavioral patterns. Affected children may also display a narrow range of focal interests and preoccupation with repetitive activities.

Bayesian reasoning: The Reverend Bayes was an 18th century cleric who had a side interest in probability theory. His theorem shows how the probability of an event is closely related to the prior probability of that event.

Behavior Intervention Plan (BIP): A written, individualized, and data-based plan which describes interventions and strategies to be implemented by school professionals to address a student's social, emotional, and behavioral development.

Bilateral hearing loss: Hearing loss that is present in both the right and left ears.

Body mass index (BMI): A measure of human body shape based on a person's weight and height. BMI can be calculated using a range of formulae. Commonly, an individual's weight is divided by the square of their height, with the resulting value expressed in kg/m^2. BMI is used as a simple parameter to express relative body weight, with criteria set for underweight, overweight, and obese classifications.

Bracing: A brace is made of rigid materials that applies corrective forces to the spine for controlling curve progression.

Central auditory processing disorder (CAPD): A deficit in neural processing of auditory stimuli that is not due to higher order language, cognitive, or related factors (note: definitions of CAPD remain controversial).

Cerebral palsy: Disorders of movement and posture due to damage to, or abnormal development of, the brain's motor control centers. It may arise as a result of prenatal, perinatal, or postnatal factors.

Cobb angle: The intersecting angle of two lines drawn from the most tilted vertebra above and below the apex of a curve.

Combination Disability Resource Class: Special education programs in which students spend up to 60% of the school day involved in special education and related services (e.g., speech therapy, occupational therapy, physical therapy, counseling). These services are typically delivered in the home school by a special education teacher who serves students with a variety of disabilities.

Conduct disorder: A behavioral and emotional disorder seen in childhood and adolescence, with inappropriate actions and expression of emotions. Violation of the social expectations of others is commonly displayed.

Conductive hearing loss: Hearing loss that is caused by a disorder in the outer ear canal or in the middle ear. A common cause of conductive hearing loss in children is otitis media with effusion.

Coryza: A contagious, acute disease including inflammation of the upper respiratory tract, e.g., the common cold.

Criterion-referenced test: An assessment that determines whether a child can perform a particular function or not. Test items are usually scored as present or absent and, in contrast to standardized tests, performance is not compared to the age-matched population.

Cystic fibrosis: A genetic disease affecting the lungs, digestive system, sweat glands, and male fertility. The pancreas is one of the main affected organs, developing fibrous scar tissue, hence, the name's origin.

Data-driven decision making: Data collected are used to guide decisions and action planning regarding effectiveness, student responsiveness, and intervention adaptations and modifications. For example, school-wide or classroom-wide data are collected and address questions regarding student behavior across multiple contexts. Student behavior support teams review progress and incident reports regularly of students receiving additional behavioral supports and interventions, and make adjustments accordingly.

dB HL: Decibels hearing level—the standard measurement unit for intensity of sound when testing human hearing. A hearing threshold of 0 dB HL equates to average normal hearing sensitivity for healthy young adult listeners. The normal threshold range is considered to be -10 to 15 or 20 dB HL.

dB SPL: Decibels sound pressure level—the standard unit for intensity of sound when measuring sound in an acoustic environment.

Dental caries: Decalcification of the tooth enamel leads to destruction of enamel and, eventually the dentin (a hole or cavity forms in the tooth).

Diabetes: Caused by disordered carbohydrate metabolism, via environmental or genetic factors, it involves inadequate secretion or usage of insulin. Symptoms may include excessive urine production, excessive blood sugar levels, thirst, hunger, exhaustion, and weight loss.

Distortion product otoacoustic emissions (DPOAEs): These evoked emissions are produced by presentation of a pair of pure tones via a probe tip inserted into the entrance of the external auditory canal. The pure tone pairs interact to produce a third tone (the distortion product). Utilized in screening and diagnostic audiology, DPOAEs are not a test of hearing per se but, rather, an assessment of the function of the cochlear outer hair cells. Their presence is indicative of normal auditory status up to the cochlea. Their absence may be associated with a hearing loss in excess of 40 dB HL and/or middle ear dysfunction, among other factors.

Eating disorders: Abnormal eating habits that involve either insufficient or excessive food consumption and which lead to physical and/or mental health conditions.

Eczema: An inflammatory skin condition whereby skin appears red, itching, and may display oozing lesions that can turn scaly and hardened.

Education record: Official and confidential information about a student that is maintained by the school and is protected under FERPA.

Efficiency index (EF): This measure is used to judge the overall performance of a system, by determining the proportion of total screening results that are correct (correct passes and correct failures).

Emergency care plan (ECP): The plan utilized by a school when a student with special healthcare needs has an emergency.

Emotional disability: A disability category defined in the 2004 Individuals with Disabilities Education Improvement Act as one or more of the following characteristics: a) an inability to learn that cannot be explained by intellectual, sensory, or health factors, b) an inability to build or maintain satisfactory interpersonal relationships with peers and teachers, c) inappropriate types of behavior or feelings under normal circumstances, d) a general pervasive mood of unhappiness or depression, and e) a tendency to develop physical symptoms or fears associated with personal or school problems. The term includes schizophrenia but does not apply to children who are socially maladjusted, unless it is determined that they have an emotional disturbance.

Enuresis: Involuntary discharge of urine.

Epilepsy: Transient disturbance of the brain's electrical activity producing episodes of impairment, lost consciousness, convulsions/fits, abnormal motor function, and/or psychic or sensory phenomena.

Equivalent ear canal volume (Vea): A tympanometric measurement parameter, Vea is the volume of the ear canal corresponding to the admittance measured at +200 daPa.

Eustachian tube dysfunction: A disorder where the eustachian tube does not properly equalize air pressure between the middle ear and the outer environment. Eustachian tube dysfunction is commonly associated with developing or resolving middle ear infections.

Expressive language: The production of language in spoken, written, or other modalities. See also "language".

False-alarm rate: Refer to the "false-positive rate" entry.

False-negative rate: The proportion of missed cases out of the total diseased/disordered cases, it is the complement of the true-positive (hit) rate.

False negatives: The number of diseased/disordered cases that have been missed by the screening system.

False-positive rate: The proportion of non-diseased/disordered cases out of the total non-diseased/disordered cases that have been wrongly failed by the screening system, it is also known as the false-alarm rate. It is the complement of the true-negative rate.

False positives: The number of non-diseased/disordered cases that have been wrongly failed by the screening system.

Family Educational Rights and Privacy Act (FERPA): A federal law that protects the privacy of student education records. The law applies to all schools that receive funds under an applicable program of the U.S. Department of Education.

Fidelity: The degree to which a strategy or intervention is implemented as intended.

Fluency: Fluency refers to the ability to produce language with normal rhythm and timing.

Forward bending test: A screening test for scoliosis. A child, who is bare-backed or in tight clothes, stands with feet together and bends forward at the waist with legs straight, arms dangling, and palms opposed. A screener then inspects the child's back, from behind and from the side, for the presence of asymmetry of or rib hump on the child's back.

Functional behavior assessment: A problem-solving process including a number of evaluation methods that allow school professionals to identify the purpose or reason for a specific behavior and then select interventions and strategies to reduce a problem behavior and increase desired behaviors.

Gingivitis: Inflammation of the gum(s).

Growth monitoring: A systematic process to identify children who are possibly underweight, overweight or obese, or who have abnormal height parameters. Growth monitoring involves regular measures of weight and height and, typically, plotting this information on a normative chart to reveal abnormal growth patterns.

Health information exchange (HIE): The mobilization of healthcare information electronically across organizations within a region, community, or hospital system. The goal of HIE is to facilitate access to and retrieval of clinical data to provide safer and more timely, efficient, effective, and equitable patient-centered care.

Health information technology (HIT): The general framework to describe the comprehensive management of health information across computerized systems, and its secure exchange between consumers, providers, government and quality entities, and insurers in the United States.

Health Information Technology for Economic and Clinical Health Act (HITECH): A federal law under which the United States Department of Health and Human Services is promoting and expanding the adoption of health information technology, including a nationwide network of electronic health records.

Health Insurance Portability and Accountability Act (HIPAA): A federal law that protects the privacy of individually identifiable health information.

Health literacy: "The capacity of an individual to gain access to, understand, and use information in ways which promote and maintain good health" (World Health Organisation, 1998, p. 10).

Hertz (Hz): Hertz (or cycles per second)—the unit for frequency of sound. Pitch is the subjective impression of frequency. Human hearing typically ranges from 16 Hz (very low tone sound) to 20 000 Hz (very high tone sound). In practice, diagnostic tests are usually confined to frequencies important for speech perception (250 Hz to 8000 Hz) and screening tests to a subset of that range (500 or 1000 Hz to 4000 Hz).

Hit rate: Refer to the "sensitivity" entry.

Hypermetropia: A disorder of the eye whereby light reaches a focus beyond the retina. Consequently, sight is better for distant rather than near objects. Also known as "hyperopia" or "farsightedness".

Idiopathic: Of unknown cause.

Impetigo: An acute, bacterial, and highly contagious infection of the skin. It can be bulbous or epidemic in form. It is characterized by bumps with vesicles that scab into a yellowish crust.

Individual health plans (IHP's): A written document that outlines school healthcare procedures and services for students with significant or chronic health problems.

Individualized education plan (IEP): Defines the individualized objectives of a child who has been found with a disability, as defined by federal regulations. The IEP is intended to help children reach educational goals more easily than they otherwise would.

Individuals with Disabilities Education Improvement Act of 2004: Reauthorization of the Individuals with Disabilities Education Act (IDEA), a federal law that governs how states and public agencies provide early intervention, special education, and related services to children with disabilities.

Informed consent: The process by which an individual is informed of the all potential benefits and harms of a procedure prior to giving consent.

Initial sound identification: A phonemic awareness skill that involves identifying the first sound of a word, real or made-up.

Intervention assistance team: A team or formal group of teachers, administrators, and other support personnel from a school building who meet regularly and follow problem-solving procedures to address student concerns ranging from academic issues, to behavioral, social, and emotional difficulties.

Keratomalacia: Induced by vitamin A deficiency, a softening and necrosis of the cornea occurs. **Language:** A rule-governed system that is used for communication. Knowledge of the linguistic rules of a certain language allow a speaker to understand the messages transmitted by others (receptive language) and make their own ideas public (expressive language). Language can have a range of modalities including spoken, written, gestural, and pictorial.

Late talking: The phenomenon whereby children between the ages of 18 to 20 months have fewer than 10 words and children between the ages of 21 to 30 months have fewer than 50 words and/or no two-word combinations. These children usually show typical comprehension ability, play skills, motor and cognitive functioning.

Learning disability: Affecting persons with normal intelligence and not a direct result of sensory or psychological impairments, a learning disability/disorder involves disruption in the basic cognitive and psychological processes needed to acquire academic skills.

Leicester Height Measure: A portable, light-weight device for measuring the height of children and adults. The measure, or similar equipment, is often used in community health situations and consists of a stand, upright sections, measuring arm, and stabilizers. Measurements are accurate to the nearest 1 mm.

Leukemia: A progressive blood disease, involving over-proliferation of immature blood cells resulting in suppression of normal blood-forming processes and infiltration of various organs. Fever, pallor, fatigue, purpura, and anorexia are common presenting symptoms.

Likelihood ratios: A measure that is used to determine how well the screening test performs in ruling in, or ruling out, the likely presence of a disease/disorder, it specifies how many times more likely particular test results will be in cases with the target condition than in those without (Deeks, 2001).

Malocclusion: An abnormality in the fit of the upper and lower teeth together when biting or chewing.

Mass screening: Refer to the "universal screening" entry.

Minimeter: see Leicester Height Measure.

Moiré topography: A screening test for scoliosis. The technique consists of a light source, a screen filter with grids of fixed width, and a camera. The light source projects contour lines, called moiré fringes, through the screen filter onto the child's back. The camera captures the moiré fringes and a photograph is used to assess the overall body shape. The asymmetry of the body surface is measured by comparing the deviation of moiré fringes on the two halves of the back.

Morphology: An area of language involving composition of words by smaller units known as morphemes.

Myopia: A disorder of the eye whereby light reaches a focus before the retina. Consequently, sight is better for near rather than distant objects. Also known as "nearsightedness" or "shortsightedness".

Myringotomy: A surgical procedure involving the cutting of the eardrum and the drainage of fluid from the middle ear space.

Narrative: An uninterrupted stream of discourse that involves telling a story. The telling of a narrative can be part of a conversation.

Negative posterior probability (Pr[N/-]): Also referred to as the negative predictive value, it is the probability that the presenting case does not have the target condition given that a negative screening test result has been obtained.

Noise-induced hearing loss (NIHL): NIHL results from exposure to hazardous noise levels, be they very high levels for short periods of time (e.g., 120 dB A for 30 seconds) or lower levels for longer periods (e.g., 90 dB A for 3 hours per day). This permanent damage to the hair cells of the cochlea produces a sensorineural hearing loss that is typically progressive, with a gradual onset, and appears on the audiogram as a high-frequency notched pattern (most notably at the test frequencies of 3, 4, or 6 kHz with recovery at 8 kHz in the early stages).

Non-lexical reading: A skill used by beginning readers (or skilled readers when they come across a word that they have not seen before) that involves reading letter-by-letter or using knowledge of letter-sound correspondences to "sound out" words.

Nonword: A made-up word that adheres to rules governing the sound patterns of a certain language but does not have meaning in that language. Frequently used in phonological awareness activities and as a measure of non-lexical reading.

Obesity: Excessive accumulation/storage of body fat relative to ideal body mass.

Odds ratio (OR): This measure describes the strength of association between two binary data values and is used to establish the risk of occurrence of a disease/disorder in one group of cases compared to another group.

Orthographic awareness: The ability to attend to, reflect upon, and manipulate the visual properties (letters, letter combinations) of words.

Other health impairment: A disability category defined in 2004 Individuals with Disabilities Education Improvement Act as having limited strength, vitality, or alertness, including a heightened alertness to environmental stimuli, which results in limited alertness with respect to the educational environment. Other Health Impairment is due to chronic or acute health problems such as asthma, attention deficit disorder or attention deficit hyperactivity disorder, diabetes, epilepsy, a heart condition, hemophilia, lead poisoning, leukemia, nephritis, rheumatic fever, sickle cell anemia, and Tourette syndrome; and must be determined to adversely affect a child's educational performance.

Otitis media: Inflammation of the middle ear.

Otitis media with effusion (OME): Inflammation of the middle ear space associated with a build-up of non-infected fluid.

Otoacoustic emissions (OAEs): OAEs result from energy leakage that is radiated out by the cochlea due to its outer hair cells actively processing and amplifying incoming low-intensity sound. They can be measured in the absence and presence of acoustic stimuli. The former class includes spontaneous OAEs (SOAEs), whereas the evoked class includes transient evoked OAEs (TEOAEs) and distortion product OAEs (DPOAEs). Testing involves placement of a small probe (containing a transducer and microphone/receiver) to achieve an acoustic seal of the external auditory canal. OAEs are performed widely for the purposes of screening (e.g., in newborn hearing screening programs) and diagnostic assessment (e.g., in the evaluation of auditory neuropathy/dys-synchrony). This electrophysiological assessment is objective, minimally invasive, pain-free, quick to perform, and easily administered and interpreted.

Patient Protection and Affordable Care Act: A federal law aimed at increasing the affordability and rate of health insurance coverage for Americans, and reducing the overall costs of health care.

Peak compensated static acoustic admittance (Ytm): A tympanometric measurement parameter, Ytm is the peak admittance value minus the admittance value at +200 daPa. Also referred to as the compliance or mobility of the middle ear system.

Pediculosis: Infection with *Pediculus humanus var. capitis*. Also known as headlice.

Pediculus humanus: A genus of lice that feed on human blood and can be found on the scalp (head lice; *var. capitis*) or body (body louse; *var. corporis*).

Periodontal disease: Affecting the tissues that support and anchor the teeth. Without appropriate treatment, it may lead to gum, bone, and/or tooth root destruction.

Permanent dentition: Also known as secondary dentition, these are the 32 teeth of adults that follow the shedding of the primary teeth.

Phoneme segmentation: The ability to segment a spoken word into all of its component sounds. A phonemic awareness task.

Phonemic awareness: An area of phonological awareness. The ability to attend to, reflect upon, and manipulate individual sounds in words.

Phonics: Knowledge of the letter-sound combinations of a language.

Phonology: The linguistic area concerned with the rules governing the sound structure of language.

Phonological awareness (PA): The ability to attend to, reflect upon, and manipulate sound units (sounds, syllables) in words.

Plaque: Mucus/bacteria on a tooth surface.

Pneumatic otoscopy: A visual examination of the outer ear and eardrum using an earlight equipped with an air-filled bulb. The bulb is squeezed to change ear canal air pressure and movement of the eardrum can be visualized and rated for normality.

Positive posterior probability (Pr[D/+]): Also referred to as the positive predictive value, it is the probability that the presenting case does have the target condition given that a positive screening test result has been obtained.

Pragmatics: The linguistic area concerned with the rules governing the way language is used.

Prevalence: The proportion of diseased/disordered cases in a particular population at a specific point in time.

Primary dentition: The first set of teeth (20) normally erupting in infancy.

Prognostic: The likely course or progression of a clinical condition.

Pruritus: Also known as itching. The sensation which causes the desire or reflex to scratch.

Psoriasis: A skin disorder which is chronic and non-contagious by nature, it is characterized by inflamed lesions cover by whitish plaques/scabs.

Public health model: A model characterized by a focus on population-wide concerns as well as providing a full continuum of services, including health promotion, prevention, intervention, and treatment. Other principles of the public health model include epidemiologic surveillance or monitoring of the general population, linkage of health and mental health with the physical and psychosocial environment, and evaluation of services.

Pure-tone audiometry: A procedure in which simple, single frequency tonal sounds (pure tones) are presented to a listener at varying or fixed intensities. The listener then responds to those tones that she/he can hear.

Readability: The ease with which material is able to be read.

Receiver operating characteristic (ROC) curve: A graphical representation of the effects of different pass/fail criteria points upon the hit and false alarm rates, the curve can also be used to judge system accuracy.

Receptive language: The comprehension or understanding of language in spoken, written, or other modalities. See also "language".

Reference standard: Also known as the "gold standard," it is used in comparison with screening or alternative tests to establish validity and other test performance measures. The reference standard may be a widely accepted diagnostic test, or an objective or subjective group of clinical findings that are capable of distinguishing those with the target condition.

Relative risk (RR): The risk of an event or developing a condition relative to exposure, it provides the probability of the condition occurring in the exposed versus non-exposed group. It is a more appropriate choice than odds ratios when prevalence of a condition is relatively high.

Reliability: This term pertains to whether tests are repeatable and precise in nature. Types include test-retest, inter-test, intra-test, subject, and instrument reliability.

Responsiveness to Intervention (RtI): An educational framework that encompasses universal screening. The National Center on Response to Intervention (NCRTI) defines RtI as the integration of "assessment and intervention within a multi-level prevention system to maximize student achievement and to reduce behavioral problems. With RtI, schools use data to identify students at risk for poor learning outcomes, monitor student progress, provide evidence-based interventions, and adjust the intensity and nature of those interventions depending on a student's responsiveness, and identify students with learning disabilities or other disabilities" (NCRTI, 2010).

Risser sign: A grade ranging from 1 to 5, made by assessing the radiograph of the iliac apophysis for the amount of calcification. A higher grade indicates a higher degree of skeletal maturity, with grade 5 indicating that the iliac apophysis has completely fused to the iliac crest.

School based health centers (SBHC): Health centers, based in schools, in which students can be treated for acute illnesses and be screened for dental, vision, and hearing problems. With an emphasis on prevention, early intervention, and risk reduction, school-based health centers counsel students on healthy habits and how to prevent injury, violence, and other threats.

School health record: A student's health-related information that allows a school nurse to communicate important health-related information to students, families, the school multidisciplinary team, emergency personnel, other health care providers, and school nurse substitutes.

School-wide positive behavior supports (SWPBS): The U.S. Department of Education's Office of Special Education Program's Technical Assistance Center of Positive Behavior Interventions and Supports defines SWPBS as a "decision making framework that guides selection, integration, and implementation of the best evidence-based academic and behavioral practices for improving important academic and behavior outcomes for all students". SWPBS emphasizes four integrated elements, including 1) data-based decision making, 2) measurable outcomes, 3) evidence-based practices, and 4) implementation support systems (TA Center on PBIS, 2009).

Scoliosis: Lateral or side-side curvature of the spine.

Scoliosis screening: The use of one or multiple screening tests to identify patients with scoliosis.

Selective screening: Refer to the "targeted screening" entry.

Semantics: The linguistic area concerned with the rules governing the meaning of words and word combinations in a language.

Sensitivity: Also known as the hit rate or true-positive rate, this common test performance measure is the proportion of cases with the target condition that are correctly identified by the system.

Sensorineural hearing loss: Hearing loss that is caused by a disorder in the inner ear. Amongst many other causes, sustained levels of high noise exposure may cause sensorineural hearing loss.

Shared decision-making: When the patient and health professional make a decision in partnership with each other. This requires communication that helps both to have a shared understanding of the intervention goals and plans.

Signal-to-noise ratio (SNR): By definition, SNR is the ratio of signal power to the noise power, with a ratio greater than 1:1 indicative of more signal than noise. However, in audiological applications, the level of the noise in dB (e.g., recorded by the probe during OAE testing) is subtracted from the signal in dB (e.g., the level of the OAE response) to produce a single value. A positive value shows the signal to be higher than the noise. Conversely, a negative value shows the noise to be higher than the signal.

Specific Language Impairment (SLI): A severe disorder of receptive and/or expressive language that is not the result of intellectual impairment or other disorders. That is, a "pure" or primary language problem.

Specificity: Also known as the true-negative rate, this common test performance measure is the proportion of cases without the target condition that are correctly rejected by the system.

Speech: The motor process by which humans turn ideas or thoughts into speech sound signals to a listener. It involves not only the ability to produce sounds or words, but also the speech rate, rhythm, intonation, and voice quality.

Speech sound disorders: A type of speech disorder in which some speech sounds in an individual's native language are not produced or used correctly.

Spinal fusion: A surgical procedure that corrects spinal curvature by fixing the spine in a balanced position with metallic rods and fusing the affected segment with onlay bone grafts.

Story grammar: The linguistic rules governing the way a narrative is structured. See also "narrative".

Stuttering: A label commonly used to describe impaired fluency of speech. In the past, stuttering was also referred to as "stammering," however, this label is now rarely used.

Subgingival calculus: Also known as tartar, this hard deposit on the exposed tooth surface is a contributing factor in periodontal disease.

Supernumerary teeth: Any teeth that are additional to the standard number of primary or secondary teeth.

Syntax: The linguistic area concerned with the rules governing the sentence and phrase structure of language.

Talipes: A congenital deformity of the foot whereby it is twisted from the normal position/shape. Sometimes referred to as "club foot".

Targeted screening: Screening tests "sort out apparently well persons who probably have a disease from those who probably do not" (Wilson & Jungner, 1968, p. 11). Targeted screening indicates the screening of selected high-risk groups within a population. It may still involve the testing of large numbers of individuals.

Test protocol: A term used to describe a battery of tests, or repeat/multistage screening.

Transient evoked otoacoustic emissions (TEOAEs): These emissions are commonly elicited by brief acoustic stimuli, such as Gaussian-shaped broadband clicks or tone bursts. Presentation of the stimulus results in a clear, frequency-dispersive response or "echo" detected in the ear canal within a short, time-locked window. Widely utilized in screening and diagnostic audiology, TEOAEs are not a test of hearing per se but, rather, an assessment of the function of the cochlear outer hair cells. Their presence is indicative of normal auditory status up to the cochlea. Their absence may be associated with a hearing loss in excess of 25 dB HL and/or middle ear dysfunction, among other factors.

True-negative rate: Refer to "specificity" entry.

True negatives: The number of non-diseased/disordered cases that have been correctly rejected by the system.

True-positive rate: Refer to "sensitivity" entry.

True positives: The number of diseased-disordered cases that have been correctly identified by the system.

Tympanogram: A graphic plot of static acoustic admittance of the middle ear system against middle ear pressure.

Tympanometric peak pressure (TPP): A tympanometric measurement parameter, TTP is the ear canal pressure corresponding to the peak admittance value.

Tympanometric width (TW): A tympanometric measurement parameter, TW is the width of the tympanogram at 50% of its amplitude from peak to tail.

Tympanometry: An objective test of the mechanical characteristics of the tympanic membrane and other middle ear structures.

"Type A" tympanogram: Described by Jerger (1970), this shape of tympanogram is characterized by normal middle ear compliance (e.g., 0.2 – 1.5 mmhos) and pressure (e.g., +50 to -100 daPa). It is usually, although not always, associated with normal middle ear function.

"Type B" tympanogram: Described by Jerger (1970), this shape of tympanogram is characterized by no changes in middle ear compliance with changes in pressure (i.e., a flat response). It is suggestive of middle ear pathology, such as OME, or tympanic membrane perforation if accompanied by an abnormally large ear canal volume.

"Type C" tympanogram: Described by Jerger (1970), this shape of tympanogram is characterized by normal middle ear compliance (e.g., 0.2 – 1.5 mmhos) in the presence of excessively negative pressure (e.g., < -100 daPa). It is indicative of Eustachian tube dysfunction.

Unilateral hearing loss: Hearing loss that is present in the right ear or left ear only.

Universal screening: Screening tests "sort out apparently well persons who probably have a disease from those who probably do not" (Wilson & Jungner, 1968, p. 11). Universal screening indicates a large-scale screening of a whole population group, where no selection within the group is made.

Usability: The extent to which a screening tool is perceived to be practical to use within a specific context with consideration for the costs associated, feasibility of administration, acceptability to multiple key stakeholders, resource demands and availability, accommodations needed, and utility of outcomes to stakeholders.

Validity: This term describes the degree in which the screening test results are consistent with the presence or absence of the target condition. In the diagnostic context, it refers to the extent to which a test measures what it was intended to measure.

Vocal folds: Two bands of muscle tissue located in the larynx, above the trachea.

Voice: Speech sound produced by the vibration of the vocal folds and modified by the resonators.

Word decoding: The ability to recognize written words. Decoding can involve either non-lexical reading (using sound-letter correspondences) or whole word reading in which a word's entire phonological form is accessed in the lexicon.

REFERENCES

American Academy of Audiology (AAA). (2011). American Academy of Audiology (AAA). (2011). *Childhood hearing screening guidelines*. Retrieved from http://www.audiology.org/resources/documentlibrary/Documents/20110926_ChildhoodHearingScreeningGuidelines.pdf

Deeks, J. J. (2001). Systematic reviews of evaluations of diagnostic and screening tests. *British Medical Journal*, *323*, 157-162.

Jerger, J.F. (1970). Clinical experience with impedance audiometry. *Archives of Otolaryngology*, *92*, 311-324.

National Center on Response to Intervention. (2010). *Essential components of RTI: A closer look at Response to Intervention*. Washington, DC: U.S. Department of Education, Office of Special Education Programs, National Center on Response to Intervention.

Rance, G. (2005). Auditory neuropathy/dys-synchrony and its perceptual consequences. *Trends in Amplification*, *9*(1), 1-43.

TA Center on PBIS. (2009). *What is School-wide Positive Behavior Interventions and Supports?* Retrieved from http://www.pbis.org/school/what_is_swpbs.aspx

Wilson, J. M. G., & Jungner, G. (1968). *Principles and practice of screening for disease*. Geneva: WHO.

World Health Organization (WHO). (1998). *Health promotion glossary*. Geneva: WHO.

INDEX

#

A

B

C

D

E

F

G

H

I

J

K

L

M

N

O

P

Q

R

S

T

Y